MW01503874

Chiron:

Trauma Key

Chiron: Trauma Key

Michael De Baker

Published in 2020 by Kindle Direct Publishing

Copyright © 2020 by Michael De Baker

This work is registered with UK Copyright Service, Registration No.: 284734358

18th May 2020

All rights reserved. No part of this publication may be reproduced or transmitted in any form or by any means, electronic or mechanical, including photocopying, recording, or by any information storage or retrieval system, without prior permission in writing from Michael De Baker.

ISBN: 9798650878292

Cover image: Pixabay - Mike Lacoste

Helix image (without shading and astrological symbols for Uranus, Neptune and Pluto) chapters 2, 3, 4, 7, 9, 10, 11, 13, 15, 16: Vectorstock

Torus image (without astrological symbol for Uranus) chapter 2: Vectorstock

Table of Contents

Preface

Chapter 1 – the Mythology of Chiron *1*

> ➤ The story of the birth of Christ: legend
> ➤ The fictional tale of Chiron: myth
> ➤ The premise of the book

Chapter 2 – Chiron and the *Trauma Helix* *11*

> ➤ Catherine's story
> ➤ Toroidal Uranus space
> ➤ the *Trauma Helix* explained
> ➤ the *Trauma Helix* in the chart of Richard Nixon

Chapter 3 – Crossing the Bridge to Saturn *29*

> ➤ Saturn as the structure of consciousness in the soul's vehicle
> ➤ Saturn in the chart of Richard Nixon

Chapter 4 – Proof, please! Abraham Lincoln *39*

> ➤ two consecutive lives created by the same soul: Anne Frank and Barbro Karlén
> ➤ two lives created by the same soul: the Himalayan yogi and Abraham Lincoln
> ➤ first encounter with the planetary nodes (Chiron and Mars)

Chapter 5 – from Lincoln to Lindbergh *61*

> ➤ the danger of telling clients about their past lives
> ➤ Soul: a Diamond held up to the Light
> ➤ *'Thematic continuity'* in Lincoln's and Lindbergh's Pluto placement
> ➤ Chiron and *the Trauma Helix* in the chart of Charles Lindbergh
> ➤ *'Trauma Continuity'* between the three lives: the Himalayan yogi, Abraham Lincoln and Charles Lindbergh
> ➤ Difference between the nodes of planets at either end of the Saturn boundary

Chapter 6 – the ´*Multidimensional Psyche*´ *85*

> ➤ The nature of the multiple self
> ➤ 'samskara' and the *Trauma Helix*
> ➤ Chiron: the subtle body imprinting form
> ➤ What message is written into Chiron's discovery chart?
> ➤ Fitting Chiron and the *Trauma Helix* into the narrative of the Evolutionary Axis
> ➤ The subtle body's memory traces of physical trauma and pain: Nixon's knees
> ➤ From '*transpersonal*' to '*multi-personal*' planets

Chapter 7 – Nina Simone *101*

> ➤ The Moon's NN ruler conjunct the SN of the Moon: a repeat assignment
> ➤ The Moon's SN ruler conjunct the NN of the Moon: a very different repeat assignment
> ➤ Chiron and the *Trauma Helix*
> ➤ *In* the trauma lies the potential for healing
> ➤ From Saturn all the way back to Mercury: determining planetary function

Chapter 8 – the "Missing Moon" *117*

> ➤ The *"Missing Moon"*. Where did it go?
> ➤ Putting the Moon back in orbit
> ➤ The natal Moon as the point of maximum resistance between its own south and north node
> ➤ Bringing in the rulers of the lunar nodes: Nixon, Lincoln and Simone
> ➤ On the evolution of evolutionary astrology

Chapter 9 – Trauma, Pain and Healing in Orbit *137*

> ➤ The nodes of Chiron, Uranus and Neptune: looking at the entire evolutionary orbit
> ➤ Placing the past of the Chiron pain against the backdrop of the Pluto, SN of the Moon and SN ruler placement: the pain does not come falling from the sky
> ➤ Simultaneity in the ´*Multidimensional Psyche*´
> ➤ What about the nodes of Pluto? The incubated soul on a 'conveyor belt'

Chapter 10 – Jim Jones *151*

> The master demagogue
> Chiron and the *Trauma Helix*: full orbits
> Jones's Moon in full orbit

Chapter 11 – Josef Mengele in Full Evolutionary Orbit *169*

> *'trauma continuity'* and *'healing continuity'*
> Mengele's revealing Moon dynamics
> Chiron aspects

Chapter 12 – Richard Nixon in Full Evolutionary Orbit *207*

> Nixon having his palm read
> Why the Sun comes last in EA chart analysis

Chapter 13 – Nina Simone in Full Evolutionary Orbit *221*

> Why Virgo should not hear the word 'forgiveness' from Pisces
> *'trauma continuity'* and *'healing continuity'* becoming the therapeutic roadmap

Chapter 14 - Jim Jones in Full Evolutionary Orbit *247*

Chapter 15 – From Barbro Karlén back to Anne Frank via the planetary south nodes: *'trauma continuity'* and *'healing continuity'* *263*

> Chiron: Trauma Key
> *'trauma continuity'* and *'healing continuity'*

Chapter 16 – Chiron Miscellaneous *295*

> Astrology and science: Chiron in a house and sign
> Chiron transits. Secondary progressions (Jim Jones, 18 November 1978, and the period leading up to the fateful day)

Endnotes *317*

About the Author *345*

Bibliography *347*

Preface

Chiron is an anomaly whichever way you look at it. Inhabitant of two distant worlds – Uranus and Saturn – which it connects, it defies categorization and is neither an asteroid nor a comet. It is a bit of both. Because of its highly elliptical orbit, Chiron spends the most time in the two opposite ends of the zodiac: Pisces and Aries, i.e. the unseen dimensions (Pisces) from which the soul descends into matter (Aries), as if trying to connect them. Initially thought to be an inactive system, scientists are now finding Chiron has rings around it. The material these rings consist of undergoes a transformation as the *asteroid-comet-icy dwarf planet* space oddity meanders deep into the orbit of Uranus and then all the way back to Saturn. In other words: a transformation takes place as it connects two realms. The very astrological glyph used for Chiron already seems to be pointing to this transformation: as the faraway worlds of Uranus and Saturn are connected, a key is turned and a door opened. In this book you will discover that turning the Chiron key will unlock the secret of how trauma, and the potential for overcoming it, travels from one lifetime to the next *as pain*. Unlocking that secret will hand you, the astrologer, a most powerful tool that will allow you to work with your clients therapeutically.

A preface is normally written to give the reader an idea of what they can expect and so ease them into the material. A certain level of trust is built that way and an agenda established. Besides what I have told you in the opening paragraph of this preface, it seems to me there is very little I can say here that would prepare you for what you are about to read.

As you learn about the specifics of how the Chiron key fits the trauma lock – and the potential for overcoming it - you are introduced to working with **the planetary nodes**. This will, out of necessity, lead to musings on a planet's - and the Moon's - full orbit and its meaning in terms of soul evolution. At this point you will be far out in space, lightyears away from your normal astrological frame of reference. I do not know if you are willing to accompany me on my journey through the decidedly unearthly surroundings of this unknown world. We shall see. The journey will be very much like Chiron's: as it moves away from the ringed planet, leaving behind the comfort of a causal and linearly ordered

Saturnian world, it ventures far out into what must be the space equivalent of Jules Verne´s *Journey to the Center of the Earth*. The Icelandic Volcano Snaefellsjökull, your point of entry, on this strangest of travels becomes the Chiron wormhole - connecting two very distant locations through spacetime curvature - and once through it, your only way of coming to the surface at the Stromboli volcano in southern Italy will be on the back of Chiron itself.

The rewards for those willing to discover how these distant worlds are connected will be many. You will learn how the Chiron myth is full of subtle references, all pointing to what exactly it is that is being carried over from one world to another. In fact, so many of them lie about the place that in the opening paragraph of this very preface we have accidentally stumbled on some of them already. You will learn how there are four major trauma indicators in any astrological chart and how to read them. You will learn how there is both **trauma and healing continuity** from one lifetime to the next. You will witness first-hand how Lincoln's and Lindbergh's seemingly non-related Pluto placements in actual fact display a high degree of what I have termed **'thematic continuity.'** You will read the powerful healing message written into Chiron's discovery chart (chapter 6).

You will also discover how the Moon went missing and how it is put back in orbit (chapter 8), how Chiron in a sign does not exist in the astrological chart (chapter 16), what it is that science does or will not understand about astrology (chapter 16), and how there is simultaneity in the 'Multidimensional Psyche.' (1)

On a more technical note, you will learn how to interpret the south node ruler conjunct the north node (Simone), how to interpret the north node ruler conjunct the south node (Simone), Chiron as a skipped step (Lincoln), the Moon as a skipped step (Lincoln), Jupiter as a skipped step (Lindbergh, Jones), Pluto as a skipped step (Jones), Uranus as a skipped step (Mengele), how to interpret the resolution node for a skipped step, how to interpret a planet conjunct the north node of the Moon (Lincoln, Mengele), how to interpret a planet conjunct the south node of the Moon (Simone, Mengele), how to interpret transits and secondary progressions from the soul perspective (Jones), how an identical planet placement can lead to vastly different conclusions (Uranus in the 3rd house Aries in the charts of Nina Simone and Jim Jones), and much, much more.

All of this is presented in chapters rich in well-referenced biographical material pertaining to the lives of the people whose charts are being discussed. The text is thoroughly sourced throughout so that you may correlate astrological conclusions to biographical fact and so verify the validity of the former. We will delve deep into the lives and charts of Richard Nixon, Nina Simone, Jim Jones, and Josef Mengele to see what happens at the turn of the **Trauma Key**.

Two sets of charts pertaining to **two consecutive lives created by the same soul** – Abraham Lincoln and Charles Lindbergh in the opening chapters of the book and Anne Frank and Barbro Karlén towards its end – are used to illustrate how, through Chiron as Trauma Key, *trauma and healing continuity* can be distilled from the chart. It is *that* continuity that will hand you a shortcut to putting your finger on your client's deepest wounds and greatest potential for healing. By the end of the book you will have added important and irreplaceable tools to your therapeutic evolutionary astrology kit.

I am most grateful to Barbro Karlén for, once more, granting me permission to use her chart and so allowing me to complete in this book the Anne Frank - Barbro Karlén comparative chart study that was begun in my first book *Intercepted Signs: Encoded Messages from the Soul.*

Abbreviations used in this book:

RR: Rodden Rating (Astrodienst, Lois Rodden)

EA: evolutionary astrology

PPP: Pluto Polarity Point

SN: south node / NN: north node

H1: 1st house, H2: 2nd house, etc.

House system used in all charts: Porphyry. True Node, Parallax Moon Correction.

Chapter 1 - The Mythology of Chiron

There is a Catholic priest sitting in our living room, drinking sherry and puffing a cigar. He seems to be outstaying his welcome. My father does not smoke cigars but keeps a stack of them in a special wooden box for when the clergy makes its twice-yearly house call. My parents seem awkward all through the visit and, as a ten-year-old boy, I wonder what the visit means and what the awkwardness means. Just like in Bible class when this same man of the cloth, with a nose like a strawberry and a belly as if he were six months pregnant, tells us stories and I wonder what they mean. I also wonder what the strawberry nose and the potbelly mean.

One day in class this priest tells us the story of the birth of Jesus. Apparently, Joseph and Mary, having travelled for a long time, are looking for a place to stay. Mary is heavy with child. They knock on the doors of several inns but are told no rooms are available. At the end of their tether and at the door of yet another inn, the innkeeper comes out and tells them they are not likely to find a place in town this time of night. They can get some rest in a stable he has out back, though. Not the most comfortable of places, but at least they will have a roof over their head. And the animals are wonderful and will not bother them. And so, Christ is born in a manger, in the presence of a donkey and an ox. Three Magi, who had followed the stars, came and brought gifts: myrrh, gold and frankincense.

"And that was it, children. On to the next story." Sorry? Could you tell us what the story means, please? Why were a domesticated member of the horse family and a bulky bovid there? And what about those three wise men? Who were they? And why bring such rare and hard to come by gifts? No explanation forthcoming. The chubby chaplain was already halfway through the next biblical yarn. As a ten-year-old I needed meaning, not facts. It took me some years to figure out that the story meant something and that its meaning would be important.

The story means, so I deduced from the somewhat unusual circumstances surrounding this birth, that when Truth needs to be born there is no place for it in this world. Truth is born in the presence of innocence, humility and stubborn, if somewhat clumsy steadfastness. Men who follow the stars, astrologers therefore, know of this birth, know where to find it and bring the parents gifts. Not the child but the parents. What good, after all, are gold, myrrh and frankincense to a newly born?

Gold and dried resins from Arabia and northern Africa are not your common gift shop items. They must represent, so my youthful thinking went, a commodity: wisdom. Three astrologers willing to travel far to find what the stars had announced while the rest of the world kept their front doors shut, Truth brought into the world amid innocence, humility and perseverance, and celebrated through wisdom provided by three wise men. I had my meaning.

The Chiron myth

Chiron, a teacher, musician, healer, gymnast, *and* a centaur, is accidentally shot in the foot by his student Hercules with an arrow poisoned by the blood of Hydra, a poison which causes wounds that cannot be healed and which come with excruciating pain. Hydra, one of the offspring of Tartarus and Gaia, was the many-headed water-beast that Hades (Pluto) had placed at Lerna, the lake that could be used as one of the entrances to the underworld, near the well of Amymone. Not to adorn the entrance but to guard it. Chopping off one of Hydra's many heads was pointless: for each one severed two more would spring forth. Being immortal Chiron could not die. What to do? Initially he retreated to the caves of his childhood, later mastering the art of healing in the Chironium, the temple of healing. In a bid to heal the pain once and for all, he gave up his immortality in a deal with Zeus (Jupiter), whereby he agreed to enter the underworld (Hades, Pluto) in exchange for Prometheus having his eternal punishment lifted.

Prometheus, tied at the top of Mount Caucasus for having stolen fire from the gods and passing it on to humans, was made to pay for his sin by eternally having his liver eaten out by an eagle at sunrise, which would then grow back on during the day and following night. Not much going on there in the way of sitting down and talking things over. Perhaps the gods had not yet heard of a written warning first. Some versions of the myth have Chiron accidentally dropping the poisoned arrow onto his own foot. Which was a human foot, by the way, showing that

Chiron was of a different lineage than his fellow centaurs, who were not only carousers, lacking Chiron's wisdom, but also had the legs and feet of a horse. Chiron's were human. He is shot *and wounded*, therefore, in a human foot.

These are the facts. Of the myth, he hastened to add. Like the story of the birth of Jesus, we are not here to corroborate their historical accuracy. We are not historians but astrologers. We are here to find out what meaning there is to be had.

The story of the birth of Christ versus the Chiron tale aptly illustrates the difference between legend and myth. Legend, which comes from the Latin *legere*, meaning 'to be read', recounts events which actually happened at some time in the past and which accrete as story. As these stories are handed down from the past, they are added to, embellished, or simplified. They are told to explain a historical event, teach a lesson, or simply to entertain. The tales of King Arthur are a good example of legend. As legend is handed down the generations it may get revised and end up as literary text. The tales of King Arthur started out as stories, then got recorded in Geoffrey of Monmouth's *Historia Regum Britanniae* around the year 1130, then popped up in romanticized form in the poems of Chrétien de Troyes towards the end of the 12th century, and finally were turned into parody in Mark Twain's 1889 novel *A Connecticut Yankee in King Arthur's Court.* (1)

Myth is much closer to folktale. Both are fictional stories and regarded as such by those who tell them and those who listen to them. No one actually believes that Chiron was born to the Oceanid Nymph Philyra, the daughter of Okeanos (Oceanus), who mated with Chronos (Saturn) who, when the two love birds were caught in the act by the goddess Rhea, leapt out of bed, took on the form of a long-maned stallion and galloped off, causing Philyra, consumed by shame, to abandon her old haunts in favor of the long Pelasgian ridges. Even the ancient Greeks themselves would have had a hard time convincing each other of the actual existence of centaurs, fresh-water nymphs, monsters and gods of the sea. Myth represents not actual but symbolic event. Mythological storytelling *points to* imagined events that carry archetypal content from which meaning can be derived. Myth, unlike legend, is a symbolic construct. The fact that as a young boy I read meaning into the story of the birth of Christ does not mean it was created as a story for people to read meaning into. It does not *point to* truth, meaning or lessons to be extracted from an interpretation of the events that make up the story. Myth does. Since symbolism is the essence of the astrologer's trade, we should not have too hard a time deriving meaning from the archetypal content the Chiron myth *points to*.

What the myth points to

The most striking feature of the myth, when looked at through eyes sensitized to symbolic meaning, is that in several places the theme of two-worldliness pops up. (2) The first instance of this we find in Chiron's parentage: Chronus (Saturn), son of Ouranus (Uranus) – the two distant worlds Chiron would connect! - mates with the daughter of Okeanos, the primordial Titan god of the river Oceanus, which, according to the most ancient notions of the Greeks, surrounded the whole earth. Time and form (Saturn), inextricably linked to earthly existence, lying with the offspring of the font of all of the earth's fresh-water rivers, wells, springs and rain clouds. An unusual liaison by any standard. Chiron, spawned forth by this union and so hideous a creature that he is immediately rejected by his mother, is half horse, half man and unites these two worlds. Wounds, of course, are seldom pretty, even when they are healed and remain as scars.

Interestingly, the word *Kairos* (Ancient Greek: καιρός) means *'the right, critical, or opportune moment.'* As such it retains its paternal lineage of chronos (χρόνος) - pointing to linear, chronological time - yet seems to combine it with the more female capability, coming in through his maternal and distinctly watery lineage, of knowing when the opportune moment for right action has come.

Already, in the very opening scene of the myth, therefore, we have the theme of two worlds coming together. The next instance of this, is the fact that Chiron, unlike his brethren, who were philanderers for the most part, is known for his wisdom and knowledge of medicine, astronomy and astrology. He comes across as distinctly human. Yet he is not, which becomes his predicament when trying to heal an incurable wound. A pact needs to be made with Zeus whereby Chiron can descend into the Underworld (Pluto) and become human. The human realm, in other words, is the only one in which this wound can be healed. In the myth: Chiron is wounded in a *human* foot.

Chiron becomes human in exchange for taking on someone else's pain (i.e. Prometheus'), a pain which is the result of a punishment that seems a bit over the top and that keeps coming back, just like Hydra's chopped-off heads. As Chiron leaves the immortal realm behind and brings his woundedness into the mortal realm, again he combines two worlds. The astronomical correlate to this is the fact that Chiron's elliptical orbit takes it deep into that of Uranus, and, on its way back, deep into that of Saturn. So much so, that its perihelion is closer to Earth than Saturn's, while its aphelion is at a greater distance from the Sun than Uranus's perihelion.

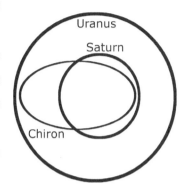

What does all of this mean? It means, I think, that Chiron seems to be picking something up from that other Uranian world and then relaying it to the known world of Saturn, with the two-pronged bit on the Chiron key already pointing to these seemingly irreconcilable worlds.

The myth translated to English: Chiron travels to a faraway world (Uranus) to pick up trauma experienced by prior-life selves (in the myth: someone else's pain) so that its eternal and maddening repetition comes to an end and his own wounding is healed by becoming mortal. Prometheus getting his liver eaten out every single day at sunrise also needs to be interpreted symbolically. It points to trauma reenacted in every new life - sunrise - created by the soul. The myth makes a more oblique reference to the recurring nature of trauma by letting us know that Chiron's incurable wound is caused by an arrow dipped in the poisonous blood of a multi-headed serpentine water monster whose very breath was lethal and who had the unique capacity to grow back two heads for each one severed.

Two of the players in supporting roles, therefore, i.e. Hydra and Prometheus, display and suffer from something that keeps coming back. One of them, Hydra, the nine-headed water-serpent who haunted the swamps of Lerna, has access to the Underworld, the world of Pluto. The world Chiron must go through if he is to cure his wound.

Conclusion: the only way to get rid of a recurring pain and move beyond its exasperating repetition is to yet again incarnate and work through it. In chapter 6 – *The Multidimensional Psyche*, we will see this message clearly reflected in Chiron's discovery chart and, more in particular, in its north node by house and sign.

Interestingly, homeopathy and regression therapy took off in a big way ever since Chiron's discovery on 1 November 1977 by Charles Kowal. (3) Like the healing of a self-inflicted wound, both homeopathy and regression therapy part from the idea that the healing is *in* the wounding, or, to be more precise, in the same stuff the wounding is made of. *Like cures like* (4) is the principle that governs both homeopathy and regression therapy. In the former it means that a substance which causes illness in healthy people, in a severely diluted form may contribute to healing in people who are ill. In the latter it means that trauma can be overcome when it is re-experienced in a therapeutic setting, which can also be said to be a diluted form of the original traumatic imprint.

Uranus in evolutionary astrology is associated with subconscious memories of events that were experienced as traumatic in prior lives. The soul carries these memories over into the current life in a bid not only to heal them but also to further its own evolution. Please allow me to give you a practical example of this using the chart of Richard Nixon. Nixon's Uranus is in the 5th house Aquarius. We assume, since trauma, until it is healed, has a tendency of repeating itself, that the subconscious memories Uranus points to have to do with *sudden dissociation from* (Aquarius) *his leadership* (5th house).

Therapeutic evolutionary astrology parts from the idea that from Saturn out, things work in a non-linear way. Chiron, the first one we run into as we move outward, is a good example of this. The *Wounded Healer* is *Like cures like* reasoning. It is non-linear. Linear reasoning would be: the wounded person needs to be healed by someone or something else. A cures B. A cures A is non-linear, circular reasoning. *In the wound is the healing* is a circular, homeopathic principle.

[6]

For Uranus this means that *in* the deepest trauma at once the potential for healing of the trauma lies. In the chart there is no need to go to the point diametrically opposite Uranus or indeed anywhere else. The healing is in the very Uranus placement by house and sign.

Translated to Nixon's Uranus: *if he manages to step back* (Aquarius) *and look objectively* (Aquarius) *at his need to always come out on top* (5th house) *and be an undisputed leader* (5th house) and how *in his leadership* (H5) *he has got dangerously dissociated* (Aquarius) *from generosity and impartiality as the more lofty expression of the Leo archetype* (H5), then he can heal the memories of trauma incurred to it.

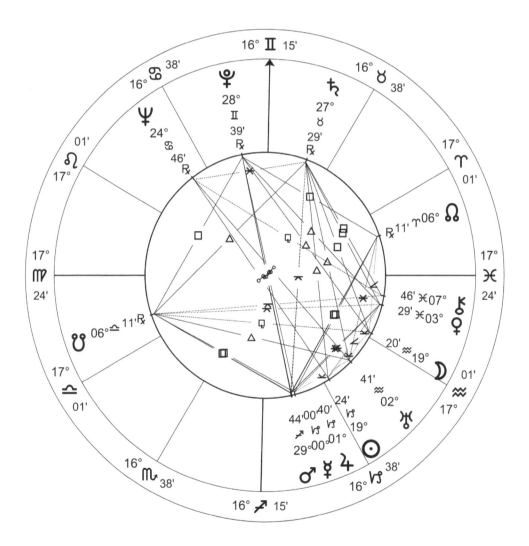

Richard Nixon, 9 January 1913, 21:35 hrs., Yorba Linda, California, RR:AA

[7]

If he does not, then he runs the risk of it getting repeated. As it did: he was *dissociated* (Aquarius) *from his leadership* (5th house) *overnight* (Aquarius). *Removed from* (dissociated) *office* (Uranus ruling the 6th house). Therapeutic evolutionary astrology posits that this circular, homeopathic principle also applies to Neptune. *In* the meaninglessness trauma of *fracturing* (11th house) *in the emotional body* (Cancer) at once lies the potential for healing it when the dissociative state in the emotional body is remedied, something of the utmost importance to a soul wishing to evolve to the emotional honesty of the 4th house Sagittarius Pluto Polarity Point.

In upcoming chapters I will explain why therapeutic evolutionary astrology associates Neptune with meaninglessness trauma.

The 11th house Neptune trauma in Nixon's case, by the way, also had to do with *prior-life selves having forced a life upon themselves*, as would Nixon in the current life, which was *in no way reflective of who they knew themselves to truly be* (11th house), *causing emotional* (Cancer) *fracturing* (H11). Nixon, who was a studious recluse with a razor-sharp mind and the gift of the gab, by forcing public life upon himself was effectively turning his life into a living lie: a dissociative (11th house) state. The healing of the Neptune trauma would have come if he had been *able to feel emotionally secure and comfortable* (Cancer) *in not being a people person but a stay-at-home, which was his true nature* (11th house). His unquenchable thirst for power through the clever use of words and misuse of information (Pluto 10th house Gemini, skipped step), however, got the better of him.

The soul has Neptune retrograde for it wants Nixon to deeply reflect on this so that the appropriate action may be taken.

The premise of this book

In comes Chiron. What it does – and this will be the premise of this book – is **travel deep into Uranus's orbit to pick up these subconscious memories, just like the centaur traveled from the immortal to the mortal world in an attempt to heal his pain. Chiron then relays these memories to Saturn. Like the mythological Chiron, he takes on someone else's pain** (i.e.

Prometheus' in the myth) **inflicted in another world and heals it in this one, transferring prior-life trauma from the Uranian realm to the Saturnian current-life one as pain.**

As we saw earlier, in Nixon's case the subconscious memories of trauma incurred in past lives have to do with *dissociation* (Aquarius) *from his leadership* (H5) *and from Leo in its highest expression* (H5). Chiron rings the doorbell. Saturn opens. *"I have a package for you. Sender is a certain Uranus."* Chiron says. *"What's in it?"* Saturn wants to know.

Chiron now reads the label on the package. On his elliptical orbit between the two distant worlds he has had tons of time to translate the Uranus trauma charge into language Saturn will understand. The translation, astrologically speaking, is in Chiron's house and sign. He now hands the package to Saturn, saying *"I bring a pain caused by a deeply engrained confusion* (Pisces) *around what true service from a place of humility* (6th house) *means."*

"Got you," Saturn replies. *"I know exactly what to do with that. My consciousness, after all, was structured by the soul so as to allow for the consolidation* (Taurus) *of truthfulness* (9th house) *and to reflect on this deeply all through my life* (Saturn retrograde)."

"Are you astrologically inclined at all?" Saturn asks Chiron. *"Very much so. I used to teach the stuff!"* (5) Chiron responds enthusiastically. *"Well,"* Saturn continues, *"then you'll be interested to know that I rule Nixon's 5th house. All of it, including his Sun and his Uranus."*

"You seem to be an expert. Uranus, I understand, because when I was out there in those faraway realms, he explained to me what happened in prior lives as he handed me this package to deliver at your doorstep. But what's this Nixon guy's Sun doing there in Capricorn?" Chiron wishes to know.

"Aha, you do well to ask after it, my learned and wounded friend! It is there because the central, integrative principle around which his whole life revolves is to develop integrity (Capricorn) *in his leadership* (5th house). *That's why the soul needs me in the 9th house Taurus, you see?"*

"I see. Could you sign here? On the dotted line, please."

The package delivered contains the full Uranus and the full Neptune trauma. But there is something else inside it. Pluto is in there too, as Saturn is soon to find out. Chiron, after all, in his pact with Zeus, did agree to descend into the Hades realm. How that works is explained in the next chapter. Chiron's physical wound, which he too carries with him as he travels from one world to the next, will have to wait till chapter 6.

Chapter 2 – Chiron and the *Trauma Helix* (1)

To give you an idea of how subconscious (2) memories of traumatic events are carried over from prior lives to the current one, I would like to tell you the story of Catherine (not her real name). The story begins on the first day of class of an astrology course Catherine had signed up for. This was still in the old days when I used to teach in brick-and-mortar classrooms, with all their corresponding inconveniences, in this case being the shape of the classroom. It was rather small and rectangular, with the teacher sitting in the front near the screen. Because of its oblong shape, the room did not allow for students to sit in a circle. Instead, they were made to sit the way we were at primary school, or at least I was, with students sitting in the back, in the middle and in the front of the room.

When all the students had got their coffees and teas and sat themselves down, it turned out some of the ones sat in the back could not see the screen because of some tall students who had chosen seats in the front. A negotiation of sorts ensued, in which one student suggested such and such could swap seats with such and such, so that everyone would be able to see what was happening on the screen.

This student suggested they all stand up to see who the tallest and who the shortest students were. At this point Catherine was already reluctant to participate and remained seated. The student who had taken the initiative was now effectively comparing heights and politely asking Catherine to stand up so that seating arrangements could be finalized and no more class time be lost on this. Catherine did so reluctantly and was clearly not happy with what was going on.

The student coordinating the comparative height study now stepped back and said something along the lines of *"Okay, now let's see who is the tallest here."* No sooner had she spoken these words than Catherine stormed out of the room angrily, saying *"I'm sorry, I'm not doing this!"* The other students looked at each other in bewilderment, not knowing what to make of what they had just witnessed and decided to just leave things as they had been. They took their seats, Catherine returned, and the class commenced as if nothing had happened.

The incident was not commented on by anyone after that. About a year or so later, Catherine requested a regression therapy session with me. She wanted to work on feeling uncomfortable when, as she said, *"men look at me in a certain way."* Although she herself did not link this issue to what had happened in class a year earlier, I immediately did. It was obvious, after all, that the classroom incident had had everything to do with appearance, and in particular with judgment made as a result of it.

During our session, we initially focused on specific times men had *"looked at her in a certain way,"* and on how this had made her feel. She recounted several and we revisited these so that she could experience these feelings again, which she did.

It turned out the feelings primarily had to do with shame and were centered, as she said: *"in my chest area."* With the feelings present on both the emotional (E) and the somatic (S) level, I asked her to go back to sometime in the past when she had experienced these very same feelings. Catherine then recounted a time when, in her first year of primary school, the teacher had asked the children to stand in line so that she could hand out aprons for an arts and crafts class. The teacher had small, medium and large-sized aprons and needed to know which to give out to who.

The worst moment for Catherine had been when the teacher had stepped back and said: *"Let's see now what we've got here."* Asked what she had wanted to do at this point, Catherine, who was sobbing and clearly in physical discomfort, said: *"I would just like to run away and never come back."*

Although she did not realize it herself, she was already in a past life. When I asked her *"Why don't you?"* she said: *"Because I can't!"*

"Why not?" I asked her. To which she replied: *"Because we are chained at the ankles."*

Although I, unlike Catherine, could not hear chains jangling, it was clear from what she subsequently told me that she was a slave. This is a good example of the kind of seamless transition from a current-life memory to a past-life one that can happen when an emotion is identified in a certain part of the body and felt strongly there. Later on in this chapter, when we come to speak of the **Trauma Helix**, you will understand why this is so. I will refer back to this point when we get there.

Further details provided by Catherine revealed she was in a line-up of slaves on a marketplace somewhere, with potential buyers comparing the slaves' bodily features. Exactly what had happened, therefore, in that astrology classroom and twenty-five years earlier at primary school. On both occasions, after all, she had been asked to stand up and be compared to others in terms of physical appearance. As a slave, she was bare-breasted and had felt shame as men came close, saw her nakedness and judged her body. She had also felt anger as the result of the powerlessness, and confusion because she did not know what would happen to her, nor where she would end up.

All three emotions – the shame, the anger and the confusion – were held in her chest area, which we now knew had to do with the fact of her having stood there with bare breasts. When I asked her what the worst moment of this experience was for her, she replied "*When the rich man steps back and says ´Now let's see what we've got here. ´*" The exact same words, therefore, that were spoken by her primary teacher and later by her fellow astrology student.

This story, which is more than a story but something that once actually happened and lives on in some distant part of Catherine's memory, could have come from the practice of any of the many thousands of regression therapists working all over the world today. (3) This is how these stories normally unfold. The shame and the anger have never gone away. They are as alive today as they were two hundred or two thousand years ago. The confusion felt at the time is secondary to the shame and the guilt - which are stronger emotions - but can be triggered by them.

Where is the origin of that anger and shame stored? Not in normal, everyday waking consciousness, otherwise we would be able to get to it through cognitive therapy or through other therapeutic modalities using linear, mercurial thought processes. But we cannot. Not just because in general it is very difficult to talk someone out of shame or anger, but also because that which caused them does not lie in this life. The incident in the astrology classroom was a re-enactment of the primary school line-up scene and both were a re-enactment of the original trauma that was incurred centuries earlier on a marketplace in some faraway country. The memories of this traumatic event are not stored in linear Mercury time

Past > Present > Future

but in the non-linear time, if we can call it that, of its higher octave Uranus. We will talk about the difference between the two in a minute. The three moments in time in Catherine's story, seemingly far removed from each other, are connected via a feeling nucleus stored at the deeper layers of the individual subconscious that is the domain of Uranus.

This nucleus can be triggered by a host of stimuli. It can be a smell, the way someone says something, or the way they look at you, a sound, certain words used, a situation, certain words used *in* a situation, a body sensation, or any combination of the above. I can walk into a room and smell something I have never smelled before in my life, but which pole-vaults me right back to a situation under an olive tree eight hundred years ago. The smell will immediately unlock all the other emotional (E), mental (M) and somatic (S) input I received at the moment of impact, that is, when the trauma was incurred. Which is why we are all of a sudden flooded with images, body pains, thought, feelings, etcetera. Just like Catherine was as she was made to stand next to others in order to be compared to them in terms of height. The whole package comes in through that one trigger, so to speak, but the memory is not accessible without an emotion.

The point of entry can be a thought or a pain, but sooner or later the therapist will want to know and ask for the emotion that comes with that thought or pain. A person might for example say: *"I always have to do everything myself."* That is not enough to go on. At some point the regression therapist will ask their client how that makes them feel. If the client responds *"sad,"* then we have got the emotion, which will be felt strongest in a certain part of the body. The sadness could be in the throat area, for example. Or, if there was anger, it could be lodged in the arms. An emotion centered in a specific body part or area will bridge memories of events belonging to different time periods. The reason for this is that these memories are not linearly grouped, Mercury wise, so to speak, but non-linearly arranged in Uranus' curved time warp, as we shall see shortly.

For Catherine there were several triggers connected to the slave trade life. The first one was the fact that in both current-life incidents, the primary school one and the later astrology class one, she was made to stand next to others in order to be compared in terms of physical appearance. The second trigger was that this comparing happened inside a classroom, that is, in a space she could not get away from, just like that marketplace hundreds of years earlier. And the third, perhaps strongest trigger, were the almost identical words spoken by the one doing the comparing in the three scenes: *"Now, let's see what we've got here,"* with the shame and anger linked to the merchandise character of these words.

Regression therapists are trained to what Roger Woolger (4) calls *"The Story behind the Story."* The sentence *"Now, let's see what we've got here,"* was identified as the worst moment by Catherine. The words and the physical action of stepping back by the one who speaks them so that they could better observe, belonging to three different stories, are what carried the strongest emotion for her. Men looking at her in a certain way, which is what she wanted to work on in therapy, triggers subconscious memories of having been treated as if she were a piece of meat. The men do not have to say the actual words. The way they look at her is enough to bring up the shame and the anger.

Anything which causes a person to behave out of character or makes them react disproportionally, may point to a story belonging to a different time period altogether. And to something unresolved coming from that story. Sometimes the story is only thirty or forty years away. Other times it goes back hundreds or even thousands of years. In Uranus' non-linear memory bank that makes little difference. In its subconscious time curvature events of three, thirty, three hundred and three thousand years ago lie side by side, united by this emotional nucleus we spoke of earlier. If that emotional core has never gone away, we could even say that regression therapy is not going back to the past at all: the past has simply always been right here and now.

Toroidal Uranus space

Uranus is the higher octave of Mercury. A higher octave is of the same make as its counterpart but vibrates at a higher frequency.

Mercury, as the lower octave of Uranus, has to do with linear, causal thought relationships. *'This'* comes before *'that'* and *"so it logically follows that ..."* etcetera. It rules our normal, waking consciousness where we need to draw logical conclusions based on discernable fact. Fact and the factual are very much part of Mercury's domain. As are language, thoughts, memories and their related imagery held in linear time. At the higher frequency of Uranus, it is still about thoughts and imagery related to memories. The difference, however, is that in Uranus' subconscious data storage these are no longer linearly arranged. Mental content in the Uranus domain follows the curved lines of warped time, so that two thousand years ago is bent and connects with twenty years away. And the curvature extends in all directions, like in a torus, where a vortex of energy is formed which bends back along itself.

In this toroidal space, linear Mercury time has become circular. Instead of A affecting B, which would be a linear Mercurial construct, the energy of the torus is continually affecting *itself*: A affecting A.

Tuesday no longer comes after Monday here. Noon no longer after morning. In curved Uranus time Catherine's marketplace scene, the primary school line-up and the astrology class thirty years 'later,' through the emotion of shame and anger they share, flow back into the torus vortex and blend into one event. The event has four components to it:

1. (**M**) a mental component (*"Now, let's see what we've got here,"* complemented by the actual images belonging to the scene and the thoughts which formed at the time)
2. (**E**) an emotional component (anger, shame, confusion)
3. (**S**) a physical component (the emotion is lodged in the chest area)
4. (**S**) a spiritual component (the meaninglessness of having your freedom taken from you)

The final component, the spiritual one, we have not talked about yet. As you can see, it has to do with meaningfulness, and its inevitable companion meaninglessness. A life lived as a slave leaves a trace in the soul narrative. It cuts a groove of hopelessness, disillusionment and despair, the same way a life spent in some Victorian kitchen does, with your hands eternally on pots and pans. After thirty years of scrubbing floors, keeping the fire going for the rich folk upstairs, without so much as a single stroll through his lordship's lush gardens, you ask yourself: *"What is the point in all of this? Why was I made to live this life? My youth is gone and so are my hopes and aspirations. If this is it, then why even bother?"*

The meaninglessness, astrologically, belongs to Neptune, Neptune being the higher octave of Venus. It vibrates at a higher frequency than its counterpart but is made of the same fabric. Meaning is related to the Taurus side of Venus. Although we find meaning in that which we relate to (the Libra side of Venus), the giving of meaning does not start out that way: initially we relate to what is meaningful to us (the Taurus side of Venus). In Taurus we give meaning to that which allows us to survive. What allows us to survive has value to us. It becomes valuable. That which is valuable to us, we ascribe meaning to. Over time it becomes our value system, that is, the inner set of values the relationship with ourselves is based on. In Libra, the outer, Yang side if Venus, we look for people who have similar values to ours, people who relate to themselves (Taurus) the way we do. It is only when we find those people and start relating to them, that we ascribe meaning to what we relate to.

Neptune, as the higher octave of Venus, points to what holds ultimate meaning to us. In therapeutic evolutionary astrology it has to do with trauma incurred to our sense of meaningfulness, carried over from prior lives to the current one. And, since from Saturn out, things operate according to the homeopathic principle of *like cures like*, <u>in</u> the trauma of the meaninglessness at once the potential for meaningfulness is found. In the chart of Richard Nixon in the previous chapter, I pointed out what this meaningfulness would consist of. Many more examples of Neptune meaning*less*ness and meaning*ful*ness will follow in this book.

The *Trauma Helix*

The four components of a past-life event experienced as traumatic, the memories of which are carried over into the current life, are:

1. (**M**) a mental component (Catherine: *"Now, let's see what we've got here."*): ***Uranus***
2. (**E**) an emotional component (Catherine: anger, shame, confusion): ***Pluto***
3. (**S**) a physical component (Catherine: the emotion is lodged in the chest area): see chapter 6 *The Multidimensional Psyche* (Chiron: the subtle body imprinting form). Also see footnote (36), chapter 6.
4. (**S**) an emotional meaninglessness component (Catherine: the sense of existential futility as a result of having your freedom taken from you): ***Neptune***

Uranus holds the actual memories of these events, the way a library stores books, with the important caveat that the storage, as we have seen, is non-linear. Like a library, it is emotionally not involved in the events. As it behooves ever-aloof Uranus, its non-linear memory vault simply tells you in what aisle and on what shelf the book is to be found. Once you find the book, open it and begin to read the story of what happened, however, you enter the domain of Pluto and Neptune.

Neptune's sense of meaninglessness as a direct result of the traumatic events, unlike Uranus, is highly laden emotionally. Where Uranus is distant, Neptune's disillusionment and despair are extremely emotive. The Neptune stuff, moreover, is gossamer, like lace: through Pluto's identification with its existential destitution and barrenness it seeps into the very nooks and crannies of the soul myth.

Pluto is the way the soul emotionally and psychologically identifies with the Uranus and Neptune strands and pulls their content into its own story. It identifies with the mental impact of the event – held in the Uranus domain as words, thoughts and images – *and* with the emotional torrents of Neptune's cascading waters, heavy with the rude awakening of disenchantment.

For our upcoming exploration of how Chiron relays this content to Saturn, it is important to know that all four components (M.E.S.S.) are held in Uranus' non-linear storage vault. Uranus, therefore, holds its own mental content (thoughts and images) linked to the event(s), Neptune's meaninglessness indentation as a direct result of it/them, the physical imprint belonging to the event(s), *and* Pluto's emotional and psychological identification with both strands curving around it.

Such is the nature of what I have termed **the Trauma Helix**, which, combined with the Chiron Key, hands the evolutionary astrologer tools that will allow him to understand how memories of traumatic events travel from one lifetime to the next. Combined with the findings provided by a careful analysis of the Evolutionary Axis (Pluto, SN of the Moon, SN ruler, PPP, NN, NN ruler, skipped steps), it will help him understand why past-life trauma is so often reenacted in the current life. The soul reenacts it not only to heal it but, equally important, also to further its own evolution. In the upcoming chapters of the book I hope to show you the combined effect of both interpretative techniques.

The *Trauma Helix* in the chart of Richard Nixon

For now, let us return to the chart of Richard Nixon for a first cursory look at what this bringing together of the Evolutionary Axis and the Chiron - *Trauma Helix* dynamic might render.

We see how the soul seems to have reached an impasse on its own evolutionary path: Pluto is ninety degrees square the Nodal Axis. This, in EA, is known as *a skipped step*. (5)

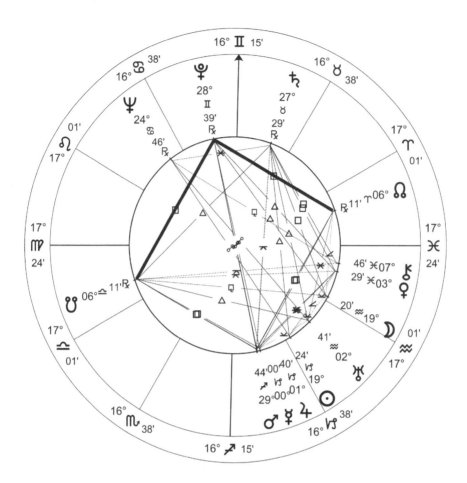

Pluto, by the way, is not the soul. The soul is too unfathomable, and yes, too sacred, to be squeezed into any one symbol, be it astrological or otherwise. Claiming that Pluto is the soul would be like saying *"OM is God."* Anyone making such a statement would immediately need to be taken to task: *"You mean, OM is God <u>too</u>."* If they then said "No, no, *OM* is God, OM *is* God!" one would feel an irresistible urge to counter *"God is everywhere, right? If he is everywhere, then surely, he is also in the snot hanging from the toddler's nose, in the bird on the wing, in the wispy clouds, in the squalor of the refugee camps."*

So, if Pluto is not the soul, then what *is* it? Pluto, like OM, is a symbol. As such it *points to* a reality. It is not that reality itself. In evolutionary astrology, Pluto points to the issues the soul has been exploring by creating multiple egos as the vehicles for said exploration, which are the same issues it comes into the current-life with and which it will hold onto for reasons of familiarity, or, to be more precise, because of the emotional security this familiarity provides.

[20]

Pluto 10th house Gemini

Pluto, then, in the chart of Richard Nixon, _points to_ the fact that the soul seems

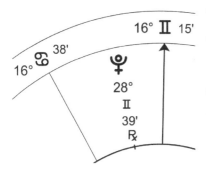

to have reached an impasse on its own evolutionary path because of the issues inherent in its house and sign placement: _to gain maximum power, status and notoriety_ (10th house) _through the clever use of words_ (Gemini) _and the underhand methods used to gather information_ (Gemini) _on others and use it against them._

SN of the Moon 1st house Libra

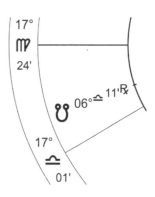

The way this issue has been explored by the soul is through prior-life selves whose modus operandi was 1st house Libra: _to engage in relationships_ (Libra) _with the sole purpose of furthering my own agenda and not having to reckon with anyone_ (1st house). Again, the SN of the Moon _is_ not those prior-life selves, the same way Pluto _is_ not the soul. The SN of the Moon _points to_ the dynamics operative in prior-life

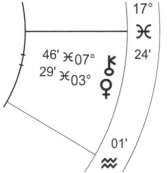

selves. Two very different things.

SN ruler 6th house Pisces

The way prior-life selves carried out this using people as pawns was by _deliberately creating confusion_ (Pisces) _in the workplace and in all matters related to work_ (6th house, literally 'in office') _in such a way as to imply shame and guilt_ (6th house) _in others in a bid to come out looking all innocent_ (Pisces) _themselves_. Very much the dynamics the soul's current-life vehicle Richard Nixon would resort to, therefore. If you have any doubts about the veracity of that statement, please read Anthony Summer's unsurpassed biography of the man: five hundred and forty pages of Nixon nefariousness. (6) As you can see, the SN ruler is glued to Chiron, so that already gives you an inkling of what that pain in all likelihood is going to be about.

Pluto Polarity Point 4th house Sagittarius

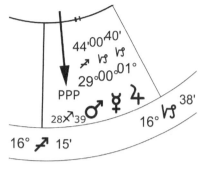

The place the soul intends to evolve towards in the current life is one of emotional truthfulness: 4th house Sagittarius. It is a place where the rigidity, the need for control and the emotional armoring proper to the hierarchical 10th house environments – having availed themselves of glib law (H10) talk (Gemini) and intellectual (Gemini) outmaneuvering – allow for *a rekindling of the emotional life (H4) so that truthfulness* (PPP in Sagittarius) *take the place of cleverness* (Pluto in Gemini) *used to get to the top*. There is a triple-headed skipped step right next to that point, as you can see. A huge boulder right in the middle of the Nodal Axis pointing to something that tripped prior-life selves up in their efforts to get to the NN of the Moon. We will get to that roadblock after we have mapped the NN of the Moon dynamics.

NN of the Moon 7th house Aries

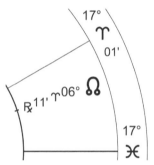

The NN of the Moon tells you how the PPP can be actualized on the Moon level in the current life, that is, in the life of the ego calling itself Richard Nixon. (7) Emotional truthfulness (PPP H4 Sagittarius) can be reached by the soul when Nixon *guarantees the other person's independence and freedom* (Aries) *within relationship* (H7) *by listening carefully* (H7) *to what they actually say*. Relationships will then be on an equal footing, which is the exact opposite, of course, of using people as pawns in your own chess game (SN 1st house Libra).

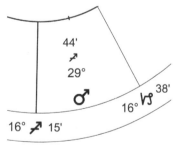

NN ruler Mars 4th house Sagittarius

The way this could have been carried out is through *emotional honesty*: 4th house Sagittarius. As it turned out, emotional dishonesty prevailed in the life of Richard Nixon: Mars is also a skipped step in this chart. That soul is okay with that, by the way, because it has all the (non) time in the (non) world: lessons not learned will simply return in the next vehicle it creates. The NN of the Moon and its ruler are an invitation only, not an imperative. An important observation, therapeutically speaking.

The fact that the NN ruler is a skipped step is significant: attempts at emotional honesty were apparently made by prior-life selves but got stranded. This information sheds light on the urgency of Pluto's retrogradation eager to get the heck out of Dodge and into the 4ᵗʰ house Sagittarius.

I am sure you are already beginning to understand how the 11ᵗʰ house Neptune trauma was formed: the fracturing in the emotional body, alongside the trauma of forcing a life upon myself which has nothing to do whatsoever with who I really am, a life that was a living lie (11ᵗʰ house dissociation).

The Mars skipped step works as a single unit with Mercury and Jupiter. The orbs are close enough for the three to be joined at the hip.

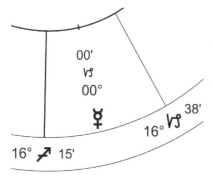

Mercury H4 Capricorn skipped step

The Mercury H4 Capricorn skipped step points to *prior-life selves having directed their thinking* (Mercury) *at the suppression* (Capricorn) *of the emotional body*, as would have been required of them in the hierarchical H10 environments the soul is so familiar with. Strict adherence to senseless rules and regulations, coupled with a lopsided emphasis on duty and obligation invariably calls for emotional armoring, and in some cases for the amputation of the emotional body.

Jupiter H4 Capricorn skipped step

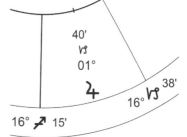

Here you see how the very *lens* (Jupiter) *through which prior-life selves looked out into the world* was cut and polished by the need to *suppress* (Capricorn) *the emotional body* (H4). The soul brings this into the current life as a major issue to be resolved, alongside those of its accomplices

Mars and Mercury. (8) And that makes sense, does it not? If this triple stumbling block has stood in the way of prior-life selves actualizing their NN of the Moon, which is the facilitator of the PPP, then obviously it has thwarted soul evolution.

How has the triple Mars-Mercury-Jupiter roadblock stood in the way of the 7th house Aries NN? That is not too difficult to see: when you are emotionally dishonest and suppress the emotional body, then obviously you are not going to be able to feel what is going on at the other end of the scale. How are you going to listen to other (H7) when you are holding back or stamping out an essential part of yourself? How is there going to be equality in your relationship with other when there is none in the relationship with yourself?

I am going through this rather quickly for it is standard EA reasoning (which I teach at my EA School Online) (9) and not the object of our investigation. It is the way to it. The object of our investigation is how the soul would have identified with the trauma charge. The answer to that is written in Pluto by house and sign. Please bear with me. We are almost there.

Although we already identified the *Trauma Helix* in this chart in chapter 1, I am going to run it by you one more time, just to refresh your memory.

The Uranus strand in the *Trauma Helix*

The Uranian toroidal space and time holds memories of events where prior-life Nixon's were *suddenly* (Aquarius) *dissociated* (Aquarius) *from a leadership* (H5) *which had become separated from* (Aquarius) *generosity and impartiality aimed*

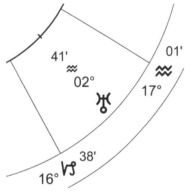

at bringing out the best in others (Leo in its higher expression). The reenactment of this trauma can be averted when and if Nixon *steps back* (Aquarius) *and looks objectively* (Aquarius) *at his need to always come out on top* (H5) *and be an undisputed leader* (H5). That would be the healing of the trauma. What needs to be objectively assessed, above all else, is *the fundamental emotional insecurity* (H5) *feeding this need*. Once seen for what it is, Uranus will impact H6, which it rules, where the Moon is commissioned with the task of *stepping back* (Aquarius) *in order to be able to look objectively* (Aquarius) *at what true service from a place of humility* (H6) *means.*

Now, folded into this Uranus strand, lies the whole Pluto and Neptune package.

The Neptune strand in the *Trauma Helix*

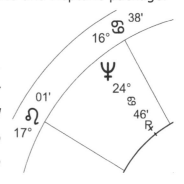

The meaninglessness trauma, as we saw in chapter 1, hinges on the *fracturing* (H11) *of the emotional body* (Cancer) as a result of *prior-life selves having forced a life upon themselves that had nothing to do with who they knew themselves to be, turning their lives into a living lie*: H11 dissociation.

{As Nixon would in this life, in all probability causing him to seek therapeutic assistance from New York psychiatrist Dr Hutschnecker early on in his career. (10) Nixon's, that is, not Hutschnecker's}

Please note how this conclusion not only resonates with the life lived by the person Nixon but also with the traumatic events – or rather with the memories thereof – around sudden dissociation from his leadership (H5 Aquarius) caused by the inability to develop any kind of objective (Aquarius) awareness of the emotional insecurity underlying his need to be Number One (H5).

The Pluto strand in the *Trauma Helix*

The way the soul would have identified emotionally and psychologically with the Uranus and with the Neptune strand is through *being deeply divided* (Gemini) *inwardly in terms of integrity* (H10), which would feel (we are talking about an emotional identification) to the soul *as if it cannot count on itself, as if it were turned against itself*. That stands to reason, does it not? When you are in this double dissociative state all of your life and incapable of observing objectively what causes it, because you simply cannot or will not (see triple Mars-Mercury-Jupiter skipped step H4) go there, then that becomes part of the soul story in the form of this *chasm* (Gemini) *in inner accountability* (H10).

Chiron 6th house Pisces relaying the trauma charge to Saturn *as a woundedness*

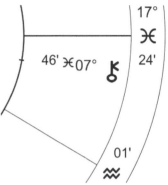

Chiron now travels deep into the Uranian realm to collect this trauma parcel (Uranus, Pluto, Neptune), then travels all the way back to Saturn and delivers it to him. On the way, which is a very long way indeed, our inhabitant of two worlds has plenty of time to study the Uranus material and translate it into language Saturn will understand. Chiron, being the master healer that he is, *would* understand his own pain, would he not? When he gets to Saturn's doorstep, he knows what is inside the package. Chiron has labeled it so that Saturn will understand at a single glance. What is named on the label is found in the jar. The label says 'H6 Pisces': *a pain caused by deeply engrained confusion* (Pisces) *around what true service from a place of humility* (H6) *means.*

Chiron's healing, by the way, is *in* the same combination of house and sign, since in the wounding the healing can be found when this mist clears and is lifted, effectively bringing about *healing* (Pisces) *in all matters service and humility* (H6).

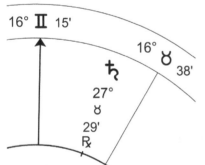

Saturn in the 9th house Taurus

When the parcel is handed to Saturn by Chiron, the soul knows exactly how the consciousness of its vehicle needs to be structured. For the soul to reach the emotional truthfulness of the 4th house Sagittarius, it is imperative that the consciousness of the vehicle created by the soul – Nixon in this case – be structured in such a way as to allow for *the consolidation* (Taurus) *of truthfulness* (H9) and that it reflect on this issue long and hard all of its life (Saturn retrograde).

[26]

I hope you see the therapeutic importance of this model. Combined with the Evolutionary Axis, it will allow you to put your finger on something that hitherto has been the exclusive domain of regression therapists: to identify how this trauma charge, heaving at the depths of the Uranian memory vault, percolates up and protrudes into the life of your client.

Chapter 3 – Crossing the Bridge to Saturn

Saturn in evolutionary astrology is the way the soul wants consciousness to operate in its vehicle. Its choice for how it wants consciousness structured in the person who is going to be its instrument for learning certain lessons is informed on the one hand by where it seeks to evolve towards and on the other by the trauma charge it brings into the current life as pain. The former we read in the Pluto Polarity Point, that is, the point diametrically opposite the Pluto placement by house and sign, whereas the latter is written in the Chiron placement and the *Trauma Helix*. I will come back to how Chiron impacts Saturn in chapter 6, under *Chiron: the subtle body imprinting form*.

Let us again use the chart of Richard Nixon to illustrate this.

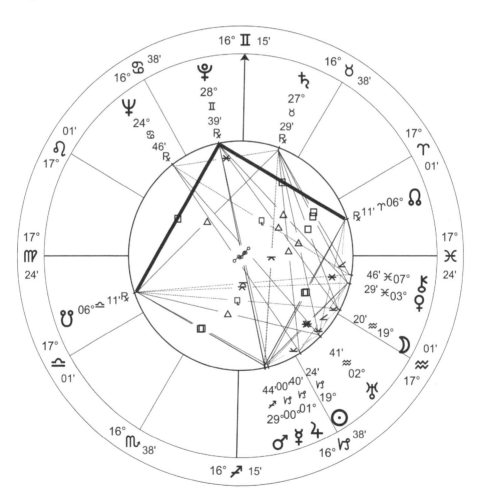

Richard Nixon, 9 January 1913, 21:35 hrs., Yorba Linda, California, RR:AA

[29]

The soul comes from a place where it would have been familiar with hierarchical environments where strict codes of conduct had to be adhered to (H10). Often, in these environments there is a lopsided emphasis on duty, obligation and functionality. As a boy Richard Nixon displayed the kind of seriousness, bordering on dourness, required of one in these stratified and highly ordered environments that the soul would have had memories of coming into this life. The sternness was never more evident than in his approach to his schoolwork, and it made him less than popular with his peers. There was always time for more learning and reading (Pluto in Gemini), little for play.

Emotional armoring is another characteristic of the kind of 10th house Capricornian environments in which the soul would have been exposed to codified rules of behavior backed by the threat of force known as 'law.' To be fully functional and fulfil your duties like clockwork, emotions can seriously get in the way and therefore need to be suppressed or amputated altogether. In Nixon this dynamic showed as an awkwardness around people, especially women. Even in the autumn of life, Nixon could feel his stomach turn by shows of affection involving physical contact with friends, family or relatives. (1) His mother, Hannah Milhous Nixon, coming from a clannish Quaker family where the exact adherence to tradition was expected of her that Richard's 10th house soul came into the current life with, never held or comforted the boy. (2) A disciplinarian, she taught him to work hard and persevere: another Capricornian trait. The young boy would sit up till late in the evening doing his homework, often with his mother around. *"My mother spent countless hours,"* Nixon would later write as he looked back on his life, *"encouraging me, helping me with homework and challenging me to learn."* (3) Discipline (Pluto H10) and knowledge (Pluto in Gemini) modelled early on in the life by the person he emotionally depended on and who could not bring herself to hug him or run her fingers through his hair. As the emotional armoring hardened and Nixon went from adolescence to adulthood, he told himself that he did not need affection, only to be held in regard and appreciated for the man he was. (4)

There can be a certain moral flimsiness to Gemini. Its fleetingness does not leave much time for lengthy moral deliberations. Hardly has the butterfly alighted on one flower than it is on the next. Gemini can be on-the-spot-decision-making,

[30]

where in a split-second action is taken that will decide whether you have a roof over your head for the night or not. The indiscriminate intake of information, something so evident in young Nixon, lacks a center around which the endless stream of data can cohere. Hence Gemini's square to Virgo, who excels at separating the wheat from the chaff so that unnecessary information is not taken in and surplus information chucked.

When you bring these 10th house traits through the filter of Gemini, you begin to get an idea of the kinds of issues the soul has been exploring, comes into the current life with and will default to for reasons of familiarity: Nixon's lifelong obsession with entitlement and social class lies squarely on the Capricorn side of the equation. On the Gemini side we find the insatiable quest for knowledge and the glib law talk. When you combine the two archetypes in the way suggested, you get *the outmaneuvering* (H10) *through clever argumentation* (Gemini), *the lack of integrity* (H10) *not only in the gathering of information* but, above all, how it is subsequently *used to defeat opponents and gain a position of maximum power and status* (H10), with *Gemini's moral frailty exacerbating Capricorn's questionable integrity*.

Although the soul will hold on to these dynamics for dear life and kick up a stink when made to leave the 10th house, it nevertheless wishes to evolve to the 4th house. There the emotional armoring can be removed so that feelings can flow unimpeded again. There the soft and vulnerable side of self can come to the fore. There the sternness in discipline can be let go of so that you can let your hair hang loose for a day and do nothing for a change, just idling the time away.

The Sagittarius half of the Pluto Polarity Point has to do with truthfulness. The soul wishes to move away from the Gemini immorality we signaled above and embrace the moral compass of being true to oneself. Please note how close we have come to Capricorn integrity with this sentence. Logically so, because truthfulness is a prerequisite for integrity. Which is why the 9th house comes before the 10th. Integrity, it could be argued, can be defined as being truthful to oneself.

If for the PPP you were to add the Cancer and the Sagittarius archetypes up, you would still not have mapped what the soul wishes to evolve towards, the same way you would not grasp the 10th house soul issues by having a bit of Capricorn on the one side and a bit of Gemini on the other. Half a kilo of apples and half a kilo of pears in evolutionary astrology a kilo of fruit does not make. To map them accurately, we need to synthesize the two archetypes in such a way as to depict the opposite of what we found in the 10th house Gemini. When we do that, we get a sentence: *if the soul manages to let go of its obsession with power and prestige, emotional security can be found within* (H4) *and the clever use of words, accompanied by underhand methods of gathering information and using it against others, can make way for truthfulness.*

As you can see in the chart, Pluto is a skipped step, indicating the soul seems to have got stuck on its own evolutionary path, unable to move back, forth or sideways. The fact that it is out of sign does not mean that it does not count as a square: if the square had been from Cancer, we would have lost the information that is key to understanding exactly what it is that got the soul to its stuck place. Through the 10th house Gemini the issue is articulated with great precision and, as we saw above, highly applicable to the life of Richard Nixon.

Pluto's retrogradation tells us that the soul in the current life will create circumstances that will cause an acceleration in the direction of the 4th house Sagittarius polarity point. In plain English: the soul wants to get the heck out of Dodge. With the clarity of hindsight, we know what those circumstances were.

Saturn and the Pluto Polarity Point

Why does the soul place Saturn in the 9th house Taurus? How would structuring a consciousness that way help it get to the 4th house Sagittarius? The soul wants consciousness in its vehicle Nixon structured in such a way as to allow for *the consolidation* (Taurus) *of truthfulness* (H9). On top of that, it wants its vehicle to reflect deeply on this issue all of its life: Saturn's retrogradation tells us the 9th house Taurus energy is turned inward for reflection. The reason for this is none other than the soul having got stuck in its 10th house Gemini predicament. It is not too difficult to see how the soul *would* need consciousness in the vehicle Nixon to ponder on how *to strengthen* (Taurus) *truthfulness* (H9) if it is ever going to get out of the ditch it finds itself in.

Through house rulership we learn that the extent to which the vehicle Nixon is willing to reflect on truthfulness will affect his leadership: Saturn rules the 5th house. Already, just by looking at three points in the chart – Pluto, the PPP and Saturn – we have learned a great deal about soul issues and the nature of the consciousness operative in the current-life self created by the soul to learn its lessons through.

Saturn and the Moon

The astrological equivalent of that self we find in the Moon in the 6th house Aquarius, commissioned with the task of *stepping back* (Aquarius: distancing) *in order to look objectively* (Aquarius) *at the issue of service from a place of humility* (H6). Immediately we understand the relationship between Saturn and the Moon, between the structure of consciousness operative in the vehicle and the vehicle itself.

Saturn and the Chiron-*Trauma Helix* dynamic

The soul´s choice to render a specific kind of structure to the consciousness

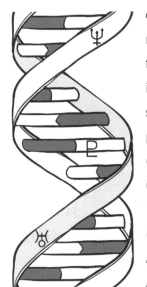

operative in its vehicle, we said, is also informed by the nature of the Chiron pain as it relays the trauma charge from one lifetime to the next. The trauma charge, after all, is caused by certain events having taken place in prior-life selves. These events do not stand by themselves: they are part of a story. The Uranus trauma of *dissociation* (Aquarius) *from his leadership* (H5) lies embedded in the unquenchable thirst for power and status we detected in the 10th house Gemini Pluto. The meaninglessness trauma (Neptune) of *forcing a life upon yourself that in no way reflects who you truly are* (H11), *causing fracturing* (H11) *in the emotional body* (Cancer) as well as *pretending before the nation* (Cancer) *to be someone you know you are not* (H11), is part of the same 10th house Gemini obsession with notoriety begotten through Machiavellian information gathering. Precisely because of this, the soul emotionally and psychologically identifies with the Uranus and Neptune strand as *a divisiveness*

(Gemini) *in integrity* (Gemini), *a split* (Gemini) *in its ability to hold itself accountable* (H10).

As Chiron moves deep into the Uranus orbit to pick this trauma charge up and translate it as pain, transferring it all the way back to Saturn, the soul has all the (non) time in the (non) world to make up its mind as to what kind of structure consciousness in its next vehicle is to have. The distinct dissociative element present in both Nixon's Uranus and Neptune trauma signature is translated by Chiron as a pain caused by *a pervasive confusion* (Pisces) *around true service from a place of humility* (H6), with the potential for healing found in the very Chiron placement (the *Like cures Like* principle I alluded to in the previous chapter) when Nixon learns to *discern* (H6) *exactly who he is serving* (H6): self or other. When he does, the Piscean mist around this issue clears and *being of service* (H6) *is healed* (Pisces).

A lot of truthfulness is needed for that. And so the soul decides it wants consciousness in the vehicle Nixon to operate in such a way as to allow for *the consolidation* (Saturn in Taurus) *of truthfulness* (Saturn H9). Whether the vehicle will heed the call is another matter altogether. It is, after all, endowed with free will. Free will, will allow it to make all the wrong choices, which, evolutionary speaking, are as important as the right choices since the soul will learn from both. Even the vehicle, in some instances, learns from both. Not always, but sometimes. (5) The soul, however, always learns from whatever choices are made. It cannot afford not to since so much planning has gone into the creation of yet another life, so many other people are involved in the intricate network of key players, some from Nixon´s own soul group and some from neighboring ones. This is why you will hear me say that the reenactment of trauma often serves an evolutionary purpose. In Nixon´s case: *the ultimate humiliation* (H6) *of getting removed from office* (Uranus H5 Aquarius - dissociated from leadership - ruling the 6th house of service through work, i.e. office) helped the soul develop emotional truthfulness (PPP H4 Sagittarius).

Saturn coloring everything within its realm

Saturn is also the outer limit of consciousness operative in the vehicle. It is a ringed planet because within its boundaries it holds several planetary functions which are all going to contribute to the soul getting to the 4th house Sagittarius Pluto Polarity Point. What I would like to do now, is specify how this works for each and every one of them: Jupiter, Mars, Venus, and Mercury. The Moon and her nodes are not subject to Saturn's rule since they are where they are for their own reasons, which ultimately are the soul's and not Saturn's. They were explicated in the previous chapter as we went through Richard Nixon's Evolutionary Axis (made up of Pluto, the SN of the Moon, the SN ruler, the PPP, the NN of the Moon, the NN ruler, skipped steps).

Jupiter saying *"I think it means this"*

When the Saturn message hits Jupiter, it is interpreted by the gas giant. This is what Jupiter does: it interprets. That is why it is so big: so that we can all have our own interpretative model, our own version of the truth (Sagittarius) instead of one, single truth proclaimed universal and imposed on everyone through whatever doctrine or creed (Sagittarius). Gemini is the facts, Jupiter the interpretation of the facts. Jupiter in therapeutic evolutionary astrology is the lens through which the soul wants its vehicle to look out into the world, to interpret it. The soul's rationale for the Jupiter placement, as for that of the other planets, needs to be understood in the light of where it seeks to evolve toward in the current life, which astrologically is expressed in the Pluto Polarity Point. In Nixon's chart this translates as:

The soul, wanting to get to the emotional truthfulness of the 4th house Sagittarius wants its vehicle – created for that express purpose and called Nixon – to look through glasses tainted by the need to bring integrity (Capricorn) to the emotional body (H4). This is the way *consolidation of truthfulness* (Saturn H9 Taurus) is interpreted by Jupiter with the 4th house Sagittarius PPP in mind.

This is one of those instances in EA, by the way, where you need to deal with a planet on two different levels: on one you deal with it as a skipped step, which we did in the previous chapter, and on the other you try and determine its function by answering the following questions: *"in what way would this planet in this house and sign contribute to the soul actualizing the evolutionary intentions it has for the current life? Why did the soul place it there? What function does it have, evolutionary speaking?"* Determining a planet's function against the backdrop of where the soul seeks to evolve towards is the one thing that can keep us away from the scourge of cookie-cutter descriptions of planets in houses and signs: bland, non-descriptive, generalized and demonstrably untrue statements (6) which are the antithesis of the specificity needed to be able to work with clients therapeutically.

Mars acting on Jupiter's interpretation

Once the Saturn message has been interpreted by Jupiter, it is passed on to Mars so that the vehicle can act on it. The planetary order makes sense, does it not? First you need to interpret the message before you can put it into action. If you do not know where you are going (Jupiter: where the arrow is pointed at), there is little point whipping the horse to make it go (Mars). In Nixon's case: *the need to grow up* (Jupiter in Capricorn) *emotionally* (Jupiter H4) *can now be acted upon by developing emotional truthfulness*: Mars 4th house Sagittarius.

Venus now knowing what kind of relationship to engage in

Now that Mars has acted, Venus is instructed to engage in a particular kind of relationship that will contribute to the soul actualizing its evolutionary intentions for the current life. That relationship is not always with people, as we will see in this and other charts to come. From Nixon's Venus in the 6th house Pisces we glean the soul placed a premium on him *healing* (Pisces) *his relationship* (Venus) *with true service from a place of humility* (H6*). "How is that relevant to where the soul seeks to evolve towards?"* you ask. It is relevant in that humility *is* a form of emotional truthfulness (PPP H4 Sagittarius). Making sentences like this is not too difficult when you apply the correct order in the filtering:

1. what is the planet about?
2. house conditions planet
3. sign contextualizes planet *in* the house

what is the planet about?	house conditions the planet	sign contextualizes house *in* planet
relationship	true service from a place of humility	to heal

[36]

This is not quantum physics. Anyone can learn it. When you string the actual sentence together, you will find that, for reasons of syntax, you sometimes need to jump between boxes a bit. In the sentence I came up with I went from box 3 to 1 and then onto 2: *to heal* (box 3) *his relationship* (box 1) *with true service from a place of humility* (box 2). Just play around with this for a bit and you will soon get the hang of it. It is actually quite good fun.

Mercury now knowing how to think

Next port of call is Mercury. In order to get to the 4th house Sagittarius, *the soul wants all thinking* (Mercury) *directed at maturing* (Capricorn) *emotionally* (H4), *allowing the emotional body* (H4) *to grow up* (Capricorn), which is the same as to say *bringing integrity* (Capricorn) *to the emotional body* (H4).

Given the close relationship between truthfulness (Sagittarius) and integrity (Capricorn), it does not take much to see how Mercury developing this kind of integrity would help the soul get to the 4th house Sagittarius. Shall we pry the sentence open again and place its parts in neat boxes? Deal. Here we go:

what is the planet about?	house conditions the planet	sign contextualizes house *in* planet
thinking	emotional body	to mature, to grow up, to develop integrity

Here you see, that in forming the actual sentence, good syntax had me start in box 1, then continue to box 2, where halfway through I jumped to box 3, picked up the information there, and then made the tail end of the sentence with what was left over in box 2: *thinking* (box 1) *directed at* (Box 2. We jump to box 3) *bringing integrity to* (back to box 2) *the emotional body*.

In the following chapters you will see just how accurate this way of forming astrological sentences is. By 'accurate,' I mean borne out by *the Life Lived*, by the actual biographical data available to us. Which is one of the reasons I am using the charts of famous people in this book instead of those of my clients. If I did the latter, you would have no way of corroborating the findings. I could be making the whole thing up. Not that you would expect me to do such a thing, I know, but still. I want to avoid you even harboring such thoughts. Using the charts of famous people forces me to constantly correlate my findings to the biographical facts available and do so in a way that is understandable to you, the reader. In short: it greatly helps me stay on course and achieve maximum clarity.

The Sun: that around which everything revolves in the current life of the soul's vehicle

We skip earth because we are on it. And so we get to the Sun. Some of you may protest heavily at this point, but it is my contention that the Sun by house and sign, although ultimately determined by the soul, does have something to do with the way it wants consciousness in its vehicle structured (Saturn).

Translated to English for Richard Nixon: there is a relationship between a consciousness structured in such a way as to allow for the consolidation (Taurus) of truthfulness (H9) and the central, integrative principle around which Nixon's whole life revolves: *to develop integrity* (Capricorn) *in his leadership* (H5).

And there you have it: Saturn, having received the Chiron parcel, coloring the whole chart. Astrologically it is important to give words to Saturn as the structure of consciousness and to then see how it affects everything coming before it. I find it a most useful exercise in understanding how the energetic field known as the 'psyche' of the vehicle is inwardly organized by the soul in such a way as to further its evolution.

Chapter 4 – Proof, please! Abraham Lincoln

To astrologically trace how trauma travels from one lifetime to the next we can use the charts of Anne Frank and Barbro Karlén. In chapter nine of my book *Intercepted Signs: Encoded Messages from the Soul* (1) I provide ample proof for my stated claim that these are two consecutive lives created by the same soul. If the Chiron-*Trauma Helix* model has any validity to it, then the Chiron, Uranus, Neptune and Pluto placements in the chart of Barbro Karlén should directly point back to trauma incurred in the life of Anne Frank, with Chiron transferring it *as pain* from one life to the other.

(see chart p.41)

Uranus in Barbro's chart is in the 12th house Cancer: *trauma suffered by a family (Cancer) in hiding* (H12). Uranus is conjunct the SN of the Moon and therefore speaks of this trauma having directly impacted prior-life selves.

The particulars of the SN of the Moon and what happened to this family in hiding are written in the 8th house Aquarius SN ruler: they were *taken to a place of death* (H8) *where large groups of people* (Aquarius) *were murdered*, which obviously constituted trauma (Aquarius).

Neptune, the meaninglessness strand of the trauma incurred as a result of these events, is in the 4th house Libra: the *disillusionment, despair and victimization* (Neptune) *as a result of what was projected* (Libra) *onto Anne's race* (H4) *and family* (H4).

Pluto, the way the soul emotionally identifies with both the Uranus and the Neptune strand, is in the 2nd house Leo: out of necessity *all of my creative energy* (Leo) *has been poured into how to stay under the radar and inside my lair* (H2).

Chiron is in the 7th house Capricorn: a pain caused by *inequality* (H7) *projected upon people* (H7) *through negative judgement* (Capricorn) *coming from dysfunctional authority* (Capricorn): the Nazi regime.

We find Barbro's **Saturn**, who is going to receive the trauma parcel from Chiron, in the 5th house Scorpio: *a deep commitment* (Scorpio) *to the solar principle* (H5) *so that it never again is betrayed* (Scorpio) *the way it was in that other life*. The commitment will manifest as an outpouring of creativity in the life of young Barbro, a published author at the tender of age of sixteen with eleven books to her name. (2) Creative energy turned inward (Pluto H2 Leo), imploded almost, is now turned outward. You can see how important that would be to a soul wishing to *open up* (PPP H8) and then *deeply merge with and commit to* (PPP H8) *a socially relevant cause* (PPP Aquarius). In chapter 15, I will expand on what that cause is. Since one swallow does not a summer make, you are going to ask more proof from me.

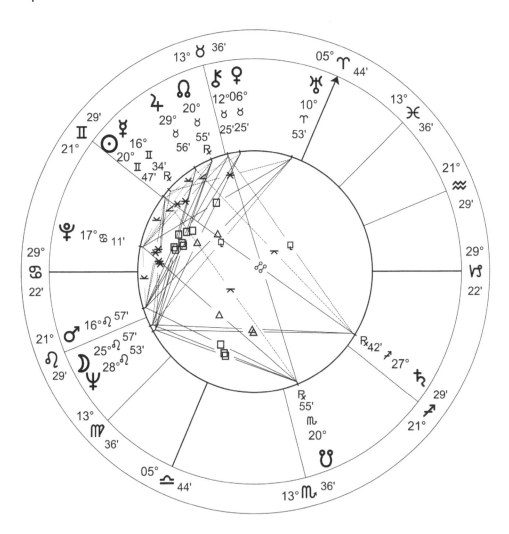

Anne Frank, 12 June 1929, 07:26 hrs., Frankfurt am Main, Germany. RR:AA

[40]

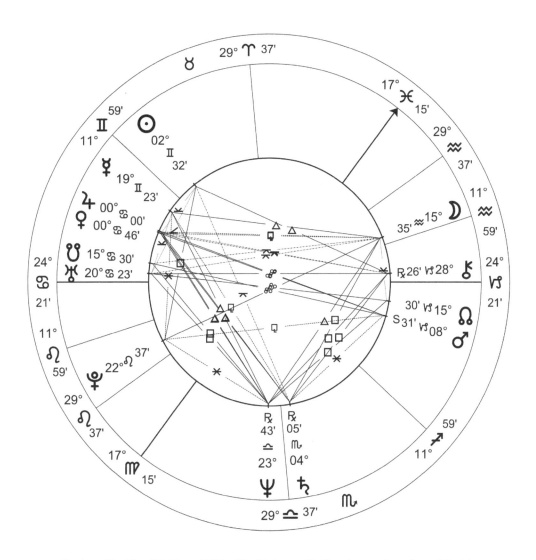

Barbro Karlén, 24 May 1954, 07:20 hrs., Gothenburg, Sweden. RR:AA

Charts belonging to two consecutive lives created by the same soul are hard to come by. I nevertheless happened to stumble on a clue to two of them as I was reading Swami Kriyananda's book *"The Path: Autobiography of a Western Yogi"* (3) and came across a quote by Paramahansa Yogananda in which he suggested that Abraham Lincoln in a prior life had been a Himalayan yogi who died with the wish of contributing to racial parity. The quote further stated that the reason for Lincoln´s life was to meet the yogi's desire of helping bring about this goal, and that Lincoln, in his turn, had returned in the twentieth century as Charles Lindbergh.

[41]

With my curiosity piqued, I was eager to find out if there were astrological correlates that could back up Yogananda's claim. And so I set about investigating them. Here are my findings. We begin with Lincoln's chart so that we may gain an understanding of where the soul was coming from when it created the vehicle Lincoln and where it sought to evolve towards.

Pluto 1st house Pisces

Unless you have set aside time to sink your teeth into Charles Darwin's chart, Louis Braille's or Edgar Allan Poe's - all born in the year 1809 - you probably will not have too much experience in interpreting Pluto placements in the sign of Pisces. It is a placement you are not going to run into in your client work.

Looking at Braille's, I was struck by the Aries nature of the Pluto-Jupiter conjunction in the 4th house Pisces: *the birth* (H4) *of a healing* (Pisces) *vision* (Jupiter), in this case one offered to the visually impaired. Jupiter rules the 2nd house, where we find all-important Mercury in Capricorn: *thinking directed at single-handedly* (Capricorn) *devising a reading system* (Mercury) *using tactile* (2nd house) *information* (Mercury) *read by the hands* (Mercury).

When first laying eyes on Darwin's chart, where Pluto is in the 3rd house Pisces, the image that came to me was that of a man trying to *devise one universal* (Pisces) *theory* (H3) *that would explain* (H3) *the diversity* (H3) *of the manifested world* (H3). When I looked at the SN in the 5th house Taurus, I literally saw *Creation* (H5) *reduced* (Taurus) *to survival* (Taurus), the bone of contention that caused Darwin's major run-in with the Church. These were first impressions, of course, of the kind that come to you when you dream your way into the chart. (4)

I even saw the *intellectual pioneer* Darwin in the SN ruler 3rd house Aries. Whether those impressions are correct or not becomes clear only after further work on the chart is done, but they often prove important pointers that can lay the intuitive foundations of one's understanding of a chart.

(see chart p.44) In similar fashion, Lincoln's Pluto in the 1st house Pisces immediately conjured up images of *the healing* (Pisces) *of freedom* (1st house) and of a soul familiar with having to *surrender* (Pisces) *its identity, freedom and*

[42]

right to exist (H1). Lincoln, born on the same day as Darwin, has that same Pluto-Jupiter conjunction in his chart, the one we also saw in Louis Braille's chart.

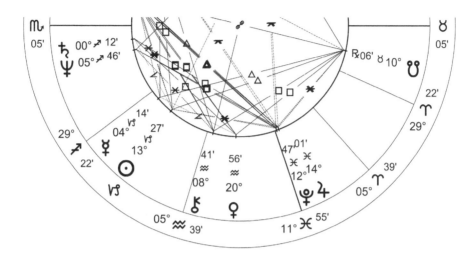

Louis Braille, 4 January 1809, 04:00 hrs., Coupvray, France. RR:AA

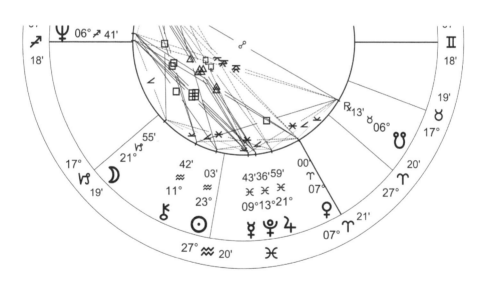

Charles Darwin, 12 February 1809, 03:00 hrs., Shrewsbury, United Kingdom. RR:DD

Here, in the first house, however, the vision (Jupiter) seemed to be about healing people's freedom. *"What house does it rule?"* I immediately asked myself. The

[43]

10th house of law, of institutionalized fairness and justice, and its flipside: hardened and calcified unfairness and injustice.

SN of the Moon 3rd house Taurus

Like Darwin's, Lincoln's SN of the Moon is in Taurus. But it is in the 3rd house instead of in the 5th: prior-life selves, created by the soul, would somehow have *experienced a limitation* (Taurus) *in their right or ability to integrate* (3rd house). (5) It would make sense for a 1st house soul exploring the issue of victimization, surrender and subsequent loss (Pisces) of identity, freedom and right to exist (H1) to create lives like that, would it not? This logic I have termed *the Inner Logic of the Soul*, and I first told you about it in my book *Intercepted Signs: Encoded Messages from the Soul*. (6)

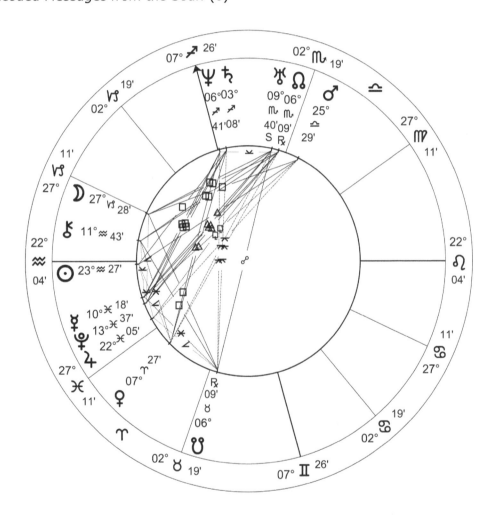

Abraham Lincoln, 12 February 1809, 06:54 hrs., Hodgenville, Kentucky. RR:B

[44]

SN ruler Venus 2nd house Aries

How did this play out? Prior-life selves were *not able to consolidate* (2nd house)

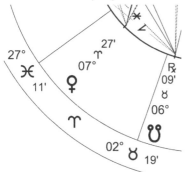

their identity, freedom and right to exist (Aries). They may even *not have survived* (2nd house) *because of their pioneering role* (Aries) *in trying to do so.* (SN ruler linked back to the SN). These are the dynamics through which the soul explored the issue of a loss of

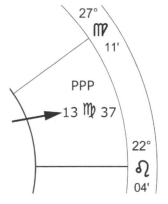

identity, freedom and right to exist (Pluto H1 Pisces).

Pluto Polarity Point 7th house Virgo

Having explored the issue of loss (Pisces) around identity, freedom and right to exist (H1), the soul wishes to evolve to a place of *equality in relationship* (7th house) where both sides truly listen to each other, to what is on the other scale. When this happens there can be no loss of identity for I am now connected (H7), (7) so that my identity is found in the mirror of other (H7). This is *the cause the soul wishes to serve* (Virgo).

NN of the Moon H9 Scorpio conjunct Uranus

The way this soul intention can be carried out on the level of self, on the Moon level of personality, is when there is *a deep, all-consuming commitment* (Scorpio) *to societal freedom*, that is, *liberty* (H9), or, in Lincoln's own words from the Gettysburg address "*a New Birth* [Scorpio] *of Freedom*" [H9]. Sagittarius'

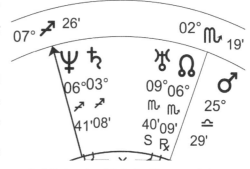

concern is societal for it knows that where the flag of truthfulness waves, principles are established which in the next house of Capricorn will lead to a fair and just society.

Through Uranus' conjunction to the NN of the Moon, you can see that in a recent prior life the NN received a major boost from Uranus the liberator to do just that:

to deeply commit to the cause of liberty (Sagittarius). (8) This is the life of the Himalayan yogi who, in all likelihood, died as a result of wanting to bring about racial equality. The life Paramahansa Yogananda referred to.

The Uranus strand of the trauma: 9th house Scorpio

The Aquarius Ascendant, the Cosmic Birth Canal through which the incarnating soul must pass, carries subconscious memories not only of this commitment but also of the consequences it had for the yogi (the Ascendant is ruled by Uranus). It constituted the trauma of *death* (Uranus in Scorpio) *because of his allegiance* (Uranus in Scorpio) *to the cause of liberty* (Uranus H9). This trauma was reenacted in the life of Lincoln when he was shot on April 14th 1865, while attending a play at Ford's Theatre in Washington, D.C., by Confederate sympathizer John Wilkes Booth as part of a larger conspiracy intended to revive the Confederate cause by eliminating the three most important officials of the United States government, that is, to undo the fight for this Sagittarian liberty.

NN ruler Pluto 1st house Pisces

Few words suffice here: the way this deep commitment to the 9th house cause of liberty was carried out by Lincoln was through him trying to *heal* (Pisces) *everyone's* (Pisces) *identity, freedom and right to exist* (1st house).

Moon 12th house Capricorn skipped step (9)

Lincoln´s mother died when he was twelve years old. Some historians state *"milk sickness"* (an illness caused by drinking the milk of cows that had eaten white snakeroot) as the cause of death, others tuberculosis. One possible translation of the astrological symbols reads: *his mother* (Moon) *disappeared from his life* (H12), *marking the onset of bouts of depression* (Capricorn) that would last a lifetime. Is this something brought in by the soul as a boulder on the road from the SN to the NN of the Moon? In other words: is it an unresolved issue that stopped the Himalayan yogi from his deep commitment to the cause of liberty (NN H9 Scorpio), in Lincoln's chart buoyed up by Uranus the liberator standing tall next to the NN and helping it scale the 9th house Scorpio wall? It does not feel like the right piece we need for this particular part of the puzzle, does it? The death of the mother as something that not only befell Lincoln but the Himalayan yogi too and sent him back to his 3rd house Taurus, that is, to the limitation experienced in their right or ability to integrate does not really make a whole lot of sense at all. So, we need to tackle this differently. The way to go about that is to

1. ask yourself what a Moon skipped step might entail
2. let the option you go for be informed by a relevant house issue
3. and place that in the context of the sign

A Moon skipped step covers a range of issues: unresolved issues to do with the family of origin, strong karmic ties with one or both parents, excessive attachment to outside sources of emotional security (often to family members or to the fact of family itself), nation, race, issues around gender, to name but a few. Which of the many options available do we go for? The economy of astrological analysis requires that we choose the one that fits the story as we have seen it unfold so far. And so we choose *race*.

In step 2 we understand that some 12th house characteristic happened to race. Is it confusion, surrender, escapism, victimization, mystic exaltation, healing, porous boundaries around self, slavery, bliss, innocence, blissful innocence, misty vagueness, purple-tinged rapture, attunement to unseen dimensions, forgiveness, despair, disillusionment, easily deluded, lost at sea like driftwood? I could pull a few more cards from the Piscean deck, but I think we have quite enough to choose from now. Which of the above did something to race that stopped the Himalayan yogi from reaching that 9th house Scorpio promise of a deep commitment to the cause of liberty? That is the question that can guide us and lead us to the answer we are looking for. I am going to go for *victimization.* Victimization happened to race. A whole race was victimized.

At this point I am not totally sure whether this piece will fit the part of the puzzle I am working on or not because I still need to place it in the context of the sign. To do this, we can ask the sign a question: *"How did this victimization of race happen?"*

The Capricorn spectrum is as broad as the Pisces one. This means that again, just like we did in step 2, we need to pick one particular characteristic from a broad archetypal spectrum that fits the story, in this case from the Capricorn deck of cards. Is it lack of integrity, rigidity, sternness, oppressive law, self-determination, futility, integrity, rectitude, responsibility, lack of responsibility, suppression of the emotional body, burden, carrying the burden all by yourself, muted grief, a lopsided emphasis on rules and regulations, duty and obligation valued over love and affection? Which one best <u>contextualizes</u> (step 3) the victimization of race?

When you think context, think about the actual circumstances Lincoln found himself in as he tried to work through this skipped step, this unresolved issue stemming from the life of the Himalayan yogi. Would that not be *oppressive law*?

what is the skipped step about?	house conditions the planet	sign contextualizes planet *in* house
race	victimization	oppressive law

After all this hard work, we now have the ingredients with which to make a sentence. The unresolved issue stemming from the life of the Himalayan yogi and which the soul brings into the life of Abraham Lincoln is *the victimization of race through oppressive law*. This is the thorn in the side which stopped the yogi from moving away from a restriction placed on integration (SN H3 Taurus) in the direction of a full commitment to the cause of liberty (NN H9 Scorpio). All of this is hard work, I know, but it pays off, would you not say? And precisely because

[48]

it pays off, we are now going to follow the exact same approach in interpreting Lincoln's Chiron skipped step.

Chiron 12th house Aquarius skipped step

A Chiron skipped step points to the fact that it was some kind of pain that thwarted the movement from the SN to the NN of the Moon. In Lincoln's chart it means that it was this pain which, in the life of the Himalayan yogi kept him away from the 9th house Scorpio promise of liberty, the one Uranus had so contributed towards (Uranus conjunct the NN of the Moon). This is the first thing we need to establish. The second thing is a little harder because we now need to pick one option from the vast 12th house/Pisces archetypal spectrum that caused the pain. What do you say we go for *slavery*? Why slavery? I go for slavery because - since this is a skipped step - I know this pain comes back in the life of Abraham Lincoln. Let us see what happens when we place '*a pain caused by slavery*' in the context of Aquarius.

Again, as we did before, we can ask the sign a question: *"In what context was this pain inflicted? How did it happen?"* An easy enough question but not such an easy answer because again we are faced with a vast array of archetypal possibilities, all of them Aquarian this time: innovative, electrical, zany, iconoclastic, cold, aloof, distant, large groups of people, stepping out of the mainstream, individuation, networking, from friendship to kinship, radicalization, liberation, groups of likeminded people, getting ousted from groups, feeling an outcast, to name but a few. As was the case with the Moon skipped step, we need to ask a question before we can pick one of these many Aquarian options. The question is twofold:

1. which of the Aquarian options provides the context for '*a pain caused by slavery*'?
2. when '*the pain of slavery*' is placed in the context of one of these Aquarian options, does the resulting sentence then represent a stumbling block on the road to the 9th house Scorpio NN of the Moon?

After trying several, I am going to go for the Aquarian option of '*large groups of people.*' The pain, so I conclude, was caused by *large groups of people getting*

[49]

enslaved. To be more precise: it was caused by one large group of people enslaving another large group of people.

what is the skipped step about?	house conditions the planet	sign contextualizes planet *in* house
a pain, a wounding	slavery	large groups of people

I am not putting 'whites' and 'blacks' in brackets after each group because this is a pain which comes from the life of the Himalayan yogi. Since we know from Paramahansa Yogananda's words that he died with a desire to bring about racial parity, I am going to add another Aquarian characteristic to the pain. The one I choose is *'liberation.'*

what is the skipped step about?	house conditions the planet	sign contextualizes planet *in* house
a pain, a wounding	slavery	large groups of people, liberation

Combining these three, I get a sentence: *the pain was caused by the yogi not having been able to liberate a large group of enslaved people.* The reason for this being that he died while fighting for the noble cause of trying to free (Aquarius) them. Did Yogananda not say he died with the unfulfilled wish of helping bring about racial equality? I know the yogi was deeply committed to this cause because it is written in Uranus conjunct the NN of the Moon: in a recent prior life the person made a major commitment (Scorpio) to the cause of liberty (9th house). Through his death - of natural causes or through assassination - the yogi got *dissociated* (Aquarius) *from the cause of liberating* (Aquarius) *those who were enslaved* (H12). That too is part of the Chiron pain. Since the soul brings the pain into the life of Abraham Lincoln as a major unresolved issue, we see him trying to heal the yogi's wounding by working tirelessly for the very same cause.

As you can see in the chart sample, the pain resolves though the NN of the Moon in the 9th house Scorpio in its conjunction to Uranus the liberator: the soul's next

[50]

vehicle (Lincoln) again makes *a deep and all-consuming commitment* (Scorpio) *to the cause of liberty* as the founding principle (H9/Sagittarius) for a fair and just society (H10/Capricorn). And (again) is killed for it.

The Moon skipped step too resolves via the NN of the Moon in its conjunction to Uranus. It makes sense that it should: the victimization of race through oppressive law does resolve via this deep commitment to the cause of liberty. It could be solved only by the kind of deep commitment Lincoln made. The NN ruler

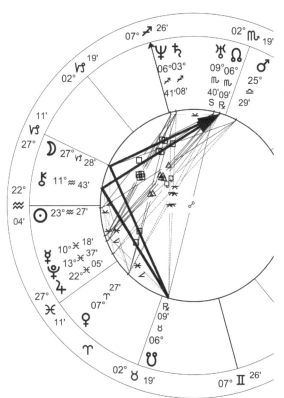

(Pluto) is part of the resolution too: the commitment was carried out (NN ruler) through *the healing* (Pisces) *of people's identity, freedom and right to exist* (NN ruler H1 Pisces).

Why do I take so much time in formulating these two skipped steps? Not just because I want to show you how precise the information is that can be obtained from them, but also because they are a big thing to the soul: if the movement to the NN of the Moon was thwarted by the skipped steps and the NN is the facilitator of the PPP, then obviously soul evolution itself was hindered

because of them. That is why it is so important to carefully map what they represent and why I take such pains to pry open the sentences for you. For our purposes it is doubly important to examine both skipped steps meticulously because already we are beginning to see a continuity (10) in Chiron content between the life of the Himalayan yogi and that of Abraham Lincoln. We can therefore expect some, if not all, of that content to somehow show up in the chart and life of Charles Lindbergh, the soul's next vehicle.

First encounter with the planetary nodes (Chiron and Mars)

[51]

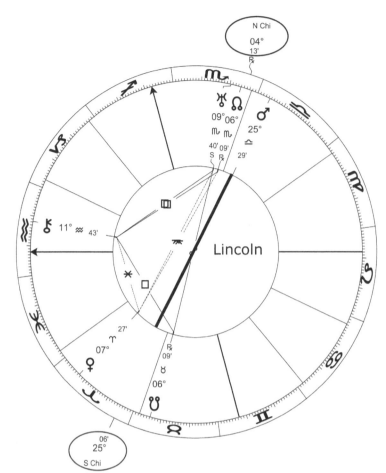

To know more about that continuity and understand how Lincoln's 12th house Aquarius pain connects to that of the Himalayan yogi, we look into its past by turning our gaze to Chiron's SN. You will be surprised to find that it is in the 2nd house at 25 degrees Aries 06 minutes and therefore exactly opposite Lincoln's Mars in the 8th house Libra.

Translation to English, please. The genesis of the Chiron pain, i.e. the past which led to Chiron's 12th house Aquarius placement in the chart of Abraham Lincoln, is found in the same issue we ran into when we looked at the ruler of the SN of the Moon, Venus 2nd house Aries: *prior-life selves were unable to consolidate (H2) their own or other people's identity, freedom and right to exist (Aries)*. They may even *not have survived (H2) because of their pioneering role (Aries) in trying to do so*. Again, from Yogananda's words we know that the Himalayan yogi died with an unfulfilled desire to help bring about racial parity. As such, the soul – and let us not forget that it is the same soul – has the past of Lincoln's Chiron pain directly oppose his **Mars in the 8th house Libra**: the soul wanting *all of Lincoln's conscious actions and desires aimed at personal and social empowerment (H8) in the context of equality in relationship (Libra)*. It makes sense for these two to be opposite each other for they represent opposing forces.

[52]

The NN of Chiron stands at 4 degrees Scorpio 13 minutes and therefore conjunct the NN of the Moon in the 9th house: *the intended healing of the Chiron pain is linked to Lincoln's deep commitment* (Scorpio) *to the cause of liberty* (H9).

Looking into the history of Mars itself in an effort to find out what the Himalayan yogi's conscious actions and desires were geared at, we turn to Lincoln's SN of Mars. We find it in his 10th house at 22 degrees Sagittarius 09 minutes: *to have the principle of liberty* (Sagittarius) *laid down in law* (H10). The NN of Mars – the evolutionary direction the soul wants Lincoln's conscious actions and desires to take (11) – is at 15 degrees Aries 59 minutes, falling in his 2nd house: *to consolidate* (H2) *my and others' identity, freedom and right to exist* (Aries), that is, the very thing the Himalayan yogi dedicated his life to (ruler of the SN of the Moon 2nd house Aries) and which he did not manage to bring about, in all likelihood because the pioneering role

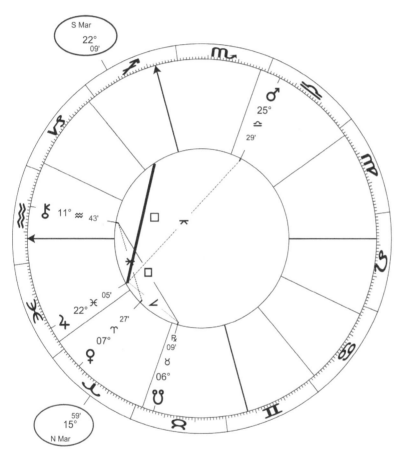

(SN ruler Aries) he played in trying to make integration (SN of the Moon H3) happen carried the price tag of non-survival (SN in Taurus, SN ruler H2). The very thing which caused his pain (Lincoln's SN of Chiron H2 Aries).

Now we understand why the yogi's desire (Mars) aimed at helping bring about racial equality by having liberty laid down in law (Lincoln's SN Mars H10 Sagittarius) is exactly square Lincoln's Jupiter in the 1st house Pisces: *the great* vision (Jupiter) *of healing* (Pisces) *people's identity, freedom and right to exist* (H1). The yogi probably had major run-ins with authority (H10) because of his relentless work on behalf of the cause and may not have survived these.

By the same logic, Lindbergh's SN of Mars is going to point back to that which Lincoln's conscious actions and desires were aimed at. And it does. We find it at 20 degrees Sagittarius 01 minute in his first house, bang on his Uranus there: to *defend people's identity, freedom and right to exist* (H1) *through an ideology* (Sagittarius) *of liberty* (Sagittarius) *as the founding principle* (Sagittarius) *for a fair and just society*, directly points back to Lincoln's Mars in the 8th house Libra. The latter, as we saw earlier in the chapter, reads as: *personal and societal empowerment* (H8) *in the context of equality in relationship* (Libra). You are now literally looking at *the continuity of the conscious desire nature between one lifetime and the next* and which has led up to Lindbergh's Mars in the 3rd house Aquarius placement. (12)

Lincoln – SN Mars H10 Sagittarius, pointing back to the Himalayan yogi's conscious actions and desires	Lincoln - Mars H8 Libra	Lindbergh – SN Mars H1 Sagittarius, pointing back to Lincoln's conscious actions and desires	Lindbergh – Mars H3 Aquarius
conscious actions and desires aimed at having the principle of liberty (Sagittarius) laid down in law (H10)	conscious actions and desires aimed at personal and social empowerment (H8) in the context of equality in relationship (Libra)	conscious actions and desires aimed at defending people's identity, freedom and right to exist (H1) through an ideology (Sagittarius) of liberty (Sagittarius) as the founding principle (Sagittarius) for a fair and just society	Conscious actions and desires aimed at distancing (Aquarius) himself from the cause of integration (H3) – through his antisemitism - and so experience first-hand the fracturing and dissociation (Aquarius) caused by his words (H3)

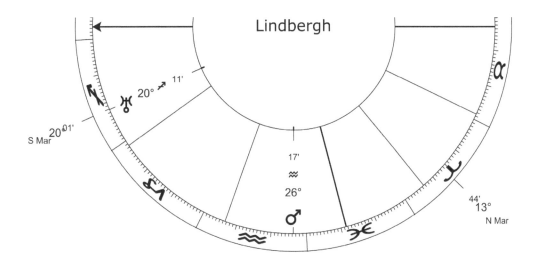

You may be more than a little surprised by the interpretation of Lindbergh's Mars in the 3rd house Aquarius. All will be explained to you in the next chapter. When we get to his *Trauma Helix* there, you will understand why his SN of Mars – pointing back to Lincoln's 8th house Libra conscious actions and desires - is bang on the aviator's Uranus in the 1st house Sagittarius, that is, on the subconscious non-linear memory vault where mental content lies stored to do with past traumatic events. It has to do with what happened to Lincoln as he fulfilled his deep commitment to the cause of liberty (Uranus H9 Scorpio conjunct NN of the Moon H9 Scorpio). I promise to expand on it there. (13)

The Neptune strand of the trauma: 9th house Sagittarius (see chart p.44)

What is the Neptune strand of the trauma about? Neptune in Lincoln's chart is in the 9th house Sagittarius: a double dose of Sagittarian optimism, faith and vison. On the flipside, we find the meaninglessness residue left behind in the soul on account of *the yogi's vision* (Neptune in the 9th house) *of liberty* (Neptune in Sagittarius) *never having come about*. For Lincoln the deepest meaningfulness is found when it does. This is the homeopathic principle I have referred to on several occasions: *in* the trauma itself lies the potential for its healing.

Sagittarius is about individual and societal truthfulness, and the vision thereof. It is about the philosophical underpinnings of what in the 10th house will harden into structures. If truthfulness is not achieved in Sagittarius, it cannot but solidify as unfair societal structures and laws in the 10th house/Capricorn. This is universal law, not something I invented on a Sunday afternoon because I had nothing better to do. Truthfulness (9th house/Sagittarius) is a prerequisite to integrity (10th house/Capricorn), both on the individual and on the collective, societal level. Which is why the 9th house comes before the 10th.

Pluto in the 1st house Pisces: the way the soul emotionally and psychologically identifies with the Uranus and Neptune strand of the trauma

The way the soul pulls these two trauma strands into its own story is written in Pluto's house and sign placement. The identification with the mental Uranus content is different in nature from that with the much more emotion-laden Neptune content. Meaninglessness, after all, is much more intensely felt than a filing cabinet saying: *"you can find it in the third drawer,"* although the mental content does have an important impact on the soul.

With regards to the Uranus strand (death as the price paid for a deep commitment to the cause of liberty), the soul registers *a loss* (Pisces) *of my right to exist* (H1). It takes note of what happened. And of the words, thoughts and images related to the event. The way it draws the Neptune meaninglessness to it is as *a tendency to give up* (Pisces) *on the cause of identity, freedom and right to exist* (H1).

The soul's emotional identification with Neptune's 9th house Sagittarius meaninglessness is a dismay so strong that it will feel this cause *slip through its fingers* (Pisces) *without being able to stop it. It will then surrender* (Pisces) *by resigning to the loss* (Pisces).

Chiron relaying the trauma package: 12th house Aquarius

All of this now lies stored in the warped time of Uranus' database ready to be picked up by Chiron. Just for good measure: what you are looking at here is the centaur - the inhabitant of two worlds as far apart as they could possibly be - relaying a trauma charge from the Himalayan yogi's life to that of Lincoln.

The way Chiron does this is by gauging this Uranian trauma charge and then translating it into language that Lincoln's Saturn will understand. On its very, very long way back to Saturn it does this as: *a pain caused by large groups of people* (Aquarius) *getting enslaved* (H12) *and the yogi not having been able to liberate* (Aquarius) *them from the enslavement* (H12).

This, I infer, is what Yogananda meant when he said the yogi died with the unfulfilled wish of helping bring about racial equality. The yogi's death dissociated

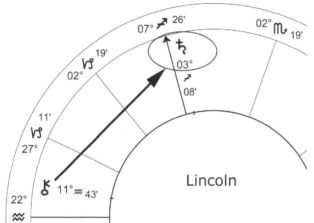

(Aquarius) him from the cause he had worked so tirelessly for. That too is part of the pain.

Saturn receiving the Chiron pain: 9th house Sagittarius

When Chiron drops this parcel off at Saturn's door – having bridged the transpersonal (14) and the personal realm – that other world and this one, the soul understands how the consciousness of its next vehicle needs to be structured: in such a way as *to bring about - through faith* (Saturn H9) - *the great promise and hope* (Saturn in Sagittarius) *of liberty* (Saturn in Sagittarius). The arduous work of the yogi will not have been in vain. The soul does not forget it.

Determining planetary function

When this Chiron-*Trauma Helix* dynamic in a chart is understood, all other planet placements in the chart can be put into words. We saw this in the chart of Richard Nixon in the previous chapter and we will see it again here.

We start with **Jupiter** since the gas giant is the first to receive the impact of how Saturn's consciousness is now structured. It interprets it as: *the healing* (Pisces) *of my and other people's* (Pisces: universal) *identity, freedom and right to exist* (H1). This is the lens (Jupiter) through which the soul wants Lincoln to interpret life. To rephrase: the glasses the soul wants him to put on his nose are tainted by this 1st house Piscean need.

[57]

The need can now be acted upon by **Mars**: to bring about *personal and social empowerment* (H8) *in the context of equality in relationship* (Libra). All conscious actions and desires are going to be directed at this.

This now establishes the nature of the relationship (**Venus**) the soul wants Lincoln to engage in. It wants him to *relate to the consolidation* (2nd house) *of people's identity, freedom and right to exist* (Aries). This is the sentence we get when we apply the steps outlined earlier correctly

1. what is the planet about?
2. house conditions the planet
3. sign contextualizes planet *in* the house

Lincoln's prime relationship (Venus), in other words, is to be with the consolidation (H2) of these 1st house/Aries issues. I hope you see how relevant that is to the commitment that was made in the life of the Himalayan yogi: to deeply commit to the cause of liberty (Uranus H9 Scorpio conjunct the NN of the Moon H9 Scorpio). The soul also wants Lincoln **to relate** (Venus) **to the consolidation of the values** (H2) **that underlie these key 1st house issues.** Please put this latest observation to simmer on a back burner, because it will prove key to understanding Lindbergh's 2nd house Jupiter skipped step and its most unusual resolution, one that will take us all by surprise (which is why the sentence is printed in bold type) in the next chapter.

Once the kind of relationship the soul envisages for Lincoln has been established, it indicates what it wants thinking (**Mercury**) in its vehicle aimed at: *the healing* (Pisces) *of people's identity, freedom and right to exist.* (H1)

It then seals the whole thing by stating the central principle around which it wants Lincoln's life to revolve (**Sun**): *to objectively assess* (Aquarius) *people's identity, freedom and right to exist* (1st house) and to then *liberate* (Aquarius) *people from what or whomever standing in the way of those.*

Once these sentences have been formulated, we can pull them into the house(s) they rule. Mercury, for example, rules the house 4th house of race and the 8th house of empowerment. In the former Mercury will seek integration (Gemini) of race (H4); in the latter it will serve (Virgo) people's empowerment (H8).

[58]

Jupiter rules the 10th house: *the healing of people's identity, freedom and right to exist needs to become law*.

The liberation the Sun seeks rules the 7th house: *the public at large*.

What I am showing you here is how you can **determine planetary function** informed by how Chiron relays a trauma charge from other lifetimes to the current one. I do so in the hope that you may apply this technique in your therapeutic work with clients.

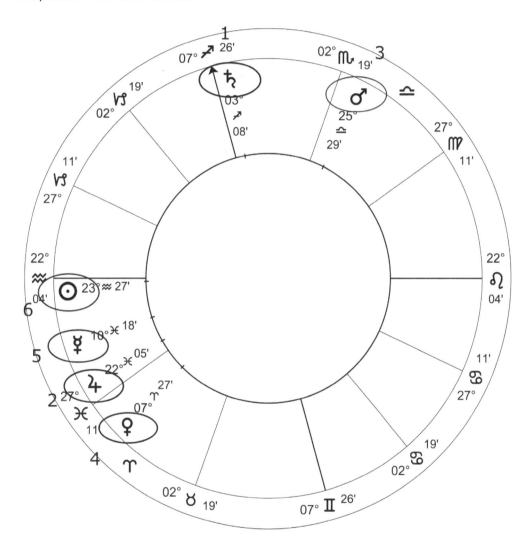

Abraham Lincoln: Determining Planetary Function

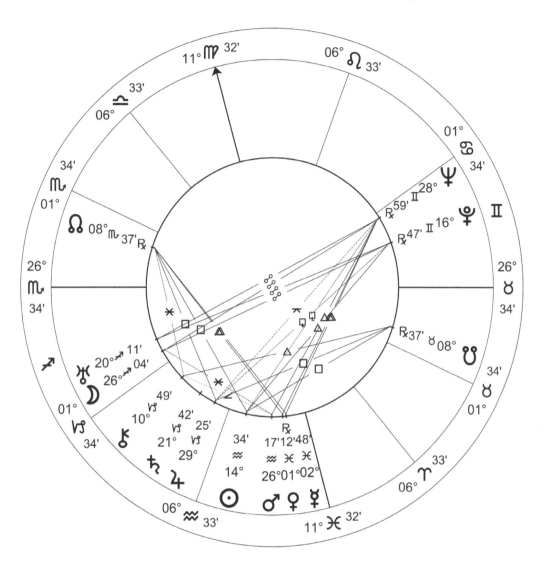

Charles Lindbergh, 4 February 1902, 01:30 hrs., Detroit, Michigan. RR:AA

The comment Swami Kriyananda refers to in his book *"The Path: Autobiography of a Western Yogi"* was one of the rare instances Paramahansa Yogananda said something about a person's past life. He was not in the habit of going around telling people who they had been in other lifetimes, what they had done there or what had happened to them. Nor did Ramana Maharshi or Jiddu Krishnamurti. These wise men understood that the soul has good reasons for putting a memory barrier in place as it pulls the veil of amnesia over the nascent personality. This barrier allows memories of past lives, if they are there to begin with, to gradually fade away as a person goes through the early developmental stages comprised between birth and roughly the age six or seven – coinciding with the first Saturn square - and marking the full birth of personality. It acts as a safety valve so that we are given the opportunity to learn afresh.

If we had full access to the content of prior lives, we would come into this life fearful, remorseful, anxious, and laden with troublesome memories. We would be robbed of the opportunity to learn since experiences handed to us by life would be viewed through the lens of the past. Life would become like taking your driving test for the seventh time. Going into life with knowledge of lessons learned and not learned would make us apprehensive and severely diminish those experiences in terms of learning opportunities. If the soul had wanted us to have access to past-life content, one wonders, would it not have provided us with a hard disk at birth?

The danger of evolutionary astrology is not that it hands the astrologer insight into the soul's deepest drives and how these were explored in past lives, but that so many of those who use the paradigm seem to part from the assumption that this automatically warrants disclosure of that information to clients. Perhaps it is time we paused and asked ourselves the question if this does not constitute an unwelcome intrusion into the soul's plan for a person's life.

In regression therapy the safety valve put in by the soul is respected at all times. A client wishing to explore their past lives out of curiosity is politely sent on their way. Regression therapy is just that: *therapy*. A past life is entered into only when a problem for which no current-life cause can be found is seriously affecting a person in one or more life areas. The same caution is taken in *Life between Lives Therapy*. (1) The barrier of death is not crossed out of curiosity ever. We do not go into the spirit world just for fun. It is simply not done.

Perhaps it is time for evolutionary astrologers to take a leaf out of the great sages' book and adopt a more cavalier approach in these matters.

Soul: a Diamond held up to the Light

We have now arrived at that crucial moment in our comparative chart study where evolutionary astrologers will ask: *"Does the soul choose the same Pluto placement in two consecutive lives"?* I fully understand the question and acknowledge its validity. After all, if we define the Pluto placement by house and sign as:

1. the issues the soul has been exploring during multiple lifetimes
2. comes into the current life with as its default setting
3. and will therefore hold onto for reasons of familiarity (read: emotional security),

then we would expect Pluto to be in the same house and sign in Lindbergh's chart as it was in Lincoln's, would we not? And even in that of the Himalayan yogi, whose chart we unfortunately do not have at our disposal. And now it turns out it is not. Problem. Big one.

Not necessarily so, I think. It is my contention that there is nothing that suggests that the soul obey the kind of linearity that would force it into the same house and sign in two consecutive lives. That would severely limit it in highlighting certain facets of its evolution, let alone in choosing the geographical location and time period most suitable to its evolutionary needs.

The soul is like a diamond held up to the light. When moving from one lifetime to the next, it will turn one of its many sides to where the light is coming from and highlight a very specific, literally, side of its overall trajectory. There are three factors involved when light hits a diamond:

1. **reflection**: part of the light that hits the diamond is reflected back out on the surface
2. **refraction**: the remaining rays of light enter or travel into the center of the diamond and bounce off its internal walls. This is what is known as "the Prism effect."
3. **dispersion**: as light exits the diamond, dispersion causes the white light to be separated into multiple colors. Some light will escape out the bottom and side, and some will escape out of the top of the stone.

[63]

As it holds itself up to the light, which in this analogy we are tempted to identify as Source, soul understands which facet of its own evolutionary path needs to be highlighted in a certain life. It reflects Divine Light and pines to be reunited with Source. All souls do. The way up for the soul is down, back to this earthly valley of tears. That is the way things are set up. I can fume at this till I go blue in the face, but that is not going to change the deal.

The refraction phase is where the soul dialogues with itself in the life between lives. According to what lessons have been learned and what lessons have not, soul, together with those in its soul group and under the loving guidance of spirit guides, designs a new life. The evaluation of a live lived is a very serious thing in the spirit world. As is the planning of yet another life. It is not done overnight, and decisions are made after lengthy consultation and careful deliberation. What comes out of these decisions is the dispersion you and I get to see. From the light that comes out of the diamond it is not always easy to see what particular facet of its own evolution the soul wishes to highlight and work on. The evolutionary astrologer sees the Pluto placement but does not get to see where it was in the chart belonging to a previous life.

Here, as was the case with the Anne Frank - Barbro Karlén comparative chart study, (2) we do, and it is a great privilege. Let us now, by way of exercise, step inside the diamond and try and understand how it receives the light and what happens in its interior during the refraction phase. Hopefully, we will then understand the way it comes out of the diamond dispersed as Lindbergh's 7th house Gemini Pluto, against all expectation perhaps.

Lincoln's soul goes Home following the assassination of the vehicle in April of 1865. I am not the one to make judgements about how much soul evolution took place in the life of Lincoln. That is for the soul to evaluate. What I do know is that he was slain in a brutal assassination. How much more would Lincoln have achieved had this event not taken place? We shall never know. It looks like a lot was achieved in one lifetime. There was incredible commitment to the cause of liberty (Uranus H9 Scorpio conjunct NN of the Moon H9 Scorpio).

The question now becomes this: can we understand, by looking at the dispersed light coming out of the diamond (i.e. Lindbergh's 7th house Gemini Pluto) what made the soul choose this placement?

'Thematic continuity' in Lincoln's and Lindbergh's Pluto placement

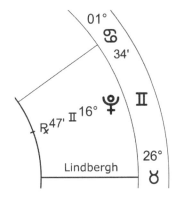

One way of finding out what happened in the refraction phase is to look at archetypal resonances between Lindbergh's Pluto-PPP axis - and even his Nodal Axis! - and Lincoln's. The first thing we realize when focusing our attention on the former is that Lindbergh's Pluto is in the house we associate with *(in)equality in interpersonal relationship as a result of (not) being able or willing to listen to what the other person has to say*: Libra. That immediately resonates with Lincoln's Pluto Polarity Point in the 7th house, does it not?

So far so good. We move slowly and tread cautiously because this is intricate stuff. It needs a great deal of reverence for the sanctity of soul.

Now comes the Gemini part. Where did we see that in Lincoln's chart? Right: SN of the Moon in the 3rd house Taurus. What did we say about it? We said: *"prior-life selves having experienced some kind of restriction, some kind of limitation* (Taurus) *in their right or ability to integrate* (Gemini) *with others."* Lives like that

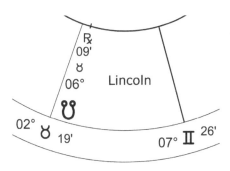

leave indentations in the soul narrative. After the rainwater has flown through the gulley, it is not the same gulley anymore. The 3rd house restriction has become part of the soul narrative. And it shows in the way the light exits the diamond: Lindbergh's Pluto 7th house Gemini.

[65]

Translated to English: *the soul has been exploring issues around inequality in relationship* (H7) *as a result of having been unable to integrate* (Gemini).

Please note how the soul's emotional and psychological identification with the Uranus and Neptune strand in the *Trauma Helix* in the chart of Lincoln, which we described as:

"... *a dissolution* (Pisces) *of one's right to exist* (H1); *a dismay so strong that it will feel this cause slip through its fingers* (Pisces) *without being able to stop it. It will then surrender* (Pisces) *by resigning to the loss* (Pisces) ..."

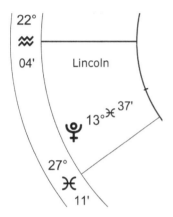

comes back in the above interpretation of Lindbergh's 's Pluto placement. The loss (Pisces) of freedom (H1) in the former is related to the inequality in relationship in the latter. Obviously, if your understanding of the Gemini archetype does not go beyond communication, thinking, curious, superficiality, connecting the dots, fleetingness, then you are not going to grasp this. Your understanding of the soul narrative is as deep as your knowledge of the astrological archetypes.

The next question is: what kinds of lives would the soul have created to explore this 7th house Gemini issue? For an answer to that question we turn to the SN of the Moon. Whatever we find there is going to point back to the life of Lincoln, of that we can be sure.

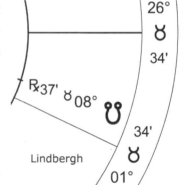

SN of the Moon in the 6th house Taurus

A life dedicated to *service to the greater whole* (6th house) and then *being restricted in that, held back* (Taurus); *not having survived* (Taurus) *because of the service* (6th house) *rendered*. Does that ring a bell in any way? Is the assassination of Abraham Lincoln going to show up in the ruler of the SN of the Moon in Lindbergh's chart? Let us head on over to it and find out.

SN ruler 3rd house Pisces

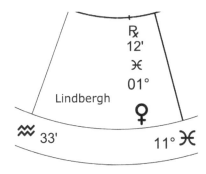

There was *a loss of self* (Pisces) *while trying to further the cause of integration* (3rd house), which is literally what happened: Lincoln was assaulted while in service (SN 6th house) to the greater whole (i.e. the American people), did not survive the assault (Lindbergh's SN in Taurus, SN ruler Pisces) and it happened while he was pouring all of his efforts into *healing* (Pisces) *integration* (3rd house). That is when the loss of self (Pisces) occurred.

Pluto Polarity Point 1st house Sagittarius

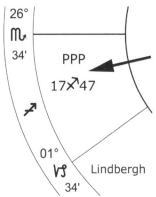

The soul wants out from under the inequality of the 7th house by *establishing its identity, freedom and right to exist* (1st house) *in the context of liberty* (Sagittarius). In other words: it wants its personal freedom and independence (1st house) to be embedded in a broader societal sense of freedom (Sagittarius).

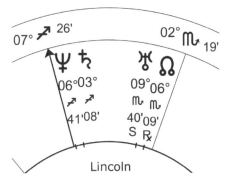

Do you feel how that resonates with all that Sagittarian energy in Lincoln's chart: Uranus conjunct the NN of the Moon in the 9th house, Saturn in the 9th house Sagittarius (a double whammy), Neptune in the 9th house Sagittarius (the deepest meaningfulness found when this kind of freedom comes about)? (3)

NN of the Moon 12th house Scorpio

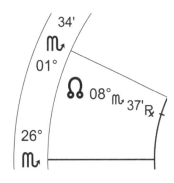

The intended evolutionary movement on the level of self, (4) on the level of Lindbergh, is for him to *deeply commit* (Scorpio) *to what is in humanity's* (H12) *best interest*, i.e. to bring about *a deep transformation* (Scorpio) *in the lives of enslaved people*. I deliberately do not say 'slaves' because I think of those who enslave others as enslaved themselves. The dissociation (Aquarius) from this cause is what caused the Chiron pain in Lincoln's chart. And his Moon skipped step: the victimization of race through oppressive law (Moon H12 Capricorn).

NN ruler 7th house Gemini

The way the NN of the Moon intention can be carried out on the Moon level of Charles Lindbergh is *when he connects, integrates* (Gemini), *strikes up a dialogue* (Gemini) *with the cause of equality in interpersonal relationship* (H7).

I would ask you to put this on a back burner for now, for this ruler of the NN of the Moon intention is at odds with something that the soul brings into the current life of Lindbergh as a major unresolved issue, pointing therefore to something harking back to the life of Lincoln: his Jupiter in the 2nd house Capricorn skipped step. Via the ruler (Pluto H7 Gemini) of its resolution node (NN H12 Scorpio) it is going to produce a very unusual answer in Lindbergh, one that seems to be coming out of left field from the human perspective yet will make perfect sense when viewed through the eyes of the soul.

Jupiter 2nd house Capricorn skipped step: the movement from the SN of the Moon to the NN of the Moon has been thwarted? By what? By *prior-life selves* (Lincoln) *not having survived* (2nd house) *for promoting an ideology* (Jupiter) *that was not to the liking of reactionary forces* (Capricorn) *or even mainstream society* (Capricorn).

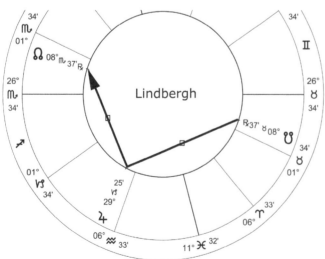

Please note how this Jupiter skipped step rules Sagittarius intercepted in the 1st house, with the very physical Uranus trauma there, which we will get to shortly.

Why does the Jupiter skipped step represent an

[68]

unresolved issue? If the movement to the NN of the Moon has been thwarted by this roadblock and the NN of the Moon is the facilitator of the PPP – which it is in the EA paradigm – then obviously that 2nd house Capricorn issue has put a spoke in the wheel of soul evolution.

Translated to English: *prior-life selves having been assassinated* (2nd house) *by reactionary forces* (Capricorn) *for promoting an ideology* (Jupiter) - in this case one of freedom through equal rights - is what kept them away from bringing about a deep transformation (NN in Scorpio) in the lives of enslaved people (H12). (5) Which is exactly what happened to Lincoln. The available biographical facts pertaining to his life tell us it is so. Before we look at the resolution node for Lindbergh's Jupiter skipped step, we are going to first try and map the Chiron – *Trauma Helix* dynamic in his chart. The reason for doing things in this order is that we will understand the Jupiter roadblock better once we grasp how the trauma charge from Lincoln's life was transferred by Chiron to Lindbergh's *as a woundedness and the potential for healing of the woundedness.*

Chiron and the *Trauma Helix*

Uranus 1st house Sagittarius: the mental content of the trauma

We are now inside the subconscious non-linear vault where memories of past-life traumatic events lie stored. The memories, so we established in Chapter 1, are of a mental nature and made up of thoughts and images. What are they? Uranus in contact with Mars, Aries or the 1st house often points to some kind of force impacting the person on a physical level, stopping cold a project barely begun. The project could be life, which is why in EA these kinds of contacts are sometimes associated with having died abruptly, young or young *and* abruptly in a past life. We will see other instances of Uranus - Mars/Aries/1st house contacts in this book, namely in the charts of Nina Simone (chapter 7), Josef Mengele (chapter 11) and Anne Frank (chapter 15). The thoughts and images held in the case of Charles Lindbergh's Uranus are related to *trauma incurred as a result of a life dedicated to people's freedom and right to exist* (1st

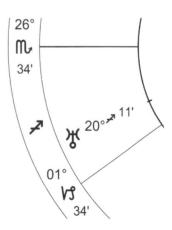

[69]

house) - *serving the cause of liberty* (Sagittarius) - *having been cut short abruptly*, a life where the person had to push against some opposing force to achieve their mission of freedom (Sagittarius), with the counterforce out to stop that mission in its tracks.

This 1st house Sagittarius trauma is Lincoln's, although it will get reenacted in the life of Lindbergh in the form of *a sudden shift* (Uranus) *in public perception of his identity* (H1) *as a result of him having expressed views* (Sagittarius) *that ran counter to those held by the majority of people*. This is why in the previous chapter I alerted you to Lindbergh's Mars having to do with him experiencing the fracturing and dissociation (Aquarius) of his words (H3). Please put this on a back burner for a moment since it is going to be of paramount importance in understanding Lindbergh's Jupiter H2 Capricorn skipped step and its rather unexpected resolution.

We know what Lincoln's mission was, and we know who the opposing forces were. We also know what the blunt instrument was they used to stop him. The opposing ideology (Uranus in Sagittarius) was voiced by Confederate Vice President Alexander Stephens as being based *"upon the great truth that the negro is not equal to the white man; that slavery, subordination to the superior race is his natural and normal condition."* (6)

John Wilkes Booth, Lincoln's assassin and an outspoken Confederate sympathizer, attended Lincoln's last public address given at the White House 11 April 1865, in which he promoted voting rights for blacks. Booth said *"That means nigger citizenship … That is the last speech he will ever give."* Four days later Lincoln was dead.

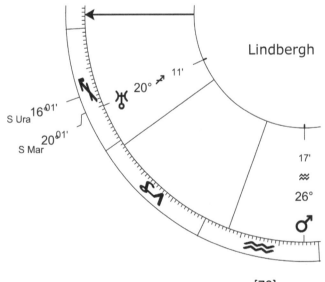

Lindbergh

Do you remember how in the previous chapter, when looking at the planetary nodes of Mars and Chiron, we noticed how Lindbergh's SN of Mars was right on his Uranus, 10 minutes shy of exact? (pp.54-55) Now you understand why: *Lincoln was assassinated for pouring all of his conscious actions and desires into fighting for people's identity, freedom and right to exist* (H1) *as part of the Sagittarian quest for liberty as the founding principle of a fair and just society.* This finding is corroborated by Lindbergh's SN of Uranus – the past of the trauma directly pointing back to what happened to Lincoln - being conjunct Uranus *and* the SN of Mars.

By the same token Lincoln's own SN of Uranus at 15 degrees Sagittarius 45 minutes in the 10 house - precariously close to the SN of his Mars - points to what must have happened to the Himalayan yogi in his relationship with *authority* (H10) as *he defended the cause of liberty* (Sagittarius): *frequent run-ins* that would not have ended well for him.

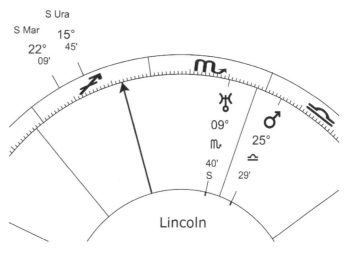

Trauma continuity

This phenomenon I have termed **'trauma continuity.'** I first noticed it in the chart of Nannerl Mozart, Wolfgang's elder sister, and that of Alma Deutscher, whom I believe to be the soul's next vehicle. Unfortunately, I cannot show you the latter's chart since my request to be provided with Alma's time of birth was denied by her family. But I *can* show it you in the case of Anne Frank and Barbro Karlén, where my request to be given her birth data was granted by Ms Karlén. I will do this in chapter 15 of the book.

Here, with Lincoln and Lindbergh, we have cut a long length of cord – Uranus - and started threading on the trauma beads of the planetary nodes. The Uranus cord itself, however, is also connected between one chart and the other: Uranus H1 Sagittarius in the chart of Lindbergh (pointing to Lincoln's *death as the price he paid for his deep commitment* – Scorpio - *to the cause of liberty* – H9) is

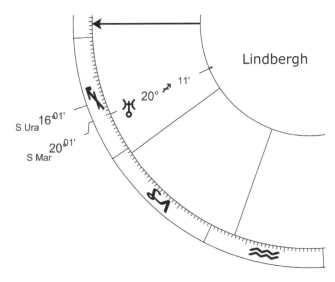

directly connected to Lincoln's own Uranus placement, which, in turn, points back to what happened to the Himalayan yogi at the hands of authority (Lincoln's SN of Uranus H10 Sagittarius) as *he directed all of his conscious actions and desires at having the principle of liberty laid down in law* (Lincoln's SN of Mars in his 10th house Sagittarius). We sense the flow between the three lives.

You can see that for both Lincoln and the Himalayan yogi, the trauma is linked to what their conscious actions and desires were aimed at: Lindbergh's SN of Mars (pointing back to the life of Lincoln) is conjunct his Uranus SN, with Lincoln's SN of Mars (pointing back to the life of the yogi) too in the close vicinity of his Uranus SN.

And so we weave the trauma story at the level of mental content in the form of thoughts and images stored in Uranus' non-linear memory vault (see table next page). You are now literally looking at the astrological correlates of how the mental component of trauma (Uranus)

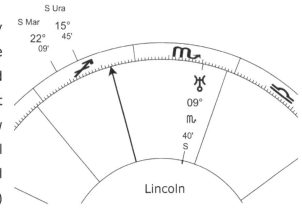

comes back in two consecutive lives and is connected to a prior, third one. The way it travels from one lifetime to the next is astrologically reflected in Chiron, which we will place under the magnifying glass in a minute.

Difference between the nodes of planets at either end of the Saturn boundary

When looking at the planetary south nodes we need to be mindful of the fact that there is a marked difference between those pertaining to Mercury, Venus, Mars,

Lincoln – SN Mars H10 Sag (close to SN of Uranus), pointing to the Himalayan yogi's conscious actions and desires	Lincoln - Uranus H9 Scorpio, pointing to trauma incurred by the Himalayan yogi	Lindbergh – SN Mars H1 Sag, pointing to Lincoln's conscious actions and desires	Lindbergh – Uranus H1 Sag conjunct SN Uranus H1 Sag, pointing to trauma incurred by Lincoln
SN Mars: the yogi directing his conscious actions and desires at having the principle of liberty (Sag) laid down in law (H10); **SN Uranus**: the yogi's run-ins with authority (H10) as he espoused his ideology of liberty (Sag), pointing back to similar trauma incurred in lives (created by the same soul) prior to his	death (Scorpio) as the price the Himalayan yogi paid for his deep commitment (Scorpio) to the cause of liberty (H9); *reenactment in the life of Lincoln*: assassinated for his deep commitment (Scorpio) to the cause of liberty (H9)	conscious desires aimed at defending people's identity, freedom and right to exist (H1) through an ideology (Sag) of liberty (Sagittarius) as the founding principle (Sagittarius) for a fair and just society	**Uranus**: sudden death (Uranus H1) of Lincoln as he pledged his allegiance to the cause of liberty (Sag); *reenactment in the life of Lindbergh*: a sudden shift (Uranus) in public perception of his identity (H1) as a result of him having expressed views (Sag) that ran counter to those held by the majority of people; **SN Uranus**: the same trauma applying to lives beyond that of Lincoln and the yogi

Jupiter and Saturn and those pertaining to Chiron, Uranus, Neptune and Pluto. Those in the first group point back to dynamics (thinking, relating, conscious action and desires, etcetera) operative in prior-life selves immediately prior to the current-life self. The south nodes in the second group indicate dynamics which go back in time much further, encompassing a far greater number of lives created by the soul, not because they are *'transpersonal'* but because they are *'multi-personal.'* I will clarify the difference between the two in the next chapter, where we will come to speak of the *'Multidimensional Psyche.'*

(see chart fragment top of p.72) Where Lindbergh's Uranus in the 1st house Sagittarius reveals information about what happened to Lincoln as he tirelessly defended people's freedom, identity and right to exist as part of the quest for liberty (H1 Sagittarius), Lindbergh's SN of Uranus in the same house and sign extends much further into the past, revealing how the 1st house Sagittarius trauma charge would have been present not just in the life of Lincoln and the Himalayan yogi but in a string of lives prior to those two.

Neptune 7th house Gemini: the meaninglessness strand of the trauma

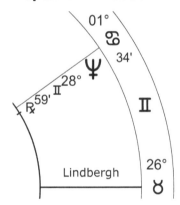

A tell-tale placement for it shows how deeply felt disillusionment, caused by *Lincoln not having been able to effectuate the much-desired equality in relationship* (7th house) *brought about by true integration* (Gemini), traveled from his to Lindbergh's life. This is the meaninglessness strand of the trauma.

'Trauma continuity'

It deeply resonates with Lincoln's Neptune in that the latter speaks of *meaninglessness caused by his vision* (Neptune H9) *of true liberty* (Neptune in Sagittarius) *never having*

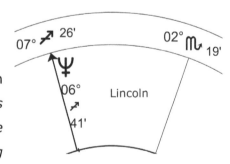

become reality (I am referring to the fact that he was assassinated by John Wilkes

Booth four days after announcing voting rights for black people). That is the trauma continuity on the level of meaninglessness.

The SN of Neptune in the chart of Lindbergh tells you how the meaninglessness trauma is related to that of Lincoln, the Himalayan yogi and beyond. We find it

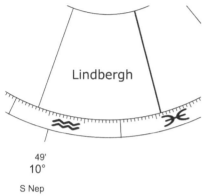

in the 3rd house Aquarius: *Lincoln was abruptly* (Aquarius) *dissociated* (Aquarius) *from the cause of integration* (H3), as we suspect the Himalayan yogi was. Is there confirmation of that in Lincoln's chart? Yes, there is: Lincoln's SN of Neptune is right on his Chiron, i.e. on the one who relayed the trauma charge from the life of the yogi to that of Lincoln. Translated to English: the past of Lincoln's 9th house Sagittarius Neptune shows how the meaninglessness trauma – reaching back into deeper

recesses of time than that belonging to the life of the yogi even – was caused by prior-life selves having been unable *to liberate* (Aquarius) *the enslaved* (H12), in all likelihood as a result of having been *suddenly dissociated* (Aquarius) *from the noble cause*. There you have the actual words linking Lindbergh's SN of Neptune in his 3rd house

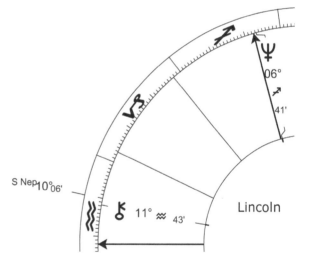

Aquarius straight back to the meaninglessness trauma incurred in the life of the yogi.

Through the south nodes and natal placement of Neptune, we are mapping the astrological correlates of how the meaninglessness component of trauma comes back in two consecutive lives, i.e. that of Lindbergh and Lincoln, and is connected to a string of prior lives, the next in line being the life of the Himalayan yogi. We have termed this phenomenon **'trauma continuity'**. Although, out of necessity,

I represent this continuity in the form of a table, it would be a good idea to visualize it as beads strung on a thread (see table next page).

Lincoln – SN Neptune (closely conjunct natal Chiron), pointing to the past of the H9 Sagittarius trauma and therefore to the yogi's life (and beyond)	Lincoln – Neptune H9 Sagittarius, pointing to meaninglessness trauma incurred by the Himalayan yogi	Lindbergh – SN Neptune H3 Aquarius, pointing to the past of the H7 Gemini trauma and therefore to Lincoln's and the yogi's life (and beyond)	Lindbergh – Neptune H7 Gemini, pointing to meaninglessness trauma incurred by Lincoln
meaninglessness caused by the same thing that caused the pain: large groups of people (Aquarius) getting enslaved (H12) and the yogi not having been able to liberate (Aquarius) them from the enslavement for getting suddenly dissociated (Aquarius) from the cause	meaninglessness caused by his vision (H9) of true liberty (Sagittarius) never having become reality	Lincoln was abruptly (Aquarius) dissociated (Aquarius) from the cause of integration (H3), as we suspect the yogi was	disillusionment and meaninglessness felt by Lincoln for not having been able to effectuate the much-desired equality in relationship (H7) brought about by true integration (Gemini)

Pluto 7th house Gemini: the soul's emotional identification with the Uranus and Neptune strands

In our *Trauma Helix* model, Pluto in the chart of Lindbergh tells you how the soul has identified emotionally both with the memories of the actual traumatic event(s) - stored in the Uranian vault as words, thoughts and images - and with

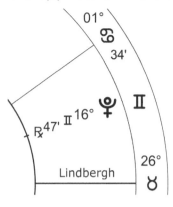

Neptune's sense of meaninglessness. It pulls them into its own narrative as *a breaking up* (Gemini*) of the cause of equality* (H7). (7)

Lincoln was meant to have stayed connected (H7) to that cause. Had he lived and not been brutally severed from it he might have been able to see his mission through and bring about true equality (H7) through full integration (Gemini). His assassination *disconnected* (the dissociative element proper to both Gemini and Libra) *the soul from its wish to serve* (PPP in Virgo) *the cause of equality* (PPP H7). (8)

The *'trauma continuity'* with Lincoln's Pluto in the 1st house Pisces is that in both there is an element of dissolution. Lincoln's Pluto, which in the *Trauma Helix*

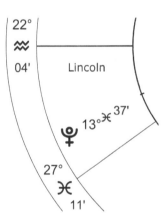

model in its turn points back to how the soul has emotionally identified with the events as they transpired in the yogi's life, speaks of *a dissolution* (Pisces) *of his right to exist* (H1) on the one hand - in all probability linked to the way he died (Lincoln's Uranus H9 in Scorpio denoting death as the price the yogi paid for his

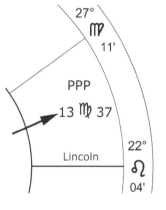

commitment) – and of *the cause of identity, freedom and right to exist* (H1) *slipping* (Pisces) *through his fingers* on the other, with him *surrendering* (Pisces) *to the loss* (Pisces). Here too, similar to what we saw with the SN of Uranus and Neptune, these deep emotional and psychological identification patterns go back way in time, far beyond the life of the Himalayan yogi. (see table p.78)

Chiron 2nd house Saturn: the one to relay the trauma charge *as pain*

Chiron will now travel deep into Uranus' orbit and pick all of this up. Not just the mental content stored in the Uranus library, but also Neptune's meaninglessness and Pluto's emotional identification with both.

Lincoln – Pluto H1 Pisces, pointing to how the soul has emotionally identified with the Uranus and Neptune strand of the *Trauma Helix*	Lincoln – PPP H7 Virgo	Lindbergh – Pluto H7 Gem, pointing to how the soul has emotionally identified with the Uranus and Neptune strand of the *Trauma Helix*
a dissolution (Pisces) of the yogi's right to exist (H1); the cause of identity, freedom and right to exist (H1) slipping (Pisces) through his fingers, with him surrendering (Pisces) by resigning to the loss (Pisces)	to serve (Virgo) equality (H7)	the breaking up (Gemini), the falling apart (Gemini) of the cause of equality (H7)

On its highly elliptical and elongated path back to Saturn Chiron will translate the trauma charge as pain and hand it over to the ringed planet: the outer limit of Lindbergh's normal, waking consciousness and the way the soul wants it structured.

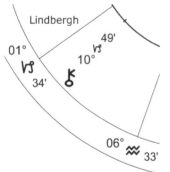

In Lindbergh's chart the Chiron pain first and foremost is about *Lincoln's non-survival* (H2) *at the hands of those who sought to revive the Confederate cause* (Capricorn) by eliminating the three most important officials of the United States government (Secretary of State William Seward, Vice President Andrew Johnson, and President Abraham Lincoln. The first two survived)

At a deeper level, the pain has to do with *the attempts at suppression* (Capricorn) *of Lincoln's values* (H2) *by those who did not support the abolition of slavery* (Capricorn). (9)

Trauma continuity

Since Chiron collects the trauma charge from Uranus and on its long way back to Saturn translates it as pain, we can expect continuity to show up in the centaur's woundedness too.

And it does. The pain of *Lincoln's non-survival* (Lindbergh's Chiron H2), *inflicted by those who opposed and actively suppressed* (Lindbergh's Chiron in Capricorn)

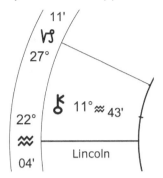

racial equality and freedom is also felt in Lincoln's 12th house Aquarius woundedness, pointing back to *the yogi not having been able to set free* (Aquarius) *the enslaved* (H12), with him in all probability getting *abruptly dissociated* (Aquarius) *from the cause of liberation* (Aquarius) the way Lincoln would.

Lincoln's Uranus in the 9th house Scorpio (death because of an ideology) rules the Chiron pain. At the time of his death the abolition of slavery, through the 13th Amendment, was a fact but its implementation was far from complete. The pain inflicted by the suppression of Lincoln's values (Lindbergh's Chiron H2 Capricorn) and his non-survival (H2) because *of* those values (H2) are going to be important in understanding the full scope of Lindbergh's Jupiter H2 skipped step, so do place this on a back burner too, if you still have any available.

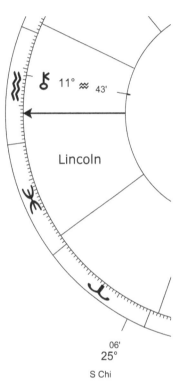

The SN of Chiron in Lindbergh's chart, pointing back to Lincoln's 12th house Aquarian pain and beyond, is at 25 degrees Aries 26 minutes in the 5th house: *a pain caused by the fact that people's identity, freedom and right to exist* (Aries) *were not honored and celebrated* (H5) *as their natural birthright* (H5).

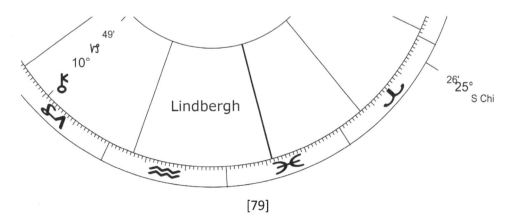

[79]

There is a **'pain continuity'** from Lindbergh's to Lincoln's chart with regards to the SN of Chiron. In Lincoln's chart it denotes the yogi's pain of *not having been able to secure and consolidate* (2nd house) *people's identity, freedom and right to exist* (Aries), and of *him possibly not having survived* (2nd house) *for trying to do so*. I hope you see how that connects to the SN of Chiron in the chart of Charles Lindbergh in the 5th house Aries as discussed above. We are, just like we did with Uranus and Neptune, threading beads on a cord, which in this case is the cord of woundedness. The woundedness is transferred from one lifetime to the next so that it may get healed, the same way the trauma it holds is carried over by the soul in a bid to overcome it so that it may evolve. This is why the Chiron-*Trauma Helix* model is key to *therapeutic* evolutionary astrology: once the pain is understood, the therapist will sense how its healing might contribute to soul growth. (10) Here is the table, ideally visualized as beads on a string:

Lincoln – SN Chiron H2 Aries, pointing to the past of the H12 Aquarius pain and therefore to the yogi's life (and beyond)	Lincoln – Chiron H12 Aquarius, pointing to a woundedness incurred by the Himalayan yogi	Lindbergh – SN Chiron H5 Aries, pointing to the past of the H2 Capricorn pain and therefore to Lincoln's life (and beyond)	Lindbergh – Chiron H2 Capricorn, pointing to a woundedness incurred by Lincoln
the yogi's pain of not having been able to secure and consolidate (H2) people's identity, freedom and right to exist (Aries), and of him possibly not having survived (H2) for trying to do so	a pain caused by the yogi not having been able to liberate (Aquarius) a large group of enslaved (H12) people, with him in all probability getting abruptly dissociated (Aquarius) from the cause of liberation (Aquarius)	a pain caused by the fact that people's identity, freedom and right to exist (Aries) were not honored and celebrated (H5) as their natural birthright (H5)	non-survival (H2) at the hands of those who sought to revive the Confederate cause (Capricorn); the attempts at suppression (Capricorn) of Lincoln's values (H2) by those who did not support the abolition of slavery (Capricorn)

Saturn 2nd house Capricorn: the one who receives the trauma charge *as pain*

As the pain is delivered to Lindbergh's Saturn by Chiron, the soul understands how consciousness in its new vehicle needs to be structured: in such a way as *to take full responsibility* (Saturn) *for the upholding* (Capricorn) *of his values, <u>whatever those be</u>.* The last three words are going to be rather important in understanding the highly unusual way in which Lindbergh resolved his Jupiter 2nd house Capricorn skipped step.

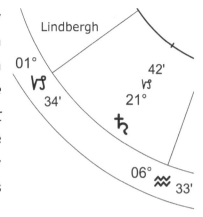

As was the case with Nixon, there is no telling whether the vehicle will actually use consciousness the way the soul intended or not. Nixon, instead of consolidating truthfulness (Saturn H9 Taurus), lived a life soaked through with lies and deception. Lindbergh, on the other hand, did honor his Saturn by upholding his values, although the net result was as shocking as Nixon *not* heeding his Saturn call.

Conclusion

The astrology in the two charts adds up, in particular with regards to Chiron and the *Trauma Helix*. Based on our conclusions, I think it is fair to say that Yogananda was right in his claim. We are indeed looking at two consecutive lives created by the same soul. But there is one thing that does not seem to make a whole lot of sense. And it is something big. How do we explain Lindbergh's antisemitism? How can we square this massively inconvenient fact with the soul's sustained efforts at bringing about racial equality?

Was Lincoln an anti-Semite? Anything but. He showed great consideration for Jewish Americans at a time when the U.S. was, to put it mildly, deeply anti-Semitic (11). Lincoln had to deal with more than one anti-Semitic general in his own ranks during the Civil War. General Benjamin F. Butler was openly anti-Semitic and regularly jailed and insulted Jews. In December 1862, future president Ulysses S. Grant issued General Orders No.11, which explicitly expelled

Jews "as a class" from territory under his command. The order came to be known as the "Jew Order" and wreaked havoc in Paducah and Kentucky.

A further problem for Lincoln was that the mid-19th century Jewish community was split on abolitionism. Many Jewish leaders supported slavery. Some Rabbis, among whom prominent ones, openly spoke out against abolitionism. Lincoln's predicament was further compounded by the fact that anti-Semitism was rife among abolitionists.

Does this complex picture explain why the soul in its next incarnation would take an anti-Semitic stance? Hardly. You would expect it to be squarely on the side of equal rights for all.

The Jupiter in the 2nd house Capricorn skipped step is something the soul brings into the life of Lindbergh as a major unresolved issue. *Prior-life selves* (Lincoln) *not having survived* (H2) *for promoting an ideology* (Jupiter) *that was not to the*

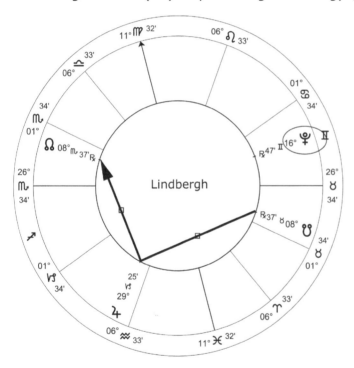

liking of reactionary forces Capricorn) is one part of the issue. Another has to do with *the inner values* (H2) *the ideology* (Jupiter) was based on. The egalitarian values Lincoln espoused went against everything not only a large segment of American society stood for but also against values held dear by Jews themselves. Just like Lindbergh's values, which he not only espoused but publicly expressed, would eighty years later.

The issue the Jupiter 2nd house Capricorn skipped step seems to hinge on is: "*to what extent can I express a vision* (Jupiter) - *based on certain inner values* (H2) *I hold - and then take responsibility* (Capricorn) *for expressing it, whether it be*

[82]

to the liking of those in power (Capricorn) – or indeed mainstream society (Capricorn) - or not? Am I going to survive (H2) if I do so?"

Why was this an unresolved issue? Well, that is not too hard to answer: did *the upholding* (Capricorn) *of his values* (H2) *not cost Lincoln his life* (H2)? It did, did it not? And so the soul says: *"see what happens next time when I open my mouth and rub everyone up the wrong way."* Do you see the soul logic in this? Do you see how, in a bid to solve the problem, it would need to make itself go through exactly the same kind of situation in the next life, i.e. Lindbergh's?

The unresolved Jupiter issue, brought into the current life of Lindbergh by the soul, resolves via the NN in the 12th house Scorpio *and its ruler in the 7th house Gemini*: *a deep commitment to* (NN Scorpio) *what is in humanity's* (NN H12) *best interest in terms of equality in relationship* (NN ruler H7) *as the result of full integration* (NN ruler Gemini) *of two sides which find themselves in a position of antagonism* (NN ruler H7 Gemini).

Lindbergh indeed takes the route to the NN of the Moon in the 12th house, getting deeply involved (Scorpio) in the political discussion on whether or not the United States of America should get involved in the second World War, but then comes out with statements no one in a million years had expected from the universally-admired aviator.

In a sense, therefore, he did exactly the same thing Lincoln had done: he aired *a vision* (Jupiter) *that went against values* (H2) *espoused by the authorities* (Capricorn) *and mainstream society* (Capricorn) *alike. What* he believed in (Jupiter) could not have been further removed from what Lincoln believed in, but the fact *that* he expressed it was exactly what Lincoln had not shied away from. *What* he believed in seemed to have been of little importance to the soul. The important thing was whether he once again would have to *pay with his life* (H2) *for having expressed views* (Jupiter) *that ran diametrically counter to public opinion* (Capricorn), in this case both at home and abroad.

Now you understand why I asked you to put that ruler of the NN of the Moon on a back burner a while back, along with all the other stuff already there: to resolve the Jupiter issue Lindbergh simply *had to* come out with something that went right against what mainstream society thought was in the best interest of humanity (resolution node for the Jupiter skipped step is the NN of the Moon H12 Scorpio).

The way he did that (NN ruler Pluto H7 Gemini) was *to cause a yawning inner chasm* (Gemini) *in the issue of equality in relationship* (H7) *through the words* (Gemini) *he spoke*. He survived, although his reputation was irreparably damaged. This is the reenactment of the 1st house Sagittarius trauma in his life: *because of the views* (Uranus in Sagittarius) *he expressed* (Uranus in Sagittarius ruling H3: fracturing and dissociation because of words willingly spoken on non-integration), *overnight* (Uranus) *Lindbergh was perceived* (Sagittarius) *to be* (H1: identity) *someone totally different* (Uranus dissociation) *from what people had believed* (Sagittarius) *him to be.*

What makes sense from the soul perspective may appear utterly reprehensible from the human perspective. At some point, however, the soul simply *had to* solve the Jupiter problem. This is how it did that.

In his later years Lindbergh would deeply regret having expressed his views, not least because they had caused so much pain to his family. In her 1998 memoir, *Under a Wing*, Lindbergh's daughter Reeve reflects on hearing her father give his Des Moines speech for the first time, during a visit to the *Lindbergh House* in Little Falls, Minnesota. Hearing his words, she could not believe they were spoken by the same man who had raised his children so lovingly, instilling altogether different values in them. (12)

Chapter 6 – the *'Multidimensional Psyche'* (1)

Richard Nixon was a quiet, studious boy. Shy and awkward around people, especially girls (getting closer than mailing distance), (2) he mostly kept to himself. Self-disciplined in the extreme, he insisted on freshly ironed shirts and his mother checking him for foul breath before leaving for school in the morning. (3) He would have the blinds down when made to do the washing up, lest the neighbors see he was doing "a woman's job." (4) The story of his youth, as would that of his later life, is shot through with lies and machinations. One day, when helping out in his father's grocery store, he cut his finger preparing hamburgers, and the meat came into contact with the open cut. When his cousin Donald suggested they dispose of the meat, Richard said, *"No way! That's the freshest-looking meat on the counter. Leave it there …"* (5) Richard was barely sixteen years old. It was around that time that he tried his hand at wiretapping for the first time, as he and his older brother Harold devised an ingenuous way of intercepting telephone conversations between a girl Harold knew and liked and a boy who was courting her. (6)

Knowledge came easily to young Richard. His elementary school teacher Mary George Skidmore reminisced *"He absorbed knowledge of any kind like a blotter. He just never had to work for knowledge at all."* She wondered how the boy had time to plough through *"no less than thirty or forty books, besides doing all of his other work."* (7) At age eleven, one of the books Richard gobbled up in his spare time was Dale Carnegie's *How to Win Friends and Influence People*, (8) the same book Charles Manson studied cover to cover so that he could ingratiate himself with the movers and shakers of his day and attract young girls from rich backgrounds who were beaten but not broken. (9) While doing a three-year prison stint at San Pedro's Terminal Island Penitentiary in Los Angeles Harbor, Manson signed up for a four-month Dale Carnegie course. In addition to attending class, enrolled students were expected to read *How to Win Friends and Influence People*. (10) By citing this book in one breath with Nixon and Manson, I am not even remotely suggesting that Carnegie's teachings are to be held accountable for the opportunism in the former or the criminal tendencies in the latter. What seems to have happened rather is that both men in their power-hungry minds appear to have read something into them that was not there and used that for their own manipulative purposes. For Nixon it seems rather tell-tale that such a young boy should be attracted to a book (Pluto in Gemini) with the words *'Influence People'* (Pluto H10) on its cover, as if he had, unwittingly, already begun building the *Dark Tower* (the ominous title of the play during whose rehearsal Nixon met his future wife Pat) that one day would become his demise. Manson was offered the course while in prison at the age of twenty-two. Eleven-year-old Nixon found the book all by himself: Pluto H10 Gemini skipped step retrograde. SN of the Moon H1 Libra: *to engage in relationships* (Libra) *with the sole purpose of furthering one's own agenda* (H1). This is exactly the way the Pluto - SN of the Moon dynamics tend to be experienced prior to the first Saturn return around the age of twenty-nine, more so with a soul having got stuck in the 10th Gemini issue. (11)

Already at the age of twelve young Nixon let his family know he aspired to be a lawyer one day. (12) Two years earlier, in an essay written after his brother Arthur's death (of encephalitis), he would state his wish *"to study law, and enter politics for an occupation, so that I might be of some good to the people."* (13)

With finances tight, his elder brother Harold dying of tuberculosis and Richard's helping hand needed at home and in the store, (14) the brilliant young student ended up attending Whittier College instead of the much more prestigious Yale. In his memoirs Nixon would write *"I had dreamed of going to college in the East."* (15) His 10th house Pluto, having made the vehicle devour all the right books by itself through the years of its tender youth, had envisaged notoriety and standing even in his studies (Pluto in Gemini), in his way *to* the top (Pluto H10), but it was not to be. For the rest of his life Nixon would compensate for the social standing he missed out on during his younger years by getting obsessed with class (Pluto H10) while at the same time harboring a deep-seated grudge against those schooled at Northeastern private universities, goading his staff in the White House to bring down the *"Eastern establishment."* (16) In a 1968 speech, he would accuse rival Hubert Humphrey of having *"come up the pharmacy way,"* having stated that *"My dad was a grocer."* (17)

A web of lies was spun around his humble beginnings, the most famous one being the oil the Nixon family had missed out on when it was supposedly discovered under its Whittier property after it had been sold. No such thing ever happened. Nor did Nixon meet his future wife Pat at a football game. They met during a school rehearsal of a Whittier amateur play with the foreboding title *The Dark Tower*. (18) Nor did he, after enlisting in April 1942, spend his U.S. navy time *"in the foxholes"* (19), *"when the bombs were falling,"* (20) as he would later reminisce. What he did do was run a beer and hamburger stand – Nick's Snack Shack - at the air strip on Green Island where he made so much money playing poker as to return from the war with considerable earnings. (21) Lying was endemic in Nixon, that much was clear by the end of the war. There had been much earlier signs of this, though.

At Whittier College Nixon's star shone brightly on the debating team. He had already excelled at debate when attending high school. His debating coach there had been worried about the boy's *"ability to slide around an argument, instead of meeting it head-on. {…} There was something mean in him in the way he put his questions, argued his points."* (22) One of his mother's friends would comment *"To get his point across he wouldn't hesitate to twist the truth."* (23)

Whittier fellow-student Lois Elliot, years later when Nixon had made a name for himself as a politician, would say of his debating strategies *"I remember it well. I sat in the gallery and I saw – when Nixon spoke in his rebuttal – that he was quoting from a blank sheet of paper. It was all against regulations and very cunning."* (24)

From 1934 to 1937 Nixon attended Duke University Law School. To Ethel Farley, one of the few female students at Duke, he came across as *"dour and aloof {…} We disliked his 'holier than thou' attitude. He was not unmoral, just amoral. He had no particular ethical system, no strong convictions {…} He was there to advance himself personally."* [SN of the Moon H1 Libra, MDB] (25) Nixon's aloofness and dourness made him less than attractive to the opposite sex. Through neighborhood talk Richard's mother would learn that when on dates her son *"talked not of romance but about such things as what might have happened if Persia had conquered the Greeks or what might have happened if Plato had never lived."* (26)

It was at Duke that Nixon got his first shot at break-ins. The aim was not to purloin documents that could be used against him or that he could use against others, as it would be in later breaking and entering, but to know about his grades, which the dean's office had been late in posting and which Richard suspected would be disappointing. Towards the end of his second year, Nixon and two fellow students broke into the dean's office, searched desks and file cabinets, found what they were looking for, and made their way out. Had the intention been to check the grades or change them? We shall never know. What we do know is that the event did not exactly claw at the edges of Nixon's conscience, for years later, in the build-up to the 1960 election, he would brag about how he had got in through the open skylight and *"moved with the finesse of a cat burglar."* (27)

Many more such break-ins and attempted break-ins would follow - the Brookings Institution one strangely often overlooked. (28) Unbeknownst to many is the fact that Nixon sabotaged the 1968 Lindon B. Johnson Vietnam peace talks for his own political gain, an act so unscrupulous that it amounts to little less than national treason. A tape made public in 1996, unequivocally shows how Nixon, a year before Watergate, gave orders for the liberal-leaning Brookings Institution break-in so that he could destroy evidence of his involvement in the 1968 sabotage attempt as well as obtaining records that would show that the halting of the bombing as proposed by Lindon B. Johnson had been a Democratic election vote-getting scheme.

White House Tape: 534-002B

Date: Thursday, July 1, 1971

Time: 8:45 a.m. - 9:52 a.m.

Participants: Richard M. Nixon & H.R. "Bob" Haldeman

Location: Oval Office

President Nixon: *Now, you do it. Shake them up! Get them off their goddamn dead asses and say, Now, this isn't what you should be talking about. We're up against an enemy, a conspiracy. They're using any means.* [banging desk for emphasis] *We are going to use any means. Is that clear?* [Haldeman acknowledges] *Did they get the Brookings Institute raided last night? No?*

Haldeman: *No Sir, they didn't.*

President Nixon: *Get it done! I want it done!* [banging desk for emphasis] *I want the Brookings Institute cleaned out, and have it cleaned out in a way that makes* [it look like] *somebody else broke in.* (29)

"I wanted it … right now," Nixon would later reminisce in his memoirs, *"even if it meant having to get it back surreptitiously."* (30)

Where did this unquenchable thirst for power obtained through collecting incriminating information on others come from? The deception - of himself and others - the obsessive chicanery, double-dealing and conniving, the almost chronic desire for retaliatory action against those who did not comply with his edicts, the hatred against those he suspected were out to get him at every corner, the disdain for anyone having enjoyed an Ivy League education, the fits of rage during which he would take his frustration out on others (on more than one occasion beating up his wife Pat so badly that she needed immediate medical care, attacking one of his own campaigners, etc.), his tendency to shift the blame on others when things fell through, the relentless self-discipline that almost destroyed both himself and his family: was all of that the result of his upbringing or did it come from deeper layers of the psyche connected to lifetimes past?

The Nature of the Multiple Self

The *'Multidimensional Psyche,'* a term coined by regression therapy pioneer Roger Woolger (31), is the self - known as "me" in this life - who carries timelines, wounding and personalities which have come through from other lifetimes, each with their own fears, anxieties, propensities, psychological dispositions, gifts, skills and need to reenact certain parts of their story in an attempt to bring them to closure. At the subconscious strata of our psyche, which knows of no time, these lives are ever present. Parts of them may percolate up into the conscious mind, pierce the semipermeable barrier between those other lives and this one and clamor for our attention. In this model of the psyche we are all multiple personalities. Not in the clinical sense of multiple personality disorder but as a

[89]

conglomerate of the wounded soldier dying on a faraway battlefield for someone else's war, the ruthless mercenary, the missionary nun who has taken a vow of poverty, the unscrupulous merchant flaunting his riches, the heretic dragged off to the dungeons, the bishop, the jilted lover, the pauper, etcetera, that live on inside of us. Rather than suppress these voices as they protrude into our normal, everyday waking consciousness, vying for prominence it seems at times, what is called for is to hear them and allow them to psycho-synthesize into a conscious self that understands exactly who of them seems to be writing and editing whole chunks of our most recurring and energy-draining life scripts. This need to bring together these dormant, half-dormant or active personalities streaming into our current-life self from other lifetimes adds a whole new level of meaning to what we commonly understand to be 'psychosynthesis': the different layers or strata of the multiple self are encouraged to strike up a dialogue with each other so that they may cohere around the unifying center I call "me". Evolutionary astrology, since it renders insight into the soul's deepest drives (Pluto by house and sign), how these have been explored in a string of past lives (SN of the Moon, ruler of the SN of the Moon), and – with the Chiron-*Trauma Helix* model I am proposing in these pages - how trauma from prior lives is brought into the current life as pain, is a seamless therapeutic fit with this kind of psychosynthesis.

If you wish to know more about this *'Multidimensional Psyche,'* I suggest you read Woolger's unsurpassed *Other Lives, Other Selves*, not just for a very clear and concise explanation of how trauma travels from one lifetime to the next, but also for its very elegant refutation of linear Cartesian-Newtonian time applied to the psyche. For a lengthier and more elaborate confutation you would need to pick up Stanislav Grof's *Beyond the Brain*. (32) Since I feel that the validity of the *'Multidimensional Psyche'* after forty years of regression therapy and a good twenty years of *Life-Between-Lives therapy* is no longer in question, I am not going to spend time and paper building a case for it.

With the wounding, fractalized parts of prior-life selves are brought into the current-life self, bits and pieces of split-off psyche: the psychic equivalent of the debris scientists at the Massachusetts Institute of Technology (MIT) now believe the rings around Chiron are made up of. The existence of a network of Saturn-like ring systems around Chiron in and of itself is surprising since until recently it was believed to be a dormant object in an inactive world. Even more surprising for our exploration of Chiron and the *Trauma Helix*, is the fact that these rings now seem to consist of numerous small pieces of rock revolving around Chiron on account of its gravitational pull: the very disparate parts and fractured pieces the psyche at the moment of trauma breaks up into. In the ´*Multidimensional Psyche*´ these split-off parts of self are brought in along with the rest of prior-life personalities: the fears, anxieties, propensities, psychological dispositions, gifts, and skills we talked about earlier. We know these segmented parts lie frozen and disconnected in the non-linear memory vault that is Uranus. Now, for the first time ever, we can literally see how in the rings of Chiron their physical counterparts are transported to Saturn.

'Samskara' and the *Trauma Helix*

In his book, Roger Woolger describes the subtle interweaving of the mental (M), emotional (E), physical (S) and spiritual (S) component of a traumatic experience carried over from a past life into the current one as a *'karmic complex'* or *'samskara.'*

Expanding Jung's concept of a *'complex'* to include prior lives, Woolger explains how the samskara is like a *'psychic scar tissue'* which has us repeat the same patterns over and over again from one lifetime to the next. (33) Citing Heinrich Zimmer, he describes this tissue as what we could call ´corrugations´ in the psyche formed by certain dispositions and propensities which, like water over rock, have run the same course during multiple lifetimes.

As he quotes Dr. Karl H. Potter, (34) Indologist from the University of Washington famous for his writings on Indian philosophy, it becomes clear in Woolger's explanation that these *'samskaras,'* these 'karmic complexes,' are made up of *'vasanas'* which, when activated, set in motion memories of the original act or event as well as their corresponding emotional dispositions. Memories (Uranus) and emotional dispositions (Neptune, Pluto) are exactly what we find in our *Trauma Helix*.

For our purposes it is interesting to read how Woolger draws his reader's attention to the fact that these *'vasanas'* in Sanskrit tend to refer to the waft left

[91]

behind on garments by perfume or cologne, with the important caveat that these *'vasanas'* come not from physical but from psychological and emotional activity. Much like the redolence of fresh coffee or the scent of freshly mown grass reveal the action that took place, from these traces we infer what emotional and psychological dispositions must have caused them. The *'vasana'* traces are subtle in nature and together form the 'samskara' or 'karmic complex' as it travels from lifetime to lifetime. (35)

Based on thousands of hours of client work, during which I have seen my astrological conclusions backed up by experiential findings through regression work, I believe **the Trauma Helix** (Uranus, Pluto, Neptune) to be the astrological equivalent of this *'samskara.'* **Chiron**, in its turn, shows us astrologically how it travels from one lifetime to the next, from one world to another. Chiron, however, does more than just deposit the pain parcel at Saturn's doorstep.

Chiron: the subtle body imprinting form

As the pain – *and* its potential for healing - comes in from the distant Uranus realm, its content produces an energy field matrix consisting of lines of force that coincide with the three components of the *Trauma Helix* (Uranus, Neptune and Pluto), complemented by memory traces of the physical impact of the traumatic events, which travel alongside the emotional impression, indentation, if you will. (36) These energy lines are the *'traces'* Woolger speaks of. Together these subtle psychic folds and creases form an etheric cast upon which physical dispositions in the vehicle's body (Saturn), in addition to its structure of consciousness (Saturn), are shaped. We could call this etheric cast *'the subtle body.'* For a proper understanding of the role of Chiron as trauma key, it is important to emphasize that this etheric mold is the template upon which both the physical disposition (Saturn) and the structure of consciousness (Saturn) operative in the soul's vehicle are anchored as the latter descends into matter. In other words: the subtle body is prior to form – whether physical or psychological - not the result of it. You cannot see the subtle body, any more than you can feel it. Yet if you could, you would find that it is an energetic blueprint the soul carries with it as it comes down and moves into form and which wraps itself around it the way an envelope does a letter. That form is the physical body (Saturn) on the one hand and the structure of consciousness (Saturn) on the other. This is why in the opening lines of chapter 3 you heard me say how Saturn by house and sign is partly determined by Chiron and partly by the Pluto Polarity Point. The same way some people have been known to train themselves to perceive the aura of a person or a plant, the therapeutic evolutionary astrologer can sensitize themselves to how this energy pattern coming in from non-form embosses form, if not person-to-person when their client sits down at the consultation table across from them, then at least astrologically. This book seeks to contribute to the latter. It is my hope that the astrological sensitization may awaken the person-to-person one.

Where Chiron in certain astrological literature has been associated with cellular memory, this is correct only in so far as the memory contained in the biological cells of the organism is the result of the subtle memory traces held in the etheric cast having been projected onto physical matter and leaving an imprint there. This is how physical disposition, part of which is a propensity to a certain type of ailment, from prior lives comes back just like emotional, psychological and spiritual one: moles, skin marks and growths appear where gunshot or knife wounds were inflicted, recurring neck pain in this life may echo death by hanging in a previous one, with the pain in some cases becoming acute at the exact age at which in that prior life the hanging occurred, etcetera.

What message is written into Chiron's discovery chart? (see chart p.94)

Interestingly, in Chiron's discovery chart we find the asteroid-comet in the 4th house Taurus, indicating, so it seems, that we are born (H4/Cancer) (37) with this pain and that there is a permanence (Taurus) to it, a fixity that may well point to the very **'trauma continuity from one lifetime to the next'** we explored in previous chapters. The 4th house takes us to an even deeper level of the pain, suggesting it is caused by the fact of *us having to go through yet another personality* (H4) *in which the woundedness needs to get anchored* (Taurus) *before it can be healed*. Chiron was retrograde at the moment of its discovery, underscoring the repeat assignment of the pain. Chiron is widely conjunct its own south node at 28 degrees Aries 33 minutes, indicating it works in unison with a past whose origins lie in our *emotional* (H4) *identities* (Aries).

[93]

Here we seem to get confirmation of the idea which lies at the heart of the Chiron - *Trauma Helix* model: the combined Pluto-Neptune emotion lies in Uranus' non-linear memory vault as an identity (Aries), an I-am-ness, waiting to be picked up by Chiron and transferred to Earth *as pain.*

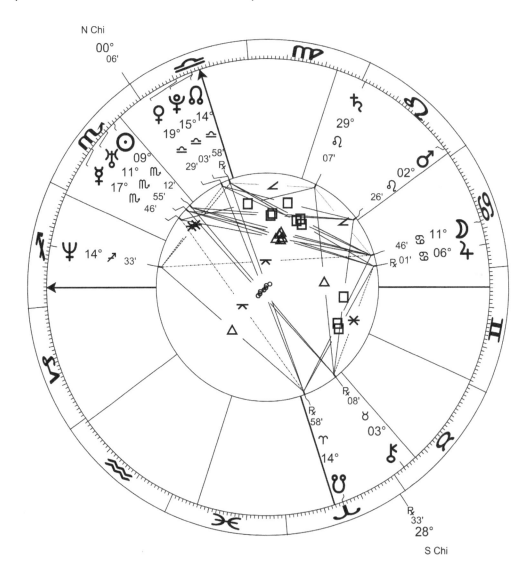

Chiron Discovery Chart. 1 November 1977, 09:56 hrs., Pasadena, California. RR: A

This point where Chiron picks up this 'feeling identity,' therefore, is literally where the Chiron pain originates (SN Chiron H4 Aries). Chiron's north node, at 0 degrees Scorpio 6 minutes falls in the 10th house, suggesting the healing of the pain asks *a deep commitment* (Scorpio) *of us in terms of maturation* (H10), consisting, so it appears, in each of us *assuming responsibility* (H10) *for our own healing*

[94]

process. Please note, that the discovery date has the master number 11 in it 8 times: 11.77. Eight is the number of infinity. Parting from the sound astrological

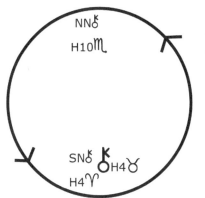

idea that nothing in the universe happens accidentally, is Chiron's discovery date perchance telling us this pain keeps coming back 'eternally' until it is mastered, i.e. healed here on earth? (38)

The subtle body's memory traces of physical trauma and pain: Nixon's knees

As an example of how memories of physical trauma contained in the *Trauma Helix* may manifest as physical ailment or a proneness to accidents to certain body parts, the case of Richard Nixon may serve. Nixon had a recurring problem with his legs and knees. The first instance of trauma to them being reenacted was at the time of his woefully unprepared televised debate with Jack Kennedy in 1960. Nixon went in convinced of a resounding victory, his only worry being that he *"might clobber that kid Kennedy too tough on the first debate and thus womp up a 'sympathy factor' for the guy."* (39) As it turned out, the debate went so bad for Nixon that it effectively cost him the election. While on the campaign trail, Nixon one day walked into a dense crowd and was thrust against the door of his limousine (40), hurting his knee. Not long after the incident, doctors at Walter Reed hospital found an infection so nasty that Nixon was at risk of losing one of his legs if he did not immediately agree to a two-week stay in hospital. (41)

Following his loss to Democratic incumbent Pat Brown in the 1962 California gubernatorial election, Nixon began traveling extensively in a bid to gain a reputation as a statesman. Going by the massive mileage he clocked up on these trips, carbon footprint did not figure large in his value system. His efforts were to no avail as more than one head of state proved less than willing to see an ex vice-president recently beaten in two major elections. On one of his many travels, Nixon suffered an inflammation of a vein in his leg (42) which would later, on a visit to the Middle East in the middle of Watergate investigations, resurface and come perilously close to ending his life. A close shave on two occasions, therefore, involving legs and knees.

The lack of moral fibre, which in chapter 3 we signaled in the soul's emotional and psychological identification with the Uranus and Neptune strand of the Trauma Helix as *a divisiveness* (Gemini) *in integrity* (Gemini), *a split* (Gemini) *in its ability to hold itself accountable* (H10), literally made his knees cave in, which astrologically, of course, are associated with Saturn, Capricorn and the 10th house (joints and skeletal system). It was as if there was insufficient moral backbone in place for his legs to carry him. (43)

Fitting Chiron and the *Trauma Helix* into the narrative of the Evolutionary Axis

Nixon's *unquenchable thirst for power obtained through collecting incriminating information on others* - a thirst that had seeped so deep into the nooks and crannies of the soul myth as to justify any means necessary *to obtain maximum status, power and prestige* - came from his Pluto in the 10th house (power) Gemini (information) skipped step.

When he had used Anna Chenault in his secret, behind-the-scenes dealings with South Vietnamese President Thieu, using her as a pawn in his attempts to sabotage the 1968 peace talks and so cast a negative light on his opponent Hubert Humphrey [SN ruler H6 Pisces], Nixon denied having had any involvement with her. With the election won, he then performed an about-face urging Thieu to come to the Paris peace talks, the very same ones he had so desperately wanted him to stay away from. Both Chenault and Thieu felt deeply betrayed by Nixon. Lindon B. Johnson knew about the ploy but did not go public with it for fear of it being construed by the electorate as dirty campaign tactics. (44)

This turning on people he had used in a bid to secure power is written in his SN of the Moon in the 1st house: *to engage in relationship* (Libra) *with the sole purpose of furthering his own agenda* (1st house). <u>*The way*</u> this was carried out by prior-life selves, as it was by Nixon, is written in the SN ruler in the 6th house Pisces: *to use information to imply guilt* (H6) *and so come out looking all innocent* (Pisces) *himself*. Nixon's merciless assault on Jerry Voorhis and Alger Hiss, not

[96]

to mention his ruthless crusade against Helen Douglas, are fine examples of this. (45) Typical of the 6th house/Virgo dynamic, of course, is the inability to clearly discern what information is to be used for what. There is an ethical component in Virgo that is absent in Gemini: the latter's concern is connecting the dots without asking the question why this is done or what the consequences of the connecting might be. In Virgo, who has her sights set on purifying the vessel in an attempt to ready it for equality in relationship (Libra), the question of which information can stay and which needs to be jettisoned - excreted - *must* be asked. With that question comes the moral issue of why and to what end the information was gathered in the first place. It is that part which in Nixon's case connects with the *implying-guilt-in-others-so-as-to-appear-innocent-myself* dynamic: 6th house Pisces.

These are the past-life dynamics as carried over into the current-life of Richard Nixon. Nixon's 6th house Pisces Chiron, so we said in Chapter 2, speaks of a pain caused by *a pervasive confusion* (Pisces) *around what true service from a place of humility* (H6) means. The pain is glued to the SN ruler's antics, and it makes

sense that it would be since it is the dynamic of *using information to imply guilt* (SN ruler H6) *in others and so come out looking all pure, blameless and squeaky-clean* (SN ruler Pisces) *oneself* which <u>caused</u> the trauma of *sudden dissociation from his leadership* (Uranus H5) *and office* (Uranus ruling H6); trauma which Chiron relays.

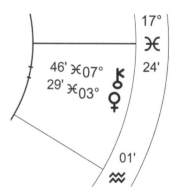

The important thing to remember when looking at the Uranus placement is that you try and understand how that trauma would have been the logical consequence of the prior-life dynamics we saw in Pluto, the SN of the Moon and its ruler. In other words: the traumatic events happened in the context of a story, as a result of actual events, in all likelihood connected *to* those dynamics.

To 'get' the story, you need to link back the SN ruler to the SN of the Moon and then back to Pluto, something I stressed the importance of throughout my first book *Intercepted Signs: Encoded Messages from the Soul*. When you do that, you get a sentence:

Using people as pawns (SN H1 Libra) *to get incriminating information on others* (SN ruler H6) *that would allow him to name and shame* (SN ruler H6) *so that he*

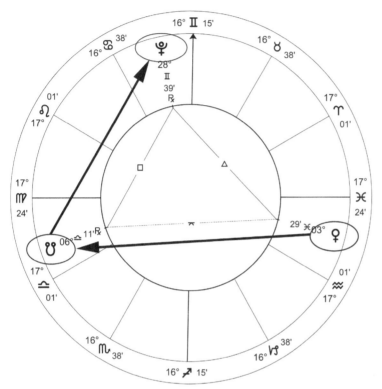

came out looking innocent (SN ruler Pisces) *is the way the soul explored its issue of getting to a position of absolute status, power and prestige through misuse of information and glib talk* (Pluto H10 Gemini).

Understanding the Neptune strand of the *Trauma Helix* against the backdrop of the actual events

reflected in the Pluto, SN and SN ruler story is equally important. Prior-life Nixons, as did the soul's current-life vehicle, would have *lived in a dissociative state* (Neptune H11) *as they made the nation* (Neptune in Cancer) *believe they were one thing when in fact they were something completely different* (H11 dissociation as deception), the price tag having been *fracturing in the emotional body* (Neptune H11 Cancer). Their lives, as did Nixon's, had become a living lie (Neptune H11): Nixon was anything but the innocent (SN ruler Pisces) do-gooder who had sworn to protect and to serve (SN ruler H6). Pieces of rock pertaining to the Neptune trauma caused by that dynamic where whizzing around Chiron as well as it hurled through space on its way to his Saturn in the 9th house Taurus, eager to deliver its parcel at Saturn's door and for the taskmaster to understand the day's work: *the imperative need to consolidate* (Taurus) *truthfulness* (H9).

Fractalized bits of Neptune meaninglessness debris in the Chiron rings may account for Nixon's paranoia since his Neptune, as it lied to the nation, was already lying to itself. This inner dissociative state got fueled by the fear of others out to remove him from office (Uranus H5 Aquarius and ruling the 6ᵗʰ house of office). Flying around in this deadly cocktail would have been bits of dissociated integrity (Pluto H10 Gemini) too, adding to its already explosive mix.

From *'transpersonal'* to *'multi-personal'* planets

The common use of the term *'transpersonal planets,'* which in astrology refers to Uranus, Neptune and Pluto, parts from the idea that these planets hold a collective energy, which is why they are sometimes called 'generational.' The idea behind this is that they are believed to point to what lies beyond – 'trans' – the personal. In the Chiron-*Trauma Helix* model, however, the term acquires a completely different meaning: what we hitherto thought lay beyond the personal, now turns out to be **multi-personal**: the self is comprised of multiple timelines - each comprised of layers of trauma charge, pain, fears, anxieties, gifts, skills, propensities - streaming into the current-life self from past-life personalities. I therefore propose renaming the three as **multi-personal planets**. Through Chiron, past-life trauma streams into the current life as pain, and with it the potential for overcoming the trauma and healing the pain.

This redefinition of the three as *multi-personal planets* does not in any way exclude their collective application. The undeniable fact that they do indeed affect the collective and events occurring on a collective level – amply demonstrated by more than one author - is soon understood when we realize that _each and every one of us **is** that collective_: in the numerous lives each and every one of us has lived – stretching back into the far recesses of time - we have all been each other's spouses, jilted lovers, disinherited black sheep of the family, teachers, students, slave owners, slaves, fathers, mothers, terror-stricken children, persecutors and victims. If nine of those lives live on inside of you and another nine inside of me, then just between you and me we are already looking at a collective of twenty (Yes, I did count correctly because you and I, as the soul's current-life vehicle are included in the count). Multiply that by 7.8 billion people all bringing in multiple past-life timelines, and all of a sudden the idea of

[99]

the collective and the individual overlapping does not seem so far-fetched anymore.

This strange simultaneity of the individual and the collective is another fine example of the kind of non-linearity we keep running into as we leave the Saturn realm behind.

In the opening chapters of the book I associated it with the *'homeopathic principle'* operative in Chiron, Uranus and Neptune. It came back in the 'trauma continuity' we spotted between the lives of Charles Lindbergh and Abraham Lincoln, as it will in chapter 15 of the book where we examine it in the charts of Barbro Karlén and Anne Frank.

It can be said to be the common thread, the leitmotiv, running through the present volume. Alerting ourselves to it is therapeutically important for it sensitizes us to the warped time reigning in these *multi-personal* planets and how it echoes psychologically inside of our and our clients' lives, piercing, as I mentioned before, through the linear barrier of Saturn - reverberating in their lower octaves Mercury (Uranus), Venus (Neptune) and Mars (Pluto) - as they enter our neatly for linearly arranged Mercurial everyday lives.

Chapter 7 – Nina Simone

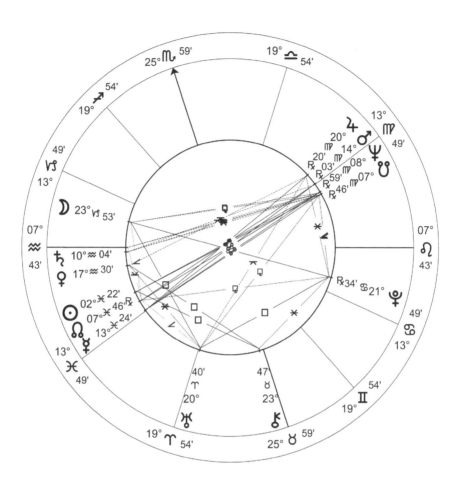

Nina Simone, 21 February 1933, 06:00 AM, Tryon, North Carolina. RR:AA

Poor, black and female. Those are the three words you would not have found on Eunice Kathleen Waymon´s audition notes when in September of 1950 the prestigious Curtis Institute of Music in Philadelphia denied her admission, in spite of an excellent performance. The denial of her application would change the course of Eunice's career and life. To be able to fund her private piano lessons with Vladimir Sokoloff, a teacher at Curtis, she performed in nightclubs. She took these lessons still hoping she would one day be admitted to Curtis, which did not happen because once she concluded her studies with him, she was past the age limit for admission. Knowing her mother, a devout Methodist minister, would not take kindly to her playing *"the Devil´s Music"* in bars, Eunice adopted the stage name Nina Simone. Nina came from *"Niña,"* meaning *"little girl,"* which is what Eunice's old boyfriend Chico had called her. *"Simone"* was after the French actress Simone Signoret, whom Eunice had seen on the big screen when she moved to Philadelphia and whom she admired.

The Curtis rejection on grounds of her race, which dashed Nina´s hopes of becoming the first great black American classical pianist - a goal she had fiercely been working toward for most of her life - became a catalyst. It helped her find her voice, not just in the figurative sense as a socially engaged musician who reflected the times, but also literally, since nightclub owners insisted she sing as well as play the piano. Not long after she had started performing at the *Midtown Bar and Grill* in Atlantic City, music lovers flocked to the club to hear a tremendously talented pianist and singer perform.

For our purposes it is important to acknowledge the fact that, in spite of the worldwide praise and acclaim that would be hers, this is not the life Eunice Waymon would have chosen. At heart she always stayed a classical pianist, incorporating the use of intricate musical lines that she had learned from Bach into pop songs and improvisation. Band members often had difficulty following not only the vertical harmonic richness of her playing but also the horizontal development of these lines. She would require her audience's full and undivided attention, refusing to play if there was so much as a whisper in the furthest corner of the hall. *"I had my music and if you didn't want to listen to it, go the hell home,"* she said. *"I wasn't making that much money that I had to compromise. […] I had that same attitude when I played bigger places. I had gotten that from being a classical pianist. You're supposed to sit down and be quiet. If you couldn't be quiet, then leave."* (1) After recording her first album *Little Girl Blue* for the Bethlehem label in late 1957, she went home, locked herself up in the piano room and played Beethoven for three days straight to get popular music out of her system. (2)

What kinds of issues had a soul choosing this kind of life been exploring? And, even more important to the subject matter of this book, how does the Chiron-

Trauma Helix dynamics fit into the soul narrative? To answer these questions, we start, as always, with an analysis of the Evolutionary Axis.

We find **Pluto in the 6th house Cancer**: *inferiority* (H6) *in the context of race*

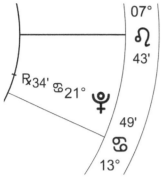

(Cancer) *and racial prejudice.*

This has been the bane of US society and the problem is far from over. Nina Simone was born in 1933, at a time when the Jim Crow laws were in place. They were state and local laws that enforced racial segregation in the Southern United States, although some northern states were not exempt from them either. Named after a black minstrel show character, the laws existed for almost 100 years, from the post-Civil War era until 1968. They were designed to marginalize African Americans in all areas of life, from voting, getting an education, to holding jobs.

You can imagine what official laws stating inferiority in black people would do to a soul trying to weed out impurities in itself (H6), a soul trying to make important adjustments in itself (H6) as it readies itself for equality in relationship. (3) A soul who, as it looks critically at itself – may fall prey to an overly self-critical stance and would have trouble clearly discerning (H6) what criticism comes from without and what from within and then, to add to the complexity, what criticism to act on and what not. The criticism and guilt implicit in the racial prejudice (Cancer) is going to seep in like a poison, reaching deep into the very fissures of the soul, depositing its nefarious message there. At a deeper archetypal level one of the issues the soul has been exploring is how the feeling of not being good enough (H6) is exacerbated by an attachment to outside sources of emotional security (Pluto in Cancer). (4)

Pluto retrograde, finally, tells us the soul will create circumstances in the current life that will cause an acceleration in the direction of the 12th house Capricorn PPP. The key question in understanding *the Inner Logic of the Soul*, now is: what kinds of lives would this soul have created to explore its 6th house Cancer issues?

The answer to that question is written in the **7th house Virgo SN of the Moon**.

The first thing we notice, is that Virgo is restated: Pluto in H6, SN in Virgo. The SN in the 7th denotes inequality in relationships as a result of what is projected onto you, or what is expected of you. At the basis of both is a state of not listening to other. (5) That is why you hear the term *projected expectations* in EA when the 7th house or Libra come up. To map the dynamics operative in prior-life selves, we are now going to bring the 7th house issues through the filter of Virgo.

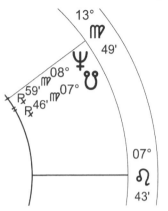

What happens to Libra when it is impacted by Virgo? To rephrase: what is going to happen to the scales when we place Virgo on one end, that is, someone who is making themselves smaller than what they actually are, either because there are convinced of their unworthiness (Virgo) or because they interject it through criticism leveled at them? (6)

Is that deflating of oneself not going to sabotage the whole weighing and comparing process before it has even started? How can I weigh myself against you when you place a diminished version of yourself on the scale opposite from where I am, possibly caused by interjected unworthiness (Virgo)? This is what actually happens when Virgo impacts the 7th house.

We are beginning to see the contours of **the Inner Logic of the Soul** emerge: lives where I self-deflated or was made smaller than what I actually was (SN in Virgo), causing inequality in relationship (SN H7), have been the means through which the soul has explored inferiority in the context of race and racial prejudice (Pluto H6 Cancer).

A planet conjunct the SN of the Moon has been a direct and decisive influence on prior-life selves and the dynamics operative in them. Here, that planet is **Neptune**, that is, the meaninglessness strand of the *Trauma Helix*.

Translated to English: *the trauma of deep disillusionment caused by relationships having been severely off kilter (H7) as a result of interjected inferiority and unworthiness – Virgo - directly impacted prior-life selves (SN of the Moon).*

Immediately we understand why **Mars is in the 8ᵗʰ house Virgo**: the soul wants

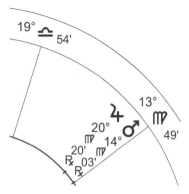

all conscious actions and desires directed at looking very critically at the issue of power, powerlessness and self-empowerment, to reflect deeply on the issue (Mars retrograde) and to then *deeply commit* (H8) *to serving* (Virgo) *empowerment* (H8).

So that the vehicle Nina Simone may reflect deeply on this 8ᵗʰ house issue, the soul will create reenactments of past-life situations in which intense powerlessness (H8) is felt: Mars retrograde. The reenactment of these situations, in other words, serves the reflection the soul seeks here. (7) The same thing applies to Jupiter: the lens through which the soul wants Simone to look out into the world is cut and polished by *the need to discern* (Virgo) *power and powerlessness* (H8), *to clearly distinguish* (Virgo) *between what one feels like and what the other feels like and to then serve* (Virgo) *self-empowerment* (H8) *by choosing* (H8) *one over the other.* The extent to which Jupiter manages to do this rules the 11ᵗʰ house of her individuation - contingent on her following her own truth (Sagittarius)- which at once is the house where large groups of people (H11) have suffered the consequences of a sick and twisted ideology (Sagittarius). Both are inextricably linked in Nina Simone's life.

My apologies for the little digression into Mars-Jupiter territory, but it is relevant to understanding the complex personality that was Nina Simone, the anger and frustration she felt at people not willing to make the same deep commitment (Mars H8) she was willing to make, anger also at people not willing to serve (Virgo) the empowerment (H8) of her people. After all, through house rulership, Mars' willingness to indeed direct all actions and desires at the 8ᵗʰ house issues affected her and her people's freedom and right to exist through full integration (Aries on the cusp of H3). In that same 3ʳᵈ house we find the Uranus strand of the Trauma Helix: **Uranus 3ʳᵈ house Aries**, ruling the Ascendant and so indicating that the soul, as it descended into matter and right before the veil of amnesia was pulled over it (the subconscious 12ᵗʰ house sleeping in adjoining quarters with the instinctive non-conscious 1ˢᵗ house), brought with it traumatic memories *of one's identity, freedom and right to exist* (Aries) *having been denied* *through non-integration* (H3). Little Eunice Waymon, *"Niña,"* won't remember

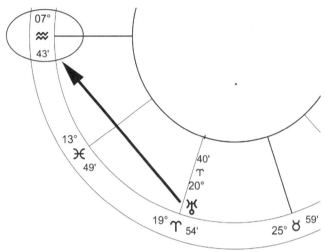

any of it, allowing her to meet the issue afresh. But circumstances will soon trigger those memories and drive home the need to take the exact kind of action written into her 8th house Virgo Mars. The reenactment of the trauma will serve an evolutionary purpose, as we shall see shortly. Please note the almost exact inconjunct (crisis) between the SN of the Moon and the Ascendant. (8)

Back to the Evolutionary Axis. How did those SN H7 Virgo dynamics play out in prior lives? To obtain that information we turn to **the SN ruler**. It is in the 1st house Pisces: *a loss and/or surrender* (Pisces) *of identity, freedom and right to exist* (H1), *possibly in the context of slavery* (Pisces).

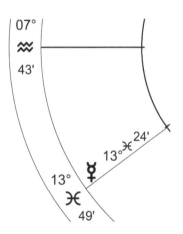

Linking back the SN ruler to the SN and then back to Pluto in an attempt to uncover the *Inner Logic of the Soul*: a loss of identity, freedom and right to exist in relationships characterized by inequality as a result of interjected unworthiness, *is the way in which* the soul has explored the issue of inferiority in the context of race and racial prejudice.

In a moment, when we have dealt with the NN and its ruler, we will come back to the SN ruler because it is conjunct the NN, indicating a very special kind of repeat assignment.

What were the evolutionary intentions this soul had for the life lived by its vehicle Nina Simone? We go to the house and sign diametrically opposite the Pluto placement and read the answer in **the Pluto Polarity Point in the 12th house**

[106]

Capricorn. Coming from this place of 6th house unworthiness, the soul wants to evolve to one where it feels the Cosmic Embrace not of forgiveness (H12) but of the fact that there is nothing to forgive to begin with, that one is perfect warts and all, that there is nothing you can do that will make God stop loving you. (9) That God's love is beyond race, creed, or gender. Once this is understood - *felt* (H12) rather - the attachment to outside sources of emotional security (Pluto in Cancer) is broken. (10) That is the maturity (Capricorn) the soul seeks in the 12th house. Did Nina Simone find that God?

When asked if she could find God in her own music (H12), she responded *"Of course, all the time. How do you explain what it feels like to get on stage and make poetry that you know sinks into the hearts and souls of people who are unable to express it? How do you talk about that? There aren't many words, but in some way you know that tonight was a good thing. You got to them. That's God. [...] I've been given the gift of being able to play by ear, having perfect pitch, having things that ordinary people do not have. When you have this gift, you must give it back to the world. That's the only way you're going to get if off your back. I don't know if I can explain any better than that what God is."* (11)

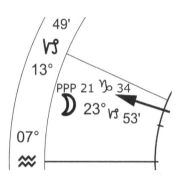

You can see the ***Moon conjunct the Polarity Point***: the soul's intentions for the current life streaming unadulterated into its vehicle, with Simone structuring (Capricorn) her music (H12) the same way her beloved master Johann Sebastian Bach had done three centuries earlier: the horizontality of counterpoint outlining the vertical Oneness of God and Man,

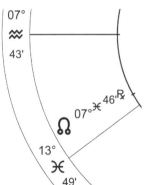

of God and Creation (12), almost as a musical illustration of the exact kind of 12th house Divine Embrace Simone needed to feel.

The way these soul intentions could be facilitated on the level of personality, on the Moon level, is through the ***NN in the 1st house Pisces***: healing (Pisces) *her identity, freedom and right to exist* (H1) by moving away from extreme inequality (SN H7) caused by interjected unworthiness (SN Virgo).

Here too, we need to uncover **the Inner Logic of the Soul**. We do that by asking this question: how would this 1st house Pisces NN help the soul get to its much-desired place of 12th house maturation (Capricorn)?

The answer to the question is: extricating herself from the 7th house inferiority-induced inequality will make the soul feel the universal Divine Love that goes beyond race, creed and gender (opening words of this chapter: *"Poor, black and female"*). The conduit for this was her music (Moon H12) and, more specifically, *the responsibility and integrity* (Capricorn) *she displayed in shaping* (Capricorn) *it*: getting up at 4:00 AM every single day, practice for four hours and then go to school. Year in, year out. Please note how this Moon rules the 6th house of craft and guild.

NN ruler conjunct the SN: a repeat assignment

The way this 1st house Pisces intention could be carried out is found in **the NN ruler**. It is in the 7th house Virgo: it seeks to *carefully examine* (Virgo) *how inequality in relationship is created through what is projected onto people* (H7). We have now reached a key moment in our analysis: Neptune fulfils a triple role and will need to be interpreted separately for each:

1. Planet conjunct the SN ruler (done)
2. NN ruler conjunct the SN
3. Neptune strand of the *Trauma Helix* (done)

The fact of the NN ruler being conjunct the SN of the Moon indicates a heavy-duty repeat assignment. It is relatively easy to see why this is so simply by looking at the symbols: every time the NN ruler wants to kick in and carry out the NN's 1st house Pisces intentions – and we have described how that can be done – it is made to revisit old dynamics (SN of the Moon). In other words: new dynamics are glued to old ones.

SN ruler conjunct the NN: a very different repeat assignment

How is this different from the repeat assignment indicated by the SN ruler being conjunct the NN of the Moon? When you see the SN ruler conjunct the NN of the Moon, what you tend to find is that somewhere in the early life of the person old dynamics are dished up by the soul in an attempt to kick start the NN of the Moon.

For Nina Simone this happened when her piano teacher Miss Mazzanovich had organized the *Eunice Waymon Fund* to raise money for her musical education. *"Miss Mazzy"* put an ad in the local newspaper, the *"Time Bulletin,"* announcing Eunice's debut recital Sunday 16th May 1943. With the entire town invited, some two hundred people showed up. Before she started playing, Eunice noticed how her parents, who had taken seats in the front row, were told to move to the back of the room so that white audience members could take these more privileged seats. Upon seeing this, young Eunice took a stand and told the organizers *"I will not be playing. My mother is a black woman. And if she can't sit where she can watch my hands, then I won't be playing."* (13)

This is the exact kind of repeat signature the SN ruler conjunct the NN can point to: again, just like she had been in prior lives, Eunice was in a situation where there was *a loss* (SN ruler Pisces) *in terms of right to exist* (SN ruler H1). As this situation was now reenacted early on in her life (Eunice was ten years old at the time), it kickstarted her NN, urging it to reclaim that right and so heal it (H1 Pisces). Which she did valiantly.

Chiron and the *Trauma Helix*

How would the soul have identified emotionally with the Uranus and Neptune strand of the trauma? Let us have a look at each of them before we answer that question.

Uranus: held in its non-linear storage vault are memories of traumatic events to do with *not having been allowed to establish one's identity, freedom and right to exist* (Aries) *because of segregation* (i.e. non-integration: H3). As Simone in

[109]

the 1960s became more and more politicized and at one point was drawn to the ideology of Malcolm X – much to the dismay of her husband and manager Andy Stroud - her response to the civil rights issue was not what you would have expected: she became increasingly convinced racial segregation was the way forward. Again, as was the case with Lindbergh, a fine example of how the soul may not evolve in linear fashion but take the exact opposite stance of the one you would expect it to take.

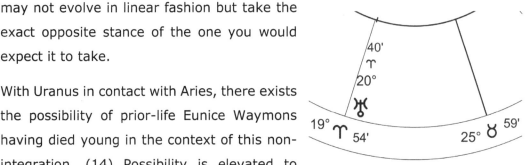

With Uranus in contact with Aries, there exists the possibility of prior-life Eunice Waymons having died young in the context of this non-integration. (14) Possibility is elevated to probability by dint of Uranus´ placement in the house of youth (H3). Quite often when this is a likely past-life scenario, in the current life the individual at a very young age seems to be pushing themselves out of a subconscious fear they will be struck down again. This would certainly apply to Nina Simone's younger years during which she displayed an unusual drivenness to accomplish extraordinary musical feats. Even Barbro Karlén, whose Uranus is not in the 1st house or in

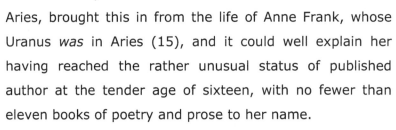

Aries, brought this in from the life of Anne Frank, whose Uranus *was* in Aries (15), and it could well explain her having reached the rather unusual status of published author at the tender age of sixteen, with no fewer than eleven books of poetry and prose to her name.

Neptune: the meaninglessness as a result of these events is related to *extreme inequality in interpersonal relationship* (H7) *as a result of projected* (H7) *and/or interjected unworthiness* (Virgo).

Pluto. How would *you* identify with these events if you were the soul? It may feel a bit strange to put yourself in the shoes of the soul, granted, but it might help you see things from its perspective. Would it not have made you *emotionally insecure* (Cancer)

in terms of self-worth (H6)? Well, that is exactly how this 6th house soul would have pulled these two strands into its own story.

All of that, the actual mental content in the forms of thoughts and images (Uranus), the meaninglessness felt as a result of the traumatic events (Neptune) and Pluto's emotional identification with both, lies in the depths of the Uranus library. Chiron travels there, takes out his library card, picks up the book and translates it on the way *as pain* so that Saturn may understand it and know how to pass the message on to the rest of the family. **How does Chiron translate the trauma charge?**

It translates it as the pain of *having been severely held back* (Taurus) *in*

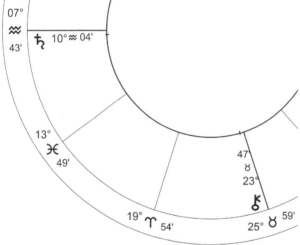

integration (3rd house).

When that pain knocks on Saturn's door, **how does Saturn receive the book**? It receives it as a consciousness uniquely structured to *step back and objectively assess* (Aquarius) *what identity, freedom and right to exist* (H1) actually mean. And then, *through* the assessment made,

liberate (Aquarius) *from any and all things standing in their way.* As such it will impact the 12th house, which it rules. The 1st house act of liberation becomes embedded in her music (H12): music as the tool for social rights activism. It could not have been any other way for Simone: a lifelong commitment to using her talent (H12 music) in the fight for racial equality (Saturn H1 Aquarius).

How does the trauma charge carried over into the life of Nina Simone and its subsequent reenactment help the soul evolve? This was the question we raised in the chapter on Nixon and we raise it again here. To experience racial inequality and gender bias all over again, and for it to happen at such a young age, activated the NN of the Moon and its ruler: Nina, in what we might call 'her Rosa Parks moment,' flatly refused to let a surrender (SN ruler Pisces) of identity, freedom and right to exist (SN ruler H1) happen again. When it raised its ugly head during her debut recital in the Tryon Library, she squashed it by refusing to have them taken away from her and her family (NN H1). Music was the weapon she brandished as she stood her ground, as if she were saying to the white community gathered there that day *"This music is God's gift to me. And so are my parents. If you have come to listen to me, then you are going to respect both."* In so doing she healed (NN Pisces) the interjected inferiority that had lain at the heart of so much inequality in interpersonal relationship (SN H7 Virgo). The resolve of that act would last a lifetime.

In the trauma lies the potential for healing

In the Uranus trauma lies the potential for healing it, which is precisely why the soul reenacts past-life trauma in the current life. Life itself, therefore, is a kind of regression therapy. Slower, granted, but it honors the same homeopathic principle regression therapy does: *in* the re-experiencing the trauma can be healed.

In chapter 4 we saw how the trauma of past-life Lincolns having paid the ultimate price for their deep commitment to the cause of liberty (**Uranus** H9 Scorpio) is overcome when Lincoln commits to it even more deeply, even more passionately.

In the deepest meaninglessness felt as a result of true liberty not having come about (**Neptune** H9 Sagittarius), the deepest meaningfulness is found for Lincoln when he works tirelessly to make it come true this time round.

In his 12th house Aquarius woundedness of having been dissociated (**Chiron** in Aquarius) from the noble cause of liberating (Aquarius) large groups of people (Aquarius) from slavery (H12), healing takes place when Lincoln faces the same obstacles he did in prior lives and then overcomes them.

For Nina Simone the same principle applies. *In* the trauma of prior-life selves not having been able to claim their identity, freedom and right to exist because of segregation (**Uranus** H3 Aries) lies the potential for overcoming it when she uses her music to do just that for herself and her people, which is what she did as she became more and more politicized.

In the deepest meaninglessness of extreme inequality in relationship as a result of interjected inferiority (**Neptune** H7 Virgo), the deepest meaningfulness can be found when she carefully examines (Virgo) the nature of equality and inequality in relationships, both interpersonal and societal. The two came together in her relationship with Andrew Stroud, an ex-policeman who became her husband and manager and who was fiercely opposed to her social involvement. The often-unbearable tension these irreconcilable interests produced in Simone and in her marriage deserves a book in and of itself. (16)

In her 3rd house Taurus **Chiron** pain of having been severely held back in all things integration, the healing of the pain can happen when she consolidates (Taurus) integration through her political engagement. Again, this is what she did and what caused said tension in her marriage.

Astrologically speaking, since Uranus, Neptune and Chiron operate according to the homeopathic principle of *Like Cures Like*, we do not have to go to the opposite house to see what the healing would consist of. It is right there, *in* the Uranus, Neptune and Chiron placement themselves.

From Saturn all the way back to Mercury: determining planetary function

(see chart p.116)

Having put into words the subconscious *Trauma Helix* charge and the way it is transferred to the Saturn realm by Chiron, it is now relatively easy to understand why the soul placed the planets the way it did. We work our way down the list and put the rationale into words for each planet.

Our first port of call is **Jupiter**. When the Chiron pain hits Saturn and the soul structures consciousness in its vehicle Eunice Waymon in such a way as to allow it to step back and look objectively (Aquarius) at all things identity, freedom and right to exist, (H1) and to then liberate (Aquarius) from anything standing in their way, this is interpreted by Jupiter. Consciousness, having been structured in a specific way (Saturn), needs an interpretative lens (Jupiter) before it can act (Mars). The lens the soul wanted Simone to look out into the world through was cut by the need *to discern* (Virgo) *power and powerlessness* (H8), *to clearly distinguish* (Virgo) *between what one feels like and what the other feels like and*

[113]

to then *serve* (Virgo) *self-empowerment* (H8) *by choosing* (H8) *one over the other.*

The fact that this Jupiter rule the 11th house, it seems to me, is tell-tale: the critical examination (Virgo) of power, powerlessness and self-empowerment (H8) rules her individuation process embedded in some larger, socially relevant cause (H11). Through house rulership you can see how Jupiter, through its careful 8th house examination, was going to help undo *the trauma inflicted on large groups of people through a distorted outlook on life*: Sagittarius on the 11th house cusp. The outlook being: blacks are second-rate citizens and need to be kept away from whites. I referred to this earlier in the chapter.

We move on to **Mars**. Now that the interpretative lens (Jupiter) is in place, that which is seen in a certain way can be acted upon: Mars. It is in the 8th house Virgo, sandwiched and exactly halfway between Jupiter H8 Virgo and Neptune H7 Virgo. The soul wants all conscious actions and desires in Nina aimed at *looking very critically* (Virgo) *at the issue of power, powerlessness and self-empowerment* (H8), *at reflecting deeply on the issue* (Mars retrograde) *and at her then deeply committing* (H8) *to serving* (Virgo) *empowerment* (H8).

How would that have helped the soul get to the 12th house Capricorn PPP? Looking critically at these 8th house issues helped the soul feel (PPP H12) that no amount of skin pigmentation could ever come between it and God's love for the soul. Nor could the fact of having been born a woman in a man's world. The fact that we are all equal in the eyes of God, and more specifically in the heart of God, is intricately linked to the commitment Simone made to the cause of equality. Through house rulership, Mars being focused on this critical examination affects the 3rd house of integration, which is where we find the Uranus strand of the *Trauma Helix* and the Chiron pain.

Now that action and desire have been directed, it is time to relate to that which they have been directed at. By placing **Venus** in the 1st house Aquarius, the soul is saying to its vehicle Simone: *"Nina, I want your prime relationship to be with your identity, your freedom and your right to exist."* To which Nina replies: *"Okay, I get that. And what would you like me to do with that?"* (sign contextualizes planet *in* the house)

Soul: "*I need you to step back* (Aquarius) *and look at these three things as objectively* (Aquarius) *as you can. And whilst you're at it, also look very objectively at how trauma* (Aquarius) *was incurred in these three areas.*"

How is that going to help the soul get to the PPP in the 12th house Capricorn? How is the soul going to mature (Capricorn) by feeling God's unconditional (H12) love – delivered as a personal message through His universal language music - when these three 1st house areas are not seen objectively? The objective awareness (Aquarius) the soul commissions Venus with, through rulership, is linked to the way *her race* (H4) *was held back* (Taurus). With the 1st house issues seen for what they are, Venus will help fortify racial self-image (Taurus on the cusp of H4). Through its rulership of the 9th house, Venus's same objective understanding (Aquarius) of the emphasized 1st house issues is going to restore balance (Libra) in societal truthfulness (H9), the same one whose absence inflicted trauma to such large groups of people (Sagittarius on the H11 cusp)

Now that the soul has indicated what it wants its vehicle's prime relationship to be with, it tells Simone what it wants thinking – **Mercury** - directed at. The soul deems it important that all thinking be directed at *healing* (Pisces) *my identity, my freedom, and my right to exist* (H1). Thinking directed this way obviously is going to be rather important to the soul. How, after all, is it going to feel this 12th house Cosmic Embrace if these three 1st house issues remain broken? With Mercury ruling the 5th house, the intended 1st house healing is going to help Simone integrate (Gemini) with the solar light (H5) of her creativity (H5) and with the right to be and shine through it (H5). It is also going to have an impact on self-empowerment since it rules the 8th house.

From all of this, we understand **the Sun** placement in the 1st house Pisces: the central, integrative principle around which her whole life revolved was *the healing* (Pisces) *of her identity, freedom and right to exist* (H1). This healing affected not only Simone but the public at large (Sun ruling the 7th house, as was the case in Lincoln's chart) making it imperative that her freedom become everyone's.

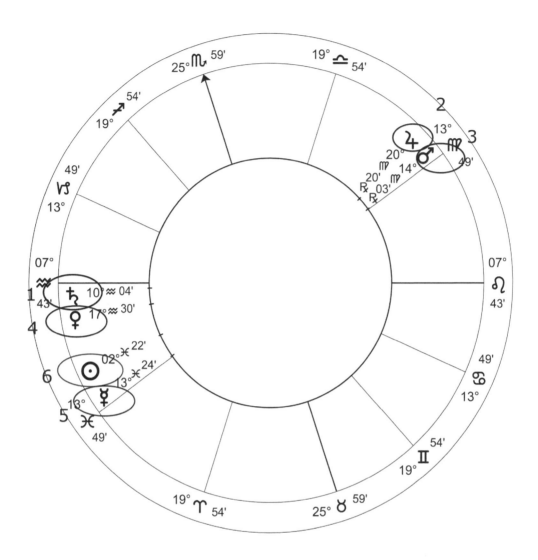

Nina Simone: Determining Planetary Function

Chapter 8 – The "Missing Moon"

In preparation for this book I took all of my astrology books off the shelf, put them on my desk and set about reading the chart analyses found in them. That is quite a few books, I can assure you. And quite a few chart analyses too. Not in a single one of them did I find the Moon defined in terms of her own south and north node. I found endless descriptions of how the SN lies in the past and the NN in the future, but the luminary to which these two belong, the Moon, was treated separately, as if it were ´from another planet´.

How was it possible that the authors of these books, experts one would imagine, treated the Moon separately as opposed to part of a single orbit on which lie her own south and north node? Which she visits every month? I pondered on this for a long time. And then I understood. The culprit was the same linearity trap we have been running into throughout this book: the nodes had been placed on a timeline, with the south node to the left in the past and the north node to the right in the future.

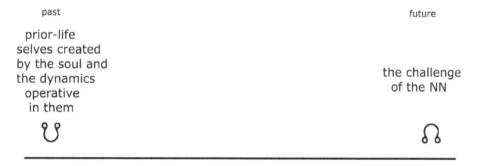

past	future
prior-life selves created by the soul and the dynamics operative in them	the challenge of the NN

In the many books I revisited over this almost month-long period, the SN of the Moon was invariably presented as an old dynamic from the past to be left behind and the north node as a future potential for growth. The Moon itself, meanwhile, would be aimlessly drifting about the edges of chart analysis. It took me some time to realize what had actually happened here. When I did, I understood why the Moon had been taken out of the equation: imagined time had been imposed on real time.

The Moon is real time: it orbits the Earth, and both orbit the Sun. Imagined time is a thought construct. Thought creates time within thought. An illusory thing within another illusory thing. It projects an imaginary line which it extends into an imaginary future and then places hope on it, the north node of the Moon, justice, or indeed whatever thought perceives of as lying in the future. It extends the same line into the past and places regret on it, frustration, pain, anything it perceives of as undesirable and not to be repeated. What thought does not realize, for doing so would mean its own undoing, is that it is in fact projecting a negative image of the past into the future, eternally perpetuating the former and denying at once the one thing that *is* real: the now.

This is exactly what had happened to the missing Moon, I now understood: the astrologer's thinking had dictated that the south node of the Moon was 'bad' and therefore placed it in the past on the timeline. The high-octane promise of the north node, as the mirror image of that undesirable thing in the past, thought had now placed in the future. The net result was the wholesale excision of the Moon we see everywhere about us, leaving a large allusive emptiness where the details of its 'now' ought to have been: the Moon by house and sign defined in terms of its own south and north node.

As I contemplated this strange phenomenon, my desperate search for the missing Moon had me frantically turning the pages of one astrology book after another, my desk piled high with them. Still there was no trace of it. Why was reality palpably not being addressed in so many authoritative books? Did the Moon's orbit not represent a single, evolutionary movement on the level of self, on the level of personality?

So where was it? Why had the middle part been cut out, leaving me with a bit of south node to the left and a bit of north node to the right? An astrological scotoma into which all real possibility of understanding the Moon orbit had vanished without trace.

Why, in all the charts I made myself plough through, was I presented with a book where all the middle chapters had been torn out? I got chapters 1 to 5 and chapters 12 to 20, but 6 to 11 were missing. What kind of author would want to do that to their readers?

How was I to make sense of the characters and the plot this way? How is a doctor to diagnose a patient when faced with limbs only and the torso missing? How are we to live a day when only morning and evening are available, with scissors and razor taken to afternoons? What kind of day is that? Is that not like going straight from childhood and adolescence to old age? What about midlife? Is that not part of the story too? So, there it was: a truncated Moon story.

Not much of a story at all, really. What to do? *"You know what,"* I said to myself *"I am going to restore the Moon to its rightful place and put it back in orbit. Out with the timeline and in with the circle."* And so I did. These are the steps I took. First, I put the Moon back on the timeline, fully aware of the fact that this was still an incorrect representation for not an orbit:

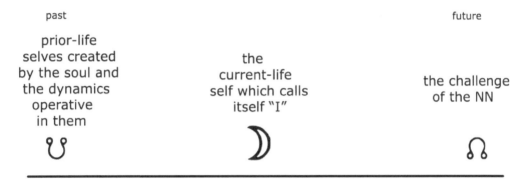

The second thing was to understand that the SN of the Moon chronologically may lie in the past but psychologically is very much present in the present. *In* the Moon.

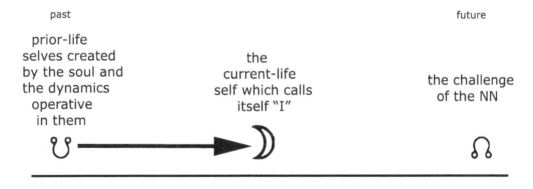

You, as I see you here and now, carry the whole of your own past inside of you. Unless you are some enlightened being who lives in an eternal now with no past luggage. With all due respect, I do not think you are that being. And I know I am not. What is more: I am not quite sure I would like to be that. I quite like the fact that I carry my past with me, with all its pain, strife, and sorrow, and to then see if I have been able to transform it into acceptance and wisdom.

My past is like the lines and wrinkles on my face. They tell a story. My past has shaped me and made me what I am today. Also, I am not quite sure I would be of much use to my clients if I did not still feel some of that past every now and then. To be reminded of it is actually not such a bad thing. How would you, my client, relate to me if you found me in a state of eternal bliss? If my answer to everything would be stillness and the pure light of consciousness? Would I be the most appropriate person for you to share your story with? Would you not be made to look straight into a bright light and be blinded by it, transfixed like a rabbit in a car's headlights? How about dimming that light a bit and feeling some empathic resonance?

So, when you meet me for the first time you are also meeting my past. More specifically, what I have done with it. I myself, of course, am very familiar with my own past. I have spent a lot of time with it and know it intimately. And, if I am not careful, I will default to it. Precisely because it is so easy to stick to the old ways and tread a smooth and well-worn path.

The Moon and her own south node are like that. Thick as thieves. **The whole of the Moon's own past is inside of the Moon**. Psychologically speaking, that is. Not chronologically. Chronologically, the south node of the Moon is in the past. There is no question.

In a chart, the past dynamics of the Moon are reflected – in good Moon fashion - in the Moon by house and sign. When you behold the Moon in a chart, you are literally looking at it. But unless your eye is trained, you will not see it. Let me show you this, using the chart of Richard Nixon. What did we say about his 1st house Libra SN? We said: *"relationships (Libra) in prior lives were engaged in with the sole purpose of furthering his own agenda (SN H1) and doing his own thing without having to reckon with anyone."*

[120]

Now, how does that past of the Moon come back in Nixon's Moon? Can we see it

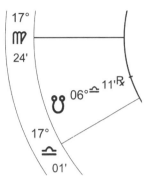

in its house and sign? Nixon's Moon is in the 6th house Aquarius: the SN dynamic of using relationships (Libra) to further my own agenda (H1) comes back in the Moon as *a dissociation* (Aquarius) *from what service from a place of humility* (H6) *means.* Nixon (the

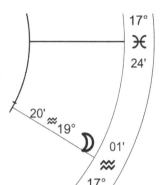

Moon) was dangerously dissociated from this. So much so that it eventually caused his demise.

The NN of the Moon wants something very different from him. It is in the 7th house Aries: it wants *to listen* (NN H7) *so carefully to what other people are saying and to what they need, that each person's*

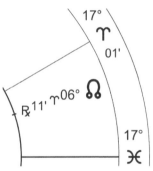

independence and freedom (Aries) *are guaranteed while in relationship* (H7). The important bit is in the tail of the sentence: *while in relationship.* Outside of relationship this goal is easily achieved: you go your way and I go mine. That is not what this Aries north node is about: it is *in* the 7th house.

The Moon, who is so familiar with her own south node, does not get any of this. She simply does not understand it because, although she visits this point every month, she will default to the known and familiar, i.e. her own south node. And so the north node has to explain to her what it is about.

To Nixon, therefore. It says: *"Mr President, look, just by looking at you it's obvious you've got seriously disconnected* [Aquarius: dissociation] *from true service and humility* [H6]. *I totally get that this is what you end up with when you use people* [SN in Libra] *as pawns in your own chess game* [H1] *for as long as you seem to have been doing,* **but if there is to be change from the old groove, then I need you to come up with a different response** *to the one I've been getting from you so far."*

"I've no idea what you're on about," says the Moon. What *would* it say?

"Really?" says the NN of the Moon. *"Seriously? Do I have to explain it to you? Just look at yourself! The answer is written in your own house and sign!"*

The 6th house Aquarius Moon looks at herself and still has no clue. No clue whatsoever. *"Okay,"* says the north node wearily, *"I'll spell it out for you then. What I need you to do is step back and look objectively* (Aquarius) *at what true service from a place of humility* (H6) *means. I need you to look dispassionately* [Aquarius] *at who you are actually serving* [H6], *self or other. It is imperative that you reach discernment* [H6] *in this issue and that you then make the necessary adjustments* [H6]. *That's your mission."*

"I don't know how to do that. How do I do that? I am not sure I even want to go there. Sounds like a lot of work. I am very comfortable with where I am, thank you very much."

"That is entirely up to you, Mr President. I'm just telling you where you seem to be coming from and where I'd like you to go. You can accept the invitation or politely decline."

The important thing for you to take away from this is that **the north node of the Moon is not in the future** but on the face of the Moon in the now. We are no longer talking straight lines here. Things are not being artificially separated anymore, with the Moon dislocated from her nodes. We are talking orbit. Real time. In each of her many changing moments the Moon, as she races through the chart and round the earth, feels how her own NN challenges her familiarity with her past, with her SN, urging her to formulate this new response. **The NN of the Moon confronting the SN and the Moon's familiarity with that SN, produces resistance in the Moon**.

To the Moon it feels as if two parties were shaking hands in the most awkward of ways, a bit like Trump and Pelosi. The meeting of the two feels distinctly uncomfortable and it is precisely this feeling of unease that will prompt it, hopefully, to come up with the new response mentioned earlier. This is how I have come to define the Moon as

"the point of maximum resistance between its own south and north node."

[122]

Although I understood it, I did not have the image that expressed it adequately. More work was needed.

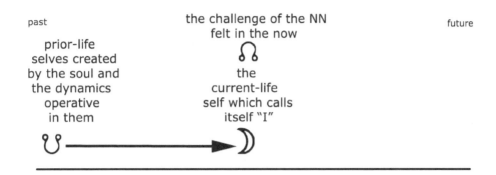

The problem with this image was that the Moon and the nodes were still on a

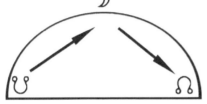

timeline, even when I brought the sky in:

Still linear and still on a timeline. How on earth was I going to get off it?

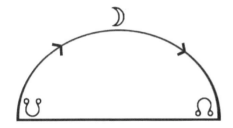

Slightly less linear but still on the darn timeline. I needed an orbit. And so I said to myself, *"You know what? I am going to live dangerously and tilt the thing."*

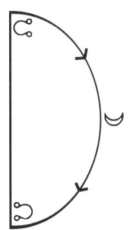

That was beginning to look more like it. The Moon was back in orbit. All I had to do now was add the sign and house placements for Nixon and Bob's your uncle.

And there she was. In all her beauty: **the point of maximum resistance between her own south and north node**.

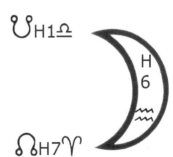

This was the Moon I knew was in the sky and which I had sorely missed as I ploughed my way through chart upon chart of truncated Moon analysis for almost a full Moon cycle.

The Moon's north node and its ruler as *the catalyst for change*; the Moon itself as *the agent of change*: Nixon, Simone and Lincoln

The inevitable consequence of contemplating the entire evolutionary orbit of the Moon is that **it is not the north node of the Moon that represents evolutionary growth but the Moon itself**. It is the Moon's new response which is going to contribute to soul growth, not the potential of her NN. All the north node of the Moon does is create resistance in the Moon through its meeting with the Moon's south node, that is, with what the Moon is so familiar with and will therefore default towards. **The NN of the Moon**, therefore, **acts as a counterweight to the old groove of the familiar and known**. Contrary to popular belief, *it is not the facilitator of soul growth*. The Moon's new response is.

Listening so carefully to what the other person says (NN of the Moon H7) - *and to what they need - that both parties' independence and freedom* (NN of the Moon Aries) *are guaranteed while in relationship,* is not going to get the soul to the emotional truthfulness it seeks in the 4th house Sagittarius. The Moon *stepping back and objectively assessing* (Aquarius) *what service from a place of humility* (H6) *means* is.

As we have seen, in Nixon's case the Moon's tug of war is between ...

		... stepping back (Aquarius) to objectively assess (Aquarius) what service from a place of humility (H6) means, looking dispassionately (Aquarius) at who I am really serving (H6), myself or others, reach discernment (H6) in this issue and then make the necessary adjustments (H6)
getting dissociated (Aquarius) from service from a place of humility (H6) and...	H 6	
... which comes about through the confrontation between		

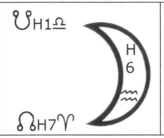

| … engaging in relationship (SN Libra) with the sole purpose of serving self (SN H1), and… | ☊H1♎ ☋H7♈ | …guaranteeing mutual independence and freedom (NN in Aries) *in* relationship (NN H7) through careful listening to other (H7) … |

in the Moon. Looking at the Moon and her nodes this way we understand that ***the Moon becomes the crucible for growth and evolution on the level of ego***, on the level of personality. And that can be said to be the tenet central to evolutionary astrology: the soul creates an ego (Moon) as the vehicle for its own evolution.

It is obvious how the Moon's new response (i.e. to step back and get an objective view of who Nixon is actually serving: self or other, to reach discernment in this issue and to then make the necessary adjustments) would be beneficial to the emotional honesty the soul seeks in its 4th house Pluto Polarity Point: *being truthful emotionally* is not going to happen as long as I am not very *clear* (Aquarius) *on who I am actually serving* (H6).

The flattened contours of the Moon have been undone. This may not be to everyone's liking, but certain changes *must* be made if a paradigm is to evolve.

Mercury 4th house Capricorn understood in its evolutionary orbit

In therapeutic evolutionary astrology we apply this same reasoning to the planetary nodes. Why? Because planets, just like the Moon, in actual fact move in orbit. They are not stills. They cross the ecliptic *in orbital movement* and are *in orbital movement* when we take a snapshot of them at the moment of birth and call that 'the astrological chart.' The particular moment in time when we, astrologers, freeze that movement shows us the planetary function (Mars: conscious actions and desires, Venus: relating etcetera) as it reaches a point of maximum evolutionary potential coinciding with the moment of birth. It is a moment which astrologers rightly ascribe much meaning to but which cannot be understood as an isolated thing, dislocated from its actual movement which comprises the two elements from which its natal position and potential derive their meaning: its south and north node. As I hope to show you in this and the upcoming chapters, the crucial information those two elements hold is quite readily to hand. Including them is the new paradigm I am building a case for in this book and which, I firmly believe, will lead us to understanding a planet's evolutionary potential against the backdrop of where the soul is coming from and wishes to evolve towards.

Let us take Nixon's Mercury as yet another example of this new approach. We find it in the 4th house Capricorn. We have already dealt with it as a skipped step. What we want to do now is look at its planetary function in terms of soul evolution. In other words: **what specific contribution to the 4th house Sagittarius PPP does it make?** The answer to that question will not be found by looking at the planet as a still, a vacuum in time, with its nodes airbrushed out of its story.

We find the SN of Mercury at 0 degrees Capricorn 54 minutes in the 4th house. Closely conjunct Mercury itself, therefore. What does this mean? It means that the past dynamic of Mercury exactly coincides with its current-life one, which in chapter 2 we described as: *thinking* (Mercury) *directed at the suppression* (Capricorn) *of the emotional body*. Mercury, just like the Moon, is very familiar with its own past wherever in the chart you find it. When you see it bang on its

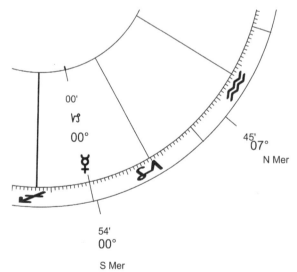

own south node, however, as is the case here, they are hand in glove.

Mercury's NN is at 7 degrees Aquarius 45 minutes in the 5th house, not too far away from Uranus: *thinking directed at stepping back to get an objective view* (Aquarius) *of the emotional insecurity that underlies Nixon's need to be an undisputed leader and come out on top* (H5). What do you think will happen when this NN impulse - ever in contact with Mercury through the planet's orbital movement - confronts a past dynamic, glued to the current-life Mercury, of suppressing the emotional body?

Is that Mercury not going to feel enormous resistance between the two and, since it is such good buddies with its own SN, going to politely decline? Yet the invitation is there and will be acutely felt by Mercury. It is challenged, in no uncertain terms, to *direct its thinking* (Mercury) *at bringing integrity* (Capricorn) *to the emotional body* (H4) *by taking on responsibility* (Capricorn) *for it as opposed to suppressing* (Capricorn) *it*, is it not? Inwardly, however, it is pulled in the exact opposite direction, and with considerably more force to boot (conjunct its own SN).

SN of Mercury H4 Capricorn	resistance	NN of Mercury H5 Aquarius
thinking (Mercury) directed at suppression (Capricorn) of the emotional body (H4)	**< >**	thinking directed at stepping back to get an objective view (Aquarius) of the emotional insecurity that underlies Nixon's need to be an undisputed leader and come out on top (H5)
the past streaming into the present and determining Mercury's old response: H4 Capricorn	**Mercury's choices**	**new response as the result of the resistance between Mercury's SN and NN and its familiarity with the former: H4 Capricorn**
thinking (Mercury) directed at suppression (Capricorn) of the emotional body (H4)	**< >**	thinking (Mercury) directed at bringing integrity (Capricorn) to the emotional body (H4) by assuming responsibility (Capricorn) for it as opposed to suppressing (Capricorn) it

It is the resistance between these two forces that will make Mercury act. Or not. Like all the other planetary functions, it has free will. Nixon has, to be more precise. He can choose to redirect his thinking or choose not to.

Here too, just like with the Moon, the important thing to understand is **that the evolutionary intention for Mercury is not its NN but Mercury's new response itself as the net result of the resistance felt.** What its NN does is remind it of the need for this new response.

We are now effectively tracing the entire evolutionary orbit of Mercury _as it serves soul evolution_. Just like the Moon's SN, Mercury's past is neither 'good' nor 'bad'. It is simply a mental dynamic the soul's vehicles in the past (SN 1ˢᵗ house Libra)

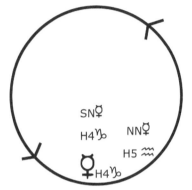 have used to explore the 10ᵗʰ house Gemini issue of gaining maximum status and power through gathering information on others and using it against them: _"I use others for that_ (SN H1 Libra) _and I cannot do that unless my thinking overrides and so suppresses my emotions_ (Mercury H4 Capricorn)."

Thinking (Mercury) _directed at getting an objective view_ (Aquarius) _of the emotional insecurity feeding Nixon's obsessive need to be seen as important_ (H5) is not going to get the soul to the emotional honesty of the 4ᵗʰ house either. Mercury's NN simply acts as a counterforce to thinking directed at the suppression of the emotional body (Mercury _and_ SN Mercury H4 Capricorn). When Mercury's NN hits the old groove, it is Mercury's new response of _bringing integrity_ (Capricorn) _to the emotional body_ (H4) which is going to be conducive to the soul actualizing the emotional honesty of the 4ᵗʰ house Sagittarius PPP.

The rulers of Nixon's lunar nodes

"What about the NN ruler?" I can hear you ask. _"How does it come into all of this?"_ The ruler of the NN of the Moon is the modus operandi of the latter. Its house and sign placement tells you how the NN intention may be carried out as a counterweight to old dynamics. For Nixon, whose NN ruler is in the 4ᵗʰ house Sagittarius, this means that the careful listening (H7) to other so that there be mutual independence and freedom (NN in Aries) _in_ relationship (NN H7) can come about _if and when he is emotionally_ (NN ruler H4) _honest_ (NN ruler Sagittarius).

As such, the NN ruler provides additional information as to how the counterweight offered by the NN will hit the old and familiar dynamics of Nixon's SN in the 1ˢᵗ house Libra, who has used relationship (SN in Libra) with the sole purpose of furthering its own agenda (SN H1). It too has a ruler and it tells you in the past this was done by *prior-life selves having deliberately created confusion* (SN ruler Pisces) *in the workplace* (SN ruler H6) *in such a way as to imply guilt* (SN ruler H6) *in others in order to come out looking all innocent* (SN ruler Pisces) *themselves*. This is the dynamic the 6ᵗʰ house Aquarius Moon brings into the present from the past and which shows in the Moon as being dissociated (Moon in Aquarius) from what service from a place of humility (Moon H6) means. The two nodes and their respective modus operandi, therefore, are:

Nixon - SN of the Moon H1 Libra	resistance	Nixon - NN of the Moon H7 Aries
prior-life selves having used relationship (SN in Libra) with the sole purpose of furthering their own agenda (SN H1)	< >	careful listening (NN H7) to other so that there be mutual independence and freedom (NN in Aries) *in* relationship (NN H7)
modus operandi (SN ruler) H6 Pisces	**resistance**	**modus operandi (NN ruler) H4 Sagittarius**
prior-life selves having deliberately created confusion (SN ruler Pisces) in the workplace (SN ruler H6) in such a way as to imply guilt (SN ruler H6) in others in an attempt to come out looking all innocent (SN ruler Pisces) themselves	< >	being emotionally (NN ruler H4) honest (NN ruler Sagittarius)
the past streaming into the present and determining the Moon's old response: H6 Aquarius	**the Moon's choices**	**new response as the result of the resistance between the Moon's SN and NN and its familiarity with the former: H6 Aquarius**
staying dissociated (Aquarius) from service from a place of humility (H6)	< >	stepping back to objectively assess what service from a place of humility means; looking dispassionately (Aquarius) at who I am really serving (H6), myself or

[129]

		others, reach discernment (H6) in this issue and then make the necessary adjustments (H6)

From the table you can see that there is resistance not just between the NN and the SN of the Moon as they meet in the Moon by house and sign but also between how they go about things (i.e. their respective rulers): you cannot be emotionally honest whilst at the same time setting up traps for people for your own gain. It is this resistance which will prompt the Moon to no longer be dissociated (Moon in Aquarius) from service from a place of humility (Moon H6) but *to step back and objectively* (Moon in Aquarius) *discern* (Moon H6) *who it* (in this case Nixon) *is actually serving* (Moon H6): self or other. **The evolutionary intention is** still **the Moon's new response, _not_ its NN and ruler**. As mentioned earlier: it is the aforementioned 6th house discernment which is going to allow the soul to move out of its power-driven 10th house and into the emotional truthfulness of the 4th house, not the counterweight offered by the NN of the Moon and its ruler. The counterweight of the NN of the Moon and its ruler is simply a new way of being which, since it clashes violently with the old way (SN of the Moon, SN ruler and Moon), will trigger a new response in the Moon.

Nina Simone's Moon dynamics: her north node of the Moon as _the catalyst for change_, the Moon itself as _the agent of change_

For Nina Simone, the same reasoning applies. (see chart p.101) Her NN of the Moon in the 1st house Pisces, bent on *healing* (Pisces) *her identity, freedom and right to exist* (H1), is not going to get the soul to a place where it *matures* (Capricorn) *for feeling unconditionally loved and accepted* (H12). What is actively going to contribute to the soul getting there is the Moon, Nina Simone herself, *taking full responsibility* (Capricorn) *for the fact that she is perfect as she is* (H12) *by becoming the embodiment* (Capricorn) *of God' universal language: music* (H12). The NN of the Moon, however, is very much needed as a counterweight to its past dynamic of *inequality in relationship* (H7) *as a result of interjected inferiority and unworthiness* (with the accompanying emotion of guilt and possibly shame) – Virgo. *Something* is going to have to pull the Moon out of the rut of *making itself next to invisible* (H12) *under the crushing weight of oppressive rule* (Capricorn): the familiarity of the Moon with its own SN and its tendency to default to it.

The rulers of Nina Simone's lunar nodes

Nina Simone's 1st house Pisces NN of the Moon avails itself of 7th house Virgo dynamics. In other words: *the healing* (NN Pisces) *of her identity, freedom and right to exist* (NN H1) can come about when she *meticulously examines* (NN ruler Virgo) *the issue of (in)equality in relationship as a result of what is projected onto people* (NN ruler H7). As such, the NN ruler provides additional information about the dynamics that are going to form the counterweight to the familiar ones of the past, which consisted of *inequality in relationship* (SN H7) *through interjected inferiority and unworthiness* (SN Virgo) *explored through a loss of self* (SN ruler Pisces) *in terms of identity, freedom and right to exist* (SN ruler H1), reflected in the Moon by her tendency to *make herself disappear* (Moon H12) *under the weight of oppressive rule* (Moon Capricorn).

As the nodes, each with their own modus operandi, meet *in* the 12th house Capricorn Moon, the resistance felt by the Moon is going to make her change things round by *maturing* (Moon Capricorn) *through deep self-acceptance* (Moon H12) *as God's universal language* (music) *flows through her and she becomes its instrument*. In this example too, as we did in the Nixon one, we clearly see how **the north node (and its ruler) is <u>the catalyst for change</u>** while **the Moon itself is <u>the agent of change</u>**.

Simone - SN of the Moon H7 Virgo	resistance	Simone - NN of the Moon H1 Pisces
inequality in relationship (SN H7) through interjected inferiority and unworthiness (SN Virgo)	**< >**	healing (Pisces) her identity, freedom and right to exist (H1)
modus operandi (SN ruler) H1 Pisces	**resistance**	**modus operandi (NN ruler) H7 Virgo**

a loss of self (SN ruler Pisces) in terms of identity, freedom and right to exist (SN ruler H1)	< >	meticulously examine (NN ruler Virgo) the issue of (in)equality in relationship (NN ruler H7) as a result of what is projected (H7) onto people
the past streaming into the present and determining the Moon's old response: H12 Capricorn	**Moon's choices**	**new response as the result of the resistance between the Moon's SN and NN and its familiarity with the former: H12 Capricorn**
make herself disappear (Moon H12) under the weight of oppressive rule (Moon Capricorn)	< >	assuming full responsibility (Capricorn) for the fact that she is perfect as she is (H12) by becoming the embodiment (Capricorn) of God's universal language: music (H12)

Lincoln's Moon dynamics: his north node of the Moon as _the catalyst for change_, the Moon itself as _the agent of change_ (see chart p.44)

Lincoln's 12th house Capricorn Moon will default to its own 3rd house Taurus south node in that the latter's memories of _having been held back_ (Taurus) _when trying to integrate or reach integration_ (H3) will make it _feel enslaved_ (H12) _and therefore victimized_ (H12) _by reactionary forces_ (Capricorn).

☊H3♉

H 12

♏

☋H9♏

That familiar dynamic is now countered by the NN of the Moon's wish - in a recent prior-life buoyed up in no small way by Uranus - to see "_a new birth_ (NN of the Moon in Scorpio) _of freedom_" (NN of the Moon H9), as Lincoln stated in his Gettysburg Address in 1863, through _a deep commitment_ (Scorpio) _to the cause of liberty_ (H9).

As the NN of the Moon hits the SN of the Moon and the Moon's tendency to default to that SN, a new response is triggered in Lincoln's 12th house Moon: _to assume_ *responsibility* (Capricorn), *through law* (Capricorn), *for the whole issue of slavery* (H12) and so set man free.

As an aside, you can see that Lincoln's Moon placement is identical to Simone's: 12th house Capricorn. That is where the similarities stop. From an evolutionary point of view, it would be impossible to interpret them identically for they form part of a different orbit. The past (i.e. the SN of the Moon) having led to the Moon's natal placement is different and the counterweight (i.e. the NN of the Moon) offered to the familiar past dynamics is different too. (1) Only an astrology which refuses to look at a planet's actual orbit can come to a generic description of a still taken out of the full picture: a lifeless thing, devoid of all meaning and non-applicable for demonstrably untrue. (2)

Lincoln - SN of the Moon H3 Taurus	resistance	Lincoln - NN of the Moon H9 Scorpio
having been held back (Taurus) when trying to integrate or reach integration (H3)	< >	a *"New Birth* (Scorpio) *of Freedom"* (H9) through a deep commitment (Scorpio) to the cause of liberty (H9)
modus operandi (SN ruler) H2 Aries	**resistance**	**modus operandi (NN ruler) H1 Pisces**
unable to consolidate (H2) their identity, freedom or right to exist (Aries); not having survived (H2) for their pioneering role (Aries) in trying to do so	< >	healing (NN ruler Pisces) people's identity, freedom and right to exist (NN ruler H1)
the past streaming into the present and determining the Moon's old response: H12 Capricorn	**Moon's choices**	**new response as the result of the resistance between the Moon's SN and NN and its familiarity with the former: H12 Capricorn**
feeling enslaved (H12) and therefore victimized (H12) by reactionary forces (Capricorn)	< >	to assume responsibility (Capricorn), through law (Capricorn), for the whole issue of slavery (H12)

Coming back to Lincoln's Moon, we see that its NN, desiring to see *"a New Birth (Scorpio) of Freedom"* (H9) effectuates this by healing (NN ruler Pisces) people's identity, freedom and right to exist (NN ruler H1). This is the counterweight to the old dynamic whereby prior-life selves experienced a limitation (SN of the Moon Taurus) in integration (SN of the Moon H3) and were unable to consolidate (SN ruler H2) their identity and freedom (SN ruler Aries), a dynamic the Moon is familiar with and which can be seen in her tendency to become the victim (Moon H12) of oppression (Moon Capricorn).

The counterforce offered by the NN of the Moon and its ruler is not enough to turn this tendency round and get the soul to the 7th house Virgo where it may serve (PPP Virgo) equality (PPP H7). For that to happen the Moon needs to feel the resistance *in herself* between the old and the new dynamic so that the coiled spring may snap and she *change victimization* (H12) *as a result of oppression* (Capricorn) *round to assuming responsibility* (Capricorn), *through law* (Capricorn), *for the issue of slavery* (H12). (3)

On the evolution of evolutionary astrology

I know this line of thought is probably at one or several removes from your standard EA frame of reference. I can only hope our vistas are expanded in tandem with the opening up of the full orbital movement of the planets as expounded in these pages. Evolutionary astrology itself is subject to the laws of evolution. We cannot shield if from this law thinking it is perfect as it is. It is not. By the very definition of evolution, nothing is. If we do shield it and think it somehow is exempt from change and growth, it runs the risk of coming to the same senseless frozen moment in time as the isolated Moon and planets taken out of their orbit, existing in a suspension of self-contradiction.

The orbital approach to understanding planets, which can be said to be overdue (4) rather than 'innovative' since they have been orbiting the Sun and intersecting with the ecliptic longer that any of them care to remember, does three things which are of importance to a therapeutic application of evolutionary astrology:

1. it recontextualizes the nodes and the planet they belong to as **one, single unit of meaning** which fulfills a specific role in the soul's evolutionary trajectory
2. it breaks with the therapeutically counterproductive practice of labeling the SN as 'bad' and the 'NN' as good (5)
3. it specifies the function of each planet (Mercury: thinking; Venus: relating; Mars: conscious actions and desires, etcetera) against the backdrop of that trajectory.

The logical and inevitable conclusion to be drawn from contemplating a planet in its orbital entirety fulfilling a specific role in the soul's plan for its evolution is that *it is not a still but a highly-charged and dynamic focal point for change*.

The chart you have, in all probability, been looking at as a series of stills so far, is in actual fact *a map of culminating points where each planet reaches its point of maximum resistance as an invitation to change*.

The snapshot of the sky taken at birth shows that particular moment in time where each orbit, lunar and planetary alike, reaches its zenith of evolutionary potential. The planet you are looking at in a chart is not a frozen point in time but rather the pointed marker of that potential.

Chapter 9 – Trauma, Pain and Healing in Orbit

We may know more about where the trauma and the pain are coming from and what their intended evolutionary direction is by looking at the entire orbit of Chiron, Uranus and Neptune as opposed to only taking into consideration their natal placement. From an evolutionary perspective not doing so makes as little sense as only looking at the nodes of the Moon and cutting the Moon bit out. (1)

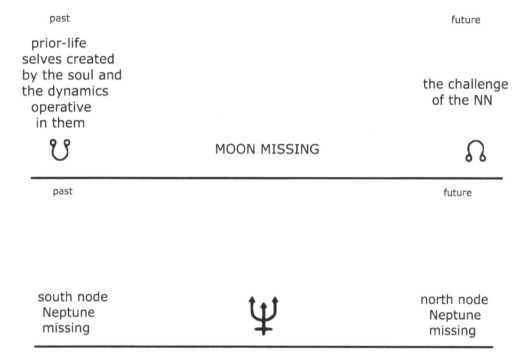

past		future
prior-life selves created by the soul and the dynamics operative in them		the challenge of the NN
☋	MOON MISSING	☊

past		future
south node Neptune missing	♆	north node Neptune missing

How are we going to understand the entire evolutionary movement of whatever planetary function when a whole chunk of it has been cut out?

How are we going to understand, for example, the meaninglessness of Richard Nixon's 's 11th house Cancer Neptune without looking at its past? We will at some point need to start asking questions about what came prior to it and has led up to the disillusionment and despair reflected in the natal planet. By the same token, to fully grasp the potential for

[137]

meaningfulness of that same 11th house Cancer Neptune, we can ill afford not to look at the counterweight to past dynamics: its own north node.

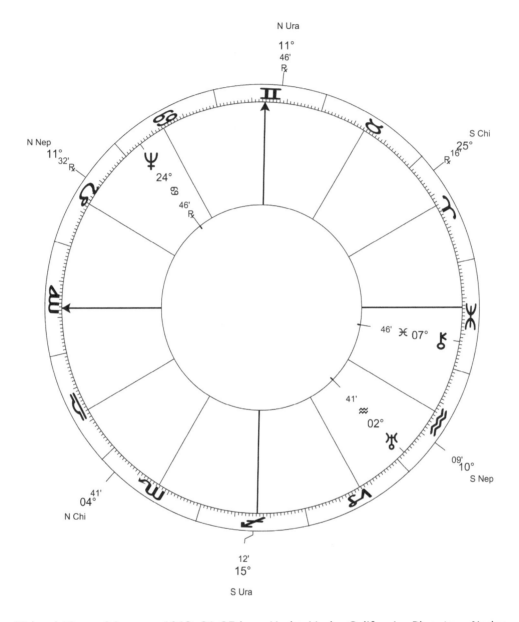

Richard Nixon, 9 January 1913, 21:35 hrs., Yorba Linda, California. Planetary Nodes chart for Chiron, Uranus & Neptune

What I intend to do in this chapter, therefore, is take you through an exploration of how trauma, pain and healing move in actual orbit, using the chart of Richard

Nixon, and how the natal placement of his Chiron, Uranus and Neptune are **culmination points of their respective orbits offering maximum potential for healing and overcoming trauma** coming in from lifetimes past and set to repeat until it is healed. A completely different approach, therefore, to the one where we look at these three as stills in the old, linear way (with rather important bits missing to boot): immovable snapshots taken at the moment of birth and ascribed frozen meaning through stale cookie-cutter descriptions. None of that applies anymore in this new, dynamic orbital approach.

The nodes of Chiron

The evolutionary orbit of Richard Nixon's Chiron pain, reaching back into more distant pasts than the life immediately prior to the current one, features a SN at 25 degrees Aries 16 minutes in the 8th house. All of our Chiron SN's, yours and mine, are more or less in that degree since they move so slowly in time. (2) The important thing is the combination of house and sign placement. For Nixon it will reveal the past that led to the 6th house Pisces pain of *a pervasive confusion around true service from a place of humility*.

The past that shaped this pain is one where *prior-life selves would have been immersed in treacherous power games* (H8) *in order to further their own agenda and not reckon with anyone* (Aries), *advancing themselves* (Aries) *at the expense of others* (H8), a finding in full accordance with the SN of the Moon in the 1st house Libra. Mindful of the fact that the SN of Chiron harks back to a multitude of prior lifetimes, we are beginning to understand how the soul would have got to its 10th house Gemini stuck place: to *gain maximum status and power through the misuse of information* (Pluto H10 Gemini skipped step). It takes many, many lives for such an impressive roadblock to form.

The important thing to take away from this is that the SN of Chiron encompasses Nixon's immediate past life and a whole string of lives prior to it. It pays, therefore, to **place the past of the Chiron pain against the backdrop of the Pluto, SN of the Moon and SN ruler placement** for it shows you part of the context in which the pain happened. The Chiron pain does not come falling from the sky. Like the centaur's wounding, it was incurred in actual circumstances. Looking at Nixon's Pluto H10 Gemini skipped step, (3) so skilled at getting its

[139]

hands on just the right kind of information (Gemini) to get to the top (H10), the slick talk (Gemini), his SN of the Moon in the 1st house Libra adroitly using relationships (Libra) to further their own agenda and do their own thing without having to reckon with anyone (Aries), and the SN ruler in the 6th house Pisces' Machiavellian ways of creating confusion (Pisces) in the workplace (H6) by implying guilt (H6) in others so that they came out looking all innocent and squeaky-clean (Pisces), it makes rather a lot of sense, does it not?, how in that scenario this 8th house Aries pain would have come into being.

Since Chiron is very familiar with its own past, at this point it is important to put into words how its past 8th house Aries dynamics are reflected in its 6th house Pisces placement. From an evolutionary point of view, it is key to grasp how the past has led to the present, which, as I hope to have shown, is impossible without

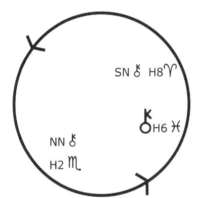

contemplating its orbital movement. I am now going to do that for you: *prior-life selves' treacherous power* (H8) *games undertaken to advance themselves* (Aries) *at the expense of others* (H8) *can be seen in Chiron's pervasive confusion* (Pisces) *around service from a place of humility* (H6).

This dynamic is countered by Chiron's NN. We find it in the 2nd house at 4 degrees Scorpio 41 minutes. Again, it is more or less in that degree for all of us. The combination of house and sign, however, reveals much about what is pulling from the other end of the rope: *a deep transformation* (Scorpio) *of the inner values* (H2) *Nixon's relationship with himself* (H2) *is based on*. (4)

Nixon's Chiron in the 6th house Pisces initially does not know what to make of this counterforce.

The NN will say to it *"Instead of these machinations and power games you've been involved in, I need you to probe [Scorpio] your set of inner values [H2] so that this mist around service and humility can clear."*

"Don't know what you're on about," Chiron responds. *"All I've ever known is that mist. How <u>could</u> it clear?"*

NN Chiron: *"That's exactly what I'm pointing out to you. You can make it go away by asking penetratingly deep questions about those values."*

Chiron: *"The confusion sure hurts and I'd like for the pain to go away but looking at my inner values as you suggest is hard work and also painful."*

NN Chiron: *"It's entirely up to you what you do with this. I'm simply indicating the route to a new response to this 6th house Pisces thing."*

Chiron: *"And what might that response be, I pray?"* (Nixon getting a tad formal here, as his 10th house Pluto would have instructed him to do)

NN Chiron: *For you to engage in a process of inner purification* (H6) *whereby you learn to distinguish* (H6) *between self-serving behavior and true service from a place of humility* (H6).

Chiron: *"And you say that requires me probing my inner values?"*

NN Chiron: *"Not just that but transforming* [Scorpio] *them after you've probed* [Scorpio] *them. Aren't they the foundation of all that self-serving behavior we've seen from you in the past?* [SN of the Moon 1st house Libra] *Just look how your pain is glued to how you used to go about that:* [ruler of the SN of the Moon Venus conjunct Chiron] *implying guilt in others* (H6) *so that you came out looking all pure and virtuous* (Pisces) *yourself."*

Chiron: *"So, what you're saying is that through discernment I can heal this pain, this confusion* [Pisces] *around service from a place of humility* [H6]*?"*

NN Chiron: *"Well, a few adjustments* (H6) *following the discernment would be nice, but yeah, that's the gist of it."*

Chiron: *"Not sure I'm up for it."*

NN Chiron: *"Again, Richard: it's entirely up to you what you do with it. I'm not the one who is going to act on this. I am just showing you <u>how</u> it can be done, that's all. It's you who is going to have to do the work."*

Nixon's Chiron is torn, literally, between these two opposing forces coming together in its 6th house Pisces placement. As the point of maximum resistance between the two, it becomes **the agent for change** if and when Chiron rises to the challenge, which would effectively bring about its healing. Again, in this example you see how the NN is _the way to_ the new response, not the new response itself. The new response is in the natal planet, as it was in Nixon's, Simone's and Lincoln's Moon in the previous chapter. (5)

Nixon - SN of Chiron H8 Aries	resistance	Nixon - NN of Chiron H2 Scorpio
prior-life selves immersed in treacherous power games (H8) in order to advance themselves (Aries) at the expense of others (H8)	< >	a deep transformation (Scorpio) of the inner values (H2) Nixon's relationship with himself (H2) is based on
the past streaming into the present and determining the old response: H6 Pisces	**Chiron's choices**	**new response as the result of the resistance between the planet's SN and NN and its familiarity with the former: H6 Pisces**
a pervasive confusion (Pisces) around service from a place of humility (H6)	< >	healing (Pisces) the pain by carefully discerning (H6) who I am serving (H6), self or other, followed by making the necessary adjustments

As always with Chiron it pays to remind oneself that it is the one who relays the trauma charge from Uranus to Saturn _as pain_. In Chiron's past dynamics, the whole of the Uranus-Neptune-Pluto _Trauma Helix_'s past is comprised, as we will get confirmed shortly when we look at the SNs of Uranus and Neptune. The healing of the Chiron pain is intimately linked to where the soul seeks to evolve towards (PPP H4 Sag) and how its vehicle is going to get it there through its new response (i.e. the Moon's, as detailed in the previous chapter): Nixon _stepping back_ (Aquarius) _and developing an objective_ (Aquarius) _awareness of who he is actually serving_ (H6) is fully aligned with the healing of the Chiron pain and will be conducive to the soul leaving behind _the misuse of information_ (Pluto in Gemini) _in order to get to the top_ (Pluto H10) – which has become its predicament: skipped step – and move to *emotional honesty* (PPP H4 Sagittarius) instead.

The nodes of Uranus (see chart p.138)

The past which has brought Uranus to where it is today in the chart of Richard Nixon can be found in the 3rd house at 15 degrees Sagittarius 12 minutes. Translated to English for you: the sudden and traumatic dissociation (Aquarius) from his leadership (H5) – or rather: the subconscious memories thereof – has to do with *prior-life selves having distorted* (Sagittarius) *the facts* (H3). (6)

This is the dynamic his Uranus is familiar with and will therefore default towards. Again, for a full evolutionary understanding of the Uranus orbit it is important to

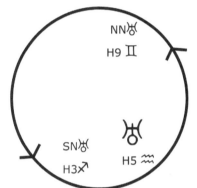

put into words how its past 3rd house Sagittarius dynamic comes back in its 5th house Aquarius placement: *through distortion of the facts, it has become dissociated* (Aquarius) *from Leo* (H5) *in its highest expression* – i.e. the impartiality and generosity of true leadership which brings out the best in everyone – *in favor of only seeing himself* (H5).

The counterforce to this past dynamic is found in Uranus' NN at 11 degrees Gemini 46 minutes in the 9th house: *to integrate* (Gemini) *with truthfulness* (H9).

The invitation the NN of Uranus sends out to Uranus in the 5th house is for him *to step back and make a dispassionate* (Aquarius) *assessment of his leadership* (H5), *allowing for impartiality and generosity to come to the fore and characterize his leadership*. If Uranus fails to integrate (Gemini) with truthfulness (H9), obviously there is no way it can step back and bring objectivity to his leadership.

This is the dialogue between the two.

NN: *"How can you step back and look objectively at your leadership, which in the past has been solely based on distortion* [SN Uranus Sagittarius] *of the facts* [SN Uranus H3], *without striking up a dialogue* [NN Uranus Gemini] *with truthfulness* [NN Uranus H9]? *Don't you see how there's nothing else for it?"*

Uranus: *"This is all I've ever known and I'm not sure I would be willing to do as you seem to suggest. What's more, I cannot afford to step back and look at my leadership because others will step right in and take it from me."*

NN: *"That's your paranoia talking. Don't listen to it. Or rather: see that for what it is too, whilst you're at it, because it's part of your style of leadership."*

Since Uranus does not understand any of this, he will refuse to engage in a dialogue with truthfulness and so further dissociate (Aquarius) from the generosity and impartiality as the higher expression of the Leo archetype (H5). It is these Leonian traits that should have characterized Nixon's leadership and which would have meant the overcoming of the trauma, which, as I have stated on several occasions, is *in* the Uranus placement itself. The ultimate dissociation, *the removal from office* (Uranus ruling the 6th house) is therefore something Nixon brings onto himself. The potential for overcoming the trauma was there all the time. He need only have heeded its clarion call.

Nixon - SN of Uranus H3 Sagittarius	resistance	Nixon - NN of Uranus H9 Gemini
prior-life selves having distorted (Sagittarius) the facts (H3)	**< >**	to integrate (Gemini) with truthfulness (H9)
the past streaming into the present and determining the old response: H5 Aquarius	**Uranus' choices**	**new response as the result of the resistance between the planet's SN and NN and its familiarity with the former: H5 Aquarius**
dissociated (Aquarius) from Leo (H5) in its highest expression – i.e. the impartiality and generosity of true leadership which brings out the best in everyone – in favor of only seeing himself (H5)	**< >**	to step back and objectively assess (Aquarius) his leadership (H5), allowing for impartiality and generosity to come to the fore and characterize his leadership

Here too it is important to place the past of trauma incurred in the context of the Pluto, SN of the Moon, SN ruler dynamics: *the distortion* (Sagittarius) *of the facts* (Gemini) *happened because of Pluto's unquenchable 10th house thirst for power, the misuse of information* (Gemini) *to get to that power not weighing on its conscience* (H10), *prior-life selves having used people* (SN Libra) *as pawns in their own chess game* (SN H1), *and the deliberate creation of confusion* (SN ruler Pisces) *while in office* (SN ruler H6) *in an attempt to imply guilt* (H6) *in others and so come out looking all pure and blameless* (Pisces).

We see very clearly now how Chiron's 8th house Aries past is part of this scenario. Tracing lines this way is part of mapping the **'trauma continuity'** we discussed earlier in the chapters on Lincoln and Lindbergh. There the continuity was between one lifetime and the next. Here it is between the pain and the trauma indicators in the chart. (i.e. Chiron, Uranus, and Neptune).

The trauma of *dissociation* (Uranus in Aquarius) *from his leadership* (Uranus H5) *and so from office* (Uranus ruling H6) is offered by the soul as an opportunity for growth in its vehicle Nixon so that it, the soul, may reach the emotional honesty of the 4th house Sagittarius. Healing of the Uranus trauma would have come about had Nixon willingly chosen to heed the call of his Uranus by getting an objective view of his leadership. Since he did not, the soul chose to learn this way. Whether Nixon indeed learned from the events I leave up to the soul and also up to you, the reader, should you decide to read his book *In the Arena: A Memoir of Victory, Defeat and Renewal,* in which Nixon looks back on his life and career. Although I have my private thoughts on the matter, I feel it is not for me to air those publicly.

Simultaneity in the ´Multidimensional Psyche' {see footnote (1) chapter 6}

"Are the nodes of Uranus not too far removed in time to have any noticeable effect on the natal Uranus in the way you suggest? On an orbit of 84,7 years, how are Uranus' nodes, or Neptune's for that matter, ever to confront each other in the planet's natal placement?" I can hear you ask. The answer is: we now find ourselves in the trans-Saturn realm of Chiron, Uranus, Neptune and Pluto where the curved time principle reigns. Linear time no longer applies here. Three thousand years ago is the same as three hundred years ago, thirty years ago and thirty hours ago. Through Pluto's and Neptune's emotional core (remember that in our model of the *Trauma Helix* Pluto's emotional identification with the emotion-laden meaninglessness of Neptune is much stronger than with the

[145]

mental images held in the Uranus realm, which we have likened to a library), Catherine's marketplace scene, her primary school scene and her astrology class scene become one, single moment highly charged in trauma content. This simultaneity of events in the subconscious strata of the psyche was first signaled

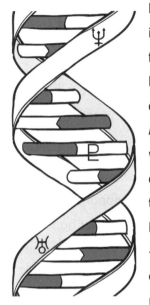

by the early psychoanalysts, of course, but it took the introduction of the *Multidimensional Psyche* (7) model for therapists to understand that its origin may well lie beyond the parameters of the current life (i.e. birth and death). In the simultaneity of the *Multidimensional Psyche,* whose astrological correlates we have associated with Chiron, Uranus, Neptune and Pluto, the many lifetimes comprised in it happen all at once. In a way we could say, therefore, that Uranus, Neptune and Pluto *are* stills, not because there is no movement - which there undeniably is – but because their trauma and potential for healing lie compressed in the eternal now of that simultaneity. The north nodes of Uranus and Neptune still confront their respective south nodes and the natal planet's familiarity with the past dynamics reflected in them, as I have begun to show you in this chapter and will continue to do in upcoming ones, but these south nodes comprise a far greater number of lives than the planets from Saturn inward do. This is why, back in chapter 6 – The *Multidimensional Psyche,* we redefined the transpersonal planets as *multidimensional*.

The nodes of Neptune (see chart p.138)

The same orbital dynamics apply to Neptune. The meaninglessness trauma of forcing a life upon yourself which does not reflect who you truly are, *causing it to become a living lie* (H11 dissociation) *and the emotional body* (Cancer) *to fracture* (H11), come from a past. We find that past at 10 degrees Aquarius 09 minutes in the 5th house: a sense of meaninglessness as a result of having been *dissociated* (Aquarius) *from leadership* (H5) *as prior-life selves, in their unstoppable self-aggrandizement, became separated* (Aquarius) *from Leo's generosity and impartiality* (H5), *that is, from the archetype in its highest expression*.

To understand how this Neptune past has led to the natal Neptune placement, it is important to give words to how the former is reflected in the latter. I will now do that for you. The dissociation from Leo in its higher expression, and through it, from leadership, is reflected in the triple dissociative state of *a life that is a living lie* (H11), *where, at the cost of fracturing* (H11) *in the emotional body* (Cancer), *the nation* (Cancer) *is led to believe Nixon is one thing when in fact he is another* (H11 dissociation through deception).

The NN of Neptune from the 11th house Leo provides the counterforce to this dynamic so that Neptune itself can come up with a new response [which, I think it is fair to say, it did not].

This is the dialogue between the two.

NN Neptune: *"Why don't you accept you were never cut out to be president? How could you be when you're clearly so extremely uncomfortable [Neptune in Cancer] in gatherings of two or more people [H11], and so extremely uncomfortable also when in the company of the opposite sex [Neptune in Cancer]?"*

Neptune: *"That's of no importance. I promised myself I would get the top job and I intend to keep that promise."* [his H10 Pluto skipped step speaking]

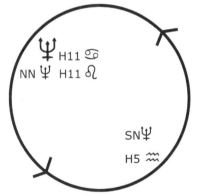

NN Neptune: *"At the cost of alienation [H11] from who you truly are [H11], risking getting permanently dissociated [H11] from that and from your family [Cancer] in the process?"* [H11]

Neptune: *"I don't know about all that. All I know is that I need to get to the top and stay there. Whatever it takes."*

NN Neptune: *"I'm offering you a better deal. Why don't you allow yourself to just be who you truly are (H11) and then shine (Leo) in whatever capacity that is? Perhaps you could be of greater use not only to yourself but also to the community (H11) that way."*

Neptune: *"And what would that be?"*

NN Neptune: "You know darn well what that is: a studious stay-at-home with a brilliant mind and the gift of the gab. Practicing law in Whittier and coming home for dinner at six would be just the ticket for you. You can be a brilliant lawyer, or a gifted speaker perhaps, although I would keep the groups small."

Neptune: "That's not going to happen."

NN Neptune: "Entirely up to you, old chum."

Nixon - SN of Neptune H5 Aquarius	resistance	Nixon - NN of Neptune H11 Leo
prior-life selves having become dissociated (Aquarius) from their leadership (H5) as they, in their unstoppable self-aggrandizement, became separated (Aquarius) from Leo's generosity and impartiality (H5), that is, from the archetype in its highest expression	< >	allow himself to be who he truly is (H11) and then shine (Leo) in whatever capacity that is
the past streaming into the present and determining the old response: **H11 Cancer**	**Neptune's choices**	**new response as the result of the resistance between the planet's SN and NN and its familiarity with the former:** **H11 Cancer**
triple dissociative state of a life that is a living lie (H11), where, at the cost of fracturing (H11) in the emotional body (Cancer), the nation (Cancer) is led to believe Nixon is one thing when in fact he is another (H11 dissociation through deception)	< >	overcoming the meaninglessness trauma when Nixon feels at home (Cancer) with who he truly is (H11)

The hand extended by the NN's 11th house Leo energy also speaks of a reinstatement of the besieged 5th house Leo qualities through a process of true individuation (H11).

Neptune in the 11th house Cancer can heal the meaninglessness trauma when Nixon *feels at home* (Cancer) *with who he truly is* (H11). This is the new response that would have undone the fracturing of the emotional body and would have greatly contributed to the emotional truthfulness the soul sought in the 4th house Sagittarius. Neptune does not get any of this and will deepen the chasm. As it does so, it will worsen the fracturing in and of the emotional body, as well as the inner lie and subsequent deception of the nation: H11 Cancer.

Again, we see how the SN of Chiron in the 8th house Aries is connected to Neptune's past, as it would be for it is the translation of that past *as pain*: the treacherous power games (SN Chiron H8) to further one's own game (SN Chiron Aries) are directly linked to prior-life selves having become dissociated (SN Neptune Aquarius) from Leo's generosity, impartiality and ability to bring out the best in others (SN Neptune H5).

Such is the single, evolutionary orbit of what constitutes deepest meaningfulness and deepest meaninglessness in a string of lives, a succession of lifetimes created by the soul to grow and evolve.

What about the nodes of Pluto? The incubated soul on a 'conveyor belt'

We have not talked about the nodes of Pluto yet. The reason for that is that they have to do with the soul's overall trajectory over a myriad of lives, all related to how it incubates on the 'Cosmic Conveyor Belt' after Source has created it. The term 'conveyor belt' may sound a little unrespectful but is not intended that way.

The image of a conveyor belt is actually used in Michael Newton's *Destiny of Souls* (8), where, in chapter 5 – *Soul Group Systems*, an advanced soul talks about its activities when at home in the spirit world. "Case 26", when prompted by Newton's subtle questioning, reveals how she works as what could be likened to a spiritual obstetrician in the place where souls are hatched. She describes how newly-hatched souls seem to come from a flowing mass of vibrating energy which she intuits to be unconditional love and behind which there is a purple darkness, adding that these souls move towards her as if on some kind of continuous, moving belt. Each soul, so she goes on to say, has its own unique individuality crafted by a perfection she cannot capture in words.

Therapeutic evolutionary astrology thinks of soul as created by Source with a specific mission through which It (i.e. Source) becomes conscious of its own Divine Nature and Unconditional Love. Through Soul Source knows Itself, the same way through Ego Soul knows itself. (9) The Pluto placement by house and sign for any given life created by the soul highlights a particular facet of this larger mission soul is working on as it seeks to reunite with Source. I do not have the wherewithal to say anything sensible about the relationship between the two in the case of any of the charts discussed in this book - or indeed any chart - and so I refrain from doing so. It is too unfathomable, too sacred for me to stick my nose in.

What I *can* say is that in our model of the *Trauma Helix* Nixon's 10th house Gemini Pluto placement emotionally identifies with the Uranus and Neptune strands as *a split* (Gemini) *in integrity and inner accountability* (H10), *as if it cannot count on itself, as if it were turned against itself.* We will have another look at this when we get to chapter 12 and look at Richard Nixon in full evolutionary orbit.

All of this work is undertaken so that we may put the wonderful paradigm of evolutionary astrology to good therapeutic use. This is my stated aim in writing this book. I hope that through the Chiron-*Trauma Helix* model, supplemented by an orbital understanding of each of its components, I am handing you a powerful therapeutic tool that you may use in your work with clients.

Chapter 10 – Jim Jones

"My power depends on your faith and willingness to serve"

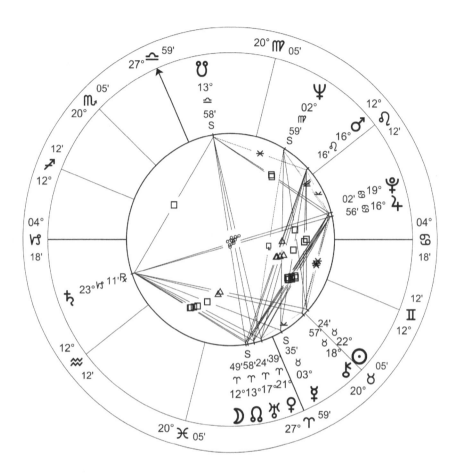

Jim Jones, 13 May 1931, 22:00 hrs., Lynn, Indiana, RR:AA

When young Jimmy was about eight or nine years old, roaming the streets of his hometown Lynn, Indiana - as young boys do - a devout Christian lady across the street from where the Jones family lived, took him in and began reading scripture to the little fellow. Unlike most residents of the Randolph County town, Jimmy´s parents were not in the habit of attending church on Sundays. This made them stand out a mile in the small community of barely a thousand inhabitants. It was surprising therefore when little Jimmy sucked up every passage that was read to him by his Bible-thumping neighbor. Even more surprising was it when not long after he took to reciting whole chunks of The Good Book at a time, as if he had

[151]

developed photographic memory in all things related to the word of the Lord. Soon he seemed to be making up for every single church service his parents had chosen not to attend by spending his Sundays going from church to church, irrespective of denomination. It was as if he could not get enough Holy Writ into his soul. This naturally raised quite a few eyebrows in Lynn. Had there been an outpouring of the Holy Spirit upon the waif? How could a young heathen be so gripped and sustained by the Gospels? How could a scruffy little scoundrel in whom such overtly pagan values had been instilled - not to mention the constant cursing and swearing in public his mother was known for in all four corners of the small rural town – have ended up on the straight and narrow? The Lord worked in mysterious ways indeed. (1)

Pluto in the 7th house Cancer skipped step conjunct Jupiter in the 7th house Cancer skipped step

The issue or issues which have brought the soul to a stuck place on its own evolutionary path are glued to something to do with faith, religion or doctrine (Jupiter), a finding which immediately makes us wonder about the SN of the Moon in the 9th house. The conjunction, which is balsamic and indicates a long story between the two drawing to a close, speaks of *dependency* (H7) *created in people through faith* (Jupiter) *by forming a close-knit family, a messianic* (Jupiter) *cult* (Cancer). Jupiter rules the 12th house, where this family may withdraw from the world and find a secluded place, a place far away from Indiana or California where Jones can wield absolute power and control over its members. (2)

SN of the Moon in the 9th house Libra

Dynamics operative in prior-life selves, created by the soul to explore this 7th house Cancer issue, point in the direction of them *having expected others* (Libra) *to abide by the tenets of a professed faith* (H9). (3) Prior-life selves would have *demanded strict compliance* (Libra) *with a doctrine* (H9)

[152]

they themselves did not believe in (H9 distortion of truth), which is exactly how things would play out this time round.

The SN of the Moon dynamics tend to be keenly felt in early youth. Sometimes they remain operative beyond one's formative years and the script may still run at the time of one's first Saturn return. Young Jimmy's religious fervor was simply the soul picking up where it had left off. His neighbor reading Biblical text to the boy must have rekindled subconscious memories in him of the kind of preaching and teaching implicit in the combined Pluto-Jupiter-SN of the Moon dynamics we had a look at just now. The truly unexpected turn came when Jones brought in socialism. In a 1977 interview (4) he let on that he had never really believed in God. That may have been the one time in his life he spoke the truth. Religion had been his way to socialism - 9th house Libra – and socialism, given the enormous social injustice young Jim Jones saw everywhere around him in the America of the 1940s and 1950s, was the way to get people to join a community where he could wield near-total control over them.

This, Jones must have sensed from a very early age. It must not have taken him long to understand that religion could be used as a Trojan horse to draw Christians into his social rights activism (5) and that the latter was the shortcut to absolutist rule. He must have vaguely sensed it as a young boy quoting biblical passages - which is how past-life dynamics tend to get reenacted - and as the years passed, he would have become more and more consciously aware of how the *slavery* (SN of the Moon Libra) *of faith* (SN of the Moon H9) could be used to his advantage.

From the biographical facts available we learn that the strategy had been perfectly laid out in Jones' mind as early on in his career as 1952, two-and-a-half years into his marriage with Marceline Baldwin, a pious Christian of the Methodist persuasion. The moment the Methodist church announced its social program targeted at, among other things, combatting poverty and promoting racial integration, Jones rejoined a church he had turned his back on years earlier, telling his wife Marceline that he now wished to become a Methodist minister. (6) She felt exalted at the news, believing her husband's faith had been restored through divine intervention. Nothing of the sort had happened. The reason he returned was not Christian faith (SN of the Moon H9), which he was disdainful of in the extreme and caused him to go on long rants against God (7). The reason was he now had the two things he needed to get to the kind of absolute sovereignty the tyrant in him craved for: **evangelical** (SN of the Moon H9) **socialism** (SN of the Moon in Libra). (8) The mountain had come to Jimmy.

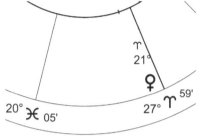

Ruler of the SN of the Moon in the 3rd house Aries

Asserting (Aries) *and imposing his will* (Aries) *via the forcefully* (Aries) *delivered word* (H3) - the entire body (Aries) accentuating the words (H3) (9) as he railed and scolded, often against the Bible as racially biased indoctrination (10) - is the way this 9th house compliance in others was created in prior lives, as it would be in this one.

Honesty compels one to also mention the more praiseworthy moments of Jim Jones' career, ones that get easily overshadowed by the tragic events of 1978. Had Jim Jones not led over 900 people to their deaths in French Guyana, he would have been remembered as an honorable social rights activist *avant la lettre* who in the late fifties single-handedly (Aries) brought about integration (H3) in the city of Indianapolis, one of the most segregated cities in the America of the fifties: years before civil rights laws, restaurant owners were urged to admit black clients and rewarded when they did so. (11). Jones also set up an in-house employment agency providing businesses with mostly black workers from his ever-growing flock who previously would not even have made it onto their job interview shortlist (12). Again, the way *to* the integration was faith (SN of the Moon H9), with Jones' Indianapolis "Community Unity" church its vehicle. Its apparent goal was social reform (SN of the Moon Libra, Pluto in the 7th house), its real goal none other than the despotism Jones craved. In Indianapolis, Jones' social reform program made him a hero. All that would change in 1965 when the flock clutched the hem of the new messiah and followed him to Redwood Valley California. There the 3rd house Aries SN ruler took on an ominously repressive hue: Jones would have followers sign blank pieces of paper (H3) so that he could later blackmail them if they defected or otherwise went against his will (Aries). (13)

Pluto Polarity Point in the 1st house Capricorn

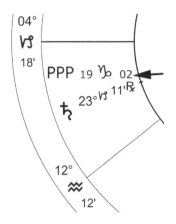

The place the soul intended to evolve towards was one where *these dependency patterns* (Pluto H7) *would be broken and with them the emotional clinginess* (Pluto in Cancer) *used to create them.* A place where the soul would *leave the immaturity of dependency* (H7) *through excessive attachment* (Cancer) *behind and assume responsibility* (PPP Capricorn) *for forging its own path*, thereby allowing others to do the same. As you can see in the chart, right next to the Pluto Polarity Point there is a Saturn skipped step. In its own sign, to boot. We will get to it in a minute.

NN of the Moon in the 3rd house Aries

We note the fact that Aries is restated, as we undoubtedly did for Libra when we moved from Pluto to the SN of the Moon. The way the 1st house Capricorn soul intention was to have been carried out on the Moon level, on the level of Jim Jones, was *for him to have allowed each and every member of his motley* (H3) *flock to connect with* (H3) *their own will and identity* (Aries) *so that they may think* (H3) *for themselves* (Aries) - (14) - instead of having to *follow the words* (SN ruler

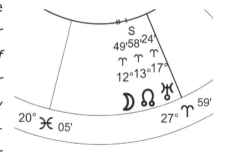

H3) *of the master demagogue* (SN of the Moon H9) *to the letter* (SN ruler H3). Allowing them *to connect* (H3) with that will and identity so that they might exercise the ability to reason (H3) would have been the kind of integration the combined Uranus the liberator conjunct the NN of the Moon conjunct the Moon 3rd house statement is imploring Jones to further. (15)

As we did in the chart of Abraham Lincoln, from Uranus´ conjunction to the NN of the Moon we glean that in a recent prior life the NN was buoyed up substantially by its liberating impetus. Why then was this not followed through in the life of Jim Jones? Is he himself, the Moon, not also conjunct that NN, in an even tighter orb than its compadre Uranus? The answer to those questions lies in the triple strangle-hold of the Saturn skipped step on one side of the chart and the Pluto-Jupiter one on the other.

NN ruler in the 8th house Leo

The way the NN of the Moon intention could have been actualized would have been to *help each and every one of the members that made up that flock* (Mars ruling H4) *self-empower* (NN ruler H8) *by generously and impartially giving of oneself* (Leo) *so that they bask in the warmth of their own sun* (NN ruler Leo). That did not happen. Instead, strict compliance (Pluto H7, SN in Libra) was expected of them by their leader (SN ruler Aries). Even, and especially, in death. Not all of the nine hundred plus people who died in French Guyana on that fateful day in November of 1978 committed suicide: some laid down their lives willingly, many others were held down and forcibly injected or made to drink cyanide-laced grape-flavored *Flavor Aid*. Over three hundred children were the first to die. (16) This is why you find the Neptune strand of the *Trauma Helix* in the 8th house: followers did not choose (H8) this death (H8). It was *required of them as an act of service* (Virgo), as *"an act of revolutionary suicide protesting the conditions of an inhumane world."* (17). Neptune's meaninglessness trauma carried over from prior lives speaks of *a severe lack of discernment* (Virgo) *in all matters self-empowerment* (H8), with *imposed death* (H8) as *the ultimate betrayal* (H8) of that 8th house Leonian empowerment.

Saturn in the 1st house Capricorn skipped step (resolving via the SN of the Moon H9 Libra)

And so we begin to understand the Saturn roadblock in the 1st house: an utter *lack of integrity* (Capricorn) *in Jones for failing to assume responsibility* (Saturn) *for his true identity* (H1) *and intentions* (H1: will): a con artist masquerading as an evangelist. The Saturn skipped step also denotes *the total and unfettered control* (Capricorn) *Jones wielded because of his presumed divine identity* (H1).

(18) He expected unquestioning obedience (Saturn in Capricorn skipped step) from his followers, most, if not all, of whom were convinced he possessed divine will (H1). Jones instilled *'situational ethics'* (Capricorn) (19) in them where the Temple's noble cause justified any and all means: stealing, twisting and turning, lying, spying and ratting on people was all perfectly fine as long as it served lofty Temple goals.

This unresolved Saturn issue, which lifetime upon lifetime had stood in the way of the 3rd house Aries NN of the Moon getting actualized, resolves via the SN of the Moon: again, just like he was in lifetimes past, life will put Jones in a place where he will run the risk of preaching (SN of the Moon H9) one thing while believing another (SN of the Moon H9: dishonesty) expecting total compliance

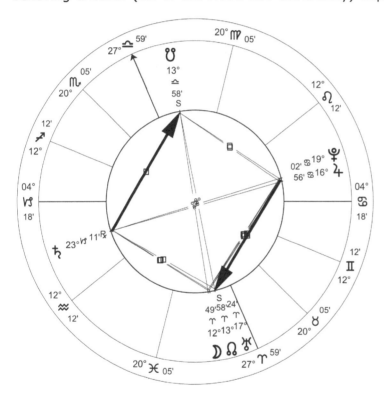

(SN of the Moon in Libra) with the lie sold as truth. (SN of the Moon H9) His hidden agenda, after all, had been socialism. And not even that. Even socialism was used as a pretext so that he could *exert his will and do his own thing* (ruler of the SN of the Moon in Aries), *cleverly cloaked in just the right rhetoric* (ruler of the SN of the Moon

H3), words that fooled thousands and thousands of devoted followers who had handed over all of their possessions to him (bank assets, the deeds to their houses, stocks, jewelry, the lot) and turned their backs on their families and friends.

The soul's rationale for sending Jones back to these old circumstances is for him to make new choices this time round: the new choice would have been *to restore*

[157]

balance (Libra) *in expecting people's compliance* (Libra) *with the lie* (H9) *by being honest* (H9). *The way* the new choice could have been made is written in the SN ruler: *to acknowledge the validity of multiple viewpoints* (H3) *so that people could connect* (H3) *with their will and identity* (Aries) *and think* (H3) *for themselves* (Aries). The exact opposite of *asserting one's will* (SN ruler Aries) *through the luring call of the spoken word* (SN ruler H3) *expressing the one, single truth* (SN H9) *all followers were expected to abide by* (SN Libra).

Pluto-Jupiter in the 7th house Cancer skipped step resolving via the NN of the Moon (see chart page 157)

Since this new choice is formulated in the 3rd house Aries, we at once understand why the NN of the Moon in the same house and sign would be the resolution node to the formidable Pluto-Jupiter skipped step in the 7th house Cancer: *only when people are allowed to connect* (H3) *with their own will and identity* (Aries) can the *clannish clinginess of a messianic cult* (Jupiter H7 Cancer) *through which total dependency* (H7) *is created be broken*. *The way* that might have been done is written in the NN ruler in the 8th house Leo: *helping people self-empower* (H8) *by generously and impartially giving of oneself* (Leo) *so that they may bask in the warmth of their fully actualized sense of self* (Leo).

(**Important notice.** From this point onward in the chapter, all NNs, whether lunar or planetary, are defined as *counterweight to past dynamics*. All natal placements, whether lunar or planetary, are defined as the *point of maximum resistance between their own south and north nodes*. The old response, coming from past dynamics and reflected _in_ the natal placement by house and sign, is given in the text, as is the new response triggered by the resistance the Moon or natal planet feels between its south and north node. It is the latter response which is the agent of change and therefore evolutionary relevant)

Chiron and the *Trauma Helix*

What I would like to do now is lift the veil of the current lifetime of Jim Jones and peek into a dimension where we know the origins of the trauma lie. Since we seek to understand the entire orbit of the planets involved as one, single evolutionary movement, we will bring in the south and north nodes of Chiron,

Uranus and Neptune as we go along, the way we did in the previous chapter for Richard Nixon.

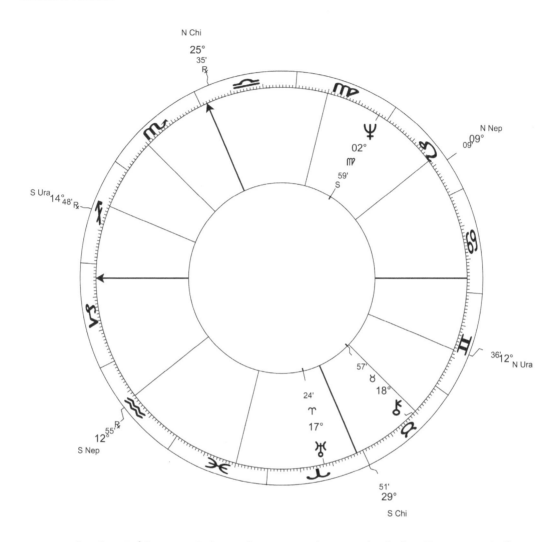

Uranus in the 3rd house Aries: the mental strand of the *Trauma Helix*

As I pointed out in the chapters on Lincoln and Lindbergh, Uranus in contact with Mars, Aries or the first house often points to *trauma incurred as a result of a project which has only just started being cut short abruptly. That project can be life itself*, which is why EA sometimes associates this kind of contact with dying young in a past life. The youthful character of the deaths is here underscored by Uranus' 3rd house placement: on that November day in 1978 *all* those who were murdered died before their time, young and old alike. The subconscious memories held in Uranus' non-linear storage vault - in the form of words,

[159]

thoughts and images - have to do with *people dying abruptly and prematurely* (Uranus in Aries) *for having come under the spell of certain words and ideas*

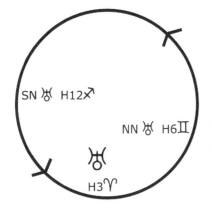

(Uranus H3). (20) Let us now look into Uranus' past to see where they originated.

We find the SN of Uranus at 14 degrees Sagittarius 48 minutes in the 12th house: *the deaths happened as part of a faith, a religion or doctrine* (Sagittarius) *in a hidden-away place* (H12), a place outside the confines of society *where people would fall victim* (H12) *to the delusions* (H12) *of a madman* (H12), as they would in the soul's current-life vehicle Jim Jones. As you gaze into Uranus' past and see how it is reflected in its 3rd house Aries placement, you realize that this 12th house Sagittarius dynamic is not new to the soul: past-life egoic structures had been there before.

Jones - SN of Uranus H12 Sagittarius	resistance	Jones - NN of Uranus H6 Gemini
the deaths happened as part of a faith, a religion or doctrine (Sagittarius) in a hidden-away place (H12) far from public scrutiny, a place where people would fall victim (H12) to the delusions (H12) of a madman (H12)	< >	to serve (H6) by acknowledging the validity of multiple viewpoints (Gemini)
the past streaming into the present and determining the old response: H3 Aries	**Uranus' choices**	**new response as the result of the resistance between the planet's SN and NN and its familiarity with the former: H3 Aries**
people dying abruptly and prematurely (Uranus in Aries) for having come under the spell of certain words and ideas (Uranus H3)	< >	allow his followers to connect with (H3) their own will and identity (Aries) and think (H3) for themselves (Aries)

The NN of Uranus we find in the 6th house at 12 degrees Gemini 36 minutes: *to serve* (H6) *by acknowledging the validity of multiple viewpoints* (Gemini), which, as we have seen, was the great promise of the NN of the Moon flanked by Uranus and the Moon itself.

The NN of Uranus is not an end in itself. It simply provides a counterforce to Uranus' familiarity with its past dynamics so that it may formulate a new response and heal the trauma carried over from prior lifetimes. Noting the Gemini archetypal resonance between Uranus (H3) and its NN (Gemini), we ourselves have formulated that new response three times already: it would have been given if Jones had *allowed his followers to connect with* (H3) *their own will and identity* (Aries) *and think* (H3) *for themselves* (Aries). (21) Desirous of knowing more about *'trauma continuity,'* we are curious to see, as we were with Richard Nixon in the previous chapter, if the past of the Uranus trauma, and indeed that of Neptune, is in any way reflected in the SN of Chiron. I will satisfy that curiosity shortly.

Neptune in the 8th house Virgo: the meaninglessness strand of the *Trauma Helix* (see chart p.159)

The natal Neptune we have already talked about. Where is the past of this betrayal of people's self-empowerment through imposed death? It sits, tellingly, in the 2nd house at 12 degrees Aquarius 55 minutes: *the holding back through confinement* (H2) *of a large group of people* (Aquarius).

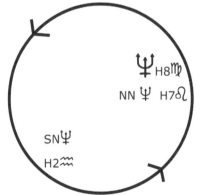

With the 2nd house we naturally think of non-survival. The issue, however, is broader than that and hinges on people's values and the value of people. The meaninglessness coming from that past, and which has accrued in the soul narrative, has to do with *holding people back in their value system* (H2) *by making them dependent on yours* (SN of the Moon H9 Libra), effectively *dissociating* (Aquarius) *them from it*. As you can see, I am placing the past of the trauma in the context of the information I glean from the SN of the Moon in terms of dynamics operative in prior-life selves. And, finally and more importantly, *holding people back by not valuing their lives.* It is *their right to survive, to live* (H2) *that prior-life Jones' got dangerously dissociated* (Aquarius) *from*. Not their own right to do so but others'. What you are literally looking at here, therefore, is *meaninglessness trauma caused by the non-survival* (H2) *of a large group of people* (Aquarius), coming in from past lives and flowing straight into the natal Neptune placement. I hope you see how this trauma is directly linked to the Uranus strand of making people die prematurely (Uranus H3 Aries) and how in the past this happened in a secluded place (SN Uranus H12) as part of a faith, religion of doctrine (SN Uranus Sagittarius), without anyone from the outside world being able to get anywhere near it (SN Uranus H12 Sagittarius). (22)

Jones - SN of Neptune H2 Aquarius	resistance	Jones – NN of Neptune H7 Leo
meaninglessness trauma caused by the non-survival (H2) of a large group of people (Aquarius); holding people back (H2) in their value system (H2), dissociating (Aquarius) them from it by making them dependent on yours (SN of the Moon H9 Libra); dissociating (Aquarius) people from both their value system (H2) and right to survive (H2), to live	< >	equality in relationship (H7) so that people may stand in their own light and bask in the warmth of that light (Leo)
the past streaming into the present and determining the old response: H8 Virgo	**Neptune's choices**	**new response as the result of the resistance between the planet's SN and NN and its familiarity with the former: H8 Virgo**
a crisis (Virgo) around taking people's power (H8) away from them, compounded by the denial (Virgo) of this fact - culminating in imposed death (H8)	< >	to truly serve (Virgo) people's self-empowerment (H8)

Here too, we see how Neptune had been down this treacherous path before. Moreover, it shows in the Neptune placement by house and sign: there is *a crisis* (Virgo) *around taking people's power away from them* (H8), *compounded by a denial* (Virgo) *of this fact – culminating in imposed death* (H8) - never more eloquently stated than by Jones himself when he said *"My power* (H8) *depends on your faith and willingness to serve."* (Virgo)

The NN of Neptune we find in the 7th house at 9 degrees Leo 9 minutes: *equality in relationship* (H7) *so that people may stand in their own light and bask in the warmth of that light* (Leo). The exact opposite, therefore, of taking that light away from them through dependency and compliance.

As this opposing force hits the familiarity between Neptune and its own SN, it triggers a new response in Neptune: *to truly serve* (Virgo) *people's self-empowerment* (H8). This is what would have constituted the deepest meaningfulness to the soul and healed the trauma. It did not happen. What in Indianapolis had started out as a temple of social empowerment in Jonestown ended in a temple of ultimate disempowerment.

Pluto identifying emotionally and psychologically with the Uranus and Neptune strand

The way the soul identifies with the Uranus and Neptune strand is as *an imbalance* (H7) *in the care for and nurturing* (Cancer) *of the flock* (Cancer).

The imbalance, through its conjunction to Jupiter, is infused – infected perhaps would be a better word – by *inequality* (H7) *cleverly dressed up as pastoral* (Jupiter) *care and counseling* (Cancer). Church members could come to Jones for anything, from plumbing to utility bills. People flocked to his church in great numbers, leaving behind black churches were they were offered sympathy for their plight and the prospect of substantially improved conditions after death, to one where their leader not only performed healings (with Jones using chicken guts for fake cancer healings) (23) but also helped out when the electricity company threatened to shut down the power supply yet insisted one keep paying the bills. Jones, unstinting with his time, offered intercessions in these cases, involving brethren in the writing of complaint letters which he subsequently personally delivered at the company's office, (24) where his smooth talking would soon convince clerks and hard-nosed higher-ups alike. With tangible results delivered he could boast that his Community Unity church cared as much for the mortal as for the eternal life.

Underneath it all, however, Jones knew full well he was creating the kind of dependency (Pluto H7, SN of the Moon in Libra) in his followers that would allow him to *use scripture* (SN of the Moon H9, SN ruler H3) *to do his own thing and not reckon with anyone* (SN ruler in Aries). The words (H3) were just that: words. Privately, he did not espouse his followers' belief in a 'Sky God.' Jones, when not on the pulpit, believed in reincarnation and kept his views to himself, knowing precious little would be achieved by shaking his followers' belief system to the core (Saturn H1 Capricorn skipped step: not owning up to who he really was). (25)

Even Jones's 'rainbow family,' consisting of several adopted children from different races – something totally unprecedented in Indiana at the time – was put together as *a lie* (Jupiter) *to create the impression of equality* (Jupiter H7) *within the family* (Jupiter in Cancer). It was a clever *marketing move* (Jupiter) *designed to have the Jones family* (Cancer) *exemplify racial* (Cancer) *parity* (H7). (26)

Chiron in the 4th house Taurus: the trauma charge relayed to Saturn *as pain* (see chart p.159)

The way the trauma charge is transferred to Saturn is as *a pain caused by the holding back* (Taurus) *and, ultimately, non-survival* (Taurus) *of the flock* (H4).

The past of this pain, inevitably, is related to the past of the Uranus and the Neptune strands. We find the SN of Chiron at 29 degrees Aries 51 minutes in the 4th house: the pain which has accrued in the soul narrative comes from *prior-life selves having imposed their will* (Aries) *at the expense of a community, a family of followers* (H4). The information could not have been etched more precisely into the chart. This dynamic comes back in Chiron in the 4th house Taurus in that

[164]

these *followers paid for their membership of the family* (H4) *with non-survival* (Taurus).

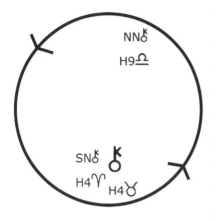

The NN of Chiron, obviously connected to the healing of the pain, is found in the 9th house at 25 degrees Libra 35 minutes and inwardly has to do with *Jones restoring balance* (Libra) *in truthfulness* (H9): <u>the</u> great predicament that lay at the heart of his Saturn in the 1st house Capricorn skipped step. Outwardly, it has to do with *him restoring balance* (Libra) *in his tendency to make people comply* (Libra) *with his truth,*

which, we now know, *was a distortion of truth* (H9): *a lie* (H9). Again, a very succinct statement by the soul. As this 9th house Libra energy hit Chiron and its SN, it hoped to trigger a new response in the former: *to secure the safety* (Taurus) *of the flock* (H4), as behooves a good pastor. The events as they transpired were the exact opposite of that.

Jones - SN of Chiron H4 Aries	resistance	Jones - NN of Chiron H9 Libra
prior-life selves having imposed their will (Aries) at the expense of a community, a family of followers (H4)	< >	restoring balance (Libra) in his tendency to make people comply (Libra) with his truth (H9) which was a distortion of truth (H9): a lie (H9)
the past streaming into the present and determining the old response: H4 Taurus	**Chiron's choices**	**new response as the result of the resistance between the planet's SN and NN and its familiarity with the former: H4 Taurus**
a pain caused by the holding back (Taurus) and, ultimately, non-survival (Taurus) of the flock (H4); followers paying for their membership of the family (H4) with non-survival (Taurus)	< >	to secure the safety (Taurus) of the flock (H4), as behooves a good pastor

[165]

The Chiron pain now arrives at Saturn's doorstep. The in**form**ation held in its subtle body will **form** Saturn (27) in such a way *as for consciousness to develop*

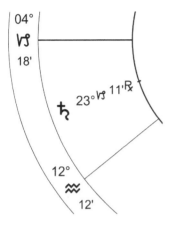

integrity (Capricorn) *in all matters will and identity* (H1) *so that Jones may own up* (Capricorn) *to who he really is* (H1 identity) *and what he is really after* (H1 will). It did not happen. He became the ultimate fraud and swindler willing to take people's lives rather than admit to (Saturn) having pulled the wool over their eyes for decades. This 1st house Capricorn lack of integrity is of extreme importance to the soul: it is a skipped step, it is retrograde (repeat assignment) *and* it rules the ascendant, meaning it colors the Cosmic Birth Canal through which the soul enters the current life of Jim Jones.

Moon in the 3rd house Aries

Jones' Moon is in the 3rd house Aries. It carries the whole of its own 9th house Libra past inside of it and is very familiar with that past. How is that written in

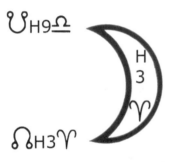

the Moon's house and sign placement? This is not immediately clear, but if you look carefully you will see it: *the near-total compliance* (Libra) *begotten through people's faith in God* (H9) *and in a better world* (Libra socialism) - *evangelical socialism as the shortcut to autocratic rule - has robbed them of their right to connect* (H3) *with their own will, identity* (Aries) *and capacity to think* (H3) *for themselves* (Aries).

What the NN of the Moon has in mind for the Moon is the exact opposite of that. When it hits the past dynamic, it hopes the Moon – Jones – will understand how important it is *to allow people to get out from under one single 'truth'* (SN of the Moon H9) *and their expected compliance* (SN of the Moon Libra) *with it* - a truth which turned out to be a gross lie - *so that they may connect* (H3) *with their own will and identity* (Aries) *and think* (H3) *for themselves* (Aries).

The Moon did not get it. (28) Not even with its nose pressed to the windowpane of its own NN and with Uranus screaming liberation from the other side of the

Plexiglas. Such was the combined force of the Saturn, Pluto and Jupiter skipped steps in the life of reverend, con artist Jim Jones.

Jones - SN of Moon H9 Libra	resistance	Jones - NN of Moon H3 Aries
demanding (Libra) strict compliance (Libra) from people with a professed faith (H9) they themselves did not believe in and which therefore was a gross distortion of truth (H9), effectively creating a *"slavery (Libra) of faith"* (H9)	< >	to allow people to get out from under one single 'truth' (SN of the Moon H9) and their expected compliance (SN of the Moon Libra) with it, so that they may connect (H3) with their own will and identity (Aries) and think (H3) for themselves (Aries)
the past streaming into the present and determining the Moon's old response: H3 Aries	**Moon's choices**	**new response as the result of the resistance between the Moon's SN and NN and its familiarity with the former: H3 Aries**
robbing people of their right to connect (H3) with their own will, identity (Aries) and capacity to think (H3) for themselves (Aries)	< >	to allow people to get out from under one single 'truth' (SN of the Moon H9) and their expected compliance (SN of the Moon Libra) with it, so that they may connect (H3) with their own will and identity (Aries) and think (H3) for themselves (Aries)

Chapter 11 - Josef Mengele in Full Evolutionary Orbit

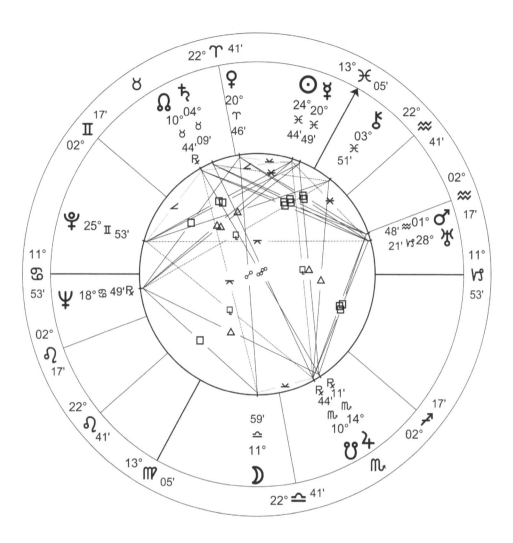

Josef Mengele, 16 March 1911, 11:45 hrs., Günzburg, Germany, RR:AA

Introduction

It would be easy and therefore tempting to portray Mengele as some Shelleyan obsessed scientist who develops a consuming interest in human genetics and, far from public scrutiny and in near total isolation, is given a free hand to experiment on as many human specimens as he wishes. The more unsettling truth, however, is that yes, Auschwitz did allow Mengele to perform these experiments without any of the restrictions that normally keep scientists within the boundaries of ethics, but rather than a wayward scientist Mengele was a faithful reflection of interbelline German society rife with antisemitism and pervaded by the notion that, as Mengele would write in his diary, *"the characteristic qualities of the German people should be freed from alien encrustation."* (1)

This notion could be found in a perception large segments of German society had of themselves and which centered around the ideas of *"Volk,* [nation] *Blut* [blood] *und Boden* [soil]", that is, the ideal of a racially defined national body (nation, blood) united with a settlement area (soil), signifying an almost mystical bond between Germans and their land. Tied to this perception was the concept of *Lebensraum* (literally "living space") i.e. the belief that the German people needed to expand into Eastern Europe and displace the native Slavic and Baltic population via the so-called *Generalplan Ost* (General Plan for the East), a plan entailing vast scale genocide and ethnic cleansing and which, when it was partially implemented between 1939 and 1943, resulted in millions of deaths of ethnic Slavs by starvation, disease and extermination through forced labor. Germany's defeat eventually prevented the full implementation of the plan.

Ultimately, the idea of *"Volk, Blut und Boden"* was inspired by Hitler's and other leading Nazis' membership of the *Thule Society*, a German occultist group founded in Munich after World War I and named after a mythical northern country in Greek legend. A primary focus of the group was the origin of the *Aryan race* and the combatting of Jews and communists. (2)

Pluto in the 12th house Gemini

It is not too difficult to see how Mengele's 12th house Pluto would have felt drawn to the supposedly rarefied air of the imagined and imaginary high culture the Nazis presumed their nation had its origins in and should be returned to.

When the young Mengele embarked on his study of medicine, genetics and anthropology in April of 1930, it was clear from the start that his science (Pluto in Gemini) would serve the collective (Pluto in the 12th house), i.e. the mythic (Pluto in the 12th house) Germany and its people. By that time Hitler had already subsumed the rights of the individual to the needs of the group, and the National Socialist German Physician's League (NSDÄB) blindly followed his edicts:

"From the first day, we have made it clear that the major turnabout in the world view of our days, an essential portion of which is vanquishing the individual through experiencing the "people" (Volk) must be the guiding principle of the morality and ethics of the medical profession." (3)

When on 5 April 1933 Hitler urged the medical profession to take center stage in the 'race question,' it did not take long for the subject of *'racial hygiene'* to show up on university curricula throughout the country. (4)

With Pluto in the 12th house Gemini, we wonder what kinds of lives the soul would have created to explore this issue of *science* (Gemini) *offered to the mystical collective* (H12) *and its presumed elevated and purified* (12th house) *culture*. The answer is written in the SN of the Moon in the 5th house in its conjunction to Jupiter.

SN of the Moon in the 5th house Scorpio conjunct Jupiter in the 5th house Scorpio

The SN in the 5th house Scorpio, in this context, denotes lives in which there would have been *genetic manipulation* (Scorpio) *of the life force itself* (5th house) *– constituting an intrusion* (Scorpio) *and betrayal* (Scorpio) *of it - in order to gain recognition, acclaim and dominance* (5th house). We know Mengele was obsessed with making a name for himself and was convinced he would end up in the annals of history as one of the greatest physicians ever. As it turned out, he would add volumes to the annals of human suffering.

A planet conjunct the SN of the Moon, as we saw in the charts of Barbro Karlén (chapter 4) and Nina Simone (chapter 7), has been a direct and decisive influence in the life of prior-life selves. Here that planet is Jupiter, associated with ideology. The ideology (Jupiter) would have been used to gain prominence (5th house) and it would have been *one that condoned the genetic manipulation* (Scorpio) *of the life force* (5th house), as would *the thoroughly perverted* (Scorpio) *Nazi ideology* (Jupiter) this time round (Jupiter retrograde: a repeat signature [5]).

[171]

The way this was carried out in past lives is written in the SN ruler. We find it in the 12th house Gemini.

SN ruler Pluto in the 12th house Gemini

Eerily, much of Mengele's work at Auschwitz, the isolated place far from the public gaze (Pluto in the 12th house), would be on twins (Pluto in Gemini). (6) But it entailed much more. All through his twenty months at the place where the Nazis laid waste to humanity, from May 1943 to January 1945, Mengele's medical activities included the treatment of *Noma facies* (a form of oral cancer which had been eradicated but resurfaced due to the abysmal hygienic conditions in Auschwitz), the investigation of heterochromia (eyes of different colors), a project on specific proteins, growth anomalies (dwarfism and giantism), physical anomalies (hunchbacks, club foot, etc.), human embryos, stillbirths and deceased newborns, as well as the anthropological study of Gypsies. (7) Many of the results of his investigations were shared with the Kaiser Wilhelm Institute for Anthropology in Berlin and with the SS Medical Academy in Graz, where the next generation of SS physicians received their training. (8)

SN ruler linked back to the SN of the Moon and to Pluto: uncovering *the Inner Logic of the Soul*

When we link the SN ruler back to the SN of the Moon and back to the Pluto placement in an attempt to lay bare **the Inner Logic of the Soul**, we find that:

the genetic manipulation of the life force (5th house Scorpio) – *constituting an intrusion* (Scorpio) *and betrayal* (Scorpio) *of it* – *seeking its justification in a thoroughly perverted* (Scorpio) *ideology* (Jupiter) *through which recognition, acclaim and dominance* (H5) *are sought, happened in the name of science* (Gemini) *offered to the delusion* (H12) *of perfection* (Pisces, H12). (9)

Pluto Polarity Point in the 6th house Sagittarius

It is understandable that we ask ourselves what evolutionary intentions the soul possibly could have had when it envisaged a life like Mengele's, a life where, instead of healing and curing, unspeakable evil was done which the person was not held accountable for. Mengele, of course, managed to escape to Argentina

[172]

after the war and lived out his days in South America (initially in Argentina, and later in Paraguay and Brazil). (10) The question here becomes if the soul indeed envisaged this life the way it turned out. From the PPP in the 6th house Sagittarius

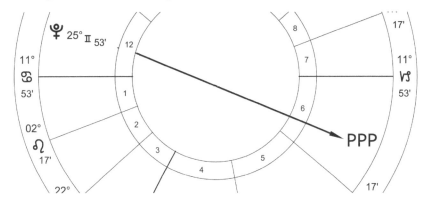

and its facilitator the NN of the Moon in the 11th house, with the ruler in the 10th house Aries, we rather get the impression it wanted to go somewhere completely different.

From being captivated by the mythical (12th house), it would have wanted to become rooted in the pragmatic (6th house). The way that could have happened was through service (6th house), alleviating the needs of everyday people in everyday situations, as the Hippocratic Oath Mengele at one point must have taken instructed him to do. From the elevated 12th house realm to the mundane 6th house one, therefore. But also, from knowledge for the sake of knowledge (i.e. science: Gemini) to truthfulness (Sagittarius). The intended evolutionary direction the soul apparently wished to take was one of *truthfulness* (Sagittarius) *through service* (H6). What actually happened was a far cry indeed from that intention. Knowledge (Pluto in Gemini) was so badly manipulated and misused (SN of the Moon in Scorpio) as to constitute the worst affront to truth (SN in Scorpio conjunct Jupiter) humanity had seen for centuries.

NN in the 11th house Taurus - facilitator of the PPP - conjunct Saturn in the 11th house Taurus

The actualization of the NN of the Moon and its ruler would have facilitated this soul movement to the 6th house Sagittarius. (11) The 11th and the 6th house – Aquarius and

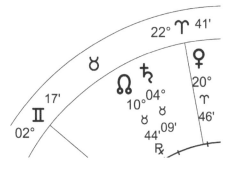

Virgo - have one thing in common: service. In the 11th house service is aimed at

[173]

some shared collective purpose. Always with the NN in the 11th house (or in Aquarius) there is an evolutionary intention to step back from and look objectively at the nature of prior-life development. It is a movement away from Leo subjectivity in the direction of Aquarian objectivity. The 11th house NN is challenging the 5th house SN to overcome its self-absorption and engage meaningfully with the collective, with some kind of humanitarian purpose.

Mengele was to have distanced himself from his megalomania and need for recognition in the medical world (Pluto in Gemini, SN in the 5th house Scorpio conjunct Jupiter) and to have offered his services to the world in such a way as to *secure the safety and survival* (Taurus) *of large groups of people* (H11) *and so consolidate* (Taurus) *his participation in a humanitarian* (H11) *cause on an egalitarian* (H11) *basis*, as opposed to the prominence his self-preoccupied 5th house SN sought.

This is how he would have facilitated his soul's 6th house Sagittarius evolutionary intentions.

From Saturn conjunct the NN of the Moon we glean that in a recent prior life responsibility (Saturn) *was* assumed for this 11th house Taurus intention. Prior-life selves turned their gaze away from 5th house self-aggrandizement in the direction of other (with Saturn's rulership of the 7th house corroborating this finding). Why then was it not followed through in this life? The answer to that question is written in the double Uranus-Mars skipped step in the 7th house, which perhaps we should place under the magnifying glass to understand this better. But before we do, there is one more thing we need to look at: the NN ruler.

NN ruler in the 10th house Aries

The 10th house is where we find Mengele's Hippocratic Oath written in capital letters: Mercury in Pisces conjunct his Sun in Pisces: *to heal* (Pisces) *the world* (H10). Together they point to the need for him to *take responsibility* (H10) *for this healing* (Pisces), which is what was made a start with in a recent prior life (Saturn conjunct the NN of the Moon 11th house Taurus).

[174]

The way *the survival of humanity* (NN 11th house Taurus) was to have been ensured, was for Mengele to have taken on *a pioneering* (NN ruler Aries) *and public* (NN ruler H10) *role so that he could be held accountable* (H10) *for his actions.* The exact antidote, therefore, to the extreme reclusiveness that typified his Pluto in the 12th house as the SN ruler: the experiments carried out in near total isolation circumventing the checks and balances of medical ethics.

Linking back the NN ruler to the NN of the Moon and to the PPP in an attempt to uncover *the Inner Logic of the Soul*

This makes sense when you link it back to the 6th house Sagittarius soul intention: the 10th house accountability that inevitably comes with being in the public eye is directly linked to truthfulness (Sagittarius) begotten *in* the act of service (6th house). In Auschwitz, after all, there were no monitoring mechanisms in place in terms of medical ethics. Mengele operated with impunity there thinking he would not be called to account.

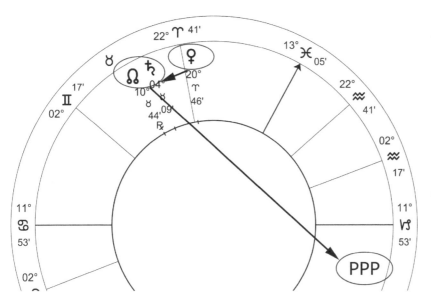

I hope you see how important it is to uncover *the Inner Logic of the Soul* this way: instead of a ragbag of three non-related pieces of information (PPP, NN and NN ruler interpreted separately), we now have a coherent whole that makes sense from the soul perspective. The PPP, the NN of the Moon and its ruler no longer float around aimlessly, like ice floes, in our analysis of the Evolutionary Axis but are connected in a meaningful way. Establishing this level of coherence in your analysis of the Evolutionary Axis is rather important therapeutically for it becomes the roadmap you fall back on in the often-stormy waters of client consultation.

Uranus in the 7th house Capricorn skipped step, conjunct Mars in the 7th house Aquarius skipped step

What you are looking at here is the boulder in the middle of the road which time and again made prior-life selves fall flat on their face when attempting to actualize their 11th house Taurus NN and its 10th house Aries NN ruler.

In previous chapters in the book, namely in the one on Lindbergh (chapter 5) and Simone (chapter 7), we saw how Uranus-Mars contacts, or Uranus in Aries or in the 1st house, can point to subconscious memories, stored in Uranus' non-linear memory vault, to do with having died young. Almost always in these contacts there is a sense of a project barely started and then coming to an abrupt, and sometimes violent end. In Mengele's chart Uranus and Aries are in contact three times:

1. Mars in Aquarius
2. Uranus conjunct Mars
3. Mars ruling the 11th house.

The 11th house is the house of large groups. Large Arian groups, in this case. Advancing armies. With this particular life script, it is not far-fetched to assume that Mengele in a past life *died as a young soldier at the hands of dysfunctional authority* (Uranus in Capricorn), *having overly projected meaning onto such authority and derived a sense of self from it* (Uranus in the 7th house), *indicating a problem around individuation.*

Enormous rage is accrued from lives that are cut short this way. It is held in the lower chakras and travels from lifetime to lifetime via the subtle body that is Chiron. The astrological correlate for that rage is Mengele's Mars skipped step. It speaks of *the will having become compromised through what was projected* (H7) *onto the person in terms of expectations* (H7) *in the context of large groups of people,* (Aquarius) again, in all likelihood, armies. It is fueled (Mars conjunct Uranus in Capricorn) by a deeper Capricorn reservoir of futility, burden and guilt, as well as muted grief, rising up from the depths of the individual subconscious, the non-linear mind stream of Uranus where all these memories of unresolved traumatic events lie dormant and dissociated: isolated pockets of rage ready to explode at any moment.

All this unresolved frustration, anger and rage as a result of an extremely impeded will in prior lives rules Aquarius in this chart: Uranus through its rulership of the 8ᵗʰ (the unspeakable transgressions) and the 9ᵗʰ house (the ideology) and Mars through that of the 11ᵗʰ house (the large groups of people). Presumably, the tree of life was felled prematurely time and again: youth slain in its prime. In this lifetime this subterranean repository of futility, grief and rage came out distorted, manifesting as Mengele's penchant for emotionally distant experimentation targeted primarily at large groups of people (Mars ruling H11), and withing those groups, you guessed it: at youth. It was also responsible for the compartmentalization of his emotional body (Moon H4 in Libra), which we shall discuss shortly.

In this life the need to provide medical care for soldiers committing atrocities while advancing through foreign territory presented itself in Mengele's frontline combat duty as a member of the Fifth Waffen-SS Viking Division. Coming directly before his assignment to Auschwitz and comprised between the end of 1940 and 1943, it is essential to understand this period as a re-enactment of trauma incurred by prior-life selves. We cannot begin to fathom the scope of the atrocities committed, the impact they must have had on Mengele or his possible participation in them.

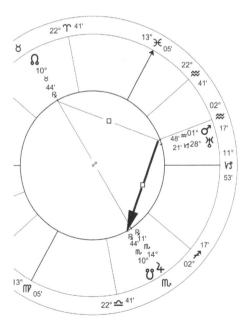

As the Viking Division advanced through Poland, unimaginable numbers of Jews were killed in town upon town.

What we do know is that a fellow physician in Auschwitz by the name of Horst Fischer, who had worked alongside Mengele in the Viking Division and had known him as unassuming and hardworking, in Auschwitz saw in him a "changed man." (12)

As you can see in the chart fragment, the double Uranus-Mars skipped step resolves through the south node of the Moon in its conjunction to Jupiter: Mengele is sent back to a situation where again he is exposed to a certain ideology (Jupiter) in his deep probing of the life force itself

[177]

(SN H5 Scorpio). This time round, however, he is invited to make new choices in those old circumstances. Those new choices are written in the SN of the Moon: Mengele is *to make a deep commitment* (Scorpio) *to the life-affirming force* (H5) *common to all of humanity as the foundational point of its existence*. The way he can go about that is expressed in the ruler of the resolution node, which we find in the 12th house Gemini: he is invited *to bring about universal healing* (12th house) *through his science* (Gemini), as opposed to using it at the exclusive service of some *deluded* (H12) *collective*.

It was not to be. With the clarity of hindsight, we can conclude that Mengele went down the old route.

Chiron and *the Trauma Helix*

With the Evolutionary Axis done and the main evolutionary issues mapped, what I would like to do now is take you through an exploration of *the Trauma Helix* and how Chiron relays the trauma charge, handed to it by Uranus, to Saturn.

Neptune in the 1st house Cancer and Uranus in the 7th house Capricorn: the two strands of *the Trauma Helix* (see chart p.169)

Having been exposed to, having embraced and, through science (Pluto in Gemini), having actively contributed to the imaginary and delusional (Pluto H12) concept of a purified collective (Pluto H12), the meaningless trauma coming in from other lifetimes has to do with *the delusion* (Neptune) *of a perfected* (Pisces) *racial and national* (Cancer) *identity* (H1).

As you can see, in constructing this sentence I follow the exact same steps I have been following all along and which I outlined in previous chapters:

1. what is the planet about?
2. house conditions planet
3. sign contextualizes the planet *in* the house

what is the planet about?	house conditions the planet	sign contextualizes planet *in* house

meaninglessness, delusion, perfection, perfected	identity (H1)	race, nation (Cancer)

I am reiterating these interpretative steps here so that you do not think I am making sentences up on the fly.

Meaninglessness is accrued in the soul through the delusional nature of this

notion. This misguided idea is what prior-life selves must have fought for in faraway trenches and paid with their lives for. *They died young as a result of what authority expected of them* (Uranus in the 7th house Capricorn), *and dying young obviously constituted trauma* (Uranus H7 Capricorn skipped step conjunct Mars H7 Aquarius skipped step)

Pluto in the 12th house Gemini: the soul's emotional and psychological identification with the Uranus and Neptune trauma strands

The way the soul pulls this double trauma charge into its own narrative is as *having sacrificed* (H12), *in vain, one's youth* (Gemini) *for a deluded* (H12) *antagonistic* (Gemini) *idea* (Gemini), something which ultimately was no more than a thought construct (Gemini).

Chiron in the 9th house Pisces (see chart p.169)

The way Chiron picks up this trauma parcel and translates it, so that the soul may know how to structure consciousness in its next vehicle, i.e. Mengele, is as *a pain caused by a severely deluded* (Pisces) *ideology* (9th house), which in this case was the ideology (9th house) of a perfected race and nation (Neptune 1st house Cancer ruling the Chiron pain). The Uranus strand of the trauma, i.e. complying (H7) with what authority (Capricorn) expects (H7) of one – with dying young as the hefty price tag (Uranus conjunct Mars) - shows up in the Chiron pain as the inability to clearly see (Pisces) the delusional (Pisces) nature of the ideology (H9) espoused by that authority. It is that part of the pain which can be traced back to Pluto's identification with the Uranus and Neptune strands as

[179]

having sacrificed (H12) *one's youth* (Gemini) *for what in the end was merely a product of the mind* (Gemini).

Again, in constructing the Chiron sentence, the same steps are followed:

what is the planet about?	house conditions the planet	sign contextualizes planet *in* house
a pain, a woundedness	ideology (H9)	delusion, the inability to see clearly (Pisces)

Saturn in the 11th house Taurus: the one to receive the pain so that consciousness in the soul's vehicle may be structured in a certain way.
(see chart p.169)

The soul, having identified with both trauma strands in the way described, knows exactly how it wants consciousness in its vehicle Mengele structured: it wants it structured in such a way as *to secure the safety and survival* (Taurus) *of the community* (H11) and so *consolidate* (Taurus) *his participation in a humanitarian* (H11) *cause on an egalitarian* (H11) *basis*. Logically so. How else is it going to get away from the 12th house elitism of the mythical land and people and into to the truthfulness (PPP in Sagittarius) begotten through everyday service to everyday, normal people (PPP 6th house)? This is the main reason why the NN ruler simply *had to* be in full public view (H10) where there would be public accountability (H10). Here, again, you see how the structure in the soul's consciousness (i.e. Saturn) is partly determined by the nature of the Chiron pain and partly by the soul's evolutionary intentions for the current life (as expressed in the PPP). Ultimately, the two are intertwined: the healing of a woundedness inflicted by a severely deluded world view has a great deal to do with whether the soul can find truthfulness through down-to-earth, pragmatic service (PPP H6 Sagittarius). To get out of the delusional 12th house mist it will have to embrace a fair bit of 6th house matter-of-factness.

The Planetary Nodes: the full evolutionary picture

What I would like to do now is bring in the planetary nodes of Chiron, Uranus and Neptune so that we may understand them in their entire evolutionary orbit, which expresses how the past of the pain and the trauma meets its intended healing in _the natal planet as the agent of change_.

(**Important notice.** From this point onward in the chapter, all NNs, whether lunar or planetary, are defined as _counterweight to past dynamics_. All natal placements, whether lunar or planetary, are defined as the _point of maximum resistance between their own south and north nodes_. The old response, coming from past dynamics and reflected _in_ the natal placement by house and sign is given in the text, as is the new response triggered by the resistance the Moon or natal planet feels between its south and north node [and its familiarity with the former]. It is the latter response which is _the agent of change_ and therefore evolutionary relevant).

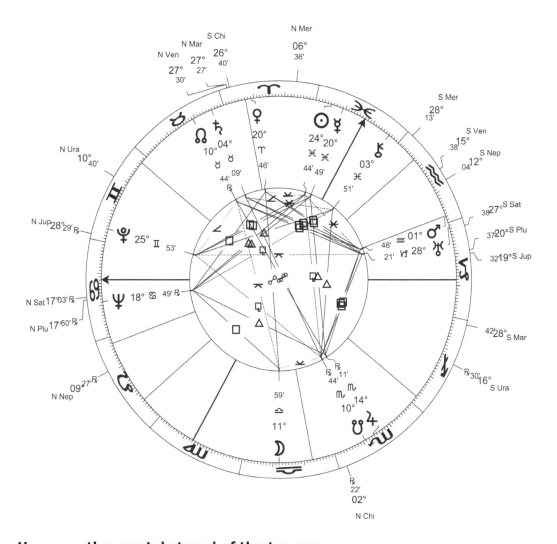

Uranus – the mental strand of the trauma

When you look at the past of the actual words, thoughts and mental images related to the 7th house Capricorn trauma, you will find **the SN of Uranus** at 16 degrees Sagittarius 30 minutes in the 6th house: *persecution* (H6) *through an ideology* (Sagittarius) *declaring people inferior* (H6). It is not too difficult to see how this dynamic got repeated in the soul's current vehicle Josef Mengele.

Why I associate Virgo with persecution may not be immediately clear to all readers, so please allow me to dedicate a few words to this. Our history is one of guilt, (13) either through the doctrine of sin and eternal damnation as part of religious teachings, or through declarations of unworthiness because you are a Catholic, a Protestant, a Jew, a Hindu, a Sunni, a Shiite, a woman, black. Whatever page of whatever history book you open, you will find the sad litany of declarations of unworthiness and inferiority, simply because someone else – from individuals to whole nations – feels you are born into the 'wrong' race, into the 'wrong' skin color, into the 'wrong' gender or because they deem you are on the 'wrong' side of some religious divide. The criticism levelled at individuals and whole swathes of the population alike in our long and bloody history is invariably followed by wholesale persecution and tends to end in war and genocide. This has become so much par for the course that we no longer realize what a profoundly sick thing it really is and how deeply it has scarred us, again both individually and collectively. We have come to expect it. Guilt and unworthiness, of course, in astrology we tend to associate with the archetype of Virgo.

Uranus' natal 7th house Capricorn placement carries the whole of that past within its combination of house and sign: *extreme inequality* (H7) *through projections*

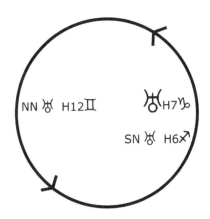

(H7) *coming from dysfunctional authority* (Capricorn) *defining one's sense of self.* This is what Uranus was familiar with and what Mengele felt drawn to as a young man: a political party (Capricorn) which projected inequality (H7) onto people, and which provided him with a sense of self. The SN of Uranus tells you he had been down the treacherous route of *persecution* (H6) *at the hands of an ideology* (Sagittarius) *which declared people inferior* (H6) before. All south nodes, whether lunar or planetary, show

[182]

you how past dynamics flow straight into the natal planet (or Moon) by house and sign and shape it.

We have now connected natal Uranus to its own past, which is half the orbit done. With the triple Uranus/Aquarius - Mars/Aries contact in Mengele's chart we should reckon with the possibility that prior-life selves died young fighting for this ideology, which, as we saw in the Chiron placement, was severely deluded.

The NN of Uranus stands at 10 degrees Gemini 40 minutes in the 12th house: the intended healing of the 7th house Capricorn trauma seems to come from *using his science* (Gemini) *to bring about universal healing* (12th house), something already present in the Hippocratic Oath of his 10th house Mercury, which he forsook upon his arrival in Auschwitz in April of 1943:

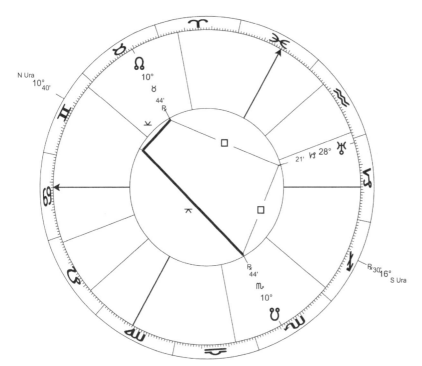

I will devise and order for them the best diet, according to my judgment and means; and I will take care that they suffer no hurt or damage. Nor shall any man's entreaty prevail upon me to administer poison to anyone; neither will I counsel any man to do so. Moreover, I will give no sort of medicine to any pregnant woman, with a view to destroy the child. Further, I will comport myself and use my knowledge in a godly manner. (14)

"To use my knowledge [Gemini] *in a Godly manner"* (H12) is perhaps the most succinct summation of Pluto H12 Gemini as the way in which the Uranus-Mars skipped step may resolve via the SN of the Moon in the 5th house Scorpio, an

[183]

intention fully supported by the NN of Uranus H12 Gemini. What Mengele did instead, was adhere to the tenets of a corrupt philosophy and use his science to gain notoriety: NN of Uranus inconjunct (in a state of crisis) SN of the Moon in the 5th house and half-sextile the NN of the Moon in the 11th house. (see chart p.183)

Uranus' natal placement now becomes the crucible for change, which in this case is the overcoming of the trauma. The natal Uranus, in other words, since it feels the resistance between its own south and north node, is spurred on to heal the trauma in a 7th house Capricorn way:

Mengele - SN of Uranus H6 Sagittarius	resistance	Mengele - NN of Uranus H12 Gemini
persecution (H6) through an ideology (Sagittarius) declaring people inferior (H6)	< >	use his science (Gemini) to bring about universal healing (H12); "to use my knowledge (Gemini) in a Godly manner" (H12)
the past streaming into the present and determining the old response: H7 Capricorn	**Uranus' choices**	**new response as the result of the resistance between the planet's SN and NN and its familiarity with the former: H7 Capricorn**
projected inequality (H7) coming from dysfunctional authority (Capricorn); the latter defining one's sense of self	< >	to assume responsibility (Capricorn) for the fundamental equality (H7) of all people

to assume responsibility (Capricorn) *for the fundamental equality* (H7) *of all people*, that is, the exact thing Mengele's son Rolf tried to convince him of when in 1977 he travelled half the globe for what was to be the last encounter with the man who had cast such a long and dark shadow over his life.

As they sat down for their first talk, Rolf, without beating about the bush, broached the subject of the Nazi worldview and raised the question why it deemed certain races and traits inferior to others. He quizzed his father on how it was that those considered inferior by the Nazis in many areas of life often shone

[184]

more brightly than those deemed superior. His father could not come up with any kind of satisfactory answer. (15)

Neptune – the meaninglessness strand of the trauma (see chart p.181)

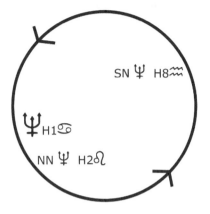

The SN of Neptune - the past of the meaninglessness trauma - streaming into the current life from multiple lifetimes - most tellingly and chillingly, sits at 12 degrees Aquarius 04 minutes in the 8th house, the house where *large groups of people* (Aquarius) *met with their deaths* (H8), rendering confirmation of our earlier assumption that prior-life selves would have been familiar with these dynamics. Needless to say, it is fully present in Neptune's natal placement, i.e. disillusionment as a result of *the delusion* (Neptune) *of a perfected* (Pisces) *racial and national* (Cancer) *identity* (H1).

The NN of Neptune, equally tellingly, we find at 9 degrees Leo 27 minutes in the 2nd house: the deepest meaningfulness can be found in *helping people survive* (H2) *in a celebration of life* (Leo).

The two opposing forces of Neptune's south and north node are now confronted with each other *in* the natal Neptune itself.

Mengele - SN of Neptune H8 Aquarius	resistance	Mengele - NN of Neptune H2 Leo
large groups of people (Aquarius) meeting with their deaths (H8)	< >	helping people survive (H2) in a celebration of life (Leo)
the past streaming into the present and determining the old response: H1 Cancer	**Neptune's choices**	**new response as the result of the resistance between the planet's SN and NN and its familiarity with the former: H1 Cancer**
the delusion (Neptune) of a perfected (Pisces) racial and national (Cancer) identity (H1)	< >	nurturing (Cancer) people's freedom and right to exist (H1)

Neptune's response to the confrontation - *nurturing* (Cancer) *people's freedom and right to exist* (H1) - is what will constitute evolution in terms of meaningfulness. The response is directly related to the PPP in the 6th house Sagittarius: truthfulness (Sagittarius) through everyday service (H6) in the world of everyday people, alleviating their everyday needs as a physician (H6), obviously needs Mengele to nurture people's freedom and right to exist (Neptune 1st house Cancer). If this response is not forthcoming and Mengele keeps subscribing to the *delusion* (Pisces) *of a perfected* (Pisces) *racial and national* (Cancer) *identity* (H1), then Neptune will not contribute to the 6th house PPP in terms of meaning. The meaning he then derives from this deluded notion will help the soul stay put in its 12th house Gemini comfort zone where it *offers its science* (Pluto in Gemini) *to a deluded* (Pluto in the 12th house) *collective* (Pluto in the 12th house) and to the equally deluded idea of some elevated and purified state (i.e. *Thule, The Third Reich*).

Chiron – the one to bring the trauma charge into the realm of Saturn (see chart p.181)

Not surprisingly (it is more or less there for all of us, see footnote [2] chapter 9), we find **the SN of Chiron** at 26 degrees Aries 40 minutes. The important information will come when we combine this with the house placement. Chiron's SN falls in the 11th house. With that we are handed the same combination of H11 and Aries we ran into with Uranus, making this a fourth contact between the two: *the past of the pain lies in having died young as part of a large group* (H11), *in all likelihood an army* (Aries: warrior). The SN of Chiron is reflected in Chiron itself, since it is the past that shaped the present: a pain caused by *the inability to clearly see* (Pisces) *the delusional* (Pisces) *nature of the ideology* (H9) they were made to defend through the sword and lost their lives for.

As we did with Richard Nixon (chapter 9) and Jim Jones (chapter 10), here too we see how the SN of the Chiron pain is directly linked to that of Uranus and Neptune: the pain caused by having died young as part of a large group (SN Chiron H11 Aries) is the necklace strung on the thread of persecution (SN Uranus H6) through an ideology (SN Uranus in Sagittarius) and large groups of people (SN Neptune in Aquarius) meeting with their deaths (SN Neptune H8).

The NN of Chiron at 2 degrees Scorpio 22 minutes falls in the 5th house: the counterweight to the past Chiron dynamics is offered by *a deep commitment*

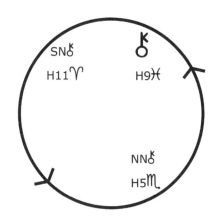

(Scorpio) *to the life force* (H5) *itself* - the very one that was so badly betrayed in the past by Mengele the physician (SN of the Moon H5 Scorpio conjunct Jupiter H5 Scorpio) – echoing the Leo signature of Neptune's NN H2 Leo: helping people survive [H2] in a celebration of life [Leo]. As one resounds in the other, we accidentally discover a kind of *'healing continuity,'* which makes sense since we have maintained all along that *in* the pain the healing is found, *in* the trauma the potential for overcoming it.

With the SN and the NN of Chiron creating resistance in the natal Chiron, the latter becomes **the crucible for healing**. The healing can be found when Mengele sees through the *delusional* (Pisces) *nature of the depraved ideology* (H9).

Mengele - SN of Chiron H11 Aries	resistance	Mengele – NN of Chiron H5 Scorpio
a pain caused by having died young as part of a large group (H11), in all likelihood an army (Aries: warrior)	< >	a deep commitment (Scorpio) to the life force (H5) itself
the past streaming into the present and determining the old response: H9 Pisces	**Chiron's choices**	**new response as the result of the resistance between the planet's SN and NN and its familiarity with the former: H9 Pisces**
a pain caused by the inability to clearly see (Pisces) the delusional (Pisces) nature of the ideology (H9) they were made to defend through the sword and lost their lives for	< >	seeing through the delusional (Pisces) nature of the depraved ideology (H9)

Healing continuity

The healing echo resounds through Uranus' NN too: to use his science (NN Uranus in Gemini) for universal healing (NN Uranus H12), or, as we saw before *"to use knowledge* [Gemini] *in a Godly manner."* (H12) These are the counterforces to the known and familiar: the natal planet and its SN as two peas in a pod. The actual healing and overcoming of the trauma will come about through the natal planets in the way we have described (resistance>new response). And, as we would expect, there is *'**healing continuity**'* there too: Chiron's healing (Pisces) potential of seeing the delusional (Pisces) nature of the ideology (H9) reverberates in the assuming of responsibility (Uranus in Capricorn) for the fundamental equality (Uranus H7) of all people and the nurturing (Neptune in Cancer) of people's freedom and right to exist (Neptune H1).

The healing of the Chiron woundedness is intimately connected to the soul's evolutionary intentions for the current life (as expressed in the 6th house PPP), as well as to the central and integrative principle around which Mengele's life revolves: *to heal* (Pisces) *my own integrity* (H10) *so that I may heal the world* (Sun 10th house Pisces, with the Hippocratic Oath glued to it: Mercury 10th house Pisces) clearly requires Mengele to see the fallacy of the ideology he subscribed to.

The opportunity for that came in September of 1977, two years before Mengele's death, when his son Rolf visited him in Brazil. Obviously, then thirty-three-year old Rolf wanted answers from his father. The trip to Brazil was hazardous for Rolf since he had to be extremely careful not to lead the Mossad, and others who had been trying to hunt Mengele down for decades, straight to his father's hiding place. During his stay with his him, Rolf broached the subject of the Nazi worldview cautiously. Challenging its premises, Mengele was not able to counter his son's arguments. When Rolf steered the discussion to Auschwitz, Mengele assumed neither guilt nor responsibility. His worldview (H9) had not changed from the days when he stood on the ramp at Auschwitz and carried out his infamous selections.

The Moon dynamics (see chart p.181)

Mengele's Moon is in the 4th house Libra. In order for him to intrude and so betray (SN of the Moon in Scorpio) the life force (SN of the Moon H5) itself and then seek to justify that trespassing through a perverted ideology (Jupiter 5th house Scorpio conjunct the SN of the Moon) - a dynamic operative in both prior-life selves and in the soul's current-life vehicle Mengele - his emotional body (H4) would have to have been seriously out of balance (Libra). No emotionally stable person could have committed the crimes Mengele did.

His NN of the Moon's efforts geared at *securing the safety and survival* (Taurus)

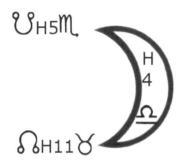

of large groups of people (H11) *and so consolidate* (Taurus) *his participation in a humanitarian* (H11) *cause on an egalitarian* (H11) *basis* would have facilitated *balance* (Libra) *in the emotional body* (H4) *getting restored*: you cannot not feel while being involved in this cause.

Those are the two forces battling it out in the Moon. There is, in other words, a constant tug of war between feeling and not feeling. Mengele felt for his son Rolf when, during a short stay with his wife Irene and child in November of 1944 in Freiburg, he had to take his son to the basement because of air raids:

"I remember so well how several times a day, during a short leave in Freiburg, I would rush – probably unnecessarily – the six-month old Rolf to the basement because of air raid warnings. I can still feel deeply – even today – that sense of worry and responsibility for the child." (16)

But he did not feel for the 1,158 Jewish men, women and children who, having been put on transport to Auschwitz from the Theresienstadt concentration camp, he sent to the gas chamber of Crematorium III only two weeks earlier, on October 20th 1944, to be followed, the very same day, by the murdering of one thousand young people between the ages of twelve and eighteen. (17)

Mengele´s emotional body (H4) *was compartmentalized* (Libra): on one end of the scales he was able to feel and on the other emotion had been disabled. This is the area where balance (Libra) needed to be restored. The compartmentalization was fueled by the unresolved frustration, anger and rage of his Mars skipped step percolating up from the subterranean depths of the Uranus realm, where it lay dissociated and fractured (Mars H7 Aquarius conjunct Uranus H7 Capricorn).

As we saw in the opening paragraphs of this chapter, the dehumanization required of the Nazis was first applied to the Nazis themselves: the collective was put before the individual at all times. A person was no more than a cogwheel in the giant clockwork of the National Socialist State. (18) The compartmentalization of the emotional body was a prerequisite for the ruthless torturing and killing that was expected of an SS soldier. Not all SS soldiers had their Moon in the 4th house Libra, of course. But Mengele did, and that is enough for our purposes.

Mengele - SN of the Moon H5 Scorpio	resistance	Mengele - NN of the Moon H11 Taurus
a deep intrusion (Scorpio) and betrayal (Scorpio) of the life force (H5) itself	< >	to secure the safety and survival (Taurus) of large groups of people (H11) and so consolidate (Taurus) his participation in a humanitarian (H11) cause on an egalitarian (H11) basis
the past streaming into the present and determining the Moon's old response: H4 Libra	**the Moon's choices**	**new response as the result of the resistance between the Moon's SN and NN and its familiarity with the former: H4 Libra**
a heavily compartmentalized (Libra) emotional body (H4)	< >	the decompartmentalization (Libra) of the emotional body (H4), thereby restoring balance (Libra) in it

I will now proceed to undertake a similar analysis for the remaining *planetary functions* in the chart of Mengele by looking at the nodes of his Mercury, Venus, Mars, Jupiter and Saturn, so that you get the full evolutionary picture of how each natal planet is invited to be an agent for the kind of change that would further soul evolution.

Mercury (see chart p.181)

The SN of Mercury - never too far away from Mercury itself since it does not stray from the Sun further than 28 degrees - is at 28 degrees Aquarius 13 minutes in the 9th house: *thinking* (Mercury) *in past-life selves was determined by an ideology* (H9) *of dissociation and fracturing* (Aquarius), an ideology of splitting people up into superior (i.e. the Aryan race) and inferior (Jews, gypsies, Communists, Roma, Slavs) and *causing trauma* (Aquarius).

That kind of thinking would have served those 5th house Scorpio past-life selves as they sought justification for their intrusion and manipulation (Scorpio) of the life force (H5) in a thoroughly perverted philosophy (SN of the Moon H5 Scorpio conjunct Jupiter H5 Scorpio): both the SN of Mercury and the SN of the Moon in its conjunction to Jupiter carry a distinctly Sagittarian signature.

Mercury's NN, also never too far away from natal Mercury, we find at 6 degrees

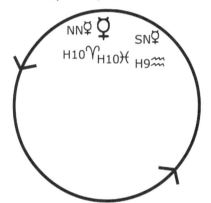

Aries 36 minutes in the 10th house: the counterforce Mercury will bring to its south node will consist of it *assuming responsibility* (H10) *for one's own independent* (Aries) *thinking*. Thinking (Mercury) itself is beckoned to grow up (H10), we could say, to mature (H10), so that it can forge its own path (Aries) instead of blindly following the tenets of an ideology (SN Mercury H9).

The past dynamic of allowing one's thinking to be determined by an ideology of dissociation and fracturing causing trauma is reflected in Mercury's *dissolution* (Pisces) *of self-determination* (H10) *in thinking* (Mercury) In other words: *assuming responsibility* (H10) *for self-rule* (H10) *in thinking* (Mercury) *gets diluted* (Pisces) as thinking hands its power over to the ideology. That information is corroborated in several places in the chart: in Neptune's delusion of racial and national identity (Neptune H1 Cancer) and in Chiron's pain of not seeing (Pisces) the delusional (Pisces) nature of the ideology (H9).

As the Mercury NN counterweight hits the old H9 Aquarius dynamic and Mercury's familiarity with it, the latter is challenged to come up with a new response: *to allow the integrity* (H10) *and self-determination* (H10) *of thinking* (Mercury) *to be healed* (Pisces), so that Mengele can dedicate himself to healing (Pisces) the world (H10) and stay true to the Hippocratic Oath (Mercury in Pisces) he took. The etymological root of the Latin word *'integra'* means *'intact,' 'whole,' 'of one piece.'* Thinking, in other words, is invited to become of itself again (H10 self-determination) and so *of one piece* (H10 integrity). This is what is in need of healing (Pisces). You can only do that when you think for yourself (NN Mercury H10 Aries): the NN *as the catalyst for change*, the natal planet as *the agent of change*.

We have now mapped the Mercury orbit as it reflects thinking patterns from the past (SN) and repeated invitations sent out to Mercury in the present (NN).

Mengele - SN of Mercury H9 Aquarius	resistance	Mengele - NN of Mercury H10 Aries
thinking (Mercury) in past-life selves was determined by an ideology (H9) of dissociation and fracturing (Aquarius) causing trauma (Aquarius)	< >	assuming responsibility (H10) for one's own independent (Aries) thinking; thinking (Mercury) itself is asked to grow up (H10)
the past streaming into the present and determining the old response: H10 Pisces	**Mercury's choices**	**new response as the result of the resistance between the planet's SN and NN and its familiarity with the former: H10 Pisces**
dissolution (Pisces) of self-determination (H10) in thinking (Mercury); assuming responsibility (H10) for self-rule (H10) in thinking (Mercury) gets diluted (Pisces)	< >	to allow the integrity (H10) and self-determination (H10) of thinking (Mercury) to be healed (Pisces)

This new Mercury response would be beneficial to the soul reaching its 6th house Sagittarius intention of truthfulness through service: *only when I disavow a false ideology and start thinking for myself, can I be of service* (PPP H6) *to those in need of help* (H6).

Venus (see chart p.181)

[192]

The SN of Venus will reveal what prior-life Mengele's primary relationship was with as they (SN of the Moon) sought to wield control over the life force itself and justify their doing so through a perverted ideology (SN of the Moon H5 Scorpio conjunct Jupiter H5 Scorpio). We find it in the 8th house Aquarius: *their primary relationship was with leading large groups of people* (Aquarius) *to their deaths* (H8). I do not think the observation is in need of further comment.

The SN of Venus dynamic of *leading large groups of people* (Aquarius) *to their deaths* (H8) can be seen in the natal Venus as *the systematic oppression* (Capricorn) *of an entire people's right to exist* (Aries) *through the structures, rules and regulations* (H10) *of a dysfunctional authority* (H10) *apparatus*. That is

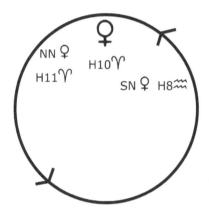

how Venus' past comes back in its natal placement, and it is where the familiarity between the two lies. It is also exactly what was re-enacted in the current life of Josef Mengele: the extermination of the Jews (SN Venus H8 Aquarius) was a highly structured and planned operation (Venus H10 Aries).

The counterforce to that dynamic - felt *in* the natal Venus H10 Aries - is going to come from the NN of Venus, which is in the 11th house Aries: Mengele's *prime relationship is to be with a humanitarian cause* (H11) *so that people are allowed their identity and right to exist* (Aries), including Mengele himself who has, so we learn from looking into several planetary south nodes, lifetime upon lifetime basically been little more than the mouthpiece of someone else's ideology. Please note how this Venus NN impulse comes back in its higher octave Neptune in the 1st house Cancer: *nurturing* (Cancer) *people's freedom and right to exist* (H1). (19)

Fellow physician Horst Fischer, later convicted for his crimes at Auschwitz and executed, in his declarations commented how Mengele was blind to any human problem and only saw that of race. He described him as *"the most convinced among us of the necessity of the destruction of the Jewish people."* (20) In other words: the one most blinded (Chiron in Pisces) by the ideology (Chiron H9) (SN of Mercury H9 Aquarius; Neptune's old H1 Cancer response; SN of Neptune H8 Aquarius, SN Venus H8 Aquarius).

Through the resistance she feels between the old dynamic and the invitation of a new one, Venus is challenged to come up with a new response: *to engage in a relationship* (Venus) *with the integrity* (H10) *needed to allow people their identity and right to exist* (Aries).

It is obvious how Venus' new, 10th house Aries response would further 6th house Sagittarius soul evolution: coming to a place of truthfulness through service (PPP H6 Sagittarius) is very much going to depend on Mengele's willingness to indeed develop the kind of inner intactness and wholeness (H10 integrity) needed to allow people their identity and right to exist.

Mengele - SN of Venus H8 Aquarius	resistance	Mengele - NN of Venus H11 Aries
prime relationship in prior-life selves was with leading large groups of people (Aquarius) to their deaths (H8)	< >	prime relationship is to be with a humanitarian cause (H11) so that people are allowed their identity and right to exist (Aries)
the past streaming into the present and determining the old response: H10 Aries	**Venus' choices**	**new response as the result of the resistance between the planet's SN and NN and its familiarity with the former: H10 Aries**
the systematic oppression (Capricorn) of an entire people's identity and right to exist (Aries) through the structures, rules and regulations (H10) of a dysfunctional authority (H10) apparatus	< >	to engage in a relationship (Venus) with the integrity (H10) needed to allow people their identity and right to exist (Aries)

Mars (see chart p.181)

Mars' SN is going to provide information on what prior-life selves' conscious actions and desires were aimed at. We find it at 28 degrees Sagittarius 42 minutes in the 6th house: *persecution at the hands of an ideology which declared certain people inferior* (H6), as it would be in this life. This past dynamic, which the natal Mars is very familiar with, is reflected in its *aloofness and non-involvement* (Aquarius) *as it projects inequality* (H7) *onto large groups of people*

[194]

(Aquarius). At the center of the Nazi ideology, after all, lay the belief in a superior Nordic race and the inferiority of other races. Especially SS members, and Mengele was one of them, were indoctrinated with the idea that they were a "master race". This is the lack of empathy Horst Fischer, himself a criminal, noted in Mengele. It is the compartmentalization in the emotional body we encountered in Mengele's 4th house Libra Moon.

Mars' NN is in the 11th house at 27 degrees Aries 27 minutes: the counterweight to this past dynamic and Mars' familiarity with it comes from an invitation *to aim conscious actions and desires at a socially humanitarian cause* (H11) *so that people are allowed their identity and right to exist* (Aries).

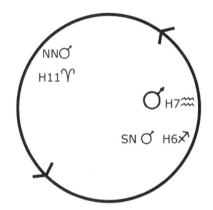

As this NN of Mars energy hits the old groove it triggers a new response in the natal Mars: *to aim conscious actions and desires* (Mars) *at looking objectively* (Aquarius) *at the whole issue of projected inequality* (H7) *and so liberate* (Aquarius) *myself from it.*

These three points are on one and the same orbit and constantly in dialogue with each other. If Mars indeed manages to come up with this new response, then that would help the soul get to the 6th house Sagittarius Pluto Polarity Point: only when one is fully seized of people's fundamental equality, can one serve them.

Mengele - SN of Mars H6 Sagittarius	resistance	Mengele - NN of Mars H11 Aries
conscious actions and desires aimed at persecution at the hands of an ideology (Sagittarius) which declared certain people inferior (H6)	< >	to aim conscious actions and desires at a humanitarian cause (H11) so that people are allowed their identity and right to exist (Aries)
the past streaming into the present and determining the old response: H7 Aquarius	**Mars' choices**	**new response as the result of the resistance between the planet's SN and NN and its familiarity with the former: H7 Aquarius**

aloofness and non-involvement (Aquarius) as he projects inequality (H7) onto large groups of people (Aquarius)		to aim conscious actions and desires at looking objectively (Aquarius) at the whole issue of projected inequality and so liberate (Aquarius) myself from it

Far-reaching conclusions can be drawn from the fact that the north nodes of Venus and Mars are closely conjunct in the 11th house Aries and both conjunct

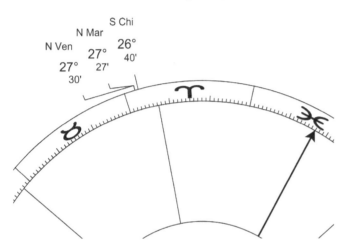

the SN of Chiron: the pain caused by having died young as part of a large group, in all likelihood an army – where my identity and right to exist would have been all but obliterated - is exactly what the soul wants undone by having all conscious actions and desires (NN Mars) as well

as the prime relationship (NN Venus) aimed at the larger humanitarian cause of allowing everyone (H11) their identity and right to exist (Aries). One is the mirror image of the other.

Jupiter (see chart p.181)

What was the lens through which prior-life selves looked out into the world? How did they see things? The answer to those questions is written in the SN of Jupiter. It sits in the 7th house at 19 degrees Capricorn 32 minutes (21): prior-life

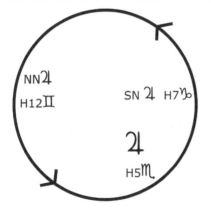

Mengele's worldview was determined by *dysfunctional authority* (Capricorn) *projecting inequality* (H7) *onto others through oppressive rule* (Capricorn). I hope you see how that lens would have served prior-life selves in executing their genetic transgressions of life itself (SN of the Moon H5 Scorpio).

This is the dynamic the natal Jupiter comes into the current life with and is familiar with. *'Familiar'* means safe and safe is what it will therefore default towards. As such this past 7th house Capricorn dynamic is recognizable in the natal Jupiter in that *it espouses a thoroughly perverted and corrupt* (Scorpio) *worldview* (Jupiter) *claiming world prominence* (H5).

The invitation coming from Jupiter's NN could not be more different. We find it in the 12th house at 28 degrees Gemini 29 minutes. The counterweight to Jupiter's familiarity with its south node is that it beckons Mengele to view the world (Jupiter) through *the need to "use his knowledge* (Gemini) *in a Godly manner"* (H12) - which is what he had sworn to do and why Jupiter's NN is so close to Pluto there as part of the resolution to the double Uranus-Mars skipped step in the 7th house. As he learns to view the world this way, Mengele will *strike up a dialogue* (Gemini) *with what is universally* (H12) *true* (Jupiter) as opposed to subscribing to a sick philosophy (Jupiter in Scorpio) that benefitted only an elitist few thinking themselves above (H5) the common heap of mankind.

Mengele - SN of Jupiter H7 Capricorn	resistance	Mengele - NN of Jupiter H12 Gemini
prior-life selves´ worldview was determined by dysfunctional authority (Capricorn) projecting inequality (H7) onto others through oppressive rule (Capricorn)	< >	the need to *"use his knowledge* (Gemini) *in a Godly manner"* (H12); to strike up a dialogue (Gemini) with what is universally (H12) true (Jupiter)
the past streaming into the present and determining the old response: H5 Scorpio	**Jupiter's choices**	**new response as the result of the resistance between the planet's SN and NN and its familiarity with the former: H5 Scorpio**
espousing a thoroughly perverted and corrupt (Scorpio) worldview (Jupiter) claiming world prominence (H5)	< >	to deeply commit (Scorpio) to life itself, to the life-affirming force (H5) common to all of humanity as its unalienable birthright (H5)

As this H12 Gemini impulse confronts the old H7 Capricorn tendencies and Jupiter's familiarity with them, it hopes to trigger a new response in Jupiter: to *deeply commit* (Scorpio) *to life itself, to the life-affirming force* (H5) *common to all of humanity as its unalienable birthright*, which can be said to be the assignment of Mengele's Hippocratic Oath: to *use his knowledge* (Mercury) *to heal* (Mercury in Pisces) *the world* (Mercury H10). The commitment in Jupiter's new response, therefore, is to 5th house Eros, understood as the need to connect with other sentient beings and celebrate (H5) that connection. If Jupiter rises to the occasion, then this deep 5th house commitment obviously is going to help the soul get out of the seclusion of the 12th house - where knowledge was put to the service of the mythical and purified nation at the exclusion of the rest of mankind - and into the kind of everyday service (PPP H6) that would lead to truthfulness (PPP Sagittarius).

Saturn (see chart p.181)

What was the structure of consciousness in prior-life selves? What would the wiring have looked like had we been able to open consciousness up and have a peek inside? We turn to the SN of Saturn for an answer to those questions. We

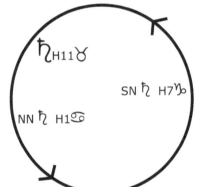

find it in the 7th house at 27 degrees Capricorn 38 minutes, a mere degree away from Mengele's Uranus there: consciousness in prior-life selves was structured in such a way as *to project inequality* (H7) *onto others from a lack of inner integrity* (Capricorn) *through the imposition of oppressive rule* (Capricorn).

This dynamic, since it shaped the natal Saturn in the 11th house Taurus, comes back in its house and sign in that it *effectuates the non-survival* (Taurus) of *large groups of people* (H11), whole swathes of society.

Saturn's NN is in the 1st house at 17 degrees Cancer 3 minutes and right on his Neptune there. It beckons Saturn *to nurture* (Cancer) *people's identity, freedom and right to exist* (H1). When it impacts the old dynamics, it hopes Saturn will be able to formulate a new response. You will find it in the table on page 199.

Mengele - SN of Saturn H7 Capricorn	resistance	Mengele - NN of Saturn H1 Cancer
consciousness in prior-life selves was structured in such a way as to project inequality (H7) onto others from a lack of inner integrity (Capricorn) and through the imposition of oppressive rule (Capricorn)	< >	to nurture (Cancer) people's identity, freedom and right to exist (H1)
the past streaming into the present and determining the old response: H11 Taurus	**Saturn's choices**	**new response as the result of the resistance between the planet's SN and NN and its familiarity with the former: H11 Taurus**
consciousness receiving the impact of past dynamics in such a way as to effectuate the non-survival (Taurus) of large groups of people (H11)	< >	consciousness structured in such a way as to secure the safety and survival (Taurus) of large groups of people (H11) and so consolidate (Taurus) Mengele's participation in a humanitarian (H11) cause on an egalitarian (H11) basis

Chiron aspects

Had Saturn risen to the occasion, then service to a larger whole (PPP H6) might have been rendered, a conclusion corroborated by its rulership of the 7th house (the public at large). Please note Saturn's sextile to Chiron in the 9th house Pisces: there is an ease in the energy flow between *Mengele seeing through the delusional nature of the depraved ideology* (Chiron H9 Pisces) and *a consciousness structured in such a way as to secure the safety and survival* (Taurus) *of large groups of people* (H11), the same way there is an ease in the energy flow between *the inability to clearly see* (Pisces) *the delusional* (Pisces) *nature of the ideology* (Chiron H9 Pisces) and *Mengele responding to the old dynamic of effectuating the non-survival* (Taurus) *of large groups of people* (H11).

[199]

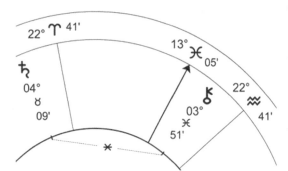

The energy is there as an invitation, a call to action. If Mengele heeds the former, there will be evolution. If he heeds the latter, there will not. All depends on which one he goes for. This is a fine example of how generalized descriptions of Chiron aspects – or indeed any aspects – go against the very heart of therapeutic evolutionary astrology: once the choice the natal planet is put before has been identified – the inevitable result of looking at its full orbit and - no two planets can be in any kind of pre-described dialogue with each other, nor can any aspect be called 'easy' or 'difficult'.

Does that mean that a sextile in therapeutic evolutionary astrology is the same as a square? Anything but. What it means is that there is the same degree of choice as in the sextile but an altogether different nature of the dialogue allowing for the choice. Unlike the ease in energy flow proper to the sextile, a square represents a dynamic tension between two planets. Mengele's Saturn is in that kind of dialogue with his Mars in the 7th house Aquarius. There is a dynamic tension between *a consciousness structured in such a way as to secure the safety and survival of large groups of people* (Saturn H11 Taurus) and *the aloofness and non-involvement as Mengele projects inequality onto a large group of people* (Mars H7 Aquarius), the same way there is a dynamic tension between *a consciousness defaulting to the old dynamic of*

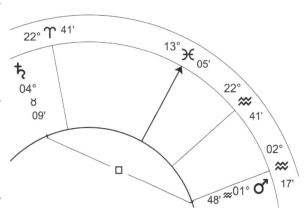

seeking to effectuate the non-survival of large groups of people (Saturn H11 Taurus) and *a conscious will aimed at looking objectively at the whole issue of projected inequality and so liberate oneself from it* (Mars H7 Aquarius). The dynamic tension of the square is there for Mengele to feel and resolve. If he does, truthfulness through everyday pragmatic service will be attained, which is where the soul desires to evolve towards (PPP H6 Sagittarius). If he does not, it will not. To say then, that a sextile is an 'easy' aspect and a square a 'difficult' one, is to miss the whole point of why the soul has calibrated the psyche of its instrument Mengele the way it has. The sextile makes a specific contribution to the possibility of soul evolution and so does the square. Their nature is different, their goal the same.

What is 'easy' about Mengele's trine between Chiron and Pluto? You are looking at a dialogue (aspect) between *science offered to some perfected collective* (Pluto H12 Gemini) *living in a mythical land* and *a severely deluded ideology* (Chiron H9 Pisces). At another level the trine is about a conversation between *having*

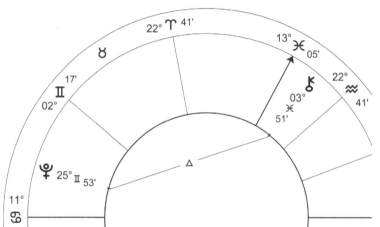

sacrificed, in vain, one's youth for a deluded, antagonistic idea, something that was no more than a thought construct - Pluto H12 Gemini as part of the Trauma Helix – and *the inability to clearly see the delusional nature of the ideology* (Chiron H9 Pisces). In addition, the exchange is between *bringing about universal healing through his science* (Pluto H12 Gemini) - Pluto as belonging to the resolution node for the double Uranus-Mars skipped step - and Mengele *seeing through the delusional nature of the depraved ideology* (Chiron H9 Pisces). All that is at play here.

The question to ask oneself when contemplating this aspect is: in what way would a dialogue between two players so much on the same wavelength contribute to the soul getting to the 6th house Sagittarius? That question can be answered for each of the three levels at which the dialogue is happening, and it would *need* to be answered if the aspect were to be understood evolutionary, that is, in terms of soul evolution. Off-the-peg interpretations of aspects, therefore, is something therapeutic evolutionary astrology has no use for. To be able to work with people therapeutically, information needs to be soul-specific, not generalized.

We have now traced the orbital movement of all the planets (and the Moon) as they relate to where the soul is coming from (Pluto by house and sign) and where it seeks to evolve towards (PPP):

Pluto H12 Gemini	natal planet as *the agent of change* conducive to evolutionary growth: the felt resistance between its south and north leading to a new response (or not, which, evolutionary speaking, is equally important)	Pluto Polarity Point H6 Sagittarius
south node		north node
the genetic manipulation of the life force (H5 Scorpio) – constituting an intrusion (Scorpio) and betrayal (Scorpio) of it - seeking its justification in a perverted (Scorpio) ideology (SN of the Moon conjunct Jupiter) through which recognition, acclaim and dominance (H5) are sought	**Moon** the decompartmentalization (Libra) of the emotional body (H4), thereby restoring balance (Libra) in it	to secure the safety and survival (Taurus) of large groups of people (H11) and so consolidate (Taurus) his participation in a humanitarian (H11) cause on an egalitarian (H11) basis, as opposed to the prominence his self-preoccupied 5th house SN sought
thinking (Mercury) in past-life selves was determined by an ideology (H9) of dissociation and fracturing (Aquarius) causing trauma (Aquarius)	**Mercury** to allow the integrity (H10) and self-determination (H10) of thinking (Mercury) to be healed (Pisces)	assuming responsibility (H10) for one's own independent (Aries) thinking; thinking (Mercury) itself is asked to grow up (H10)
prime relationship in prior-life selves was with leading large groups of people (Aquarius) to their deaths (H8)	**Venus** to engage in a relationship (Venus) with the integrity (H10) needed to allow people their identity and right to exist (Aries)	prime relationship is to be with a humanitarian cause (H11) so that people are allowed their identity and right to exist (Aries)

	Mars	
conscious actions and desires aimed at persecution through an ideology (Sagittarius), which declared certain people inferior (H6)	to aim conscious actions and desires at looking objectively (Aquarius) at the whole issue of projected inequality and so liberate (Aquarius) myself from it	to aim conscious actions and desires at a humanitarian cause (H11) so that people are allowed their identity and right to exist (Aries)
	Jupiter	
prior-life selves´ worldview was determined by dysfunctional authority (Capricorn) projecting inequality (H7) onto others through oppressive rule (Capricorn)	to deeply commit (Scorpio) to life itself, to the life-affirming force (H5) common to all of humanity as its unalienable birthright	the need to *"use my knowledge (Gemini) in a Godly manner"* (H12); to strike up a dialogue (Gemini) with what is universally (H12) true (Jupiter)
	Saturn	
consciousness in prior-life selves was structured in such a way as to project inequality (H7) onto others from a lack of inner integrity (Capricorn) and through the imposition of oppressive rule (Capricorn)	consciousness structured in such a way as to secure the safety and survival (Taurus) of large groups of people (H11) and so consolidate (Taurus) Mengele's participation in a humanitarian (H11) cause on an egalitarian (H11) basis	to nurture (Cancer) people's identity, freedom and right to exist (H1)
	Chiron	
a pain caused by having died young as part of a large group (H11), in all likelihood an army (Aries: warrior)	seeing through the delusional (Pisces) nature of the depraved ideology (H9) and so heal the Chiron pain	a deep commitment (Scorpio) to the life force (H5) itself
	Uranus	
persecution (H6) at the hands of an ideology (Sagittarius) declaring people inferior (H6)	to assume responsibility (Capricorn) for the fundamental equality (H7) of all people and so overcome the Uranus trauma	use his science (Gemini) to bring about universal healing (H12); *"to use my knowledge (Gem) in a Godly manner"* (H12)
	Neptune	
	nurturing (Cancer) people's freedom and right to exist	

large groups of people (Aquarius) meeting with their deaths (H8)	(H1) and so overcome the Neptune trauma	helping people survive (H2) in a celebration of life (Leo)
Pluto H12 Gemini		**Pluto Polarity Point H6 Sagittarius**
south node	**natal planet as _the agent of change_ conducive to evolutionary growth: the felt resistance between its south and north leading to a new response (or not, which, evolutionary speaking, is equally important)**	**north node**

The central and integrative principle around which Mengele's life and all planets revolve (Sun) is: *to heal* (Pisces) *integrity* (H10) *so that he may heal* (Pisces) *the world* (H10) *and stay true to the Hippocratic Oath* (Mercury H10 Pisces conjunct the Sun) *he took.*

On 17 January 1945, when Mengele fled the Auschwitz concentration camp as the Russian troops were closing in, his transiting Cancer-Capricorn Nodal Axis was squared by his natal Venus H10 Aries, ruler of the NN. The transiting Capricorn SN had already touched Uranus in the 7th house Capricorn while its counterpart was bang on his Neptune in the 1st house Cancer and therefore on the NN of his Saturn and Pluto there: a clear invitation for him to see through his delusions (Neptune) about racial and national (Cancer) identity (1st house). Venus squaring his transiting Nodal Axis was yet another invitation to finally assume responsibility (10th house) for his actions (Aries). He would run away from that responsibility for the rest of his life, even when in his final years his own son travelled half the globe in a last-ditch attempt to persuade him to do otherwise.

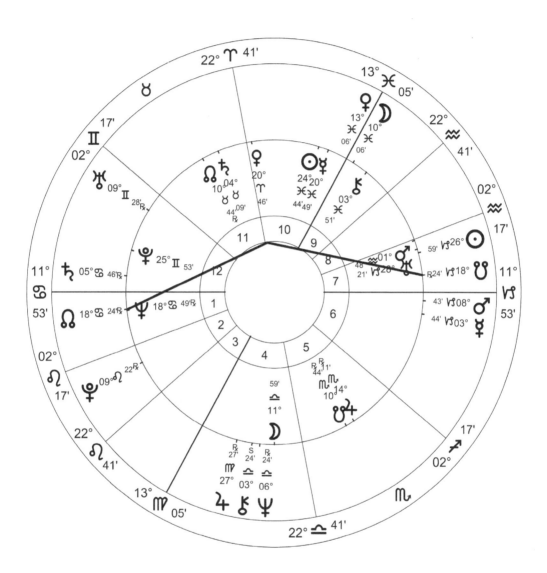

Josef Mengele, transits 17 January 1945

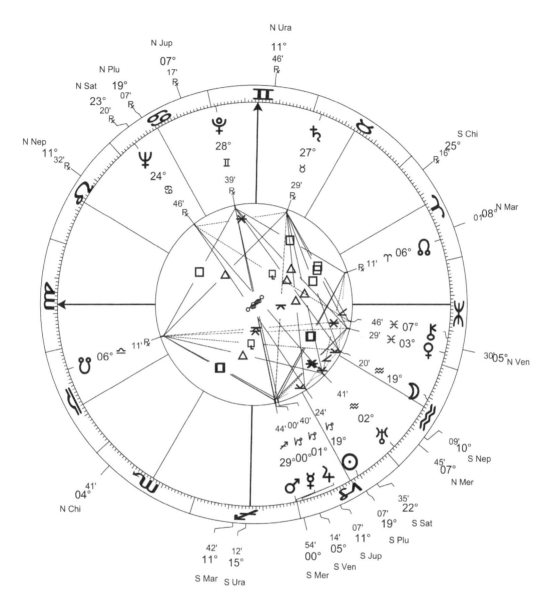

Richard Nixon, 9 January 1913, 21:35 hrs., Yorba Linda, California, RR:AA

"Let us begin by committing ourselves to the truth, to see it like it is and to tell it like it is, to find the truth, to speak the truth and to live the truth. That's what we will do." (1)

A few years before Richard Milhouse Nixon took up law practice in his hometown Whittier, he had his palm read by a youngster by the name of Dorothy Welch, who had a knack for fortunetelling. What she saw was a high-flying career that would suddenly come to a screeching halt by some sort of disaster or accident. Not wanting to cause distress in the young Nixon, whom she thought of as rather serious, she decided to give him a watered-down version of the sharp curve-off she had seen. (2) She may also have wanted to spare him the full version for being the sister of the woman Nixon had fallen in love with and planned to marry: Ola Florence Welch. How would young Nixon have reacted had Dorothy Welch given him chapter and verse? She might just as well have because Ola would eventually reject Richard, not least because he two-timed her. How would he have taken a full account of what she saw, having expressed from a very early age his wish to occupy high political office? How would he have responded had an astrologer been around with access to the kind of analysis we are about to embark on in this chapter? An astrologer who understood the full evolutionary picture for having looked at the entire orbit of each of the planets in his chart. We shall never know.

Mercury (see chart p.207)

To know what thinking was directed at in the soul's 1st house Libra prior-life egoic structures, prior-life selves, in other words, we turn to the SN of Mercury. We find it in the 4th house at 0 degrees Capricorn 54 minutes closely conjunct Mercury itself: to engage in relationships (SN of the Moon Libra) with the sole purpose of furthering their own agenda (SN of the Moon H1), *prior-life selves would have directed their thinking* (Mercury) *at the suppression* (Capricorn) *of the emotional body* (H4). Logically so, because when I exploit people, I cannot allow myself to feel.

We need not formulate how this past dynamic is reflected in Mercury in the 4th house Capricorn since we are handed the information on a silver platter: they are identical. The important information that can be had from this fact, however, is that the natal planet – by definition familiar with its own SN irrespective of where it is in the chart – is now seen to be hand in glove with its own past. What that means in practical terms is that it is going to be rather difficult for this

Mercury to bid farewell to the other pea in the pod, so to speak. With all that 4th house Capricorn Mercurial energy we get a fairly good idea of how the Mercury skipped came to be.

Looking at Mercury orbitally, the opposing force to Mercury treading the same well-worn path is going to come from its NN. It is in the 5th house at 7 degrees Aquarius 45 minutes: *thinking directed at stepping back and objectively*

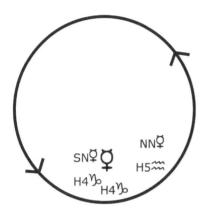

assessing (Aquarius) *the emotional insecurity that underlies Nixon's need to be an undisputed leader and always come out on top* (H5).

What happens when this counterforce hits Mercury and its SN, who are like jam and bread, is that it will cause the former to *direct thinking* (Mercury) *at maturing* (Capricorn) *emotionally* (H4). This is its new response. Instead of holding (Capricorn) the ball of emotion (H4) under water, Mercury is now invited to *allow the emotional body* (H4) *to grow up* (Capricorn). That way integrity (Capricorn) is brought to it, and integrity is what is needed if the soul is to get to the emotional truthfulness of the 4th house Sagittarius Pluto Polarity Point. Seeing the emotional insecurity feeding the craving for attention for what it is (NN of Mercury H5 Aquarius) is needed to trigger that kind of response in the natal Mercury (the planetary NN as *the catalyst for change*, the new response of the natal planet as *the agent of change*).

Nixon - SN of Mercury H4 Capricorn	resistance	Nixon - NN of Mercury H5 Aquarius
prior-life selves would have directed their thinking (Mercury) at the suppression (Capricorn) of the emotional body (H4)	< >	thinking directed at stepping back and objectively assessing (Aquarius) the emotional insecurity underlying Nixon's need to be an undisputed leader and come out on top (H5)
the past streaming into the present and determining the old response:	**Mercury's choices**	**new response as the result of the resistance between the planet's SN and NN and its**

H4 Capricorn		familiarity with the former: H4 Capricorn
thinking (Mercury) directed at the suppression (Capricorn) of the emotional body (H4)	< >	thinking (Mercury) directed at maturing (Capricorn) emotionally (H4), allowing the emotional body (H4) to grow up (Capricorn)

We have now understood Mercury's orbital movement as it relates to where the soul (and its prior-life egoic structures) is coming from and where it seeks to evolve towards. Our next port of call is Venus.

Venus (see chart p.207)

The SN of Venus is going to tell us what prior-life selves' prime relationship was with. We find the SN of Venus at 5 degrees Capricorn 14 minutes in the 4th house: *the prime relationship was with the suppression* (Capricorn) *of the emotional body* (H4). We are not surprised to find this: to work your way up the ladder in the hierarchical 10th house environments through the clever use of words (Gemini) and the equally clever use of information (Gemini), the emphasis would have been entirely on thinking and scheming as opposed to feeling.

This dynamic can be seen in Venus by house and sign: for me to relate (Venus)

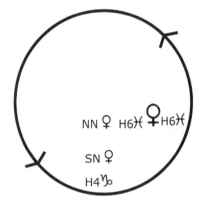

to how I can imply guilt (H6) in others so that I can come out looking all pure and virtuous (Pisces), the emotional body (SN Venus H4) would have had to be turned into a bock of granite (SN Venus Capricorn).

The back-force to this dynamic comes from the NN of Venus in the 6th house at 5 degrees Pisces 30 minutes, sandwiched between Venus and Chiron

and closely conjunct the former, therefore: *to relate* (Venus) *to discerning* (H6) *who I am actually serving* (H6), self or other, and to then *make the adjustments* (H6) *needed to offer* (Pisces) *the right kind* (H6 discernment) *of service* (H6).

When this NN impulse hits the SN of Venus and Venus' familiarity with it, it will cause the latter to formulate a new response: *to heal* (Pisces) *my relationship* (Venus) *with true service from a place of humility* (H6). This healing (Pisces) will come about when Nixon develops the kind of discernment (H6) the NN of Venus seeks: the moment I know what or whom I should *not* be serving (Virgo: not this but that), I can make the adjustments (H6) required to serve what or whom I should be serving. (the planetary NN as *the catalyst for change*, the new response of the natal planet as *the agent of change*).

Here we have the opposite of what we encountered in Mercury: where with Mercury it was its own SN that stood by its side, with Venus it is its NN who flanks it. And for good evolutionary reasons: to break the dynamic of relating to the suppression of the emotional body it is imperative that this 6th house discernment impulse receive a double dose.

When acted upon, it is going to help the soul actualize the intended 4th house honesty (Sagittarius) in the emotional body (H4): when my relationship (Venus) with service from a place of humility (H6) is healed (Pisces), the soul discovers what it is like to be emotionally truthful.

Nixon - SN of Venus H4 Capricorn	resistance	Nixon - NN of Venus H6 Pisces
the prime relationship in prior-life selves was with the suppression (Capricorn) of the emotional body (H4)	< >	to relate (Venus) to discerning (H6) who I am actually serving (H6), self or other, and to then make the adjustments (H6) needed to offer (Pisces) the right kind (H6 discernment) of service (H6)
the past streaming into the present and determining the old response: **H6 Pisces**	**Venus's choices**	**new response as the result of the resistance between the planet's SN and NN and its familiarity with the former: H6 Pisces**
relate (Venus) to how I can imply guilt in others (H6) so that I can come out looking all pure and virtuous (Pisces)	< >	to heal (Pisces) my relationship (Venus) with true service from a place of humility (H6)

This is the entire Venus orbit understood against the backdrop of where the soul is coming from and where it wishes to go. Let us now do the same for Mars.

Mars (see chart p.207)

The conscious actions and desires of prior-life selves are found in the SN of Mars in the 3rd house at 11 degrees Sagittarius 42 minutes: *the distortion* (Sagittarius) *of facts* (H3) *and dishonest* (Sagittarius) *use of information* (H3). (3) Again, we are not surprised. When I use people as pawns in my own chess game (SN of the Moon H1 Libra) to get my hands on information that can be used (against others) to get to the top (Pluto H10 Gemini), then I am going to use that information as I see fit and twist it to serve my purposes.

When trying to formulate a given planetary south node, it is important to understand how the dynamic you are looking at would have served prior-life selves. We did this for Mercury (thinking, thought patterns), for Venus (relationship), and now we are doing it again for Mars (conscious actions and desires). Whatever you find for whatever planetary function you are looking at,

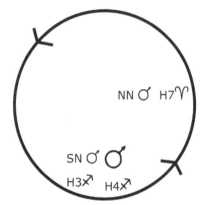

the conclusion needs to fit the dynamics you found when you looked at the SN of the Moon and its ruler.

Since the natal Mars is entirely shaped by its 3rd house Sagittarius past, this tendency to do with the facts as I please can be seen in the natal Mars in that it would need to be emotionally dishonest, not just to others but primarily to itself.

The resistance to this familiar dynamic now comes from the NN of Mars at 8 degrees Aries 1 minute in the 7th house [*on* the NN of the Moon!]: it is telling Mars and its SN in no uncertain terms to *aim its conscious actions and desires at equality in relationship* (H7) - as a result of truly listening to other - *so that both parties' independence and freedom* (Aries) *while in relationship* (H7) *are guaranteed.*

When this counterforce hits the SN of Mars and Mars itself in its familiarity with that SN – and it cannot but do so since it is on the same orbit with them - it

[212]

creates resistance in Mars in the 4th house Sagittarius. Through the resistance Mars is now challenged to *turn emotional dishonesty into emotional honesty*. That is the new response that is going to help the soul get to the 4th house Sagittarius.

Nixon- SN of Mars H3 Sagittarius	resistance	Nixon - NN of Mars H7 Aries
conscious actions and desires in prior-life selves aimed at the distortion (Sagittarius) of facts (H3) and dishonest (Sagittarius) use of information (H3)	< >	conscious actions and desires aimed at equality in relationship (H7) - as a result of truly listening to other - so that both parties' independence and freedom (Aries) *while in relationship* (H7) are guaranteed
the past streaming into the present and determining the old response: **H4 Sagittarius**	**Mars's choices**	**new response as the result of the resistance between the planet's SN and NN and its familiarity with the former:** **H4 Sagittarius**
being emotionally (H4) dishonest (Sagittarius) both to myself and others	< >	conscious actions and desires aimed at turning emotional dishonesty into emotional honesty

Such is the Mars orbit understood against the backdrop of what the soul is familiar with and seeks to evolve away from. On to Jupiter.

Jupiter (see chart p.207)

The SN of Jupiter will tell us what glasses H1 Libra prior-life selves would have looked out into the world through. We find it, not surprisingly, in the 4th house at 11 degrees Capricorn 7 minutes: *prior-life selves would have seen the world through the lens of suppression (Capricorn) of the emotional body (H4)*. I hope you see how this recurring 4th house Capricorn theme sheds light not only on the emotional armoring we so often find in the hierarchical 10th house environments the soul knows so well but also on Neptune's meaninglessness trauma caused by *the fracturing (H11) of the emotional body (Cancer)*, that is, *a dissociative state (H11) in the feeling nature (Cancer)*. Quite often, when working with the

[213]

planetary nodes, you get confirmation of earlier findings, which is why I am drawing your attention to this here.

Jupiter's SN is what has shaped the natal Jupiter. Through their 4th house Capricorn placement they speak exactly the same language, shedding light on how the Jupiter skipped step came to be. A situation similar to what we

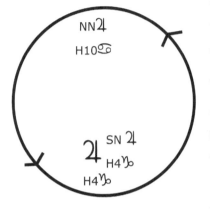

encountered with Mercury, the difference being that with Mercury and its SN we found a close conjunction whereas here we do not.

The NN of Jupiter is going to pick the needle up and gingerly place it away from the scars and scratches across the grooves of the old record. As you can see in the chart, it is doing so from the 10th house at 7 degrees Cancer 17 minutes: *the lens needs to be refocused so that integrity* (H10) *becomes Nixon's home* (Cancer).

Nixon- SN of Jupiter **H4 Capricorn**	resistance	Nixon - NN of Jupiter **H10 Cancer**
prior-life selves would have seen the world through the lens of suppression (Capricorn) of the emotional body (H4)	< >	a refocusing of the lens so that integrity (H10) becomes Nixon's home (Cancer)
the past streaming into the present and determining the old response: **H4 Capricorn**	**Jupiter's choices**	**new response as the result of the resistance between the planet's SN and NN and its familiarity with the former: H4 Capricorn**
seeing the world through the lens of suppression (Capricorn) of the emotional body (H4)	< >	restore integrity (Capricorn) in the emotional body (H4), to make it of one piece again, whole, intact (Capricorn)

As it confronts the old dynamic, the NN of Jupiter will turn it round to one in which the lens through which Nixon sees things is cut by the need to *restore integrity* (Capricorn) *in the emotional body* (H4), to make it *of one piece* again, *whole, intact* (Capricorn). For that it will need to *mature, grow up* (Capricorn).

Only when it matures can the soul get to the emotional truthfulness of the 4th house Sagittarius Polarity Point.

Such is the Jupiter orbit understood evolutionary. As we progress, it is important to keep reminding ourselves that the planetary north node, contrary to what is generally believed, is **not** the evolutionary intention. The evolutionary intention is the new response triggered in the planet itself as it feels the resistance between its own north and south node. Only this way we can understand **the natal planet as the agent of change** and **its NN as the catalyst for change**. The moment we depart from this notion, we are back in linear the-north-node-is-the-solution thinking.

Saturn (see chart p.207)

Saturn's SN is going to reveal how consciousness was structured in prior-life selves (SN of the Moon) out to use relationships with people (SN of the Moon in Libra) to further their own agenda (SN of the Moon H1). We find the SN of Saturn in the 5th house at 22 degrees Capricorn 35 minutes: *consciousness operated in such a way as to obtain leadership and prominence* (H5) *through a lack of integrity* (Capricorn).

Having shaped it, this past dynamic is fully present in Saturn in the 9th house

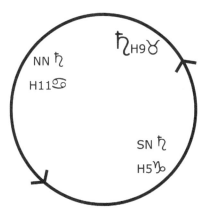

Taurus: obtaining leadership and prominence through a lack of integrity has led to *a curbing, a holding back* (Taurus) *of truthfulness* (H9). This is not what Saturn's NN envisages for Saturn.

The counterweight it offers comes from the 11th house at 23 degrees Cancer 20 minutes, closely conjunct Neptune: it wants *consciousness structured in such a way as for Nixon to feel at home* (Cancer) *with who he truly is* (H11), which in his case was a studious stay-at-home and a smooth talker cut out to be a lawyer but not a president. (4)

[215]

When this 11th house Cancer energy hits Saturn and its 5th house Capricorn buddy, it will produce a resistance in the former that will urge it to *consolidate* (Taurus) *truthfulness* (H9). Why? Because to feel at home (Cancer) with who you truly are (H11), you need to be truthful to yourself. (5)

Consolidating truthfulness (Saturn H9 in Taurus), needless to say, is going to be tremendously beneficial to the soul reaching a state of emotional truthfulness (4th house Sagittarius).

Nixon - SN of Saturn H5 Capricorn	resistance	Nixon - NN of Saturn H11 Cancer
consciousness in prior-life selves operated in such a way as to obtain leadership and prominence (H5) through a lack of integrity (Capricorn)	< >	consciousness structured in such a way as for Nixon to feel at home (Cancer) with who he truly is (H11)
the past streaming into the present and determining the old response: H9 Taurus	**Saturn's choices**	**new response as the result of the resistance between the planet's SN and NN and its familiarity with the former: H9 Taurus**
the curbing (Taurus) of truthfulness (H9)	< >	consciousness structured in such a way as to allow for the consolidation (Taurus) of truthfulness (H9)

We have now traced the entire Saturn orbit and understood it from the soul's perspective. With that we have reached the outer limit of Richard Nixon's everyday waking consciousness, the very one at whose doorstep Chiron will deposit its pain.

Quite often, when working on the planetary nodes I begin to grasp **the Chiron - Trauma Helix dynamic** or am led to a deeper understanding of it. My now comprehensive overview **of how each planet** in Richard Nixon's chart **is the focal point of either the kind of change needed to help the soul evolve or of resistance to it** will lead me into sensing how the trauma charge is brought into the Saturn realm *as pain*.

[216]

In the case of Nixon, I quite follow the soul's rationale for bringing the trauma around getting dissociated from his leadership (Uranus H5 Aquarius) coupled to the emotional fracturing as the inevitable consequence of living a life that is a lie (Neptune H11 Cancer) - identified with by the soul as a split in inner integrity (H10 Gemini) - into the current life of Richard Nixon as *a pervasive confusion around what true service from a place of humility* (Chiron H6 Pisces) means.

Failure to act, as we have seen, in terms of evolution, is as relevant as heeding the call for change. Nixon consistently failing to act on what the soul was screaming at him eventually led to the kind of demise where he suffered the ultimate humiliation (H6) in the house were Chiron had sought to be healed: the humiliation took place while in office (H6), something that was already part of the hand he had been dealt through Uranus' rulership of the 6th house (Uranus H5 Aquarius: *dissociation from his leadership* ruling the 6th house of office). It was up to him to play his cards right. Had he played the Uranus card to its full potential, he would have *stepped back and developed some degree of objective awareness* (Aquarius) *of the emotional insecurity underlying his need to be Number One* (H5), to have the top job. As it turned out, he chose not to.

As my understanding of the Chiron - *Trauma Helix* dynamics begins to take shape, I then turn my attention to the south nodes of Chiron, Uranus and Neptune and look into the past that led up to their natal placements. That will almost always clinch the deal. Further corroboration of my conclusions then comes from looking at the full evolutionary orbit for each of the planetary functions. I might also do this the other way round, starting with the planetary nodes form Saturn inward and *then* looking at the full evolutionary Chiron, Uranus and Neptune orbit. (as I do in the next chapter for Nina Simone). Things tend to add up either way. For a detailed description of the Chiron, Uranus, Neptune *and* Moon dynamics for Nixon, you can go back to Chapter 9 - *Trauma, Pain and Healing in Orbit* and read up on them there.

Pluto H10 Gemini (skipped step)		Pluto Polarity Point H4 Sagittarius
	natal planet as *the agent of change* conducive to	

south node	evolutionary growth: the felt resistance between its south and north leading to a new response (or not, which, evolutionary speaking, is equally important)	north node
Moon		
engaging in relationship (SN Libra) with the sole purpose of serving self (SN H1)	step back (Aquarius) and objectively assess (Aquarius) what service from a place of humility (H6) means	guaranteeing mutual freedom and independency (NN Aries) *in* relationship (NN H7) through careful listening to other (H7)
Mercury		
prior-life selves would have directed their thinking (Mercury) at the suppression (Capricorn) of the emotional body (H4)	thinking (Mercury) directed at maturing (Capricorn) emotionally (H4), allowing the emotional body (H4) to grow up (Capricorn)	thinking directed at stepping back and objectively assessing (Aquarius) the emotional insecurity that underlies his need to be an undisputed leader and come out on top
Venus		to relate (Venus) to discerning (H6) who I am actually serving (H6), self or other, and to then make the adjustments (H6) needed to offer (Pisces) the right kind (H6 discernment) of service (H6)
the prime relationship in prior-life selves was with the suppression (Capricorn) of the emotional body (H4)	to heal (Pisces) my relationship (Venus) with true service from a place of humility (H6)	
Mars		
conscious actions and desires in prior-life selves aimed at the distortion (Sagittarius) of facts (H3) and dishonest (Sagittarius) use of information (H3)	conscious actions and desires aimed at turning emotional dishonesty into emotional honesty	conscious actions and desires aimed at equality in relationship (H7) – as a result of truly listening to other - so that both parties' independence and freedom (Aries) *while in relationship* (H7) are guaranteed
Jupiter		
prior-life selves seeing the world through the lens of	restore integrity (Capricorn) in the	a refocusing of the lens so that integrity (H10)

suppression (Capricorn) of the emotional body (H4)	emotional body (H4), to make it of one piece again, whole, intact (Capricorn)	becomes Nixon's home (Cancer)
Saturn		
consciousness in prior-life selves operated in such a way as to obtain leadership and prominence (H5) through a lack of integrity (Capricorn)	consciousness structured in such a way as to allow for the consolidation (Taurus) of truthfulness (H9)	consciousness structured in such a way as for Nixon to feel at home (Cancer) with who he truly is (H11)
Chiron		
prior-life selves immersed in treacherous power games (H8) in order to advance themselves (Aries) at the expense of others (H8)	engage in a process of inner purification (H6) whereby Nixon learns to distinguish (H6) between self-serving behavior and true service from a place of humility (H6) so that the latter be healed (H6), and with it the pain	a deep transformation (Scorpio) of the inner values (H2) Nixon's relationship with himself (H2) is based on
Uranus		
subconscious memories of trauma incurred as a result of prior-life selves having distorted (Sagittarius) the facts (H3)	overcoming the trauma by stepping back and objectively assessing (Aquarius) the emotional insecurity underlying the need to come out as Number One (H5), allowing for impartiality and generosity to come to the fore and characterize his leadership	integrating (Gemini) with truthfulness (H9)
Neptune		
prior-life selves having become dissociated (Aquarius) from their leadership (H5) as they, in their unstoppable self-aggrandizement, became separated (Aquarius) from Leo's generosity and impartiality (H5), that is,	overcoming the trauma by feeling at home (Cancer) in who he knows himself to truly be (H11)	allowing himself to simply be who he truly is (H11) and then shine (Leo) in whatever capacity that is

from the archetype in its highest expression		
south node	**natal planet as _the agent of change_ conducive to evolutionary growth: the felt resistance between its south and north leading to a new response (or not, which, evolutionary speaking, is equally important)**	**north node**
Pluto H10 Gemini **(skipped step)**		**Pluto Polarity Point H4 Sagittarius**

Why does the Sun come last in EA analysis?

It comes last because we need all of the above information to understand why the soul wants _integrity in leadership_ (H5 Capricorn) to be the central, integrative principle around which everything in Richard Nixon's life revolves. As far as the soul is concerned, the Sun, just like all the planets, is articulated the way it is for one reason only: the actualization of the PPP in the 4th house Sagittarius. It is not too difficult to see how integrity in leadership would be beneficial to emotional truthfulness.

[220]

Chapter 13 – Nina Simone in Full Evolutionary Orbit

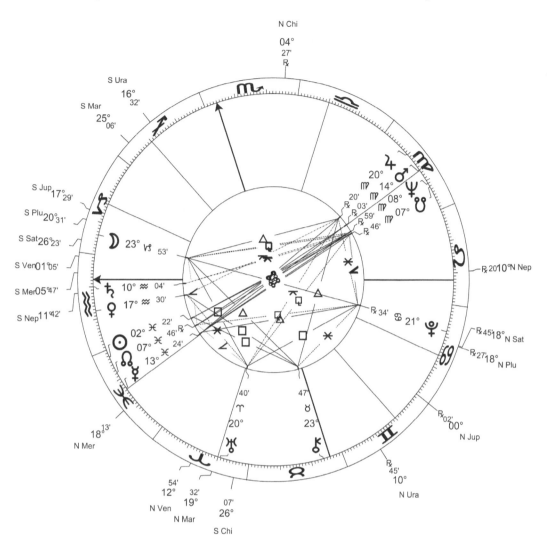

Nina Simone, 21 February 1933, 6:00 AM, Tryon, North Carolina. RR:AA

The watershed moment in Eunice Waylon's life was not the rejection by the Curtis Institute of Music but her claiming her parents' right to sit front row during their daughter's much anticipated musical debut age ten. To understand where Eunice's unusual resolve came from, we need to grasp how her 12th house Moon is the point of maximum resistance between its 7th house Virgo SN and its 1st house Pisces NN and how, as a result of that resistance, the Moon – Simone herself - was urged to act in a certain way. Urged to come up with a response radically different from the one it had known for so long and was apt to default to. Since this principle, as we have seen in the previous two chapters on Richard Nixon and Josef Mengele, applies from Mercury right up to Neptune, it is good best practice to always first put it into words for the Moon, especially since the planetary south nodes refer to dynamics operative in prior-life selves and, via those prior-lives, to the issues the soul has been exploring.

In our first exploration of the chart of Nina Simone in chapter 7, we saw how prior-life egoic structures (SN of the Moon) created by the soul were marked by *inequality in relationship* (H7) *as a result of interjected inferiority and unworthiness* (with the accompanying emotion of guilt and possibly shame). Neptune tagging along at the heels of the SN of the Moon told us that *feelings of meaninglessness caused by relationships having been severely off kilter* (H7) *as a result of projected* (H7) *and/or interjected unworthiness* - Virgo - directly impacted prior-life selves (SN of the Moon).

Further particulars pertaining to those lives were provided by the ruler of the SN of the Moon (Mercury), informing us of how there had been *a loss* (Pisces) *of their identity, freedom and right to exist* (H1) in the context of this 7th house inequality.

Our premise in working with the nodes, whether they are the Moon's or a planet's, is that past dynamics are reflected in the natal placement by house and sign since in reality we are not looking at three distinct points (i.e. natal planet/Moon, its SN, its NN) but rather at a single orbital movement in which prior dynamics are constantly brought into the Moon or planet itself. Trailing along in the SN's wake is the Neptune meaninglessness. That too shapes the current life Moon.

How then, does this SN of the Moon-Neptune 7th house Virgo dynamic come back in Nina Simone's 12th house Capricorn Moon? It can be seen in her Moon in its tendency *to make oneself/become invisible* (H12) *under the crushing weight of oppressive power* (Capricorn). I am phrasing this in general terms because it would be easy, and therefore tempting, to jump straight to 12th house slavery. Slavery might very well have been part of the story, especially with the SN ruler Mercury speaking of *a loss* (Pisces) *of freedom* (H1), but I feel the narrative is broader than that. In its broadest sense the 12th house Moon implies an unseenness, a sense of going unnoticed. Perhaps we should bear that in mind when from the Moon's new response we see this very strong and, at times, even overbearing personality emerge.

The Moon, we have said, is far more familiar with her own SN than she is with her NN. Just like the soul, she will default to what is familiar and known. On her orbit, however, her own NN is constantly reminding her, *and* her SN with which she is on such good terms, of a new dynamic. This new dynamic clashes with both the Moon *and* her familiarity with her own history, her own background, so to speak, and so produces resistance in the Moon itself. What Nina Simone's NN of the Moon has in mind is *to heal* (Pisces) *all matters identity, freedom and right to exist* (H1). The way it will go about that is written in the NN ruler in the 7th house Virgo: *to meticulously examine* (Virgo) *the issue of inequality in relationship as a result of what people project onto each other* (H7).

As the NN of the Moon confronts the Moon and her SN with this new approach, the Moon is challenged to come up with a new response. The new response is: *to take full responsibility* (Capricorn) *for the fact that she is perfect as she is* (H12) and that there can therefore be no question of inferiority and unworthiness. It would be a grave mistake to associate Pisces with forgiveness. In its sextile to Capricorn you could get away with that: when he assumes responsibility for something he has done wrong, then Pisces can say to Capricorn *"You are forgiven."*

Those words are the last thing Virgo needs to hear. What Virgo needs to hear from Pisces is that there is nothing to forgive to begin with. That is what guilt-ridden Virgo cannot seem to get through her thick skull. The Mercury frenzy turned inward in its self-incriminatory fault-finding quest keeps hollowing Virgo out until there is a big, gaping hole right in the middle of her psyche that says: *"You are not good enough. There is something chronically wrong with you."* Virgo then turns to Pisces in the hope that its presumed perfection can fill that hole. What do you think happens to that void, squatting at the center of the maiden's consciousness, when Pisces says to her

"There is nothing wrong with you, never has been and never will be. There is nothing you can do that will make God stop loving you." It will disappear, will it not?

This is why Nina Simone's Moon is in the 12th house. *Taking full responsibility for the fact that she is perfect as she is* - Moon H12 Capricorn - for the fact that she is a child of God, who does not care for gender or race (Pluto in Cancer), is something Nina Simone can do through her music – H12. Through *becoming the embodiment* (Capricorn*) of God's universal language* (H12: music), shaping and sculpting (Capricorn) it, through endless hours (Capricorn: time) of study. Which is what young Eunice did: she used to get up at four in the morning and put in three hours of practice before she went to school. She put in the hard graft of her own accord (Capricorn) and not because she was told to. That is why that Sunday in May of 1943 was such a big deal to her and why there was so much at stake, making her resolve at that crucial moment in her life all the more poignant.

Simone - SN of the Moon H7 Virgo	resistance	Simone - NN of the Moon H1 Pisces
prior-life egoic structures (SN of the Moon) created by the soul were marked by inequality in relationship (H7) as a result of interjected inferiority and unworthiness (Virgo)	< >	to heal (Pisces) all matters identity, freedom and right to exist (H1)
the past streaming into the present and determining the Moon's old response: H12 Capricorn	**the Moon's choices**	**new response as the result of the resistance between the Moon's SN and NN and its familiarity with the former: H12 Capricorn**
going unseen, unnoticed (H12) under the crushing weight of oppressive power (Capricorn)	< >	to take full responsibility (Capricorn) for the fact that I am perfect as I am (H12) by becoming the embodiment (Capricorn) of God's universal language: music (H12)

Now we understand the true significance of what happened there: on the very same day of her musical debut, the day, therefore, when she was to share God's language with the world, in one fell swoop she reclaimed her parents' right to exist (NN H1) along with her own and so healed (NN in Pisces) it. Exactly the new response the NN of the Moon was hoping she would come up with.

The important thing for you to take away from this is that, contrary to popular belief, **the intended evolutionary direction on the level of self is not the NN of the Moon but rather the Moon's new response**. The NN of the Moon simply provides the counterforce to the familiar (the Moon and the SN of the Moon). Were we to postulate the NN of the Moon as the intended evolutionary direction, we would immediately be out of orbit again and find ourselves back in the linear projection of the NN at some point on the imaginary timeline called _'future.'_ It would instantly turn the Moon into a lame duck, devoid of all internal friction and therefore incapacitated to act. That would take the heart out of the tenet central to evolutionary astrology, namely that the soul creates finite lives (astrologically represented by the Moon) through which to learn its lessons.

The same principle applies to the south node of Mercury right up to that of Neptune. **A planet in a house and sign is the point of maximum resistance between its own south and north node**. As it feels the tug of war going on between the known and unknown, between the familiar and unfamiliar, it becomes the agent for change per excellence, a vibrant and marked point in which its entire orbit culminates and cries out for change. By opening up its orbit in these pages we move from what I would call _'stills astrology'_ to three-dimensional astrology and we begin to think of the orbit as a single, evolutionary statement comprised of past and present. Not _future_, but _present_. There is no future potential on this orbit: only counterforce (NN) felt in the now as it holds on to the past.

Holding on to the known

If this model shakes up everything you are familiar and therefore comfortable with, then I do apologize. I know the feeling. It happened to me years ago and felt like I was transiting from what I then labeled _'flat-Earth astrology'_ to what was actually happening in the Heavens. If you happen to still practice this kind of *'stills astrology'* (i.e. the orbit halted and the planet taken out as a fragment, a dead thing), then please know that it is not my intention to offend anyone. The term is not used in any kind of derogatory manner whatsoever, proof of which is the fact that I applied it to my own thinking first, many years ago now when these ideas germinated and were tested in many hours of client work. The approach outlined in this book will be anathema to the very essence of what the Moon and the planets have been assumed to be, and assimilation requires a shift of perspective that is not easy for anyone to accomplish. I know how difficult it is to let go of - or even make adjustments in - something you have invested in emotionally, intellectually etc. My brief, however, is to establish a therapeutic evolutionary astrology, and to be able to do so, I need to redefine certain concepts. This is one of them and it is a big one.

To show you how these new nodal dynamics work for Mercury right up to Neptune in Nina Simone's chart, I will now guide you through an exploration of the orbital movement of each of those planets.

Mercury (see chart p.221)

When looking at Mercury, we first of all try to establish where it is coming from. In other words: what were the thought patterns or ways of thinking operative in prior-life selves (SN of the Moon) as they experienced this inequality in relationship as the result of interjected inferiority and unworthiness? That is the question we are trying to answer, ever mindful of the fact that these prior-life selves were created by the soul to explore its issue of inferiority in the context of race and gender (Pluto H6 Cancer).

We find the SN of Mercury in the 12th house. At 5 degrees Aquarius 47 minutes, to be precise. *Thinking in prior-life selves was aimed at making oneself invisible (H12) as part of a large group of people* (Aquarius). Speaking of Aquarius, it pays to remind oneself that the flipside of everyone being equally unique in the sign of the Water Bearer can mean that everyone is made equally *un*important. Aquarius gone wrong can show a leveling tendency where anyone sticking their head above the parapet is mowed down, especially when, as we often find in 11th house group dynamics, *'some pigs are more equal than others.'* With the SN of Mercury in the 12th house Aquarius, slavery is therefore beginning to become a

[226]

possibility to seriously reckon with. This often happens when working with the planetary nodes: as the past of each planetary function reveals itself, earlier assumptions are confirmed or proven unwarranted. Whatever happens, it is always a fascinating journey and can feel as if you stumble upon a box of long-forgotten photographs in the attic. Whole new timelines come into view, similar perhaps to the view you would get if you were allowed to contemplate the planets' orbits from the vantage point of a spaceship. I do not want to get all Star-Trekky here, but that is what is feels like at times.

The next step is to ask yourself how this 12th house Aquarius dynamic comes back in Mercury in the 1st house Pisces. This is not too hard to put into words: *having had to make myself invisible* (SN Mercury H12) *as part of a large collective* (SN Mercury Aquarius) *where everyone is equally unimportant* (SN Mercury Aquarius) has shaped the dynamic of *surrendering* (Mercury in Pisces) *my identity, freedom and right to exist* (Mercury H1). Current-life thinking would default to this past dynamic, in addition to allowing itself to *get confused* (Pisces) *in terms of these 1st house issues*. Thinking could also lean towards *victimization* (Pisces) around them. This is how the past dynamic might operate in the current-life Mercury. Remember that these Mercury dynamics operative in 7th house Virgo prior-life selves ultimately were created by the soul as the way in which it sought

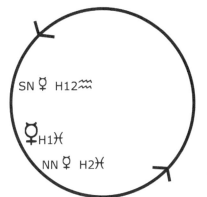

to explore the issue of inferiority in the context of race and gender (Pluto H6 Cancer). Be sure to never lose sight of the bigger soul picture.

In comes Mercury's NN. You will find it at 18 degrees Pisces 13 minutes in the 2nd house. Its counterweight to the past dynamics operative in the SN of Mercury and in Mercury itself says: "*direct your thinking at healing* (Pisces) *the value* (H2) *you place on the relationship you are in with yourself* (2nd house) *and with the inner values* (2nd house) *that relationship is based on*."

What an incredible statement for one told to make herself invisible, do you not think? Now, the next step is equally if not more important. We need to determine what will happen in Mercury itself when this statement hits the old groove. At one end of the rope we have got the NN of Mercury insisting on healing the value placed on self (H2 Pisces), and at the rear end we have a Mercury directing its thinking at remaining unseen (SN Mercury H12) within a large group of equally *un*important people (SN Mercury Aquarius), leading to a dissolution (Mercury in Pisces) in one's sense of self (Mercury H1).

What is going to happen when the 2nd house Pisces self-affirming energy hits this self-effacing unseenness? Is it not going to urge Mercury in the 1st house Pisces *to heal all things identity, freedom and right to exist?* And *direct its thinking* (Mercury) *at placing those important 1st house issues in the context of music* (Pisces) *so that the vehicle Simone, through its music, may come to think of itself as God's instrument?* It is my contention that it would.

"I didn't get interested in music. It was a gift from God and I know that." (1) *"Music is a gift and a burden I've had since I can remember who I was. I was born into music. The decision was how to make the best of it."* (2)

You can see how relevant Mercury's new response would be to the soul getting to this 12th house Capricorn place where *it matures* (Capricorn) *through feeling the total acceptance* (H12) *of the way it is.* And more than that even: where *it matures in the full knowledge that the way it is, is exactly what God intended.* Would healing who I am and how I have every right to be what I am (Mercury H1 Pisces) not be tremendously beneficial to the soul getting there?

Simone - SN of Mercury H12 Aquarius	resistance	Simone - NN of Mercury H2 Pisces
thinking in prior-life selves was aimed at making oneself invisible (H12) as part of a large group of people (Aquarius) where everyone was equally *un*important	< >	direct your thinking at healing (Pisces) the value (H2) you place on the relationship you are in with yourself (H2)
the past streaming into the present and determining the old response:	**Mercury's choices**	**new response as the result of the resistance between the planet's SN and NN and**

[228]

H1 Pisces		its familiarity with the former: H1 Pisces
having had to make myself invisible (SN Mercury H12) as part of a large collective (SN Mercury in Aquarius) has led to a dynamic of surrendering (Mercury in Pisces) my identity, freedom and right to exist (Mercury H1)	< >	heal all things identity, freedom and right to exist and direct thinking (Mercury) towards placing those H1 issues in the context of music (Pisces) so that the vehicle Simone, through its music, may come to think of itself as God's instrument

This is the Mercury orbit understood evolutionary, and it reveals much about the towering musical figure Nina Simone we used to see on stage. Doing things this way is hard work, I know, but I do feel it is worth it if we are to apply the wonderful EA paradigm therapeutically. It is a great privilege for me to be allowed to guide you through this exploration for I know you will use it in your own chart and that of your clients. That means this great art and science of ours, this *Sacred Science*, can finally become a full-fledged therapeutic discipline in its own right, which is my stated aim in writing this book and teaching this material at the EA School Online.

Venus (see chart p.221)

For information on what kind of relationships 7th house Virgo prior-life selves would have engaged in we turn to the SN of Venus. The relationship does not always have to be with people, as we saw in the chapters on Nixon and Mengele. It can be with nature, with a value system, with a system of thought, etcetera. We shall see. For Nina Simone we find the SN of Venus at 1 degree Aquarius 5 minutes in the 12th house: to explore the issue of inequality in relationship as a result of interjected inferiority and unworthiness (SN of the Moon H7 Virgo), *prior-life selves' prime relationship seems to have been with the hidden-awayness, the unseenness (H12) of or within a large group of people where everyone was equally underimportant* (Aquarius). Evidence in support of our earlier assumption of slavery is mounting.

Having shaped it, how is this dynamic reflected in Venus in the 1st house Aquarius? In the following way: *having had to relate to the unseenness* (SN Venus H12) *of or within a large collective of equally <u>un</u>important people* (SN Venus Aquarius), *has led to trauma* (Venus in Aquarius) *incurred to my identity, freedom and right to exist* (Venus H1). As was the case with Mercury, the current-

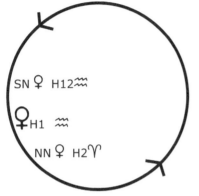

SN ♀ H12♒

♀H1 ♒

NN ♀ H2♈

life Venus, for reasons of familiarity, might default to this past dynamic by *relating* (Venus) *to the dissociation* (Venus in Aquarius) *from my identity, freedom and right to exist* (Venus H1) and to the trauma (Aquarius) caused by it.

The counterforce to this beaten track comes from the NN of Venus at 12 degrees Aries 54 minutes in the 2nd house telling Simone *to relate to consolidating and strengthening* (H2) *her identity, freedom and right to exist* (Aries), *to the fortification* (H2) *of these* in a Taurean 2nd house way, I would almost say, which makes rather a lot of sense when in the past you have related to the exact opposite of that, that is, to your unseenness within a large group of people. As this new and unfamiliar dynamic confronts the old one – present in both Venus *and* its SN – *Simone is challenged to objectively observe* (Aquarius) *her relationship* (Venus) *with her identity, her freedom and her right to exist* (H1) and, *through* the observing, *to relate* (Venus) *to the liberation* (Aquarius) *of these 1st house issues*. (3) This new response serves the current-life egoic structure created by the soul and which goes by the name of Nina Simone: the Moon in the 12th house Capricorn out to assume full responsibility for accepting herself unconditionally through God's Divine language (music). Via *that* Moon, Venus' new response ultimately allows the soul to mature (PPP Capricorn) through feeling the total acceptance (PPP H12) of the way it is.

By the same token, the old 12th house Aquarius Venus dynamic operative in prior-life selves ultimately served the soul exploring its issue of (interjected) inferiority and unworthiness in the context of race and gender (Pluto H6 Cancer). It is important to draw these lines, otherwise we would lose sight of why the Venus orbit is as it is. Its exquisite precision was calibrated by the soul for one reason only: to further evolution in the direction of the 12th house Capricorn PPP. Here

[230]

again we see how south nodes, whether lunar or planetary, are not 'bad' and north nodes 'good.' To be able to evolve the soul needs one as much as the other.

Simone - SN of Venus H12 Aquarius	resistance	Simone - NN of Venus H2 Aries
prior-life selves' prime relationship was with the hidden-awayness, the unseenness (H12) of or within a large group of people (Aquarius) where everyone was equally _un_important (Aquarius)	< >	to relate to consolidating and strengthening (H2) her identity, freedom and right to exist (Aries), to the fortification (H2) of these in a Taurean 2nd house way
the past streaming into the present and determining the old response: H1 Aquarius	**Venus's choices**	**new response as the result of the resistance between the planet's SN and NN and its familiarity with the former: H1 Aquarius**
having had to relate to the unseenness (SN Venus H12) of, or within a large collective (SN Venus Aquarius) constitutes trauma (Venus in Aquarius) in terms of my identity, freedom and right to exist (Venus). I relate (Venus) to the dissociation (Venus in Aquarius) from my identity, freedom and right to exist (Venus H1) and to the trauma (Aquarius) caused by it	< >	challenged to objectively observe (Aquarius) her relationship (Venus) with her identity, her freedom and her right to exist (H1) and, _through_ the observing, to relate (Venus) to the liberation (Aquarius) of these 1st house issues

Such is the full Venus orbit seen through the eyes of the soul.

Mars (see chart p.221)

What would conscious actions and desires have been directed at in prior-life egoic structures experiencing inequality in relationship as a result of interjected inferiority and unworthiness (SN of the Moon H7 Virgo)? That is the question with which we approach the SN of Mars. We find it in the 11th house at 25 degrees

Sagittarius 6 minutes: they would have been directed at *following the distorted truth* (Sagittarius) *of some ideology* (Sagittarius) *affecting large groups of people* (H11). At this point of our analysis the evidence for slavery is somewhere between persuasive and convincing.

As was the case with the Moon, Mercury and Venus, the SN of Mars too is fully present in Mars itself. Its 8th house Virgo placement speaks of *powerlessness* (H8) *in the context of interjected inferiority and unworthiness* (Virgo).

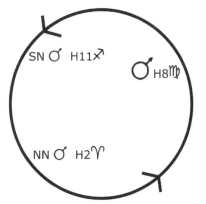

The counterweight to this familiar dynamic Mars in the 8th house will default to comes from the NN of Mars at 19 degrees Aries 32 minutes, squeezed, interestingly, into the far corner of the 2nd house: *the soul wishes all conscious actions and desires in its vehicle Eunice Waylon to be directed at the strengthening and fortification* (H2) *of her identity, freedom and right to exist* (Aries).

As it confronts the old groove, the NN of Mars will generate a new response in Mars: *to direct all conscious actions and desires at looking very critically* (Virgo) *at the issue of power, powerlessness and self-empowerment* (H8), to reflect deeply on the issue (Mars retrograde) and to then *deeply commit* (H8) *to serving* (Virgo) *empowerment* (H8).

That, one could argue, sums up Nina Simone's life's work. This is what she actually did through her music and person. These are the conscious actions and desires the soul knew would help her (i.e. the Moon) *take full responsibility* (Moon in Capricorn) *for the fact that she is perfect as she is* (H12), *allowing the soul to mature* (PPP Capricorn) *through feeling the total acceptance* (PPP H12) *of the way it is*. As you can see, I have not changed a word: Simone will have to direct her conscious will at this critical examination if she is to become *of one piece* (Capricorn's integrity coming from the Latin *'integra'*: whole, intact) *in her unconditional self-acceptance as a child of God* (Moon H12 Capricorn), gifted with perfect pitch so that she may speak His universal language (i.e. music).

Simone - SN of Mars H11 Sagittarius	resistance	Simone - NN of Mars H2 Aries
conscious actions and desires directed at following the distorted truth (Sagittarius) of some ideology (Sagittarius) affecting large groups of people (H11)	< >	conscious actions and desires to be directed at the strengthening and fortification (H2) of her identity, freedom and right to exist (Aries)
the past streaming into the present and determining the old response: H8 Virgo	**Mars's choices**	**new response as the result of the resistance between the planet's SN and NN and its familiarity with the former: H8 Virgo**
powerlessness (H8) in the context of interjected inferiority and unworthiness (Virgo)	< >	to direct all conscious actions and desires at looking very critically (Virgo) at the issue of power, powerlessness and self-empowerment (H8), to reflect deeply on the issue (Mars retrograde) and to then deeply commit (H8) to serving (Virgo) empowerment (H8)

With that we have understood the Mars orbit against the backdrop of where the soul is coming from and where it wishes to go. We shall now do the same for Jupiter.

Jupiter (see chart p.221)

The SN of Jupiter sits in the 12th house at 17 degrees Capricorn 29 minutes: the lens through which prior-life selves looked at the world, or were made to look at the world, was tainted by *making myself invisible* (H12) *under the crushing weight of suppression and exploitation* (Capricorn). With that finding, evidence for prior lives as a slave has moved from convincing to compelling.

The natal 8th house Virgo Jupiter defined by its own past shows as *powerlessness* (H8) *in the context of interjected inferiority and unworthiness* (Virgo).

[233]

The NN of Jupiter is going to pull hard at this from the other end of the rope. That other end is in the 5th house at 0 degrees Cancer 2 minutes. What the soul intends here is so obvious that you might not see it: it wants Eunice Waylon to look through glasses of a different kind altogether. Glasses tainted by *the birth* (Cancer) *of her solar energy* (H5). In other words: *the ultimate being seen and getting noticed* (H5) *through the creative act* (H5) as opposed to the unseenness of the past that we have run into at every corner we turned.

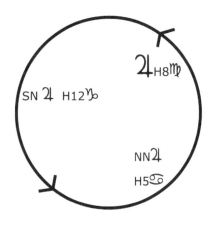

When the 5th house Cancer energy hits the worn-out H8 tune, the new glasses, the new lens through which Simone sees the world, is going to be cut by the need *to know how to discern* (Virgo) *power and powerlessness* (H8), *to clearly distinguish* (Virgo) *between what one feels like and what the other feels like and to then serve* (Virgo) *self-empowerment by choosing* (H8) *one over the other.*

It is fairly obvious how Jupiter's NN would be the catalyst for this new response: birthing herself (NN Jupiter Cancer) through the creative act (NN Jupiter H5) and *as* a creative act is going to trigger Simone discerning between power and powerlessness and then choose the former over the latter (Jupiter H8 Virgo): the planetary NN as *the catalyst for change*, the new response of the natal planet as *the agent of change*.

Jupiter's is a wonderful orbit. The soul could not have spoken more clearly. The information is all there for the astrologer who wishes to see.

Simone - SN of Jupiter H12 Capricorn	resistance	Simone - NN of Jupiter H5 Cancer
making myself invisible (H12) under the crushing weight of suppression and exploitation (Capricorn)	< >	the birth (Cancer) of her solar energy (H5). Being seen and getting noticed (H5) through the creative act (H5) and *as* a creative act

the past streaming into the present and determining the old response: H8 Virgo	Jupiter's choices	new response as the result of the resistance between the planet's SN and NN and its familiarity with the former: H8 Virgo
powerlessness (H8) in the context of interjected inferiority and unworthiness (Virgo)	< >	to know how to discern (Virgo) power and powerlessness (H8), to clearly distinguish (Virgo) between what one feels like and what the other feels like and to then serve (Virgo) self-empowerment by choosing (H8) one over the other

Saturn (see chart p.221)

What would the structure of consciousness in prior-life selves have been like? How would that consciousness have operated as it went through a life of inequality as a result of interjected inferiority and unworthiness (SN of the Moon H7 Virgo)? The answer comes from Saturn's SN, which we find in the 12th house at 26 degrees Capricorn 23 minutes: *a consciousness structured in such a way as to be able to endure the unseenness of self* (H12) *under the crushing weight of suppression and exploitation* (Capricorn).

As this old dynamic flows into the natal Saturn in the 1st house Aquarius, it manifests there as: *"I dissociate* (Aquarius) *from my identity, my freedom and my right to exist* (H1)*."*

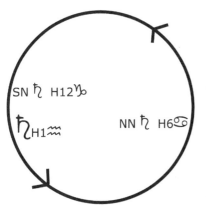

"No such thing," says the NN of Saturn from the 6th house at 18 degrees Cancer 45 minutes. *"Consciousness in the vehicle Simone is to go through this whole issue of interjected inferiority and unworthiness* (H6) *with a fine-toothed comb* (H6) *so that a new self-image* (Cancer) *be born, a new 'me.' "*

When this opposing force hits the old consciousness, it will create resistance in Saturn in the 1st house Aquarius since it is hand in glove with its own past. The resistance will prompt it to operate in an entirely new way: *it will internally be wired* (structured) *to liberate* (Aquarius) *Simone from the trauma* (Aquarius) *incurred to her identity, her freedom and her right to exist* (H1).

This is the Saturn orbit seen through the eyes of the soul. I hope you appreciate its beauty. There is nothing 'good' or 'bad' about any of its moments. They simply are what they are and have served and *are* serving the soul as it evolves from the 6th house Cancer to the 12th house Capricorn.

Simone - SN of Saturn H12 Capricorn	resistance	Simone - NN of Saturn H6 Cancer
a consciousness structured in such a way as to be able to endure the unseenness of self (H12) under the crushing weight of suppression and exploitation (Capricorn)	< >	consciousness in the vehicle Simone is to go through the issue of interjected inferiority and unworthiness (H6) with a fine-toothed comb (H6) so that a new self-image (Cancer) be born, a new 'me.'
the past streaming into the present and determining the old response: **H1 Aquarius**	**Saturn's choices**	**new response as the result of the resistance between the planet's SN and NN and its familiarity with the former: H1 Aquarius**
"I dissociate (Aquarius) *from my identity, my freedom and my right to exist."* (H1)	< >	consciousness internally wired to liberate (Aquarius) Simone from the trauma (Aquarius) incurred to her identity, her freedom and her right to exist (H1)

We have now traced the full evolutionary orbit for all the planetary functions operative within Nina Simone's everyday waking consciousness, the outer limit of which is Saturn. We have seen how there are evolutionary reasons for the soul wanting the nature of thinking (Mercury), the nature of relationship patterns

(Venus), the nature of conscious actions and desires (Mars), the nature of the lens through which the vehicle Simone looks out into the world (Jupiter), and the way its consciousness is structured (Saturn) to be the way they are.

Into the outer limit of that consciousness (Saturn) Chiron now brings a subconscious trauma charge translated *as pain*. To the cursory sketch of Chiron, Uranus and Neptune offered in chapter 7, we are now going to add the granular detail of their respective south and north nodes so that we get the full evolutionary picture of how timelines from multiple other lives, from multiple other selves, stream into the current-life egoic structure created by the soul (i.e. the Moon H12 Capricorn) going by the name of Nina Simone.

Chiron (see chart p.221)

The past of the Chiron pain will tell us how it was formed. We find the SN of Chiron at 26 degrees Aries 7 minutes in the 3rd house, not too far away from Uranus there: *the pain was inflicted to her identity, freedom and right to exist* (Aries) *as a result of not having been allowed to integrate* (H3). At this point it is important to remind yourself that what you are looking at with Chiron is the way the soul relays a trauma charge from prior-life selves to the current one *as pain*. The pain in one way or another is therefore going to reflect the Uranus and Neptune strands of the *Trauma Helix*, as well as the soul's emotional and psychological identification with them. When we get to Uranus, Neptune and Pluto we shall see if this is indeed the case and if the theory holds up. If it does, we will have gathered further evidence of the kind of ´**trauma continuity**´ we first ran into in chapter 5 - *From Lincoln to Lindbergh*.

Chiron's past pain comes back in Chiron in the 3rd house Taurus in that it speaks of *having been limited, held back* (Taurus*) in the context of integration* (H3) *because of segregation* (H3). As you can see, the information handed the astrologer here is becoming rather unequivocal. There remains little doubt indeed now as to what happened in prior lives. Both Chiron's familiarity with its past and the past itself lie squarely on the side of 7th house Virgo prior-life selves as the vehicle through which the soul explored its 6th house interjected inferiority in the context of race and gender (Cancer). That is something to always keep your eye on.

[237]

The NN of Chiron is going to bring a counterclaim into the court of pain. It is

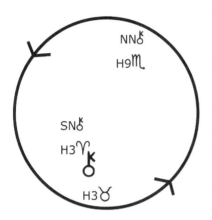

submitted from the 9th house, at 4 degrees Scorpio 27 minutes: *to heal the pain from a deep commitment* (Scorpio) *to the cause of liberty* (H9), understood not as my freedom but as everyone's: the archer's arrow is aimed at overarching principles written in the firmament. 'Liberty' understood, therefore, as *being free from oppressive constriction by a government or other power, free from confinement, servitude and forced labor*. Arresting songs like *To Be Young, Gifted and Black*, *Four Women*, *Revolution*, and *Are You Ready, Black People?* all speak of that commitment and Simone's political thrust. In the 9th house, as we saw in the chapters on Lincoln and Lindbergh, the focus is entirely on the principles which in the 10th house will harden into either fair or unfair societal structures. The catalyst for the healing of the Chiron pain for Simone cannot but be political.

As it confronts the pain's past and Chiron's tendency to default to it, the NN of Chiron triggers a new response in Chiron which will enable it to heal the pain by *consolidating and strengthening* (Taurus) *integration* (H3), understood as the right to freely exchange ideas with others, to be with others, learn in what way they are different from you and in what way the same.

We understand why the soul would put a premium on this: how is it to mature (PPP Capricorn) through unconditional self-acceptance (H12) when its vehicle is kept away from a large segment of the population? Is the realization that we are all children of God not dependent on the vehicle being allowed contact with each and every one of them?

Simone - SN of Chiron H3 Aries	resistance	Simone - NN of Chiron H9 Scorpio
a pain was inflicted to her identity, freedom and right to exist (Aries) as a result of not	< >	to heal the pain from a deep commitment (Scorpio) to the cause of liberty (H9)

the past streaming into the present and determining the old response: H3 Taurus	Chiron's choices	new response as the result of the resistance between the planet's SN and NN and its familiarity with the former: H3 Taurus
having been allowed to integrate (H3)		
being limited, held back (Taurus) in the context of integration (H3) because of segregation (H3)	< >	to consolidate and strengthen (Taurus) integration (H3)

Uranus (see chart p.221)

Uranus in the 3rd house Aries, we said in chapter 7, denotes subconscious memories – stored in its warped-time vault – to do with *prior-life selves having been denied their identity, their freedom and their right to exist* (Aries) *because of non-integration* (H3), i.e. segregation.

It fits the picture of slavery. Where is the past of that trauma? How did it come about? The answer to that question lies at 16 degrees Sagittarius 32 minutes in the 10th house: *oppressive worldly power* (H10) *taking away my liberty* (Sagittarius) *through laws* (H10) *that are a lie* (Sagittarius), *a distortion of truth*

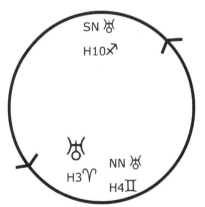

(Sagittarius). There is your confirmation of the past Chiron pain: sick and twisted laws, crowing like roosters, stopped her from integrating. We are hearing south node voices beginning to sing in unison.

The call for overcoming this trauma comes from the NN of Uranus, although it is Uranus itself who is going to have to do the actual work. Eloquent and articulate, Uranus' NN speaks to us from the 4th house at 10 degrees Gemini 45 minutes, saying: *"I want my race* (H4) *to be allowed to integrate* (Gemini) *so that there be an integrated* (H3) *nation* (H4)."

Just think what that kind of counterweight is going to trigger in Uranus in the 3rd house Aries. Is it, in a bid to overcome the trauma, not going to insist on *claiming its identity, its freedom and its right to exist* (Aries) *through full integration* (H3)? The astrological symbolism definitely seems to be pointing in that direction.

How overcoming the trauma this way would be relevant to the soul actualizing its 12th house Capricorn intentions is the same as what we said for Chiron: how can it mature (Capricorn) through unconditional self-acceptance (H12) when it is segregated (H3) from others?

Simone - SN of Uranus H10 Sagittarius	resistance	Simone - NN of Uranus H4 Gemini
oppressive worldly power (H10) taking away my liberty (Sagittarius) through laws (H10) that are a lie (Sagittarius) and reflect a distortion of truth (Sagittarius)	< >	*"I want my race (H4) to be allowed to integrate (Gemini) so that there be an integrated (H3) nation (H4)."*
the past streaming into the present and determining the old response: H3 Aries	**Uranus' choices**	**new response as the result of the resistance between the planet's SN and NN and its familiarity with the former: H3 Aries**
being denied an identity, freedom and the right to exist (Aries) because of non-integration (H3), i.e. segregation	< >	claiming my identity, freedom and right to exist (Aries) through full integration (H3)

With that we have traced the Uranus orbit and understood it from the soul perspective.

I hope you see how *a pain inflicted through having been limited, held back* (Chiron in Taurus) *in the context of integration* (Chiron H3) *because of segregation* (Chiron H3) reflects the Uranus strand of the *Trauma Helix* – where the words, thoughts and images are held – of *being denied an identity, freedom and the right to exist* (Aries) *because of non-integration* (H3), i.e. *segregation*. This is the **'trauma and pain continuity'** we set out to investigate. Direct lines can be drawn from Uranus to what shows up in Chiron's woundedness, providing validation of the premise of this book first stated back in chapter 1 (i.e. in bold on pages 8-9). We head on over to Neptune.

Neptune (see chart p.221)

Neptune in the 7th house Virgo, we said in chapter 7, speaks of the trauma of deep disillusionment caused by inequality in relationship as a result of interjected inferiority and unworthiness. From its conjunction to the SN of the Moon we learned that its felt sense of meaninglessness was a direct and decisive influence on lives lived by prior-life selves. Neptune's south node is going to tell us about the past and therefore origin of that meaninglessness. It is going to provide us with information on how and where it started. We find the SN of Neptune at 11 degrees Aquarius 42 minutes in the 1st house: *the meaninglessness trauma was incurred through prior-life selves having been dissociated* (Aquarius) *from their*

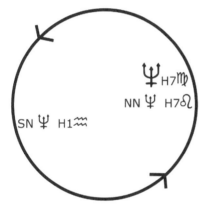

identity, freedom and right to exist (H1). (4) Again, we are provided with rather strong evidence in support of past lives as a slave.

This past dynamic is what has shaped Neptune by house and sign and is recognizable there in that it denotes *extreme inequality in relationship* (H7) *through humiliation* (Virgo) *whilst in a situation of servitude* (Virgo). This is how the past streams into the present.

Meaningfulness is going to come from a surrounding street, the soft breeze sweeping calliope music into a muddle of screams and laughter. The street is the 7th house. The music playing is at 10 degrees Leo 20 minutes: *equality in relationship* (H7) *as a result of true listening* (H7) *so that I may shine* (Leo) *and bask in the full light of my creative self* (Leo). We are beginning to understand the drivenness behind Eunice Waylon's desire to become the first black classical pianist to play Carnegie Hall. She would play there, although not as a classical pianist. But people listened (H7) and her light shone (Leo).

When that light hits the old tune, it will generate the new Neptune response of *deriving ultimate meaning* (Neptune) *from serving* (Virgo) *equality in relationship* (H7): music at the confluence of personal empowerment and political engagement.

Much depended on her willingness to serve this cause: how was the soul to mature (PPP Capricorn) through the inner equality of self-acceptance (PPP H12) if Nina remained impervious to social ills and racial barriers? She was not an island. The acceptance *had* to be all around her too. It had to be social. This is how her music got politicized. It was never meant to be merely pleasing. To Nina Simone her music *and* person reflecting the times in which she lived was imperative.

"[...] *Now I change my direction from love songs and things that are not related to what's happening, to something that is happening for my people. I can use my music as an instrument, a voice to be heard all over the world for what my people need and what we really are about."* (5)

Simone - SN of Neptune H1 Aquarius	resistance	Simone - NN of Neptune H7 Leo
meaninglessness trauma incurred through prior-life selves having been dissociated (Aquarius) from their identity, freedom and right to exist (H1)	< >	equality in relationship (H7) as a result of true listening (H7) so that I may shine (Leo) and bask in the full light of my creative self (Leo)
the past streaming into the present and determining the old response: H7 Virgo	**Neptune's choices**	**new response as the result of the resistance between the planet's SN and NN and its familiarity with the former: H7 Virgo**
extreme inequality in relationship (H7) through humiliation (Virgo) whilst in a situation of servitude (Virgo)	< >	deriving ultimate meaning (Neptune) from serving (Virgo) equality in relationship (H7)

Here too, as was the case with Uranus, we see how the Neptune strand of the
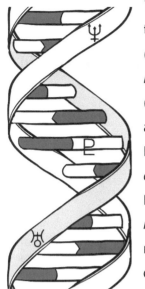
Trauma Helix – the extreme inequality in relationship (H7) through humiliation (Virgo) whilst in a situation of servitude (Virgo) – is reflected in a Chiron *pain inflicted through having been limited* (Taurus*) in the context of integration* (H3) *because of segregation* (H3). Finally, Pluto's emotional and psychological identification with the Uranus and Neptune strand comes back in the Chiron pain too: *feeling emotionally insecure* (Pluto in Cancer) *in self-worth* (Pluto H6) shows up in *the pain of having been held back* (Taurus) *in your integration with others*. After all, is that self-worth not gained as you exchange with your environment (H3) in open interaction and dialogue (H3)? As we lay bare these strata of *'trauma and pain continuity'* in the soul narrative, weight and substance is given to our premise of Chiron indeed being the one to relay a trauma charge coming from past lives to the current one *as pain*.

Trauma and healing continuity: the therapeutic roadmap

Equally, if not more important to therapeutic evolutionary astrology is the **'healing continuity'** as reflected in the new Chiron, Uranus and Neptune responses. For Nina Simone it consists of:

1. **Chiron**: to consolidate and strengthen (Taurus) integration (H3)
2. **Uranus**: claiming my identity, freedom and right to exist (Aries) through full integration (H3)
3. **Neptune**: deriving ultimate meaning (Neptune) from serving (Virgo) equality in relationship (H7)

Together with the *'trauma continuity,'* this *'healing continuity'* becomes a therapeutic roadmap as you work with your client.

All through writing this chapter I heard Bach's music in my inner ear, the music Nina Simone so loved. Tracing the full orbital movement of each of the planets has sounded like the counterpoint of multiple voices weaving in and out of each other, with their harmony understood from the soul holding all of them together:

[243]

astrology as a *Music of the Spheres*. Through this chapter I would like to pay tribute to Nina Simone the classical pianist. The pianist she was meant but not allowed to be.

Pluto H6 Cancer		Pluto Polarity Point H12 Capricorn
south node	**natal planet as _the agent of change_ conducive to evolutionary growth: the felt resistance between its south and north leading to a new response (or not, which, evolutionary speaking, is equally important)**	north node
	Moon	
prior-life egoic structures (SN of the Moon) created by the soul were marked by inequality in relationship (H7) as a result of interjected inferiority and unworthiness (Virgo)	to take full responsibility (Capricorn) for the fact that I am perfect as I am (H12) by becoming the embodiment (Capricorn) of God's universal language: music (H12)	to heal (Pisces) all matters identity, freedom and right to exist (H1)
	Mercury	
thinking in prior-life selves was aimed at making oneself invisible (H12) as part of a large group of people (Aquarius) where everyone is equally _un_important (Aquarius)	heal all things identity, freedom and right to exist and direct thinking (Mercury) towards placing those H1 issues in the context of music (Pisces) so that the vehicle Simone, through its music, may come to think of itself as God's instrument	direct your thinking at healing (Pisces) the value (H2) you place on the relationship you are in with yourself (H2)
	Venus	
prior-life selves' prime relationship was with the hidden-awayness, the unseenness (H12) of or within a large group of people (Aquarius) where	challenged to objectively observe (Aquarius) her relationship (Venus) with her identity, her freedom and her right to exist (H1) and, *through* the observing, to relate	to relate to consolidating and strengthening (H2) her identity, freedom and right to exist (Aries), to the fortification (H2) of these in a Taurean 2nd house way

[244]

everyone was equally _un_important (Aquarius)	(Venus) to the liberation (Aquarius) of these 1st house issues	
	Mars	
conscious actions and desires directed at following the distorted truth (Sagittarius) of some ideology (Sagittarius) affecting large groups of people (H11)	to direct all conscious actions and desires at looking very critically (Virgo) at the issue of power, powerlessness and self-empowerment (H8), to reflect deeply on the issue (Mars retrograde) and to then deeply commit (H8) to serving (Virgo) empowerment (H8)	conscious actions and desires to be directed at the strengthening and fortification (H2) of her identity, freedom and right to exist (Aries)
	Jupiter	
making myself invisible (H12) under the crushing weight of suppression and exploitation (Capricorn)	to know how to discern (Virgo) power and powerlessness (H8), to clearly distinguish (Virgo) between what one feels like and what the other feels like and to then serve (Virgo) self-empowerment (H8) by choosing (H8) one over the other	the birth (Cancer) of her solar energy (H5). Being seen and getting noticed (H5) through the creative act (H5) and _as_ a creative act
	Saturn	
a consciousness structured in such a way as to be able to endure the unseenness of self (H12) under the crushing weight of suppression and exploitation (Capricorn)	consciousness internally wired to liberate (Aquarius) Simone from the trauma (Aquarius) incurred to her identity, her freedom and her right to exist (H1)	consciousness in the vehicle Simone is to go through the issue of interjected inferiority and unworthiness (H6) with a fine-toothed comb (H6) so that a new self-image (Cancer) be born, a new 'me.'
a pain was inflicted to her identity, freedom and right to exist (Aries) as a result of not having been allowed to integrate (H3)	**Chiron** to consolidate and strengthen (Taurus) integration (H3) and so heal the pain	to heal the pain from a deep commitment (Scorpio) to the cause of liberty (H9)
	Uranus	
oppressive worldly power (H10) taking away my liberty (Sagittarius)	claiming my identity, freedom and right to exist (Aries) through full	"_I want my race (H4) to be allowed to integrate (Gemini) so that there be_

through laws (H10) that are a lie (Sagittarius) and reflect a distortion of truth (Sagittarius)	integration (H3) and so overcome the trauma	*an integrated* (H3) *nation* (H4)."
	Neptune	
meaninglessness trauma incurred through prior-life selves having been dissociated (Aquarius) from their identity, freedom and right to exist (H1)	deriving ultimate meaning (Neptune) from serving (Virgo) equality in relationship (H7) and so overcome the trauma	equality in relationship (H7) as a result of true listening (H7) so that I may shine (Leo) and bask in the full light of my creative self (Leo)
Pluto H6 Cancer		**PPP H12 Capricorn**
south node	**natal planet as _the agent of change_ conducive to evolutionary growth: the felt resistance between its south and north leading to a new response (or not, which, evolutionary speaking, is equally important)**	**north node**

At this point, I feel, it would be an insult to you, the reader, if I pointed out to you why Nina Simone's Sun is in the first house Pisces. So, I will not.

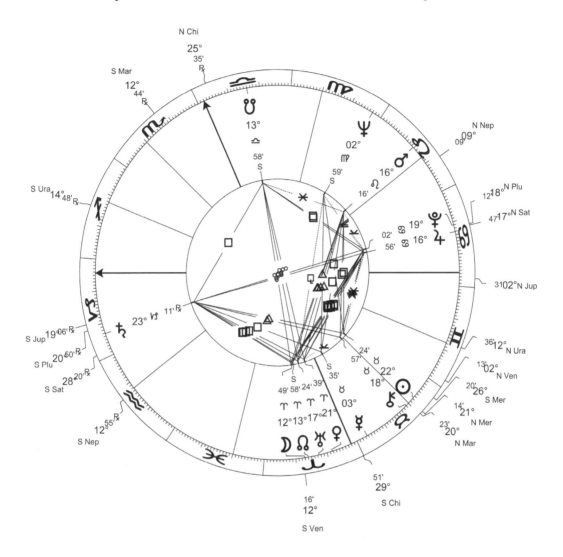

Jim Jones, 13 May 1931, 22:00 hrs., Lynn, Indiana, RR:AA

From those who somehow managed to escape the Jonestown massacre that fateful day of November 1978, or who left the church's fold as early as in Indiana or later in San Francisco, we hear time and again how with Jim Jones you always heard the message you needed to hear. It was, they say, as if he intuitively knew what your greatest hopes and deepest fears were. Mercury in the chart of a born demagogue like that obviously is going to be of some importance. How did he manage to draw such crowds in? Was it the connection with spirit, the fact that so many of his followers were disenfranchised, or both? Or was it the fact that he cleverly used religion as the Trojan horse for social reform (SN of the Moon H9 Libra), so that people felt seen and heard both at the mundane and the spiritual level?

Mercury (see chart p.247)

The SN of Mercury points to the intellectual and verbal tactics used by prior-life selves (SN H9 Libra) to enforce maximum compliance (Pluto-Jupiter H7 Cancer, SN H9 Libra) with the forcefully delivered spoken word (SN ruler H3 Aries). We find it in the 5th house at 26 degrees Taurus 20 minutes: *the word* (Mercury) *was used to solidify* (Taurus) *their absolutist leadership* (H5) *as well as their megalomania* (H5).

These are the Mercury dynamics those 9th house Libra prior-life selves availed themselves of. Full translation of the symbols to English: so as to compel in followers maximum observance (SN Moon Libra) of a professed faith (SN Moon H9) they themselves did not believe in and which therefore was a gross distortion of truth (SN Moon H9), prior-life selves *used the word* (SN Mercury) *to strengthen* (Taurus) *their self-inflation and self-aggrandizement* (H5). This is what was rekindled as young Jimmy, through a neighbor, got exposed to lengthy Biblical passages and began to recite them, as far as anyone could tell, effortlessly.

Doing this kind of linking back is rather important since without it you might lose track of *why* the SN of Mercury is where it is in Jones' chart. You need to uncover how these particular SN of Mercury dynamics fit the ones operative in 9th house Libra prior-life selves, which, as we have seen on several occasions, consisted of creating a *"slavery* (Libra) *of faith"* (H9). (1)

This is the Mercury dynamic which from the past shaped the natal Mercury in the 4th house Taurus and can therefore be seen in it. It is one unbroken line coming from the past and leading to *the word* (Mercury) *being used to put the blinkers* (Taurus) *on members of the flock* (H4) *so that they do not rely* (Taurus self-reliance) *on their own thinking* (Mercury). Brainwashing, in other words. Through brainwashing Jones got people so far in they could not imagine ever getting out (2).

[248]

The NN of Mercury is the counterforce that will create resistance in Mercury via its confrontation with the SN dynamics *and* Mercury leaning toward them. It

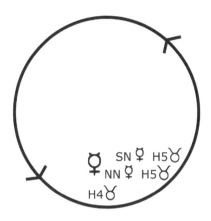

stands at 21 degrees Taurus 14 minutes in the 5th house, very close to the Sun. Since it is in the same house and sign as the SN of Mercury, you may initially find it challenging to put into words. It gets easier when you think of what it is Leo energy is trying to achieve elsewhere in the chart. Mars, who also happens to be the ruler of the NN of the Moon, is in the 8th house seeking to empower people (H8) so that they may stand in the full light of their sun (Leo). The NN of Neptune in the 7th house finds it deepest meaningfulness when through equality in relationship (H7) people come into their full sense of self (Leo). The NN of Mercury in the 5th house Taurus wants *to consolidate* (Taurus) *thinking* (Mercury) *directed at bringing out this full sense of self* (H5) *in others*. Leo in its higher expression can do that. It can bring out the best in you for it does not feel threatened by your specialness.

You can see how that would be a challenge for Jim Jones, whose ego was at the helm from the very beginning. It was always only about him exerting total and absolute control on every level. Control through the imposition of will is written in capital letters in his Saturn in the 1st house Capricorn skipped step. (3)

The NN of Mercury confronts Mercury with its 5th house Taurus energy in the hope of triggering a different response from it to the one it is so comfortable with: *to direct all of its thinking* (Mercury) *at how to secure the survival* (Taurus) *of the flock* (H4) *by allowing its members to rely on their own* (Taurus self-reliance) *thinking* (Mercury). What Jones did instead was a far cry from that intention indeed: he *conjured up* (Mercury) a diabolic plan designed *to secure* (Taurus) *the non-survival* (Taurus) *of his loyal flock* (H4) *having already taken the means to their intellectual* (Mercury) *self-reliance* (Taurus) *away from them.* How? Firstly, by moving them to an enclave outside of U.S. jurisdiction from which they could not escape, not just because their passports and worldly possessions had been confiscated but also because the jungle was an impenetrable booby-trap where dangers lurked from every imaginable corner.

And secondly, once held prisoners there, by using the word to drill into them, *White Night* after *White Night*, the false belief that they were surrounded by a capitalist enemy who would torture them and then take their and their children's lives so that it was preferable to take one's own.

Here too it is important to draw lines from this new Mercury response to the Moon's new response (as *the agent of change*) and then from there to the PPP. The premise in EA, after all, is that the soul creates an egoic structure (Moon) with the express intention of actualizing its evolutionary intentions for the current life (as expressed in the PPP). The question then becomes: **how would this new Mercury response serve the Moon in its efforts to allow people to get out from under one single 'truth'** (SN of the Moon H9) **and their expected compliance** (SN of the Moon Libra) **with it, so that they may connect** (Moon/NN of the Moon H3) **with their own will and identity** (Moon/NN of the Moon Aries) **and think** (Moon/NN of the Moon H3) **independently** (Moon/NN of the Moon Aries)? And: **how is that going to help the soul evolve?** It is these kinds of questions that constitute the fine art of evolutionary astrology chart analysis. The answer to these particular ones is not too difficult to obtain: thinking directed at securing the survival and intellectual self-reliance of the flock is going to help the Moon foster independent thinking in its members, which in turn will help the soul break the 7th house Cancer dynamic of creating extreme dependency in people through the clannish clinginess of a messianic cult (Pluto conjunct Jupiter) so that it may forge its own independent path (PPP H1) and so mature (PPP Capricorn), allowing others to do the same.

This is how you connect the new Mercury response to the new Moon response and to the PPP.

It is my hope that by drawing these lines you may appreciate how there is **a soul logic** behind lunar and planetary placements, both natal and nodal. Each planetary function – Mercury (thinking), Venus (relating), etc. – carries within it old dynamics streaming into their natal placement via their respective south node, with the latter directly connected to dynamics operative in prior-life selves (SN of the Moon, SN ruler). These, in turn, were the means through which the soul explored its issues, astrologically reflected in Pluto by house and sign. The new planetary response - Mercury (thinking), Venus (relating), etc. - given as a result of the resistance felt between its own south and north node, serves **the Moon's new response as *the agent of the kind of change conducive to soul evolution*.** This is what I have tried to put into words for you in the above paragraphs using the Mercury example.

Jones - SN of Mercury **H5 Taurus**	resistance	Jones - NN of Mercury **H5 Taurus**
the word (Mercury) was used to solidify and strengthen (Taurus) his absolutist leadership (H5) as well as his megalomania (H5)	**< >**	to consolidate (Taurus) thinking (Mercury) directed at bringing out a full sense of self (H5) in others
the past streaming into the present and determining the old response: **H4 Taurus**	**Mercury's choices**	**new response as the result of the resistance between the planet's SN and NN and its familiarity with the former:** **H4 Taurus**
the word (Mercury) is used to put the blinkers (Taurus) on members of the flock (H4) so that they do not rely (Taurus self-reliance) on their own thinking (Mercury)	**< >**	to direct all thinking at how to secure the survival (Taurus) of the flock (H4) by allowing its members to rely on their own (Taurus self-reliance) thinking (Mercury)

Venus (see chart p.247)

The SN of Venus is going to reveal the prime relationship 9th house Libra prior-life selves - availing themselves of a 3rd house Aries modus operandi - engaged in. We find the SN of Venus at 12 degrees Aries 16 minutes in the 3rd house: prior-life selves' prime relationship was *the imposition of their will* (Aries) *through the forcefully* (Aries) *delivered word* (H3). (4)

You can see these SN dynamics reflected in Venus itself in that it shows the exact same modus operandi: *the imposition of will* (Aries) *through the forcefully* (Aries) *delivered word* (H3). There is no difference between the two: same house, same sign. The important thing, again, is to understand how this imposing one's will through the forcefully delivered word would have served 9th house Libra prior-life

[251]

selves as they demanded strict compliance (SN Moon Libra) with a professed faith they themselves did not believe in (SN Moon H9).

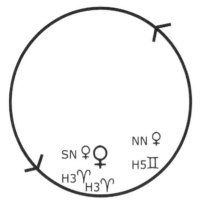

The NN of Venus is pulling hard from the other end in the 5th house at 2 degrees Gemini 13 minutes by urging Jones *to establish a relationship* (Venus) *with bringing people into their fullest sense of self* (H5) *through the spoken word* (Gemini). The Leo energy that seeks to be reinstated here is the impartiality and generosity the archetype in its higher expression is known for. As Jones connects (Gemini) with it, he will bring out the best in himself and so in others. (5)

When the old 3rd house Aries dynamics are confronted with the 5th house Gemini pull, Venus is challenged to *relate to the validity of multiple viewpoints* (H3) *so that people are allowed to connect with* (H3) *their own will and identity* (Aries) *and think* (H3) *for themselves* (Aries).

This is the new relationship (Venus) response which is going to help the Moon's new response of allowing people to connect (H3) with their own will and identity (Aries) so that they may think (H3) for themselves (Aries), facilitating, in its turn, the evolution of a soul wishing to extricate itself from dependency created in others (Pluto H7) through smothering attachment (Pluto in Cancer) cleverly dressed up in pastoral care (Pluto conjunct Jupiter H7 Cancer, both a skipped step). We are, as we were a moment ago with Mercury, **uncovering Soul Logic**. We put these dynamics into words mindful of the fact that in the contemplation of the full orbital movement not only of the Moon but also the planets, *the north node is **the catalyst** for change* while *the natal placement's new response is **the agent** of change*.

Jones - SN of Venus H3 Aries	resistance	Jones - NN of Venus H5 Gemini
relationship was with the imposition of will (Aries) through the forcefully (Aries) delivered word (H3)	< >	to establish a relationship (Venus) with bringing people into their fullest sense of self (H5) through the spoken word (Gemini)

the past streaming into the present and determining the old response: **H3 Aries**	Venus' choices	new response as the result of the resistance between the planet's SN and NN and its familiarity with the former: **H3 Aries**
relationship is with the imposition of will (Aries) through the forcefully (Aries) delivered word (H3)	< >	relate to the validity of multiple viewpoints (H3) so that people are allowed to connect with (H3) their own will and identity (Aries) and think (H3) for themselves (Aries)

Such is the Venus orbit seen through the eyes of the soul. On to Mars.

Mars (see chart p.247)

The SN of Mars is going to tell us what conscious actions and desires in prior-life selves were aimed at as they sought to assert their will (ruler SN of the Moon Aries) through the forcefully (ruler SN of the Moon Aries) delivered word (ruler SN of the Moon H3) as the way in which (SN ruler) maximum compliance was created through the false profession of faith (SN of the Moon H9 Libra).

Not surprisingly we find it at 12 degrees Scorpio 44 minutes in the 10th house: *conscious actions and desires were aimed at wielding maximum control* (H10) *over people through psychological and sexual abuse* (Scorpio). The SN of Mars placement sheds much light on Jones' Saturn in the 1st house Capricorn skipped step in which rigorous control over people through the imposition of the sexual will is implicit.

In Deborah Layton's book *Seductive Poison: A Jonestown Survivor's Story of Life and Death in the Peoples Temple* we read how this imposition played out in the current life of Jim Jones. In the back of one of the twelve Greyhound buses Jones had purchased to travel all over America to places where recruitment needed to be done or appearances made - Bus Seven - he had his own private space, furnished with a bed, a small sink and a cooler. On one trip, traveling back to San Francisco, he told nineteen-year-old Deborah she was beautiful, that she did not realize just how beautiful, that he was attracted to her and that she was to go into the back compartment of the bus. She waited there, the door opened, Jones came in and raped her, telling her *"I am doing this for you, Deborah … to help you."* (6)

Since this past dynamic is what shaped the natal 8ᵗʰ house Leo Mars, you can see it reflected there: *by dint of my perceived specialness* (Leo) *I can use people sexually and psychology* (H8) *as I see fit.* First-hand accounts of Jones' sexual proclivities abound. In Redwood Valley, as his wife Marceline got bedridden because of recurring and persistent backache and after having officially started a relationship with twenty-four-year-old Carolyn Layton since his spouse "could no longer satisfy him," he embarked on a string of sexual adventures with mainly female but also male followers, maneuvering and manipulating couples and bachelors alike into such tight corners that they had no choice but to do his bidding. Peoples Temple had now, in all but name, become an absolutist mini state. (7)

These are the dynamics pertaining to will (Mars) that allowed prior-life 9ᵗʰ house Libra selves to demand strict compliance (SN Moon Libra) with a professed faith they themselves did not believe in (SN Moon H9).

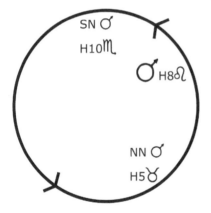

The NN of Mars tells a different story. It is in the 5ᵗʰ house at 20 degrees Taurus 23 minutes (8) and seeks *to aim conscious actions and desires at consolidating* (Taurus) *the impartiality and generosity* (H5) *that characterize a true leader* (H5), *bringing out the full creative potential in others* (H5) which, as the Sun is letting you know in no uncertain terms, is the central and integrative principle around which the life of Jim Jones revolves.

Is Mars in the 8ᵗʰ house Leo going to get this? Is it going to understand that what the soul envisages is for Jones *to help people self-empower* (H8) *so that they may bask in the light and warmth of their full sense of self* (Leo)? The question, sadly, answers itself.

Jones - SN of Mars H10 Scorpio	resistance	Jones - NN of Mars H5 Taurus
conscious desires and actions were aimed at wielding maximum control (H10) over people through psychological and sexual abuse (Scorpio)	< >	to aim conscious actions and desires (Mars) at consolidating (Taurus) the impartiality and generosity (H5) that characterize a true leader (H5), bringing out the full creative potential in others (H5)
the past streaming into the present and determining the old response: H8 Leo	**Mars' choices**	**new response as the result of the resistance between the planet's SN and NN and its familiarity with the former: H8 Leo**
by dint of my perceived specialness (Leo) I can use people sexually and psychology (H8) as I see fit	< >	to help people self-empower (H8) so that they may bask in the light and warmth of their full sense of self (Leo)

Had he understood it, then Mars' new 8th house Leo response would have helped the Moon's new response in its efforts to allow people to connect (Moon H3) with their own will and identity (Moon Aries) so that they may think (Moon H3) for themselves (Moon Aries).

Such is the Mars orbit understood from the soul perspective.

Jupiter (see chart p.247)

The SN of Jupiter will reveal what particular glasses prior-life selves looked through as they viewed the world. I am not talking about the sunglasses Jim Jones used to wear to shield followers from his 'piercing eyes so full of the glory of God,' which in reality he needed to conceal from them eyes that were bloodshot and watery from amphetamine and tranquilizer drug abuse (9), not to mention the fact that during his so-called 'miracles' he used crib notes handed him by his cronies furnishing him with the personal details of the person he was about to cure. I am talking about how prior-life selves viewed the world so that they could do their SN of the Moon 9th house Libra, ruler of the SN of the Moon 3rd house Aries thing.

The SN of Jupiter speaks to us from 19 degrees Capricorn 6 minutes in the 1st house, dangerously close to Jones' Saturn skipped step there. What it says is: *"the way I see things is that I can control people* (Capricorn) *in every way imaginable because of who I am. I am Divine* (Jupiter) *will* (H1), *bestowed with Divine* (Jupiter) *authority* (Capricorn)."* That is what the SN of Jupiter is saying there.

This is how prior-life selves viewed (Jupiter) the world as they demanded strict compliance (SN Moon Libra) with a professed faith they themselves did not believe in (SN Moon H9), enforcing it through the forcefully (SN ruler Aries) delivered word (SN ruler H3).

Via the planet's orbit these past dynamics stream straight into in the 7th house Cancer Jupiter skipped step – revealing much about how it came to be - and are recognizable there as *a near-total dependency* (H7) *created through messianic World Teacher behavior* (Jupiter) *festering in an ambience of suffocating clannish proximity* (Cancer) – expecting Temple members to extend the reach of the evangelizing claw to family, relatives and friends (10) - as the perfect environment in which this unfettered 1st house Capricorn control could be wielded.

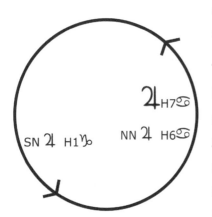

This is not what the NN of Jupiter has in mind. From the far corner of the 6th house Cancer, at 2 degrees 31 minutes to be precise, it seeks *to serve* (H6) *the family of followers, the flock* (Cancer). I hope you see the clarity of the statement the soul is making here: the NN could have been in the 7th house Cancer, along with that of Saturn and Pluto. But it is not. It is in the 6th house Cancer, nuancing the imperative need for Jones to see (Jupiter: the glasses, the interpretive lens) that he is there *to serve* (H6) *the parish* (Cancer) instead of the other way round (a need restated in Mercury H4 Taurus and in Chiron H4 Taurus).

Is Jupiter in the 7th house Cancer going to heed the call? Is it going to understand that lifetime upon lifetime it has blocked evolution (Jupiter skipped step) by *creating extreme dependency* (H7) *in people through the creation of a stifling clan culture* (Cancer)? Is it going to understand that what is required of it is to change the lens to one where there is *equality in the relationship* (H7) *with each and every one of the members that make up this family* (Cancer)? Is it going to produce that response by placing new glasses on its nose? With the clarity of hindsight, we know that the answer to those questions unfortunately must be in the negative.

Jones - SN of Jupiter H1 Capricorn	resistance	Jones - NN of Jupiter H6 Cancer
"*the way I see things* (Jupiter) *is that I can control people* (Capricorn) *in every way imaginable because of who I am*" (H1)	< >	to serve (H6) the family of followers, the flock (Cancer)
the past streaming into the present and determining the old response: H7 Cancer	**Jupiter's choices**	**new response as the result of the resistance between the planet's SN and NN and its familiarity with the former: H7 Cancer**
near-total dependency (H7) created through messianic World Teacher behavior (Jupiter) festering in an ambience of suffocating clannish proximity (Cancer)	< >	equality in the relationship (H7) with each and every one of the members that make up this family (Cancer)

Saturn (see chart p.247)

For prior-life selves to demand strict compliance with a professed faith they themselves did not believe in (SN Moon H9 Libra), enforcing it through the forcefully delivered word (SN ruler H3 Aries), consciousness would need to have been structured in a certain way. That way is written in the SN of Saturn in the 1st house at 28 degrees Capricorn 20 minutes: *total and absolute control* (Saturn) *through the imposition of will* (H1) *coming from a lack of integrity* (Capricorn) *in terms of my true identity* (H1) *and will* (H1), i.e. the not owning up (Capricorn) to the fact of being a fraud and a con artist.

It is not too difficult to see how those dynamics show up in the Saturn in the 1st house Capricorn skipped step, the block of granite in which oppression and suppression came together and which kept past-life selves away from actualizing their 3rd house Aries NN potential.

The NN of Saturn, squarely on the side of the Moon's new H3 Aries response in service of the Pluto Polarity Point in the 1st house Capricorn, is at 17 degrees

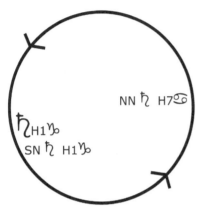

Cancer 47 minutes in the 7th house and therefore right on the Jupiter skipped step, of which it is the exact reverse. It seeks *the new birth* (Cancer) *of equality in relationship as a result of truly listening* (H7) *to each and every member of the flock* (Cancer).

As this 7th house Cancer energy hits the 1st house calcified tissue, it undoes the hardening, challenging it to *develop integrity* (Capricorn) *in all matters will and identity* (H1), *relinquishing the control so that Jones may own up* (Capricorn) *to who he really is* (H1 identity) *and what it is he is really after* (H1 will). Nothing of the sort happened. Nine hundred plus followers had to die so that he could avoid this owning up. Even in death Jim Jones proved it was never about socialism and equal rights at all but always and only about himself: while his followers lay writhing on the ground, foaming at the mouth and dying an agonizingly slow and painful death, he chose the quick way out from a single gunshot to the head.

This is Saturn's orbit understood evolutionary, that is, against the backdrop of where the soul is coming from and where it intends to evolve towards. And with that we have come to the outer limit of everyday, waking consciousness in the vehicle Jim Jones. As I commented on in the chapter on Nixon, here too studying these dynamics, more often than not, leads to a direct understanding of the Chiron - *Trauma Helix* dynamic.

Jones - SN of Saturn	resistance	Jones - NN of Saturn
H1 Capricorn		H7 Cancer

total and absolute control (Saturn) through the imposition of will (H1) coming from a lack of integrity (Capricorn) in terms of my true identity (H1) and will (H1), i.e. not owning up (Capricorn) to who I really am (H1 identity) and what it is I am really after (H1 will)	**< >**	the new birth (Cancer) of equality in relationship as a result of truly listening (H7) to each and every member of the flock (Cancer)
the past streaming into the present and determining the old response: **H1 Capricorn**	**Saturn's choices**	**new response as the result of the resistance between the planet's SN and NN and its familiarity with the former: H1 Capricorn**
total and absolute control (Saturn) through the imposition of will (H1) coming from a lack of integrity (Capricorn) in terms of my true identity (H1) and will (H1) i.e. not owning up (Capricorn) to who I really am (H1 identity) and what it is I am really after (H1 will)	**< >**	to develop integrity (Capricorn) in all matters will and identity (H1), relinquishing the control so that I may own up (Capricorn) to who I really am (H1 identity) and what it is I am really after (H1 will)

From what we have seen in this chapter, we totally get why the soul would bring the trauma charge of lives cut short prematurely as a result of people having come under the spell of certain words and ideas (Uranus H3 Aries), with its corresponding meaninglessness as a result of the betrayal of people's self-empowerment through imposed death (Neptune H8 Leo) - identified with by the soul as *an imbalance* (H7) *in care for and nurturing* (Cancer) *of the flock* (Cancer) - into the current life as *a pain caused by the holding back and, ultimately, non-survival* (Chiron in Taurus) *of the flock* (Chiron H4). It is one, unbroken line of **trauma and pain continuity**, pulled taut by the soul as an invitation to healing. The potential for healing, of paramount importance to therapeutic evolutionary astrology and the very reason for writing this book, is indicated in the table on the following pages.

Pluto 7th house Cancer (skipped step)	natal planet as _the agent of change_ conducive to evolutionary growth: the felt resistance between its south and north leading to a new response (or not, which, evolutionary speaking, is equally important)	Pluto Polarity Point 1st house Capricorn
south node		north node
	Moon	
demanding (Libra) strict compliance (Libra) from people with a professed faith (H9) they themselves did not believe in and which therefore was a gross distortion of truth (H9)	to allow people to get out from under one single 'truth' (SN of the Moon H9) and their expected compliance (SN of the Moon Libra) with it, so that they may connect (H3) with their own will and identity (Aries) and think (H3) for themselves (Aries)	to allow people to get out from under one single 'truth' (SN of the Moon H9) and their expected compliance (SN of the Moon Libra) with it, so that they may connect (H3) with their own will and identity (Aries) and think (H3) for themselves (Aries)
	Mercury	
the word (Mercury) used to solidify and strengthen (Taurus) his absolutist leadership (H5) as well as his megalomania (H5)	to direct all thinking at how to secure the survival (Taurus) of the flock (H4) by allowing its members to rely on their own (Taurus self-reliance) thinking (Mercury)	to consolidate (Taurus) thinking (Mercury) directed at bringing out a full sense of self (H5) in others
	Venus	
prime relationship was with the imposition of will (Aries) through the forcefully (Aries) delivered word (H3)	relate to the validity of multiple viewpoints (H3) so that people are allowed to connect with (H3) their own will and identity (Aries) and think (H3) for themselves (Aries)	to establish a relationship (Venus) with bringing people into their fullest sense of self (H5) through the spoken word (Gemini)
	Mars	
conscious desires and actions were aimed at wielding maximum control (H10) over people through	to help people self-empower (H8) so that they may bask in the light and	conscious desires and actions aimed at consolidating (Taurus) the impartiality and generosity

psychological and sexual abuse (Scorpio)	warmth of their full sense of self (Leo)	(H5) that characterize a true leader (H5), bringing out the full creative potential in others (H5)
	Jupiter	
"*the way I see things* (Jupiter) *is that I can control people* (Capricorn) *in every way imaginable because of who I am*" (H1)	equality in the relationship (H7) with each and every one of the members that make up this family (Cancer)	to serve (H6) the family of followers, the flock (Cancer)
	Saturn	
total and absolute control (Saturn) through the imposition of will (H1) coming from a lack of integrity (Capricorn) in terms of my true identity (H1) and will (H1), i.e. not owning up (Capricorn) to who I really am (H1 identity) and what it is I am really after (H1 will)	undoing the hardening, challenging consciousness to develop integrity (Capricorn) in all matters will and identity (H1), so that Jones may own up (Capricorn) to who he really is (H1 identity) and what it is he is really after (H1 will)	the new birth (Cancer) of equality in relationship as a result of truly listening (H7) to each and every member of the flock (Cancer)
	Chiron	
prior-life selves having imposed their will (Aries) at the expense of a community, a family of followers (H4)	a pain caused by the holding back (Taurus) and, ultimately, non-survival (Taurus) of the flock (H4); followers paying for their membership of the family (H4) with non-survival (Taurus). Healing of the pain through securing the safety (Taurus) of the flock (H4)	restoring balance (Libra) in his tendency to make people comply (Libra) with his truth (H9) which was a distortion of truth (H9): a lie (H9)
	Uranus	
the deaths happened as part of a faith, a religion or doctrine (Sagittarius) in a hidden-away place (H12) far from public scrutiny, a place where people would fall victim (H12) to the delusions (H12) of a madman (H12)	trauma incurred as a result of people having come under the spell of certain words and ideas (H3) and dying abruptly and prematurely (Aries) as a consequence. Overcoming the trauma by allowing people to connect (H3) with their own will and identity (Aries) and think	to serve (H6) by acknowledging the validity of multiple viewpoints (Gemini)

	(H3) for themselves (Aries)	
	Neptune	
spiritual trauma caused by the non-survival (H2) of a large group of people (Aquarius); holding people back (H2) in their value system (H2), dissociating (Aquarius) them from it by making them dependent on yours (SN of the Moon H9 Libra); dissociating (Aquarius) people from both their value system (H2) and right to survive (H2), to live	a crisis (Virgo) around taking people's power (H8) away from them, compounded by the denial (Virgo) of this fact - culminating in imposed death (H8). Overcoming the trauma by truly serving (Virgo) people's self-empowerment (H8)	equality in relationship (H7) so that people may stand in their own light and bask in the warmth of that light (Leo)
south node	**natal planet as _the agent of change_ conducive to evolutionary growth: the felt resistance between its south and north leading to a new response (or not, which, evolutionary speaking, is equally important)**	**north node**
Pluto 7th house Cancer (skipped step)		**PPP 1st house Capricorn**

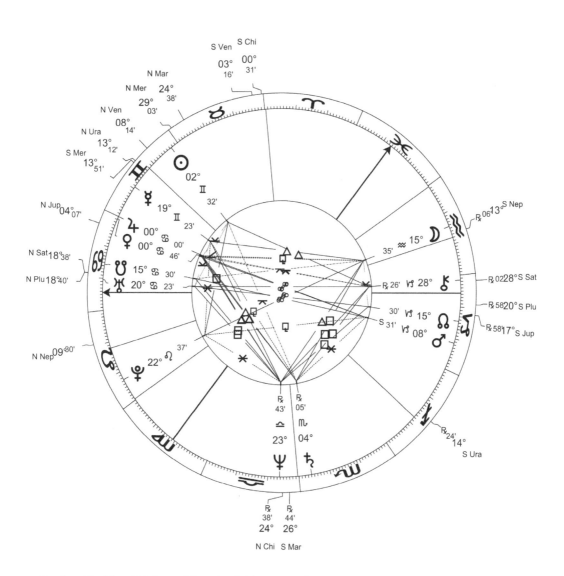

Barbro Karlén, 24 May 1954, 07:20 hrs., Gothenburg, Sweden. RR:AA (birth time supplied to the author by Ms Karlén)

I feel I owe you one more thing before we bring this book to a close: to link the planetary south nodes in the chart of Barbro Karlén back to the chart of Anne

Frank and so provide definitive and conclusive astrological proof for my claim that these are indeed two consecutive lives created by the same soul.

This chapter will not hold much meaning to you unless you have read chapter 9 of my book *Intercepted Signs: Encoded Messages from the Soul*. In it I embark on a comparative study of the charts of Barbro Karlén and Anne Frank to show how the intercepted and duplicated signs in the former have their origin in the latter.

What I would like to do in this chapter is delve even deeper into these two charts and show you, through an exploration of full orbital movements, how the planetary functions in one chart are connected to those in the other. We already tiptoed into this kind of approach in the comparative chart study of Abraham Lincoln and Charles Lindberg in chapters 4 (p.55) and 5 (pp.70-71) of this book where we saw how the SN of Mars in the chart of Lindbergh was on his Uranus in the 1st house Sagittarius: *conscious actions and desires in Lincoln coincided with his relentless efforts to guarantee people's freedom and right to exist* (Uranus H1) *as essential to the noble cause of liberty* (Uranus in Sagittarius), with the 1st house Uranus at once pointing at Lincoln having been abruptly and violently dissociated from this cause.

To look at what I have termed **'trauma continuity between one life and the next'** I would like to start with Barbro Karlén's Chiron - *Trauma Helix* dynamic and see how it relates back to Anne Frank. When that has been mapped, we will look at the planetary nodes from Saturn all the way in to Mercury.

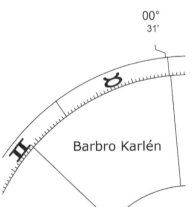

S Chi
00°
31'

Barbro Karlén

Chiron (see chart p.263)

The SN of Chiron in Barbro Karlén's chart is at 0 degrees Taurus 31 minutes in the 11th house: the past of Barbro's 7th house Capricorn *pain was caused by the non-survival* (Taurus) *of a large collective* (H11) *upon whom all sorts of things were projected* (H11/Aquarius: group projections), in this case the Jewish race. (1)

The 7th house Capricorn Chiron pain itself speaks of *projections* (H7) *in the form of negative judgement* (Capricorn) *coming from dysfunctional authority* (Capricorn): the Nazi regime. It is the 11th house Taurus past of the pain which has led to Barbro's natal Chiron in the 7th house Capricorn, and it shows: a history of all kinds of things being projected onto a collective which does not survive as a result of those projections (SN Chiron H11 Taurus) has led to the pain of projections in the form of negative judgement coming from dysfunctional authority (Chiron H7 Capricorn). Let us not forget that what we are looking at

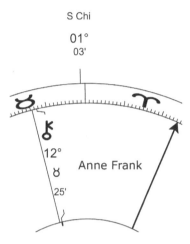

with Chiron is the trauma charge extracted from the *Trauma Helix* and transferred to Saturn *as pain*. This is the premise of the book and we are, one final time, testing it through astrological findings corroborated by biographical fact pertaining to actual lives lived.

If this past of Chiron is fully present in its natal 7th house placement, then how do both relate to Anne Frank's Chiron in the 10th house Taurus? (see Planetary Nodes chart Anne Frank page 293) They relate in that the latter speaks of *non-survival*

(Taurus) *at the hands of dysfunctional authority* (H10). That pain too has a past (i.e. SN) and it points to a pain dating back to more distant pasts, to lives prior to that of Anne's. We find it in the same house and sign, at 1 degree Taurus 3 minutes, speaking the exact same language as Anne's natal Chiron: *non-survival* (Taurus) *at the hands of dysfunctional authority* (H10). The pulse playing through the woundedness narrative, as you can see in the table on the next page, is negative judgement issued by dysfunctional authority (Capricorn) coming down on past and current-life selves like a ton of bricks and squashing (Taurus: non-survival) them.

Chiron: Trauma Key

This is the **'trauma continuity between one lifetime and the next'** which we first ran into in the Lincoln-Lindbergh chart comparison (chapter 4 & 5) and then complemented with **'healing continuity'** in the chapters on Jim Jones (chapter 11) and Nina Simone (chapter 13), as we will in this chapter. Understanding both is the key to healing the Chiron pain and overcoming the trauma relayed inside of it. Chiron, therefore, indeed is the **'Trauma Key'**. The title of the book may sound jazzy or fancy to you, but it was chosen for legitimate reasons.

Anne Frank – SN Chiron H10 Taurus, pointing to wounding incurred in lives prior to that of Anne's	Anne Frank – Chiron H10 Taurus, pointing to wounding incurred in a life prior to that of Anne's	Barbro Karlén – SN Chiron H11 Taurus, pointing to the past of the H7 Capricorn pain and therefore to Anne's life (and beyond)	Barbro Karlén- Chiron H7 Capricorn, pointing to a wound inflicted in Anne's life
non-survival (Taurus) at the hands of dysfunctional authority (H10)	non-survival (Taurus) at the hands of dysfunctional authority (H10); **reenactment in the life of Anne:** non-survival (Taurus) at the hands of dysfunctional authority (H10)	a pain caused by the non-survival (Taurus) of a large collective (H11) upon whom all sorts of things are projected (H11/Aquarius: group projections)	projections (H7) in the form of negative judgement (Capricorn) coming from dysfunctional authority (Capricorn): the Nazi regime; **reenactment in the life of Barbro:** unstoppable barrage of false accusations by those in authority

In Barbro's chart you can see how Chiron squares its own south node, (2) indicating that this is an important unresolved issue the soul brings into the current life of Barbro Karlén, a finding fully corroborated by the relentless persecution Barbro would have to endure as a member of the Swedish Mounted Police force. (3) Chiron relaying a trauma charge *as pain* points to (an) unresolved issue(s) by definition, of course, but through the square the unresolved nature of the issue(s) is stressed quite dramatically. (4) How it played out in Barbro's life you can read in her book *And the Wolves Howled*, which I strongly recommend you read to gain a fuller understanding of the **'trauma continuity'** we are looking into in these pages.

Chiron's NN, prompting a response from Chiron that will contribute to healing of the pain, we find at 24 degrees Libra 38 minutes in the 4th house, smack-dab on her Neptune skipped step: *to restore balance* (Libra) *in the extent to which she allows these projections* (Libra) *on her and her people* (H4: race) *to occur*. This is one of those occasions where through a planetary node you are handed a

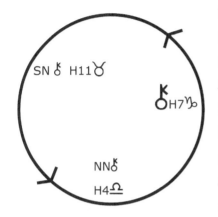

trump card which, if you know how to read it, provides major corroboration of an earlier finding made during your analysis of the Evolutionary Axis: lifetime upon lifetime the movement to the 6th house Capricorn NN was thwarted by the Neptune boulder in the middle of the road: *deep disillusionment and despair*, ultimately leading to *a sense of meaninglessness* (the Neptune strand of the *Trauma Helix*) *as a result of what was projected* (Libra) *upon her race* (H4) now turns out to have the NN of Chiron right on it. The catalyst for healing (NN of Chiron), obviously, is going to be the exact opposite of what caused the meaninglessness: *to restore balance in the degree in which she allows the projections to happen* or, if they do happen – and they did - *to affect* (Libra) *her*. (5)

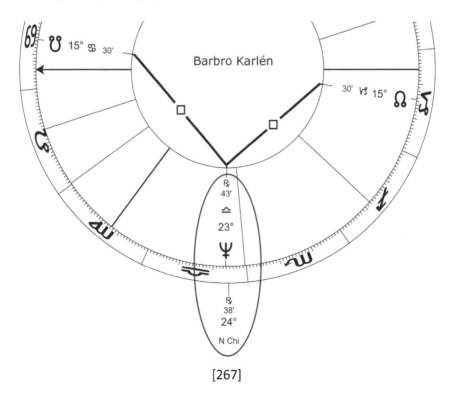

[267]

Karlén - SN of Chiron H11 Taurus	resistance	Karlén - NN of Chiron H4 Libra
a pain caused by the non-survival (Taurus) of a large collective (H11) upon whom all sorts of things are projected (H11/Aquarius: group projections)	< >	to restore balance (Libra) in the extent to which she allows projections (Libra) on her person and her people (H4: race) to occur
the past streaming into the present and determining the old response: H7 Capricorn	**Chiron's choices**	**new response as the result of the resistance between the planet's SN and NN and its familiarity with the former: H7 Capricorn**
projections (H7) in the form of false accusations (Capricorn: negative judgment) coming from those in authority (Capricorn)	< >	to assume responsibility (Capricorn) for stopping the false allegations (Libra: projections) by taking her accusers to court (Capricorn)

Chiron's NN confronting the past dynamics will engender a new response in Chiron, one that is intimately linked to its NN: healing will come when she *assumes responsibility* (Capricorn) *for stopping the false allegations* (Libra: projections) *by taking her accusers to court* (Capricorn). (6)

Personally, I feel at this point I could already rest my case: the evidence at this early stage of our analysis is persuasive, if not compelling. But I am not going to. We are going to go the whole hog and look at all the planetary south nodes in Barbro's chart and link them to the life and chart of Anne Frank. And whilst we are at it, we will turn our gaze to Barbro's planetary north nodes as well, so that we may understand all orbital movements in her chart in their full evolutionary meaning.

In an earlier chart fragment (p.265), we saw how both Anne's Chiron and its SN are in the 10th house Taurus: ***non-survival*** (Taurus) ***at the hands of dysfunctional authority*** (Capricorn). As you can see in the chart fragment below, Anne's NN of Chiron is at 22 degrees Libra 52 minutes in her 4th house,

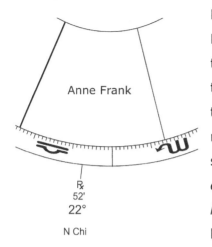

Anne Frank

℞
52'
22°

N Chi

less than one degree away from where Barbro's Neptune skipped step would show up and less than two degrees removed from Barbro's NN of Chiron: the healing of Anne's pain clearly is linked to what the soul would bring into the life of Barbro as a major unresolved issue (i.e. her Neptune skipped step H4 Libra): *restoring balance* (Libra) *in the extent to which Anne allowed these projections on her race* (H4) *to happen*. By looking carefully at how these placements connect in terms of content we lay bare **'pain – and the potential for healing - continuity'** between one lifetime and the next (7), which, ultimately, is what we are after as we seek ways I which we might use Chiron therapeutically.

In the table on the next page, I have sketched the Chiron orbit for Anne Frank. We know what the pain was, what the past of the pain was, and what the counterforce provided by Chiron's NN was. What we do not know, since Anne's life was wrenched away from her, is if her Chiron would indeed have been able to come up with the new response given in the table. But it *was* given by the soul in its next incarnation: Barbro Karlén very much put a stop to the negative judgements coming at her in a barrage of false accusations by those in authority (the Swedish Mounted Police, character assassination by newspaper journalists, etcetera). The human body withers and dies or is killed. The soul is never born and never dies. From its home in the spiritual world it contemplates its lessons and then steps into the exact right set of circumstances which will further its evolution. The soul of Anne Frank chose gender discrimination, personal vendettas, onslaught by the media, libel and attempted murder in Sweden in the latter half of the twentieth century as the perfect environment in which to continue its lessons and heal the trauma and pain. And healed they were.

We move on to Uranus, which is where Chiron picks up the trauma charge. Perhaps in its past too we will find traces of *'trauma continuity'* the way we did for Chiron.

Frank - SN of Chiron H10 Taurus	resistance	Frank - NN of Chiron H4 Libra
non-survival (Taurus) at the hands of dysfunctional authority (H10)	**< >**	restoring balance (Libra) in the extent to which Anne allows these projections (Libra) on her race (H4) to happen
the past streaming into the present and determining the old response: H10 Taurus	**Chiron's choices**	**new response as the result of the resistance between the planet's SN and NN and its familiarity with the former: H10 Taurus**
non-survival (Taurus) at the hands of dysfunctional authority (H10)	**< >**	to survive (Taurus) in the world (H10) *in spite of* suffering the consequences of dysfunctional authority coming down on one (H10)

Uranus (see chart p.263)

The Uranus placement in Barbro's chart is one of the strongest pieces of astrological evidence in support of her indeed being the reincarnation of Anne Frank: it literally speaks of *trauma incurred to a family* (Cancer) *in hiding* (H12),

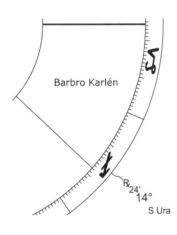

Barbro Karlén

with its conjunction to the SN of the Moon in the same house and sign underlining how this trauma had a direct and decisive impact on prior-life selves.

With the SN of Uranus, we move deeper into the rabbit hole and catch a glimpse of where this kind of trauma originated. We find it at 14 degrees Sagittarius 24 minutes in the 6th house: *wholesale persecution* (H6) *by a twisted ideology* (Sagittarius). The SN of Uranus is not on a natal planet belonging to the *Trauma Helix*, as was the case with Barbro's NN of Chiron, but the information we get from its house and sign is no less tell-tale. In Uranus' past lies the mental content – in the form of thoughts, words and images – pertaining to persecution by some depraved and aberrant world view, which has led to the trauma of a family in hiding (Uranus H12 Cancer), streaming into Barbro's Uranus as *the threat of dissolution* (H12) *of her person* (Cancer), *her home* (Cancer) *and everything she had emotionally* (Cancer) *invested in through discrimination, personal vendettas, character assassination in the media, libel, & attempted murder.* The past shaping the present is one, unbroken arc in orbit and it tells the story of this kind of trauma going way back in time, much further than the life of Anne Frank even. As you can see, Uranus' SN is inconjunct the SN of the Moon in the 12th house Cancer.

There is a crisis (inconjunct) between the two and we totally get why: there *would*

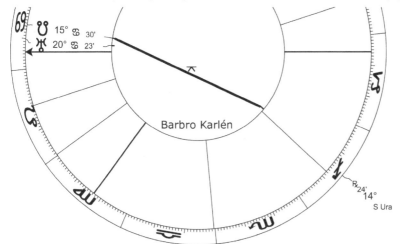

be a crisis between lives where a family was in hiding (SN Moon H12 Cancer) and persecution on a large scale by a sick and perverted ideology (SN Uranus H6 Sagittarius), would there not? A life directly impacted by the trauma inflicted upon that family (Uranus H12 Cancer conjunct the SN of the Moon).

Does this trauma connect to Anne Frank's Uranus placement in any way? Very much so: it tells us *trauma was incurred through dying young* (Uranus in contact with Aries) *at the hands of dysfunctional authority* (H10). In my book *Intercepted Signs: Encoded Messages from the Soul* I point out how through house rulership this 10th house Aries trauma rules the house of death (H8) in Anne's chart. As you can see, the SN of her Uranus is in the 5th house at 13 degrees Sagittarius 14 minutes: dying young at the hands of dysfunctional authority (Uranus H10 Capricorn) has its origins in lives from more remote pasts during which *the light of the Sun* (SN Uranus H5) *was put*

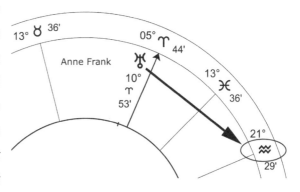

[271]

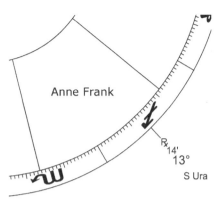

Anne Frank

out by sick and aberrant ideologies (SN Uranus Sagittarius), its fire doused the way it would be in Anne's. Through the SN of Uranus we are also looking into lives prior to that of Anne, the same way with the SN of Uranus in the chart of Abraham Lincoln we were handed information about the life of the Himalayan Yogi *and beyond*. Using the table below, a single 'trauma line' can now be drawn from lives prior to that of Anne Frank's to the life of Barbro Karlén. This is how we astrologically unravel *'trauma continuity between one lifetime and the next.'*

Anne Frank – SN Uranus H5 Sagittarius, pointing to trauma incurred in lives prior to that of Anne's	Anne Frank – Uranus H10 Aries, pointing to trauma incurred in a life prior to that of Anne's	Barbro Karlén – SN Uranus H6 Aquarius, pointing to the past of the H12 Cancer trauma and therefore to Anne's life (and beyond)	Barbro Karlén - Uranus H12 Cancer, pointing to trauma incurred by Anne Frank
the light of the Sun (H5) put out by sick and aberrant ideologies (Sagittarius)	dying young (Uranus in contact with Aries) at the hands of dysfunctional authority (H10); *reenactment in the life of Anne:* dying young (Uranus in contact with Aries) at the hands of dysfunctional authority (H10)	wholesale persecution (H6) by a depraved ideology (Sagittarius)	a family (Cancer) in hiding (H12); *reenactment in the life of Barbro:* the threat of dissolution (H12) of her person (Cancer), her home (Cancer) and everything she had emotionally (Cancer) invested in through discrimination, personal vendettas, character assassination in the media, libel, and attempted murder

Uranus' NN in the chart of Barbro Karlén is going to point to ways of overcoming and therefore healing the trauma. It will leave the actual work to Uranus in the

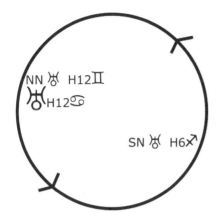

12th house Cancer, of course, but it will place a big weight at the other end of the see-saw, one that will hopefully get Uranus to indeed formulate a new response. We find the NN of Uranus at 13 degrees Gemini 12 minutes in the 12th house: *the written or spoken word* (Gemini) *offered* (H12) *to help humanity* (H12) *heal* (H12) is going to be the way out for Uranus. And guess what: Barbro Karlén at age 12 had written two books that did just that: *When the Storm Comes* and *A Moment in the Blossom Kingdom,* major works of literature which we will come back to in a moment. (8)

Karlén - SN of Uranus H6 Sagittarius	resistance	Karlén - NN of Uranus H12 Gemini
wholesale persecution (H6) by a depraved ideology (Sagittarius)	< >	the written or spoken word (Gemini) offered (H12) to help humanity (H12) heal (H12)
the past streaming into the present and determining the old response: H12 Cancer	**Uranus' choices**	**new response as the result of the resistance between the planet's SN and NN and its familiarity with the former: H12 Cancer**
the threat of dissolution (H12) of her person (Cancer), her home (Cancer), everything she had emotionally (Cancer) invested in	< >	overcoming the trauma by making humanity (H12) my family, my home (Cancer)

The NN of Uranus administered a counter dose, an injection of 12th house Gemini energy. When it got into the veins of the Uranus system, laden with trauma, it triggered a new response in Uranus itself. The new response is written in its house and sign: *"I am going to overcome this trauma by making humanity* (H12) *my family, my home* (Cancer). (9) The writing (NN Uranus Gemini) is going to be about how the soul (NN Uranus H12) cloaks itself in many lives, how it travels from lifetime to lifetime, from Anne Frank to Barbro Karlén. "I am going to *tell this story* (NN Uranus Gemini) *for the healing* (NN Uranus H12, Uranus H12) *of the family* (Uranus in Cancer) *of mankind* (NN Uranus H12, Uranus H12)." (10)

In a moment you will learn how the NN of Uranus is bang on the SN of Mercury: 13 degrees Gemini, and you will understand why.

Neptune (see chart p.263)

The meaninglessness strand of the *Trauma Helix* tells of disillusionment accrued in the soul narrative as a result of events the subconscious memories of which

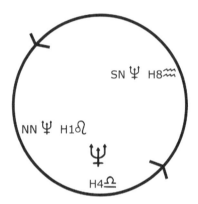

are held in Uranus' non-linear storage vault. We have seen what those events are. The meaninglessness that has folded around them, as we saw just now with Chiron's NN right on it, has to do with *what was projected* (Libra) *upon an entire race* (H4) *by an entire nation* (H4): 4th house Libra. (11) It too, just like Chiron and Uranus, has a past and it tells a story. The past of Neptune, its SN, we find in the 8th house at 13 degrees Aquarius 6 minutes, perilously close to the ruler of the SN of the Moon there, who informed us of what happened to that family in hiding: *it was taken to a place where large groups of people* (Aquarius) *were murdered* (H8). (12) Through the SN of Neptune's proximity to the ruler of the lunar SN, you see how meaninglessness

trauma spanning a myriad of lives far beyond Anne's - i.e. *the powerlessness* (H8) *of a large collective* (Aquarius) *beset through the ages by persecution ending in attempts at annihilation* (H8) *of that collective* (Aquarius): *genocide* (the

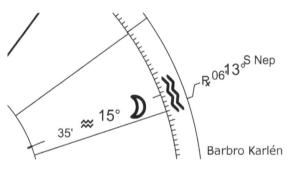

Barbro Karlén

Inquisition, the Chmielnicki Massacre, the Pogroms, the Shoah) – is connected to what happened to the Frank family (ruler of the SN of the Moon H8 Aquarius) and the subconscious memories thereof held in Uranus's non-linear memory vault (Uranus H12 Cancer conjunct SN of the Moon H12 Cancer). It streams straight into the person Barbro (i.e. the Moon), offering yet another explanation for why memories of these events haunted young Barbro at night. The memories encompass an entire history of a large collective facing annihilation (SN Neptune H8 Aquarius), part of which are the ones belonging to the soul's most recent life, i.e. that of Anne Frank (ruler of the SN of the Moon).

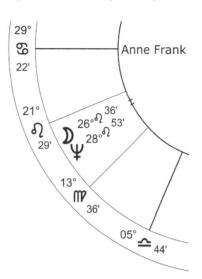

Can this trauma be detected in Anne's Neptune placement? Let us see and find out. Neptune in Anne's chart is in the 2nd house Leo and it is a skipped step, closely aligned with the Moon and therefore indicating how the meaninglessness trauma would have streamed unadulterated into the vehicle Anne. (13) Neptune tells the story of both Anne and prior-life 'Annes' *having had to pour all of their creative efforts* (Leo) *into survival* (H2). Neptune's SN in Anne's

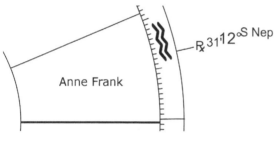

chart – pointing to the origin of this survival issue - is in the 7th house at 12 degrees Aquarius 31 minutes: *trauma* (Aquarius) *incurred by a large collective* (Aquarius) *ostracized* (Aquarius) *through projected inequality* (H7).

Barbro's 4th house Libra Neptune and its SN in the 8th house Aquarius directly point back to Anne's 2nd house Leo meaninglessness trauma: even *when* in hiding they were found out and led to their deaths. For the Neptune strand of the *Trauma Helix* too we are handed proof in support of the **'trauma continuity'** we are seeking to uncover.

In the meaninglessness lies the potential for meaning*ful*ness when Barbro manages to put a stop to these projections, that is, *restores balance* (Libra) *in the extent to which she allows them to happen, or – if they cannot be stopped – affect* (Libra) *her person, her self-image* (H4). (14)

Anne Frank – SN Neptune H7 Aquarius, pointing to meaninglessness trauma incurred in lives prior to that of Anne's	Anne Frank – Neptune H2 Leo, pointing to meaninglessness trauma incurred in a life prior to that of Anne's	Barbro Karlén – SN Neptune H8 Aquarius (on the ruler of the lunar SN), pointing to the past of the H4 Libra trauma and therefore to Anne's life (and beyond)	Barbro Karlén – Neptune H4 Libra, pointing to meaninglessness trauma incurred by Anne Frank
trauma (Aquarius) incurred by a large collective (Aquarius) ostracized (Aquarius) through projected inequality (H7)	having had to pour all of one's creative efforts (Leo) into survival (H2); **reenactment in the life of Anne:** having had to pour all of her creative efforts (Leo) into survival (H2)	the powerlessness (H8) of a large collective (Aquarius) beset through the ages by persecution ending in attempts at annihilation (H8) of the collective (Aquarius): genocide	subjected to projections (Libra) upon an entire race (H4) by an entire nation (H4); **reenactment in the life of Barbro:** subjected to projections (Libra) upon her person (H4)

This she does by dispelling each and every one of the false accusations - and it is a true fusillade - leveled at her and which almost bring her to her knees, the account of which you can read in

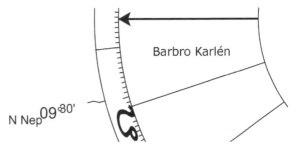

Barbro Karlén

N Nep 09°30'

her book *And the Wolves Howled*. This new response of Neptune is triggered by its NN at 9 degrees Leo 30 minutes in the 1st house, beckoning her *to claim her right to exist*, that is, *to come out of her hiding place, through the creative act*. This is how Barbro came to *establish her creative identity* (NN Neptune H1 Leo) at such an unusually early age in this life.

Karlén - SN of Neptune H8 Aquarius	resistance	Karlén - NN of Neptune H1 Leo
the powerlessness (H8) of a large collective (Aquarius) beset through the ages by persecution ending in attempts at annihilation (H8) of the collective (Aquarius): genocide	**< >**	claim her right to exist (H1) *through* the creative act (Leo), that is, to come out of her hiding place and bask in the light of her creative self (Leo)
the past streaming into the present and determining the old response: H4 Libra	**Neptune's choices**	**new response as the result of the resistance between the planet's SN and NN and its familiarity with the former: H4 Libra**
allowing projections (Libra) onto her person and self-image (H4) to continue (and affect her)	**< >**	restoring balance (Libra) in the extent to which she allows projections (Libra) to happen, or – if they cannot be stopped - affect her person, her self-image (H4)

Ultimately this new Neptune response serves the soul in its efforts to get to the 8th house Aquarius PPP: to stop directing all of her creative efforts (Pluto in Leo) at survival (Pluto H2) by staying under the radar (Pluto H2), come out of her den and trust enough (PPP H8) to deeply share with others (PPP H8) in the context of some larger collective need, some socially relevant cause (PPP Aquarius).

Barbro, subconsciously driven by an authorship taken away from Anne Frank, does this between the ages of 10 and 12, even before her first book was published, by writing *When the Storm Comes* and *A Moment in the Blossom Kingdom*. In the former, with the visionary clarity of one able to see far into the future, young Barbro writes about the inevitable consequences of humanity exploiting the earth. In the latter, she depicts a world where humans live in harmony with nature. The maturity of the writing in both works is far beyond her years in earthly time but not in soul time. When reading the gossamer-like prose and poetry, filled with love and respect, one gets the distinct impression young Barbro is holding the pen that was snatched from Anne's hand.

Barbro's Pluto identifies with the Neptune and Uranus strand emotionally and

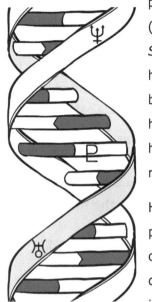

psychologically as *having had to pour all of its creativity* (Leo) *into survival* (H2). As pointed out in *Intercepted Signs: Encoded Messages from the Soul*, Anne's triple-headed Mars-Moon-Neptune in Leo skipped step comes back in highly condensed form in Barbro's Pluto in the 2nd house Leo, which is another fine example of what can happen during the refraction phase of *the Diamond Self* as referred to in the chapter on Lindbergh (pp.63-66).

Here too, at the level of the soul's emotional identification patterns, there is continuity with Anne's Pluto: pouring all of one's creativity into survival (Barbro's Pluto H2 Leo) is directly related to feeling emotionally secure (Anne's Pluto in Cancer) in remaining unseen (Anne's Pluto H12), the hiddenness (H12) becoming one's home (Cancer). We are getting strong confirmation here of how the *Trauma Helix* model shows these identification patterns at the level of the Deep Self and how they feature the same continuity we find in the Uranus and Neptune strands.

Anne Frank – Pluto H12 Cancer, pointing to how the soul identifies with the Uranus and Neptune strands	Barbro Karlén – Pluto H2 Leo, pointing to how the soul identifies with the Uranus and Neptune strands
feeling emotionally secure (Pluto in Cancer) in remaining unseen (Pluto H12), the hiddenness (H12) becoming one's home (Cancer)	having had to pour all of one's creativity (Leo) into survival (H2)

Trauma and healing continuity: the therapeutic roadmap

Since the whole point of therapeutic evolutionary astrology is to help clients heal and evolve, mapping **'healing continuity'** is as important as tracing *'trauma continuity.'*

1. **Chiron**: assuming responsibility (Capricorn) for stopping the false allegations (H7: projections) by taking her accusers to court (Capricorn).

2. **Uranus**: making humanity (H12) her family, her home (Cancer)

3. **Neptune**: restoring balance (Libra) in the extent to which she allows projections (Libra) to happen, or – if they cannot be stopped - affect her person, her self-image (H4)

Here, with Barbro Karlén, the common thread in the healing potential seems to be for her to stand up to her accusers and, through her writing, sublimate the suffering by offering to humanity what both she and Anne have learned from it. This is what Barbro's life has been about, and it is beautifully chronicled in her books.

From Chiron to Saturn

In our model of Chiron and the *Trauma Helix*, the former now relays the trauma charge held in the Uranus domain to Saturn, the outer limit of consciousness. When it gets there, the pain envelops Saturn in the form of the energy field matrix which in chapter 6 (*The 'Multidimensional Psyche'*) we called *'the subtle body'*, structuring it for two reasons:

1. to heal the pain
2. to have consciousness operate in a way conducive to soul evolution

What does that mean in practical terms? It means consciousness in the vehicle Barbro is structured in such a way as to allow for *a deep commitment* (Scorpio) *to the profundity* (Scorpio) *of life* (H5) *and to its celebration* (H5). How would that heal the pain? Firstly, it heals Anne Frank's SN in the 5th house Scorpio, which speaks of *a deep betrayal* (Scorpio) *of the child* (H5), *and with it, of the child's blossoming creativity* (H5). (15) Secondly, it heals the trauma incurred to a family in hiding (Barbro's Uranus H12 Cancer); the withdrawnness and unseenness of the hiding (Anne's Pluto H12) having become one's permanent home (Anne's Pluto in Cancer). Thirdly, it heals the trauma incurred through projections *upon an entire race by an entire nation* (Barbro's Neptune H4 Libra skipped step) - reenacted in Barbro's life as an unstoppable onslaught of false accusations against her person - with all of the above transferred to the life of Barbro Karlén as the woundedness of projections (Chiron H7) in the form of

[279]

negative judgement (Chiron in Capricorn) coming from dysfunctional authority (Chiron in Capricorn).

That same 5th house Scorpio structure of consciousness, in its celebration of life, is going to help the soul leave its 2nd house lair behind and trust enough to deeply open up (PPP H8) and commit to some larger collective and shared purpose (PPP Aquarius), which is exactly what we saw Barbro do at a very young age.

Saturn (see chart p.263)

The structure of consciousness in Barbro did not come falling from the sky. It too has a past and that past is going to have a lot to do with the soul's vehicle Anne Frank. We find the SN of Saturn at 28 degrees Capricorn 2 minutes in the 7th house, bang on Chiron there at 28 degrees Capricorn 26 minutes: in the life of Anne Frank consciousness was structured in such a way as *to withstand* (Capricorn) *inequality projected upon a people* (H7) *through negative judgement* (Capricorn) *coming from dysfunctional authority* (Capricorn): the Nazi regime.

What was projected onto Anne Frank and her people, through orbital movement, from the past is brought into the present of Barbro's natal Saturn in the 5th house Scorpio in that it constitutes *a deeply felt sense of betrayal* (Scorpio) *of the life force itself, of Eros, understood as the need to celebrate life in direct contact with other sentient beings*. This affront to life itself conjures up uncomfortable images of Josef Mengele's SN of the Moon in the 5th house violating that force, with the thoroughly perverted ideology too close for comfort (conjunct Jupiter H5 Scorpio, see chapter 11, p.171).

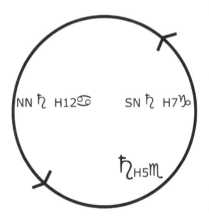

In Barbro's chart the NN of Saturn sits at 18 degrees Cancer 38 minutes in the 12th house, firmly wedged between her SN of the Moon and the trauma content streaming unadulterated into it, into young Barbro as she, in the small hours of the night, is haunted by dreams of that other life, without the young girl able to comprehend why she seems to be living two lives. As she was plagued by these persistent nightmares of the horrors which befell that other girl, in too came the gifts of Anne Frank. And in came the great unfulfilled dream of the books she would have written had she been allowed to live. All of that flowed straight into not only Barbro's SN of the Moon but also into her Saturn NN, producing the most exquisite prose and poetry. Never is this consciousness felt more keenly than in young Barbro's *When the Storm Comes* and *A Moment in the Blossom Kingdom.* There is a strong element of her wanting *to heal* (H12) humanity's co-existence with its host *Mother Earth* (Cancer) in these early works, an element of wanting to care (Cancer). These are books that seem to come from unseen 12th house dimensions, from Anne speaking through the pen of Barbro, bearing testimony to Mercury having moved from the 11th house in Anne's chart to the 12th in Barbro's, almost as if the soul in the Bardo – where it planned the next life - became fully seized of the need to write not only about the soul but also about one of the biggest perils humanity would face during Barbro's lifetime. (16)

Karlén - SN of Saturn H7 Capricorn	resistance	Karlén - NN of Saturn H12 Cancer
consciousness structured in such a way as to withstand (Capricorn) inequality projected (H7) upon a people through negative judgement (Capricorn) coming from dysfunctional authority (Capricorn): the Nazi regime.	< >	healing (H12) the family (Cancer) of mankind (H12); wanting to heal humanity's co-existence with its host Mother Earth (Cancer)
the past streaming into the present and determining the old response: H5 Scorpio	**Saturn's choices**	**new response as the result of the resistance between the planet's SN and NN and its familiarity with the former: H5 Scorpio**
a deeply felt sense of betrayal (Scorpio) of the life force itself (H5), of Eros (H5), understood as the need to celebrate life in direct contact with other sentient beings	< >	a deep commitment (Scorpio) to the profundity (Scorpio) of life (H5) and to its celebration (H5)

This is what happened to Saturn as it received the impact of its H12 Cancer NN: it decided *to deeply commit* (Scorpio) *to the profundity* (Scorpio) *of life and to its celebration* (H5). Through the creative act (H5) of writing Barbro would let people know that instead of death (Scorpio) there is constant rebirth (Scorpio) from lifetime to lifetime. Anne picking up her pen again, would inform them there is no irate and vengeful God, only the soul lovingly evaluating its own evolution.

Jupiter (see chart p.263)

The SN of Jupiter in Barbro's chart is at 17 degrees Capricorn 58 minutes in the 6th house. It reveals how Anne Frank's interpretative lens, the lens through which she looked out into the world, was cut by *the need to shape* (Capricorn) *her craft* (H6) *as a writer*, something she had made a start with on her 13th birthday, 12 June 1942, (17) when she received an autograph book, bound with red-and-white checkered cloth and with a small lock on the front, which she decided she would use as a diary and began writing in almost immediately. From her diary entry 5th April 1944, we learn how she had hoped to one day become a journalist. In it she mentions how she cannot see herself as a housewife dedicated only to a husband and children. She aspires to be of use to a much larger collective and feels that the gift of writing has been bestowed upon her to bring fulfillment and meaning to people around the world so that her name may outlast her life. (18)

This interpretative lens (Jupiter) belonging to the soul's vehicle Anne Frank is

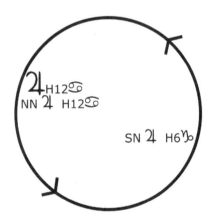

reflected in Barbro's Jupiter in the 12th house Cancer in that *she offers her craft to caring* (Cancer) *for humanity* (Cancer). Its intention resounds in Anne's wish to bring meaning to humankind. The flip side of the 6th house Capricorn past dynamics - the *being able to withstand* (Capricorn) *the relentless persecution* (H6) *at the hands of dysfunctional authority* (Capricorn) - also streams into it however, tainting Barbro's 12th house Cancer lens (Jupiter) with *the dissolution* (H12) *of her home* (Cancer), *her persona* (Cancer) *and everything she has invested in emotionally* (Cancer).

Karlén - SN of Jupiter H6 Capricorn	resistance	Karlén - NN of Jupiter H12 Cancer
the need to shape (Capricorn) her craft (H6) as a writer at loggerheads with the need to be able to withstand (Capricorn) persecution (H6) at the hands of dysfunctional authority (Capricorn)	< >	to care for (Cancer) humanity (H12)
the past streaming into the present and determining the old response: H12 Cancer	**Saturn's choices**	**new response as the result of the resistance between the planet's SN and NN and its familiarity with the former: H12 Cancer**
the dissolution (H12) of her home (Cancer), her persona (Cancer) and everything she has invested in emotionally (Cancer)	< >	to care for (Cancer) humanity (H12)

The need *to care for* (Cancer) *humanity* (H12) is restated by Jupiter's NN at 4 degrees Cancer 7 minutes in the 12th house: Jupiter and its NN convey the exact same message. Both seem fully seized of the importance of this orientation to the greatest common good if the soul is to open up and connect deeply (PPP H8) with a humanitarian cause (PPP Aquarius).

Mars (see chart p.263)

We can expect Barbro's SN of Mars to point to what conscious actions, desires and aspirations in Anne Frank were aimed at. We find it at 26 degrees Libra 44 minutes in the 4th house, near Barbro's Neptune skipped step and the NN of Chiron: they were aimed, as Anne's diary attests to, primarily at *understanding relationship patterns* (Libra) *within her family* (H4) whose members quarreled and exchanged insults in their confined space, with Anne often depicting her mother and sister as self-righteous complainers.

Had Anne be allowed to live, however, it would have become apparent how this focus would have expanded to *understanding relationships* (Libra) *in the wider family* (H4) *of humanity*, with particular interest in *how people project inequality* (Libra) *onto each other*: the great predicament of Barbro's Neptune skipped step.

Barbro's SN of Mars being so close to her Neptune skipped step also points in the direction of *Anne's conscious will having been subjugated* (made to comply: Libra) *to what people projected* (Libra) *onto her race* (H4), a finding corroborated

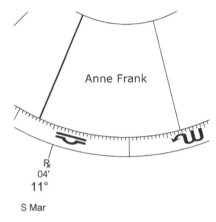

by Anne's SN of Mars at 11 degrees Libra 4 minutes in the 4th house and indicating the same dynamic having been operative in a life immediately prior to Anne's: **a continuity in the nature of will from one lifetime to the next.** (19) I will sum this continuity up for you in the form of a table at the end of this section on Mars.

The attention to the wider social aspect of life beyond that of an adolescence in wartime, can be seen in the diary's portrayal of Jewish life in central and western Europe. Anne's budding social consciousness is evident when she makes changes in her diary, following a call from the then exiled and London-based Minister of Education Gerrit Bolkestein - whom Anne heard during a broadcast from London by the Dutch underground Radio Oranje - urging Dutch citizens to keep documentation and, if possible, diaries so that history might be written after the war and war criminals brought to justice. Heeding the call, Anne kept writing in her diary hoping it would one day bear witness.

The past of Barbro's Mars dynamics define her natal H6 Capricorn Mars, the same way any planet's present is defined by its past, and show up there as the old response of *a will directed at being of service* (H6) *through her craft* (H6) - very recognizable in the child prodigy writer Barbro, right up to the shaping (Capricorn) and honing

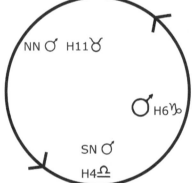

(H6) of her talent – *and all of that youthful ebullience then getting all but crushed by ossified Capricornian unresponsiveness in the form of libel, slander, and obstruction by those in authority* (a lot of which was concentrated in the Swedish

Mounted Police and in certain segments of the Swedish press - in cahoots with it - bent on committing full-blown character assassination).

The NN of Mars we find at 24 degrees Taurus 38 minutes in the 11th house: *to ground* (Taurus) *her efforts at putting her personal talent into service of some socially relevant cause* (H11), *some shared Aquarian purpose*, almost, one gets the impression, in an attempt at transcending the narrow confines of a particular society (Capricorn) - in this case Sweden - and finding abiding safety (NN Mars in Taurus) through a larger humanitarian perspective (H11). All the traumatic memories haunting young Barbro, after all, had their origin in judgment (Capricorn) issued by a particular society (Capricorn) – Germany - at a particular and critical juncture in history (Capricorn: time).

When this new H11 Taurus impulse hits Mars and its tendency to get crushed all over again, it triggers a new response in Barbro's will: it gets directed at *being of service* (H6) *through her gift and craft* (H6) *come hell or high water* (Capricorn: assuming responsibility for), *however much opposition* (Capricorn) *from the authorities* (Capricorn) *she meets with*.

Karlén - SN of Mars H4 Libra	resistance	Karlén - NN of Mars H11 Taurus
the conscious will having been subjugated (made to comply: Libra) to what people projected (Libra) onto her race (H4)	< >	to ground (Taurus) her efforts at putting her personal talent into service of some socially relevant cause (H11), some shared Aquarian purpose
the past streaming into the present and determining the old response: H6 Capricorn	**Mars' choices**	**new response as the result of the resistance between the planet's SN and NN and its familiarity with the former: H6 Capricorn**
the will to be of service (H6) through her craft (H6) getting all but crushed by ossified Capricornian obstruction	< >	to be of service (H6) through her gift and craft (H6) come hell or high water (Capricorn: assuming responsibility for), however much opposition

		(Capricorn) from the authorities (Capricorn) she meets with

Mars in orbit in Anne Frank's chart (see chart p.293)

Frank - SN of Mars H4 Libra	resistance	Frank - NN of Mars H11 Gemini
the conscious will having been subjugated (made to comply: Libra) to what people projected (Libra) onto her race (H4)	**< >**	to use her writing (Gemini) in service of a socially relevant cause (H11), some shared collective purpose (H11)
the past streaming into the present and determining the old response: H1 Leo	**Mars' choices**	**new response as the result of the resistance between the planet's SN and NN and its familiarity with the former: H1 Leo**
not being allowed to show (Leo) one's true identity (H1) (20)	**< >**	establishing my identity (H1) through the creative act (Leo), at once asserting my identity (H1) *as* a creative act (Leo)

Continuity in the nature of will from Barbro's life to Anne's

Anne – SN Mars H4 Libra, pointing back to what will was aimed at (or subjected to) in the life prior to Anne's	Anne – Mars H1 Leo	Barbro – SN Mars H4 Libra, pointing to what will was aimed at (or subjected to) in Anne's life	Barbro – Mars H6 Capricorn
the conscious will having been subjugated (made to comply: Libra) to what people	conscious actions and desires directed at establishing my identity (H1) through the creative act (Leo), at once asserting one's identity (H1) *as* a	understanding relationships (Libra) in the wider family (H4) of humanity, with particular interest in how people project inequality (Libra)	to be of service (H6) through her gift and craft (H6) come hell or high water (Capricorn: assuming responsibility for),

projected (Libra) onto her race (H4)	creative act (Leo). Anne's SN of Mars' subjugation coming back in her Mars as not being/having been allowed to show (Leo) one's true identity (H1)	onto each other; Anne's will having been subjugated (made to comply: Libra) to what was projected (Libra) onto her race (H4)	however much opposition (Capricorn) from the authorities (Capricorn) she meets with

Venus (see chart p.263)

The SN of Venus in the chart of Barbro Karlén is going to reveal what Anne Frank's primary relationship was with. The information comes from the 11th house, at 3 degrees Taurus 16 minutes to be precise: Anne's prime relationship - a budding one but a relationship all the same - was with *grounding* (Taurus) *her efforts at putting her personal talent into service of some socially relevant cause* (H11), *some shared Aquarian purpose* (H11). The exact same thing, therefore, her conscious will was directed at. Barbro´s SN of Venus, however, also denotes *Anne´s relationship* (Venus) having been *with the survival* (Taurus) *of a marginalized and ultimately ousted and traumatized collective* (H11) *upon whom non-survival* (i.e. extermination) *is projected* (H11: group projections).

This past dynamic comes back in Barbro´s 12th house Cancer Venus in that it shows *victimization* (H12) *of an entire race* (Cancer), with *the imminent threat of its annihilation, its disappearance* (H12).

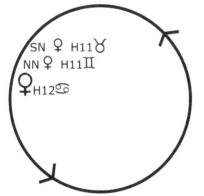

The NN of Venus at 8 degrees Gemini 14 minutes in the 11th house provides the counterweight to the latter part of this past dynamic: it stresses *the need for Barbro's prime relationship to be with a humanitarian cause* (H11) *through her writing* (Gemini), fully in accord, therefore, with her NN of Mars intentions there. The dispute between a relationship with a particular collective (i.e. the Jewish race) - out of necessity limited (Taurus) to that collective - and a larger humanitarian purpose going beyond the needs of that collective is settled by the new response of Barbro's Venus in the 12th house Cancer urging it *to make*

humanity (H12) *her home, her family* (Cancer). Which is exactly what happened between the part personal part historical writing in *The Diary of Anne Frank* and Barbro's *When the Storm Comes* and *A Moment in the Blossom Kingdom.* The writing, matured in the Bardo, acquires universal relevance as it concerns itself with the fate of humanity as a whole, echoing the shift from Anne´s Mercury in the 11th house Gemini to Barbro´s Mercury in the 12th house Gemini, which we shall have a closer look at shortly.

This new Venus response is beneficial to the actualization of Barbro's 8th house Aquarius PPP of deeply merging (H8) with and committing to (H8) a humanitarian cause (Aquarius) in that *it redirects its energy to the nurturing* (Cancer) *of mankind itself* (H12), coinciding with the lens through which the soul wishes Barbro to see things (Jupiter H12 Cancer closely conjunct Venus).

Karlén - SN of Venus **H11 Taurus**	resistance	Karlén - NN of Venus **H11 Gemini**
prime relationship with grounding (Taurus) her efforts at putting her personal talent into service of some socially relevant cause (H11); relationship with the survival (Taurus) of a marginalized and ultimately ousted and traumatized collective (H11) upon whom non-survival (i.e. extermination) is projected (H11: group projections)	**< >**	the need for Barbro's prime relationship to be with a humanitarian cause (H11) through her writing (Gemini)
the past streaming into the present and determining the old response: **H12 Cancer**	**Venus' choices**	**new response as the result of the resistance between the planet's SN and NN and its familiarity with the former: H12 Cancer**
victimization (H12) of an entire race (Cancer), with the imminent threat of its annihilation, its disappearance (H12)	**< >**	to make humanity (H12) her home, her family (Cancer); to nurture (Cancer) mankind (H12)

Mercury (see chart p.263)

Barbro's SN of Mercury is going to lead us directly to the kind of thinking and the nature of thought patterns operative in the soul's vehicle Anne Frank. As you can see in the chart on page 263, it sits in the 12th house at 13 degrees Gemini 51 minutes:

thinking and writing in Anne Frank already directed at mankind and the human condition (H12). It also denotes, however, *the writing* (Gemini) - *from the hiding place* (H12) - *dissolving* (H12), *disappearing* (H12) because of the events as they transpired: the diary stops the day German and Dutch SS men led by Oberscharführer Josef Zilberbauer raided the hiding place and its occupants were deported to Auschwitz and from there to Bergen Belsen: 4th August 1944. The transport arrived in Birkenau from Westerbork camp August 5th, with 1,019 Jews from the Netherlands. If Josef Mengele was on ramp duty that day, which we cannot ascertain, he would have seen the Frank family and decided their fate with a single gesture of the thumb.

At the time, Mengele's wife Irene had fallen ill with diphtheria while visiting her husband at Auschwitz and was receiving top care in a newly-built SS hospital, with her husband sitting at her bedside three times a day and reading Balzac's *Le Diamant* out loud. (21) A month later, when she had convalesced, the couple would embark on their second honeymoon in a recently refurbished house only hundreds of yards away from where people were tortured and gassed. You can read all about it in Gerald Posner's *Hitler's Children: Sons and Daughters of Leaders of the Third Reich Talk About Their Fathers and Themselves* (22).

The book will help you understand the compartmentalization (Moon in Libra: from one extreme to the other) in Mengele's emotional body (Moon H4) needed to go from henchman to caring parent in a single day. (see pp.188-190)

Barbro's SN of Mercury in the 12th house Gemini connotations come back in her Mercury (in the same house and sign) in that young Barbro is bullied and ridiculed (H12 victimization) upon publication of her early work. The fact that she becomes known as a child prodigy causes problems at school and in the media alike, especially when, as a twelve-year-old, she decides to write a letter to a college professor who on national television had expressed his fear of dying and *"the*

thought that his whole self was dead for ever when his life on earth was over."
(23)

Karlén - SN of Mercury H12 Gemini	resistance	Karlén - NN of Mercury H11 Taurus
the writing (Gemini) directed at mankind and the human condition (H12); the writing (Gemini) - from the hiding place (H12) - dissolving (H12), disappearing (H12)	< >	thinking and writing directed at the permanence (Taurus) of the individual core (H11) of one's being as it travels from lifetime to lifetime
the past streaming into the present and determining the old response: H12 Gemini	**Mercury's choices**	**new response as the result of the resistance between the planet's SN and NN and its familiarity with the former: H12 Gemini**
the writing (Gemini), done mostly at night (H12), leading to victimization (H12) after it has been published	< >	thinking (Mercury) is going to be directed at writing (Gemini) about the spiritual life (H12)

In her *"Letter to the Man who was Afraid to Die,"* Barbro tells the reader she would like to take the learned professor into the woods so that he could see for himself – if his fear would let him - how the autumn leaves are not afraid to die for they know they will be born again the following year and the year after. The letter was never meant for publication but when the media got hold of it, the twelve-year-old schoolgirl met with derision as her peers started calling her 'the poet' and 'the writer' and teachers began to treat her unfairly.

Barbro's NN of Mercury, in all likelihood, is going to want to do everything to stop the undoing of the writing (SN Mercury H12 Gemini) from ever happening again. Where in the chart do we find it? We find it in the 11th house at 29 degrees Taurus 3 minutes.

The soul could not have etched it into its narrative more eloquently: ***thinking and writing are to be directed at the permanence*** (Taurus) ***of the individual core*** (H11) ***of one's being as it travels from lifetime to lifetime***, aptly expressed by Thomas Meyer in the afterword to Barbro Karlen's *And the Wolves Howled*, where he mentions how the life of Barbro Karlén shows the imperishable nature of what lies at the heart of one's being seeking expression across multiple lifetimes in spite of genocide and attempts at annihilation. (24)

The message Anne sought to convey was picked up again by the soul's next vehicle Barbro.

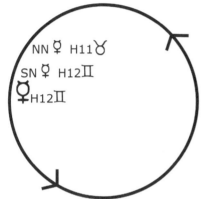

As the 11th house Taurus counterforce confronts the old dynamics of dissolution (SN Mercury H12) of one's writing (SN Mercury in Gemini) and Mercury's familiarity with it manifesting as victimization (Mercury H12) because *of* the writing (Mercury in Gemini), the NNs invitation to direct it at expressing the immutability (NN of Mercury in Taurus: permanence, stability, durability) of one's indivisible selfhood (NN of Mercury H11) will trigger a new response in Mercury in the 12th house Gemini:

thinking (Mercury) ***is going to be directed at writing*** (Gemini) ***about the spiritual life*** (H12), reflected also in Mercury's already signaled move from the 11th house Gemini in the chart of Anne to the 12th house in that of Barbro.

Mercury's new response is never more clear than in Barbro's early works *When the Storm Comes* and *A Moment in the Blossom Kingdom,* produced between the ages of 10 and 12, where she writes about how the soul cloaks itself in many bodies, about how we die and are born again until we have learned enough to forever live in heavenly realms. The writing at times is reminiscent of William Wordsworth's *Ode: Intimations of Immortality*, especially where, in stanza 5, he reminds us that prior to our descent to earth we dwell in more elevated realms, ones whose purity reverberates throughout our childhood years:

Our birth is but a sleep and a forgetting:

The Soul that rises with us, our life's Star,

Hath had elsewhere its setting,

And cometh from afar:

Not in entire forgetfulness,

And not in utter nakedness,

But trailing clouds of glory do we come

From God, who is our home:

Heaven lies about us in our infancy! (25)

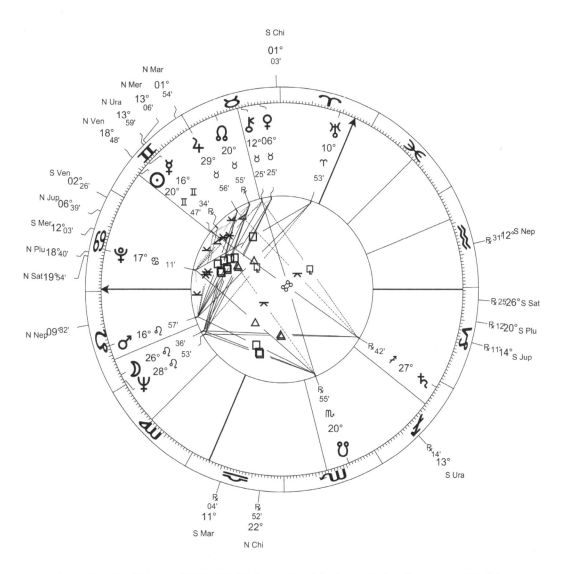

Anne Frank, 12 June 1929, 07:26 hrs., Frankfurt am Main, Germany. RR:AA

Chapter 16 – Chiron Miscellaneous

Astrology and science: Chiron in a house and sign, part 1

Modern science as taught at today's universities and institutions of higher education thinks of astrology as decidedly unscientific. The reason it does this is none other than the fact that astrology's results in its view are not universally applicable and therefore repeatable. Let me give you an example. When in the chart of Nina Simone I describe her Chiron pain as *having been caused by a limitation* (Taurus) *in the degree in which she and prior-life selves were allowed to integrate* (H3), modern science expects this same description to apply to anyone who has their Chiron in the 3ʳᵈ house Taurus.

That is not how astrology works. Astrology works on the premise that the combined 3ʳᵈ house and Taurus spectra allow for a plethora of vastly different conclusions which, when checked against *the Life Lived*, are applicable in each individual case. You and I know how vast the Gemini spectrum is and how vast the Taurus spectrum. At the very mention of the word 'Gemini' the astrologer's mind is flooded by all sort of words and images, ranging from:

... breaking down reality into distinct units, classifying and categorizing these, the dissociation between the knower and reality itself, the mental attempt at synthesis of what Gemini has broken up into parts, the wish to engage with the world through words and the exchange of ideas, curiosity, the indiscriminate intake of ideas and information, spreading oneself thin, to ...

... Gemini's improvisational nature, how the latter can border on immorality, connecting the dots, its inability to see the overall picture (drawing by numbers), its fear of what lies beyond the mind, its youthfulness, siblings, etcetera.

This is just a small segment of the ABC for Gemini that the astrologer uses to construct his sentences with. The list is by no means exhaustive. For Taurus, the astrologer draws from an equally broad gamut of possible manifestations:

...the need for survival, playing it safe, having your back covered at all times, insistence on dependability and predictability, a narrowing of focus, steadfastness, contingency plans in place, fixity in inner values, patience and perseverance, simplicity, trusting and valuing one's senses, sensuality, stubbornness, valuing material possessions, laziness, and many more.

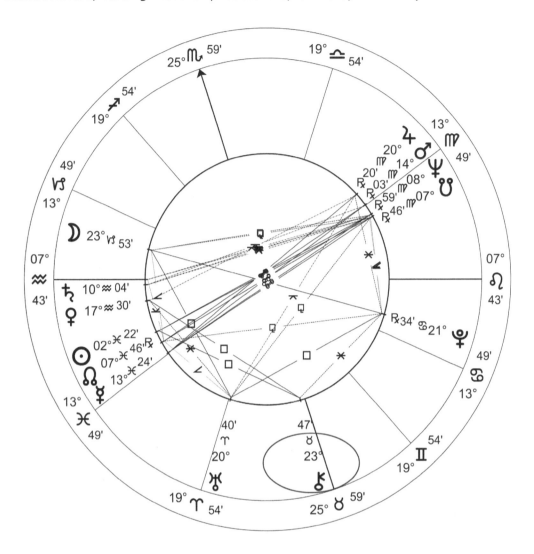

Nina Simone, 21 February 1933, 06:00 hrs., Tryon, North Carolina. RR:AA

I have not counted the words I used for each of the two archetypes and so I do not know how many possible combinations they render, but it must be well over a hundred. Now watch what happens when the astrologer looks at a different life and chart and draws a conclusion for Chiron in the 3rd house Taurus. Let us say the chart they produce is that of Jacques Chirac, President of France from 1995 to 2007. The astrologer, not necessarily an evolutionary astrologer but of any

[296]

denomination, studying the life and chart of Jacques Chirac could come up with the following description:

"*Jacques Chirac's pain was caused by the fact that he was an only child as his sister Jacqueline* (H3: siblings) *had died in infancy* (Taurus survival, and, inevitably, non-survival) *before he was born. All through his younger years he felt limited* (Taurus) *in the kind of exchange of ideas and information* (H3) *he would have enjoyed had his sister lived.*"

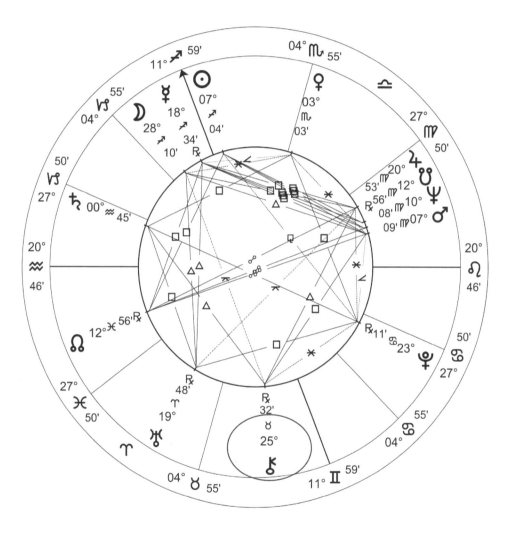

Jacques Chirac, 29 November 1932, 12:00 hrs., Paris, France. RR:AA

I am not saying that this conclusion is in any way borne out by the biographical facts available. That is not the point. The point is that *if* the astrologer were indeed to stumble on such biographical facts - through Chirac's memoirs, through a biography of the man, or because Chirac had told them in person during consultation - then they would be warranted in drawing this conclusion for the former President's Chiron in the 3rd house Taurus.

At this point the modern scientist will begin to protest rather heavily, perhaps even uncontrollably, with veins bulging at both temples. *"Having been limited* (Taurus) *in the degree in which she was allowed to integrate* (H3)" and *"a sibling* (H3) *who died* (Taurus) *in infancy so that he felt limited* (Taurus) *in exchanging ideas and information* (H3)" are two conclusions so far apart that in the scientist's mind they cannot possibly meet what would be their immediate demand in this case: a strict correlation between the statements and *any* 3rd house Taurus Chiron. To the astrologer, however, both are perfectly valid conclusions. How is this possible?

Since the conclusion drawn is fully corroborated by the biographical data available to the astrologer, he does not feel he is making any of this up. Why would it be invalid when the facts confirm it? When presented with this line of argumentation, the modern scientist would hold that the conclusion drawn is invalid for not repeatable.

They would insist on the astrologer submitting data proving either that Nina Simone had also lost a brother or sister before she was born and, as a result of that, felt limited in the extent to which she was able to exchange ideas and information, or, conversely, they would insist on demonstrable fact proving that Jacques Chirac had been limited in integrating with his immediate environment. In the unlikely scenario that the astrologer were able to submit such proof, the modern scientist would then start looking for other people who had Chiron in the 3rd house Taurus and demand that both these conclusions be applicable to their lives. Their quest would also lead them to form a control group made up of people who did *not* have Chiron in the 3rd house Taurus to make sure subjects in that group did not display any of the descriptions used for Chiron in the 3rd house Taurus in the experimental group.

Obviously, the astrologer and modern scientist are parting from different premises. The astrologer would argue that the degree of correlation between conclusion and fact is high – even strict - in both cases yet not repeatable because they refer not only to demonstrable fact (not having been able to integrate for Simone and a sibling's death for Chirac) but also to human behavior (having been stopped or stopping oneself from integrating for Simone and growing up as an only child for Chirac) and, in Chirac's case, human emotion (*feeling* limited in one's exchange with a sibling). That is a nice try but, although certainly relevant, the argument does not carry enough weight to make the scientist re-examine their objections. It needs something more.

What we would need to make the scientist see is the fact that symbols, like myth, *point to* a reality whereas scientific fact *coincides* with it. That is the first observation. The second observation has to do with the astrologer's earlier brave attempt at defending his art: since what astrological symbols point to is human behavior, the conclusions drawn from them are valid *thanks to* their unrepeatability, not *in spite of* it. Or, using a different approach, precisely *because* the combined gamut of any two given archetypes covers such a vast range of human behavior, the level of correlation between astrological conclusion and observed reality – i.e. *the Life Lived* – remains consistently high *irrespective of* how many cases are studied, creating its own kind of repeatability, one that is of an altogether different kind than science's. I am not saying *'more elevated kind,'* but *'different kind,'* treading cautiously for now.

Science's kind, since it insists on conclusion and observable fact coinciding literally so that the correlation shown between the two be applicable in an infinite number of cases, out of necessity must limit the number of variables that might pose a threat to it. Human behavior is one big variable. Variability, and therefore unpredictability, is human behavior's middle name. And so science, to get its repeatability, must kill it. Halt its changeability. Freeze it in time. A bit like astrology has done with planets by ignoring their orbit: we take a piece out of the pie and then do as if there never was a pie. The fact that the piece is now devoid of meaning does not matter. The important thing is that we now have a still, a dead thing, that we can make generalized statements about which we can apply in all cases. As I write these sentences, the realization is beginning to dawn on me that many an astrologer has been 'scientific' all along without knowing it. There is one snag, though: their cookie-cutter descriptions of planets in a house

[299]

and sign do *not* apply in all cases, providing science with much grist for the mills of ridicule and mockery.

Let us imagine, for example, that an astrologer - undoubtedly with the best possible intentions - were to say of Chiron in Sagittarius that it points *to "a wound around faith and optimism, causing one to become acerbic."* David Duke – the infamous white supremacist – has this placement and so the astrologer happily applies his conclusion to David Duke. Why does a statement like this fly in the face of astrological integrity? Why is it so utterly unwarranted? It is unwarranted not just because the house placement has been left out - a serious enough offence in and of itself - but foremost because Chiron in Sagittarius is a placement

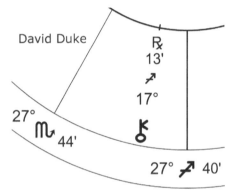

which can be found in the charts of 1/12 of the world's population, meaning sixty-two million five-hundred thousand people on the planet would be walking around carrying that kind of wound with them, a conclusion which can be disproven instantly by checking correlation in a small sample of that vast collective. A handful would suffice. In a

sample of ten people, you would be lucky if you got to person number three before the fallacy of your conclusion would become painfully evident.

Chiron in Sagittarius in a chart, of course, does not even exist: it is always in a house. The chart is only partially a reflection of the sky since the moment someone is born and a chart drawn, the snapshot taken of the sky at the moment of birth inevitably, and fortunately, results in houses. This is the second reason the above conclusion is unwarranted: what the astrologer effectively has done, is take a generalized meaning they ascribe to Chiron in Sagittarius and plonk it in an individual chart. They have therefore not only taken the heart out of astrology but also done exactly what modern science expects them to do: show repeatability by imposing the general onto the specific. Since you cannot fit a square astrological peg into a round astrological hole without violating specificity and applicability, the astrologer comes up short and then kicks up a terrible stink when the scientist calls his art 'unscientific.' The inevitable conclusion to be drawn from this is that by extrapolating the general to the specific and so making the

[300]

non-applicability of its findings painfully obvious not only to science but to all and sundry, it is astrology itself which causes society to view its noble art with rank suspicion and which plays right into the hands of its most vitriolic detractor: science.

In Duke's case, Chiron in Sagittarius falls in his 3rd house and *points to* a *pain caused by divulging* (H3) a *distortion of truth* (Sagittarius), i.e. *the lie of setting cultural differences* (Sagittarius) *against each other* (H3), relaying a trauma charge comprised of *deriving emotional security from wanting the nation to follow*

archconservative ideas and have these implemented through rigid and oppressive authority (Uranus H10 Cancer), *projecting all kinds of things onto people's identities* (Neptune H1 Libra), and, finally, the soul emotionally identifying with the Uranus and Neptune strand as *not getting the attention it so craves* (Leo) *because of the egalitarian principle* (H11) *by which everyone is equally special*, the reaction to said emotion being *the soul imposing its prominence* (Leo) *by declaring whole swathes of the population* (H11) *equally unimportant* (the downward equalizing tendency as the less lofty side of the Aquarius archetype). I provide Duke's birth data in the Endnotes so that you may generate his chart yourself. (1) In someone else's chart each of these four placements (Chiron, Uranus, Neptune, Pluto) may lead to vastly different interpretations, warranted by *the Life Lived*, by the actual circumstances of the observable and observed life of a real person and not by some generalized description. Astrology, if it is to have any validity, needs to be specific, never generalized.

Chiron in a house and sign, part 2

Another fine example of identical planet placements leading to vastly different astrological conclusions whilst maintaining a strict correlation to verifiable biographical fact can be found in this very book: Nina Simone's Uranus in the 3rd house Aries versus Jim Jones'. Why did I interpret the former as *trauma incurred to her identity, freedom and right to exist* (Uranus in Aries) *through non-*

[301]

integration (i.e. segregation, Uranus H3), and the latter as *trauma incurred as a result of people dying abruptly and prematurely* (Uranus in Aries) *for having come under the spell of certain words and ideas* (Uranus H3)?

I did so primarily because the conclusions drawn for each fit the findings produced by my analysis of their respective Evolutionary Axis. This is what I referred to in earlier chapters when I said: *"trauma does not come falling from the sky."* It happens in the context of certain events, of certain dynamics playing out. What also played a role in formulating them as I did, however, was what I would like to term *Trauma's Thread of Ariadne*: since trauma, until it is healed, tends to repeat itself, all I had to do was look at the biographical facts for each of the two lives and see how it was reenacted. For Simone that was as easy to see as it was for Jones: the singer suffered the direct consequences of racial segregation, while the con man masquerading as evangelist led over nine hundred people to a certain death as a result of his words. Linking

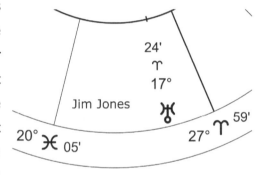

back astrological conclusions to verifiable biographical fact is the first rule of astrological chart interpretation. Astrological symbols, as do all symbols, point to a reality, which I have termed *the Life Lived*. If the conclusions drawn from interpreting them are not backed up by the facts pertaining to that life, then there can be no validity to them.

Chiron transits. Secondary progressions

Because of the demonstrable fallacy of cookie-cutter descriptions, you will find no chapters listing Chiron aspects, transits or progressions in this book. Let us take the chart of Jim Jones to see how the therapeutic evolutionary astrologer deals with the latter two. Aspects were dealt with in chapter 11 (pp. 199-201). On that fateful day of 18 November 1978, Jones' Chiron transit was in the vicinity of his Mercury in the 4th house Taurus, which in chapter 14 we defined as the evolutionary choice between *directing his thinking at how to secure the safety* (Taurus) *of the flock* (H4) and *using the word* (Mercury) *to put the blinkers* (Taurus) *on members of the flock* (H4) *so that they do not think* (Mercury) *for themselves*.

The choice had been raging in his mind for months and reached fever pitch in the weeks leading up to the inescapable denouement. Whatever house or planet *in* a house a transit or secondary progression visits, **it is always going to carry with it the original imprint of its natal position**. This is a key tenet of therapeutic evolutionary astrology. The house or planet *in* a house is going to feel the impact of *that* imprint. What does that mean in this case? It means that the stark choice Mercury was put before received the impact of a wound that would either continue to fester if the flock was led to their deaths (Chiron H4 Taurus) or be healed if their safety and survival were procured (Chiron H4 Taurus). The Chiron transit would have been felt by Jones the moment it entered the 4th house, which happened in February of 1977. Fortunately, what happened around that time is very well documented.

Without specifying all the events as they transpired between Chiron´s entry in the 4th house Aries and its position at 6 degrees Taurus 29 minutes on the day of the Jonestown massacre, I can summarize them for you by saying that from the moment Jones arrived in Jonestown he implemented a well-thought-out strategy designed to convince his flock of settlers (H4) of the need to commit suicide (Taurus: non-survival). To be able to do so, he schemed a series of what came to be known as ´White Nights.´ (2)

Via the prison camp's PA system (it had effectively become a prison camp since people's passports and possessions had been confiscated, no one was allowed to leave and everyone ratted on everyone else) and after a 12-hour shift laboring the unforgiving jungle soil where only things that slithered or crawled seemed to thrive, settlers were summoned to attend Jones' endless paranoid rants in the central pavilion well into the small hours of the night - depriving them of much-needed sleep - and often until dawn. (3) If anyone paid less than full and undivided attention or, God forbid, fell asleep, they were punished on the spot through ridicule and beatings.

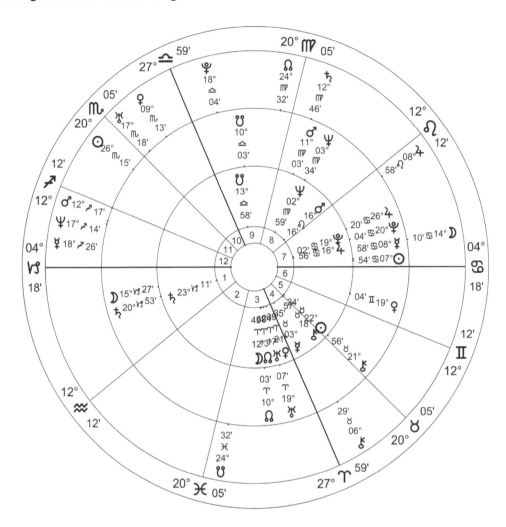

Jim Jones, transits (outer ring) and secondary progressions (middle ring) 18 Nov. 1978

The idea conveyed on these nights was always the same: Jonestown was under siege from mercenaries, C.I.A. and F.B.I. agents out to put a stop to their wonderful Guyana socialist experiment and it was more dignified to take one's own life as a last revolutionary stand than to be captured by capitalist pigs who would torture and kill everyone. What occupied Jones' mind at the time, unbeknownst to the majority of Jonestown residents, was a series of incriminatory magazine articles back in the States, a custody battle over a child Jones had fathered by one of his many concubines, and Congress asking serious questions about American citizens' wellbeing at Jonestown, (4) all causing Jones'

[304]

amphetamine-induced paranoia to spiral out of control. Investigations by journalists and politicians alike were aimed at finding out whether or not people in Jonestown were held there against their will.

On the first of such *White Nights*, 5 September 1977, Jones sent his adopted black son Jimmy Junior out into the bush and had him fire shots at his cabin while he stood near one of its windows. Security guards immediately came to Jones' rescue and found him lying on the floor, disheveled and disoriented. Asked what had happened, Jones told them that, whilst standing at the window, he had had a feeling in the pit of his stomach telling him something bad was about to happen and he had better duck and seek cover. Not much later *"Alert! Alert! We are under attack!"* was heard from speakers throughout the camp and surrounding fields. All settlers, young and old alike, were ordered to assemble in the pavilion, where they were told the camp was surrounded by mercenaries ready to invade and snatch their children. (5) This, Jones would never allow to happen. Socialism dictated that if one were taken, all would be taken. This, of course, was the necessary prelude to the next step: rather than *be* taken, followers would take their own lives. *All* followers, in good socialist fashion.

On 5 September 1977, the Chiron H4 Taurus transit was retrograde and inching ever closer to Mercury in the same house and sign, which it had already visited in May of that year in direct motion.

The astrological implication is clear: Chiron's critical choice between *plotting the non-survival* (Taurus) *of the flock* (H4) and *securing the safety and survival* (Taurus) *of the flock* (H4) was now directly impacting Mercury's equally critical choice between *using the word* (Mercury) *to put the blinkers* (Taurus) *on members of the flock* (H4) *so that they do not think* (Mercury) *for themselves* and *directing thinking at how to secure*

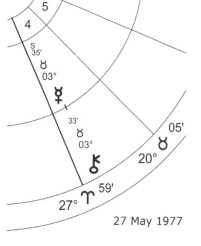

5 Sept.1977

27 May 1977

[305]

the safety (Taurus) *of the flock* (H4) *by allowing its members to become self-reliant* (Taurus), not only agriculturally but in every other way possible.

Please note the Pluto transit in the 9th house having already touched Jones' south node of the Moon there. This is a slow transit. It moves like a freight train: it builds up very slowly and has a notoriously long braking distance, meaning it would have been felt long before and long after its exact contact with the SN of the Moon. The original 7th house imprint of *creating extreme dependency in others* (Pluto H7) *through clannish clinginess* (Cancer) - a major unresolved issue at the level of soul: Pluto skipped step - now impacting the Moon's past dynamic, i.e. the modus operandi in prior-life selves, of *demanding strict compliance* (Libra) *with a professed faith* (H9) *they themselves did not believe in* (H9 distortion of truth), *effectively creating a "Slavery* (Libra) *of Faith"* (H9). (6) It is a very poignant transit - one that would be exact 4 October 1977, not long after the first 'White Night' and coinciding with Chiron retrograde making its way back to Mercury - for it was the congregation's hope of a better world based on Christian principles that made it follow the lies of a man who privately, and by 1977 increasingly publicly, decried God, Christianity and the Holy Bible. As early as fall of 1949 in Bloomington, he had ripped God to shreds and chucked Him out. (7) He had kept this a secret from his followers all these years and now, in a jungle 4,000 kms. from home which had effectively turned followers into camp prisoners, the cat was out of the bag: Jim Jones never believed in God to begin with (8) and his socialism was fake too.

This first *White Night* marked the beginning of what would come to be known as *the Six Day Siege*. Jones's aids handed out hoes, pitchforks, and cutlasses so that settlers could defend themselves and their offspring against the imaginary foe. Exhausted, trembling and shaking, they formed a human wall facing the impenetrable jungle, another and more formidable one. The first, frail wall of sleep and food depraved settlers stood well into the following day. Jones then allowed his disciples to take it in turns to get some sleep. People left in pairs so that one could rest and the other stand guard. Anyone who tried to abandon ship would get their throats slit with a single stroke of the cutlass. (9) Jonestown, once a parish's dream of Eden, had turned into a living hell.

Many such nights would follow. Shots would emanate from the jungle, Jones would call the alert and panic would grip the camp. All would be ordered to convene in the pavilion where they were invariably told parachutes would soon appear, upon which Jonestown would be invaded by mercenaries on a killing spree. When followers had got used to the idea of mass suicide and all voices of dissent had been squelched, Jones during these *White Nights* began to introduce dress rehearsals for the final act. Vats of fake poison would be brought in – the concoction having been prepared by camp physician Larry Schacht - followers made to line up and forced to drink the potion. When no one convulsed or foamed at the mouth – with the exception of a few who had fallen victim to auto-suggestion - the congregation would be told that this was Jones' way of testing their loyalty to the cause. (10) People who refused to ingest the liquid were severely punished (11) so that after several test-runs over a period of as many months, with followers asking themselves repeatedly whether this was now finally the real thing, by early fall 1978 nearly all were on board and ready to die. When on the 18th of November a large drum was brought in from the kitchen after its personnel had been summoned to the pavilion, everyone knew that this time round Jones was making good on his promise.

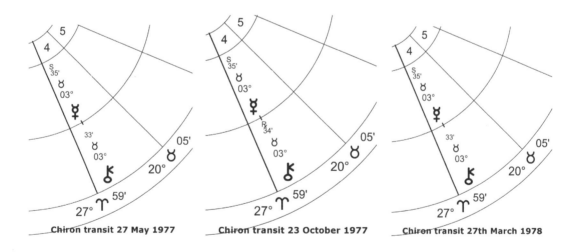

Chiron transit 27 May 1977   Chiron transit 23 October 1977   Chiron transit 27th March 1978

When the day came, the Chiron 4th house Taurus transit had touched Mercury three times as part of its back-and-forth retrograde dance: the first contact was made in May of 1977 when Chiron was still direct, the second one via retrogradation in October of that year, and the final one when it had gone direct again and landed on it in March of 1978. It turned retrograde once again Mid-August of the marked year, almost as if it wished to issue Jones with one final warning of what was at stake. It receded all the way back to 5 degrees Taurus in January 1979, at which point it would have realized there was no point anymore in going all the way back to Mercury at 3 degrees Taurus. The curtain had been drawn. Nine hundred people had suffered the ultimate betrayal and a great evolutionary opportunity been missed.

Jones' Uranus during those portentous days is in the 10th house Scorpio, spurring him on *to deeply commit* (Scorpio) *to* the kind of *integrity* (H10) his Saturn skipped step in the 1st house Capricorn had been walking away from lifetime upon lifetime. This is the impact of one end of the Uranus H3 response on the 10th house, namely the healing end telling him to *allow his followers to connect with* (H3) *their own will and identity* (Aries) *and think* (H3) *for themselves* (Aries). As it turned out, the other end of Uranus, the old response, won out: *people dying abruptly and prematurely* (Uranus in Aries) *for having come under the spell of certain words and ideas* (Uranus H3). The impact of this old response on the 10th house would lead him to once again *betray* (Scorpio) *his inner accountability* (H10).

On close inspection, we notice that this 10th house Uranus transit, but for a few minutes' arc, is exactly inconjunct the natal Uranus in the 3rd house Aries and therefore in a state of crisis with it. The nature of the crisis has to do with him assuming 10th house responsibility or not *with regards to* the original 3rd house Aries trauma on the one hand and the overcoming of it on the other.

Speaking of the 10th house, please note Jones' Saturn transit in the 8th house Virgo. When interpreting it, we apply the same principle: the original 1st house Capricorn imprint is now brought to bear on the 8th house. Translated to English: *a consciousness structured in such a way by the soul as to allow the vehicle Jones to develop the integrity* (Capricorn) *needed to assume responsibility* (Saturn) *for who he really is* (H1: identity) *and what it is he is really after* (H1: will) is now challenged *to carefully discern* (Saturn transit in Virgo) *why people should live rather than die* (Saturn transit H8) *and to then make the right* (Virgo: not this but that) *choice* (H8). If the call is not heeded and the lack of integrity prevails – the imprint of the old response now also coming into the 8th house – then *the crisis* (Virgo) *around taking people's self-empowerment* (H8) *away by imposing death* (H8) *on them* will become acute.

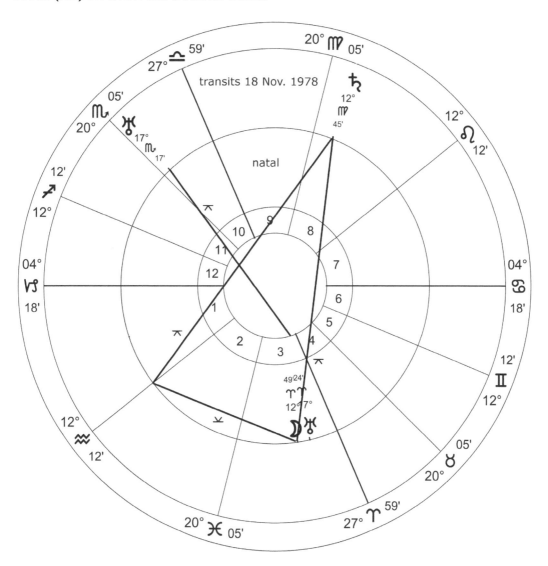

As you can see in the chart, the Saturn transit in the 8th house Virgo is (almost exactly) inconjunct the Moon in the 3rd house Aries, that is, in a state of crisis with Jones himself as he is torn between the old response of *robbing people of their right to connect* (Moon H3) *with their own will, identity* (Moon in Aries) *and capacity to think* (Moon H3) *for themselves* (Aries) and *allowing people to get out from under one single 'truth'* (SN of the Moon H9) *and their expected*

[309]

compliance (SN of the Moon Libra) *with it, so that they may connect* (H3) *with their own will and identity* (Aries) *and think* (H3) *for themselves* (Aries).

If you are so inclined, you can draw another inconjunct to the cusp of the 2nd house at 12 degrees Aquarius - the trauma of the non-survival (H2) of a large group of people (Aquarius) - ruled by Uranus in the 3rd house Aries, i.e. *trauma incurred as a result of people having come under the spell of certain words and ideas* (H3) *and dying abruptly and prematurely* (Aries) *as a consequence* – and from there form a Yod with a sextile to the Moon H3 Aries and back to Saturn again as its apex, with all the energy from the double crisis streaming into the tip of the dowsing rod. As you can see from the two players involved, the sextile here is anything but an *'easy aspect'*. It is, in fact, a highly charged energy vortex between the 2nd house trauma and a Moon put before a choice that encapsulates much, if not all, of Jones' life. It is the highly uncomfortable ease in energy flow between the two which fuels the double crisis, combusting at the base of the Yod and driving the two inconjuncts to come to a head in Saturn as its apex: the grand finale of a life of shirking one's responsibility (Saturn H1 Capricorn skipped step) now affecting almost a thousand lives (Saturn transit H8 Virgo).

20° ♍ 05'   18 November 1978

♄ 12° ♍ 45'

12°

transits

♂ 11° ♍ 03'   ♌ 12'

second. progr.

natal

16° ♂

16° ♌

8

On top, Jones' Saturn transit for 18 November 1978 was right on his secondary progressed Mars in the 8th house Virgo, its original 1st house Capricorn imprint now funneling into it. What were the old and the new response that Mars was made to choose between? It could opt, so we found out in chapter 14, for *(ab)using people* (H8) *in any which way it saw fit by dint of its perceived specialness* (Leo) or go for *helping people self-empower* (H8) *so that they may bask in the light and warmth of their full sense of self* (Leo). Those were the options. Why was Mars' internal programming (secondary progression) in the 8th house Virgo at the time of the tragic events and the period leading up to them? How did it know it had to be aligned with Saturn, the lightning rod on the roof of that Yod? That is not too difficult to see once we apply the same principle to Mars as we did to Saturn: **the planet via transit or progression carries its original imprint and brings it to bear on whatever house or planet in a house it touches**. In the case of Mars, it is a house. In the case of Saturn, a house (i.e. the 8th) *and* a planet (i.e. Mars secondary progressed). Mars' original choice – which I reiterated for you above – is now brought to bear on *the critical* (Virgo) *choice* (H8) *between life or death* (H8). Opting for his people's self-empowerment so that they may bask in the light of their full sense of self (natal Mars H8 Leo) will have Jones choose life over death. Doing one final time with them as he sees fit by dint of his perceived specialness (Mars H8 Leo), will push him in the exact opposite direction. *That* critical choice is now impacted by Saturn the lighting rod, and so the internal genetic code (secondary progressed) of Jones' conscious actions (Mars) gets sucked into the final act, the apogee, of the monumental crisis his life has been building up to.

As the events unfolded, the transiting Nodal Axis lay splayed on the H3-H9 axis (see chart next page). The original SN of the Moon´s 9th house Libra imprint of *expecting people to comply* (Libra) *with a professed faith* (H9) *which in reality was a gross distortion of truth* (H9) (12) via transit was now impacting the 3rd house as *the dissolution* (Pisces) *of reason* (H3), and, equally important, as *the dissolution* (Pisces) *of multiple voices* (H3) *heard*. Its ruler, squaring the axis from the 12th house Sagittarius, informs us of how this played out: *disappearance, dissolution and ending* (H12) *as a result of a twisted truth, a lie* (Sagittarius). The transiting NN of the Moon impacting the 9th house through Virgo and bringing with it its original 3rd house Aries intention of *allowing people to connect* (H3) *with their own will and identity* (Aries) *so that they may think* (H3) *for themselves* (Aries) was now bidding Jones *to serve* (Virgo) *truth* (H9) *by discerning* (Virgo) *truth and distortion of truth*, i.e. lie (H9). Its ruler too was squaring the transiting nodal axis from the 12th house Sagittarius: *to heal* (H12) *through truth* (Sagittarius). Fleeting as it was and having freed itself from the clutches of Neptune by a mere minute only, Mercury proved too weak to turn the tide.

You can see how from the rear end the transiting Nodal Axis is squared by secondary progressed Venus in the 6th house Gemini. (13)

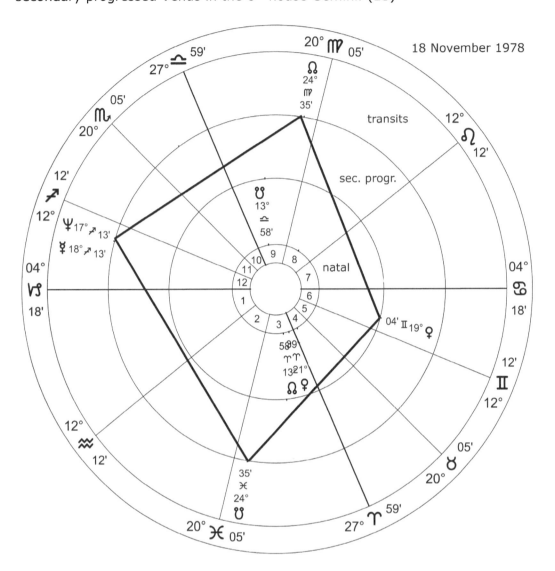

Venus' natal choice between the old response of *a relationship with the imposition of will* (Aries) *through the forcefully* (Aries) *delivered word* (H3) and the new response of *relating to the validity of multiple viewpoints* (H3) *so that people are allowed to connect with* (H3) *their own will and identity* (Aries) *and think* (H3) *for themselves* (Aries) in its internal programming now having reached a point where its relationship is with *serving* (H6) *the validity of a multiplicity of angles from which to look at things* (Gemini), echoing *not only its own Gemini NN but also the 3rd house Uranus-NN of the Moon-Moon conjunction.*

[312]

The effect Venus' choice via progression is going to have on the 6th house can be described but not predicted, so I will limit myself to the former, although with hindsight we know which one she went for. If people are indeed allowed to connect with their own will and identity so that they can think for themselves, and different voices (Gemini) are heard, then *true integration* (Gemini) *is served* (H6). If the imposition of Jones' will through the forcefully delivered word carries the day, then *a deep chasm* (Gemini) *in service* (H6) opens up.

I give you the words spoken by a Jonestown resident in a bid to restore the voice of reason in a situation which was rapidly getting out of hand through Jones' erratic behavior, words which deeply resonate with his secondary progressed Venus in the 6th house discerning (H6) the options put before it.

The only resident who spoke up for herself and defended life on Jonestown's final day, especially that of the children, was sixty-year-old Christine Miller from Brownsville, Texas. In a last-ditch attempt to prise some of the power from the madman's hands, she spoke these words: *"I think we all have a right to our own destiny as individuals. I have a right to choose mine, and everybody else has a right to choose theirs."* (14) She was soon heckled by 'true believers' accusing her of being afraid of dying, her voice a faint echo of truth and dignity.

It is the subtle interplay between transits and secondary progressions – between actual movements in the sky and the inner genetic programming of a planet, its inner unfolding, so to speak – which we need to grasp if we are to understand the evolutionary opportunities that presented themselves at this particular and crucial juncture in Jones' life.

Back to astrology and science

Science's insistence on repeatability of findings seems to lack the adaptability - or should I say *imagination*? - needed when applied to human behavior. For astrology to be viewed as 'scientific' the term 'repeatability' would need to be redefined: if both for Simone and Chirac the astrological conclusion drawn for Chiron in the 3rd house Taurus is accurate – in the sense outlined earlier – then 'repeatability' in astrology means the applicability of its findings is shown *thanks to* as opposed to *in spite of* the richness and variability in human behavior. In simpler terms: the respective archetypal spectra of Gemini and Taurus are broad enough to accommodate for an almost infinite number of combinations, each of which will more than meet science's demand in terms of demonstrable correlation. That is its repeatability.

The question remains, of course, whether astrology is in any need of genuflecting to science. Perhaps, after centuries of meeting astrology with derision, it is science's turn to take the above line of argumentation seriously and leave behind its one-way street of causal tolerance. I would contend that it is decidedly unscientific to reject proof that does not fit one's paradigm and only admit proof that does.

Astrology is both an art and a science. It requires vast knowledge yet at the same time it needs the kind of playful, imaginative and intuitive approach we find in the arts. Before the darkness of the Enlightenment set in, science combined these two approaches: astronomers were often astrologers.

The Church's beef with astrology we have talked about elsewhere in this book: the moment the Cosmos within reveals your inner God to you, you cannot be manipulated. From that moment on the Church cannot put 'the fear of God' into you anymore through the prospect of fire and brimstone.

Science's grumble on astrology is very different. What it cannot abide by is the fact that astrology moves right at the interface of the left and right hemisphere, that it walks the razor's edge of logical thinking and intuition, of art (right hemisphere) and science (left hemisphere). Science feels threatened by the fact that astrology leaves room for the mystery of life, for the unfathomable and therefore unquantifiable. It needs to control life at all cost. Incredible technological advancements have been made because of its approach. However impressive these are, they cannot embrace the totality of life. For that we need to be able to say *"I do not know. I surrender. I bow and allow the mystery to speak."* And that is the one thing modern science cannot and will not do.

The beauty of this situation, however, is that science itself, as it moves deeper into the mystery of matter and driven by its unstoppable compulsion to know, has come perilously close to the point where it will have to admit, and already seems to have admitted, that matter is consciousness. And with that we have come full (Trismegistus) circle. It is closing Hermetically. We can sit back and watch astrology being restored to its former glory as an Art and a Science. All we have to do is bide our time.

Endnotes

Preface

(1) The term is not mine but Roger Woolger's and used in his book *Other Lives, Other Selves: A Jungian Psychotherapist Discovers Past Lives* (Bantam Books, 1988), chapter 5: *The Multidimensional Psyche*.

Chapter 1 – The Mythology of Chiron

(1) As an aside, Jim Jones, whom we will learn much more about in chapters 10 and 14, believed his mother to have been Mark Twain in a previous life. He himself, so he would let followers know, had been Vladimir Lenin. See Layton, Deborah. *Seductive Poison: A Jonestown Survivor's Story of Life and Death in the Peoples Temple*, p.45. Also see Guinn, Jeff. *The Road to Jonestown: Jim Jones and Peoples Temple*, p.146.

(2) Even astronomically Chiron inhabits two worlds: observing behavior characteristic of a comet having already labeled it an asteroid, astronomers pronounced Chiron both asteroid *and* comet, assigning a number to each: 2060 Chiron and 95P/Chiron.

(3) Chiron was discovered on 1 November 1977 by Charles Kowal from images taken on 18 October of the same year at Palomar Observatory (located in San Diego County, California, 145 kilometers southeast of Los Angeles, in the Palomar Mountain Range).

(4) Latin: *Similia Similibus Curantur*

(5) A great healer, astrologer, and respected oracle, Chiron was much revered as a teacher and tutor. Among his pupils were: Asclepius, Aristaeus, Ajax, Aeneas, Actaeon, Caeneus, Theseus, Achilles, Jason, Peleus, Telamon, Perseus, Oileus.

Chapter 2 – Chiron and the *Trauma Helix*

(1) The term *Trauma Helix*, as is the content of the present volume, is copyright Michael De Baker.

(2) By 'subconscious' I refer to content that lies below the surface of the conscious mind. 'Unconscious' in my vocabulary refers to a state where waking consciousness is temporarily lost, for example when one faints or sleeps.

(3) A good introduction to regression therapy can be found on Youtube. It is called *Why Regression Therapy?* and was produced by the European Association for Regression Therapy (EARThassociation)

(4) Woolger, Roger. *Other Lives, Other Selves: A Jungian Psychotherapist Discovers Past Lives* (Bantam Books, 1988)

(5) The fact that Nixon's Pluto skipped step is 'out of sign' in therapeutic EA does not disqualify it as a square. Therapeutic EA parts from the notion that the soul, by having Pluto in the 10th house Gemini as opposed to in the 10th house Cancer, is indicating with great precision what the unresolved issue is: it is a 10th house Gemini one, not a 10th house Cancer one. Also see chapter 4, footnote (9).

(6) Summers, Anthony. *The Arrogance of Power: The Secret World of Richard Nixon* (Viking Publ., Penguin Group, 2000)

(7) In chapters 8 & 9 I will rather drastically redefine the NN of the Moon – and the Moon itself for that matter – but for now we will go with the more traditional EA approach.

(8) Since the three are joined at the hip, the suppression (Capricorn) of the emotional body (H4) found in the Mercury and Jupiter skipped step goes a long way towards explaining how Mars as the NN ruler got stranded in its efforts to reach emotional (H4) honesty (Sagittarius).

(9) https://www.easchoolonline.com

(10) Summers, Anthony. Op. cit., chapter 10.

Chapter 3 – Crossing the Bridge to Saturn

(1) See Summers, Anthony. Op. cit., p.9. Also see Aitken, Jonathan. *Nixon: A Life* (Regnery Publ., Washington D.C., 1993), p.15. Also see Abrahamsen, David. *Nixon versus Nixon: An Emotional Tragedy* (Farrar, Straus & Giroux, New York, 1977).

(2) See Summers, Anthony. Op. cit., p.9.

(3) Nixon, Richard. *In the Arena: A Memoir of Victory, Defeat and Renewal* (Easton Press, New York, 1990), p.103.

(4) See Summers, Anthony. Op. cit., p.9. Also see Abrahamsen, David. Op. cit.

(5) If Nixon indeed learned from choices made can be most clearly seen in his book *In the Arena* [see footnote (3)], where he shares his thoughts and feelings on his life and career.

(6) Why these generalized "cookbook" descriptions are 'demonstrably untrue' is explained at length in chapter 16 – *Chiron Miscellaneous*.

Chapter 4 – Proof, please! Abraham Lincoln

(1) De Baker, Michael. *Intercepted Signs: Encoded Messages from the Soul* (Kindle, Publ. 2019).

(2) If you wish to know more about Barbro Karlén, you are kindly directed to her website www.barbrokarlén.com

(3) Kriyananda, Swami. *The Path: Autobiography of a Western Yogi* (Ananda Publications, Nevada City, Cal., 1977).

(4) The process of *'Dreaming Your Way Into the Chart'* is explained in my first book *Intercepted Signs: Encoded Messages from the Soul* (Kindle, Publ. 2019).

(5) Why do I associate Gemini with *integration*? A comprehensive understanding of the Gemini archetype tells us it first brings together two worlds (upper and lower, left and right, inside and outside) through the act of synthesis, after which it seeks integration of the two: what is from within strikes up a dialogue with what is from without, and vice versa. An exchange (integration) takes place following the bringing together. **Synthesis** and **integration**, therefore, are the key words for Gemini, and in that order. The often-made association of synthesis with the archetype of Sagittarius is erroneous: Sagittarius does not bring together (synthesis) distinct units but rather gets the big picture in one go, as a *Gestalt*, to use a term coined by Fritz Perls. Gemini, who connects the dots, is painting by numbers. Even before pen is put to paper, Sagittarius already knows it is going to be a horse (or, in his case, half-horse, half-human). A thorough exploration of the twelve astrological archetypes is offered in Module 1 of the EA School Online, https://www.easchoolonline.com

(6) De Baker, Michael. *Intercepted Signs: Encoded Messages from the Soul* (Kindle, Publ. 2019).

(7) The archetype of Libra has nothing to do with connect**ing**. It has to do with being connect**ed**. This can be seen by contemplating both scales in the object the astrological glyph for Libra refers to: they are welded together. Why are they welded together? They are welded together so that there is nothing else for it than to listen to each other. With Libra we find ourselves in the social arena where man seeks to find a form (Libra square Capricorn) in which to live together meaningfully. To do so, he *must* listen to other. Not listening is no longer an option. Leo could still afford to do so, Virgo was busy purifying herself in preparation for equality in relationship – listening intensely to herself - and now, in Libra, the option to not listen is no longer available. Not Libra but Gemini has to do with connect**ing**: two worlds are brought together (synthesis). Once they are connected, they are made to integrate. Again, this more thorough exploration of the twelve astrological archetypes is undertaken in Module 1 of the EA School Online, https://www.easchoolonline.com The twelve astrological archetypes are the ABC of evolutionary astrology. Without a comprehensive knowledge of them, erroneously associating Sagittarius with synthesis or Libra with connecting – to name but two frequently

encountered errors - you will lack the words to make sentences with. As pointed out in elsewhere in the book, your understanding of the soul narrative is as deep as your understanding of the archetypes.

(8) Several examples of planets conjunct the NN of the Moon can be found in my book *Intercepted Signs: Encoded Messages from the Soul*, namely in chapter 5 (David Bowie: Uranus conjunct the NN of the Moon); chapter 7 (Nannerl Mozart: Saturn conjunct the NN of the Moon); chapter 9 (Barbro Karlén: Mars conjunct the NN of the Moon). In this book you will find one in chapter 11 - *Josef Mengele in Full Evolutionary Orbit* (i.e. Saturn conjunct the NN of the Moon H11 Taurus).

(9) Do not think the Moon does not qualify as a skipped step for being 'out of sign.' As you will learn soon, the soul, by having the Moon skipped step in Capricorn rather than in Aquarius, is being very articulate in pointing out (we are still looking at symbols prior to translation into English!) what the roadblock to the H9 Scorpio NN of the Moon consisted of in the life of the Himalayan yogi. What it was will be revealed to you shortly when we bring the 12th house and Capricorn together. Also see chapter 2, footnote (5).

(10)   This continuity in future chapters will be referred to as **'trauma continuity.'**

(11)   In chapter 8, *The Missing Moon* I will show you how the NN of the Moon, or indeed a planetary NN, *does not represent the evolutionary intention of the Moon* (or of the planet in question). Until this has been explained, though, I am formulating the NN in the traditional way adhered to by most evolutionary astrologers. If at this point you feel I seem to be going against everything you hold dear and believe in astrologically, I would ask of you not to put the book down or tear it to pieces. I promise: you will be rewarded for your patience.

(12)   The continuity for all planetary functions between two consecutive lives created by the soul will be explored in chapter 15: *From Barbro Karlén back to Anne Frank via the planetary south nodes: 'trauma and healing continuity.'*

(13)   What I am anticipating here is the *'trauma continuity'* in the Uranus strand of the *Trauma Helix* stretching back from the life of Charles Lindbergh, via that of Abraham Lincoln, to that of the Himalayan yogi.

(14)   A term we will redefine in chapter 6: *The 'Multidimensional Psyche*.' (See footnote {1}, chapter 6)

Chapter 5 – From Lincoln to Lindbergh

(1) If you wish to know more about Life Between Lives Therapy, I kindly refer to the official Michael Newton website https://www.newtoninstitute.org/

(2) De Baker, Michael. *Intercepted Signs: Encoded Messages from the Soul* (Kindle Publ. 2019), chapter 9. We will pick the Frank-Karlén comparative chart study up again in chapter 15 of this book, where the planetary south nodes of the latter will be linked back to the chart of the former.

(3) This is not the place to go into the intercepted signs of Gemini and Sagittarius in the chart of Charles Lindbergh for it does not fall within the remit of this book. Suffice it to say, though, that they archetypally resonate with the house placement of Lincoln´s Nodal Axis and with Lindbergh´s Pluto-PPP axis by sign and represent an area in the life of Lincoln where growth was thwarted. Also note the archetypal resonance between Lincoln's Libra-Aries interception and Lindbergh's emphasized H1-H7 axis, where we find the Pluto-PPP placements in the intercepted signs of Gemini-Sagittarius. Further pointers are the duplicated Scorpio-Taurus pair in Lindbergh's chart coinciding with the Scorpio-Taurus signature of Lincoln's Nodal Axis. Based on the work undertaken in my first book *Intercepted Signs: Encoded Messages from the Soul*, specifically that in chapter 9: Anne Frank and Barbro Karlén - where I show you how Anne's thwarted 11th house NN of the Moon potential becomes Barbro's Taurus intercepted there (and, of course, at the rear end Scorpio) - you may be able to work out for yourself what that area is.

(4) Again, the NN as the intended evolutionary intention on the level of self will be redefined in chapter 8: *The Missing Moon*. For now, I follow traditional EA reasoning.

(5) I am almost giving away here how the intercepted Gemini-Sagittarius pair in the chart of Lindbergh is related to the life of Lincoln.

(6) Stephens, Alexander. *"Cornerstone Speech"* a.k.a. the *"Cornerstone Address"* was given by Confederate Vice president Alexander H. Stephens at the Athenaeum in Savannah, Georgia on March 21, 1861. In it, Stephens defended slavery and highlighted the fundamental differences between the constitutions of the Confederacy and that of the United States. The term *'cornerstone'* was used to describe what Stephens thought of as the *"great truth"* of white supremacy and black subordination.

(7) An even closer look at the Gemini archetype tells us that prior to the signaled synthesis and integration, what Gemini does is break reality up into distinct parts. So, the steps and therefore key words for Gemini are: 1. break up into distinct parts (dissection) 2. bring the parts together (synthesis) 3. have the parts communicate with each other (integration). Or, in less formal English: breaking up, bringing together, communicate.

(8) Dissociation is found in all three air signs. In Gemini it happens during the first phase described in the previous footnote: as reality is broken up into distinct parts, they get dissociated from each other. Hence the Geminian need to bring them back together (synthesis). In Libra dissociation

happens when both scales do not listen to each other. As they fail to register what happens on the other side they literally move away from the center, i.e. from the point where there would be equilibrium as the result of true listening to each other. In Aquarius, finally, dissociation happens on a number of different levels. The first level is proper to the essence of the archetype, which is to step back in order to look at something objectively. It is this stepping back that causes the dissociation from that which needs to be looked objectively at. At a different level, dissociation in Aquarius happens at the moment of trauma when the mental (M), emotional (E) or physical (S) component of an experience dissociates from consciousness in order to protect the survival (square Aquarius-Taurus) of the organism as a whole. These dissociated, fractalized parts of self, many lives after the fact can still lay split-off at the deeper levels of the psyche, i.e. the ones which in the *Trauma Helix* we associate with Uranus.

(9) If you get a chance to read Stephens "Cornerstone Speech" you will get an idea of just how reactionary the Confederate cause was. The speech is discussed in detail in Jaffa, Harry V. *A New Birth of Freedom: Abraham Lincoln and the Coming of the Civil War* (Rowman & Littlefield, Publ., Lanham, Maryland, 2000) *"A New Birth of Freedom,"* by the way are words taken from Lincoln's Gettysburg address and seem to perfectly encapsulate his NN of the Moon in the 9th house (Freedom) Scorpio (A New Birth).

(10)   It is also why the words **Therapeutic Evolutionary Astrology** feature on the cover of this book, something I feel I would not have been able to justify had I put them on the cover of my first book *Intercepted Signs: Encoded Messages from the Soul.*

(11)   See Sarna, Jonathan D. and Shapell, Benjamin. *Lincoln and the Jews: A History* (Thomas Dunne Books, New York, 2015).

(12)   See Lindbergh, Reeve. *Under a Wing: A Memoir* (Simon & Schuster, New York, 1998)

Chapter 6 – the '*Multidimensional Psyche*'

(1) The term is not mine but Roger Woolger's and used in his book *Other Lives, Other Selves: A Jungian Psychotherapist Discovers Past Lives* (Bantam Books, 1988), chapter 5: *The Multidimensional Psyche.*

(2) As I write these words, half in jest, I am reminded of Nixon's Pluto skipped step in the 10th house Gemini. In the top-down, hierarchical and austere environments the soul has memories of, behavior with regards to gender would have been highly codified, causing males to live on one side of the Plexiglas and females on the other. These divided worlds show up not only in the Gemini signature of Nixon's Pluto placement but also, and perhaps more importantly, in *the distance* (H11) *from the female side of life*

(Cancer) as part of the meaninglessness trauma of his 11th house Cancer Neptune placement. Thinking and then writing the words *"closer than mailing distance"* somehow placed me with one foot in the 11th house Cancer and with the other in the 10th house Gemini, allowing me to gauge the separation (H11 dissociation) from the opposite sex and, in terms of character, from the malleable and impressionable side of self. To our earlier interpretation of Neptune as *"fracturing in the emotional body"* we can now add this more literal facet of those rigid 10th house environments. The observation not only renders depth to the truthfulness the soul wishes to evolve towards (PPP Sagittarius) when the soft, pliable and feminine side of self (PPP H4) is allowed to come to the fore, but also shows how in Nixon's case meaninglessness trauma can be understood from the impasse of his Pluto skipped step.

(3) See *Good Housekeeping* magazine, June 1960: *My Son Richard Nixon. A Mother's Story*, by Hannah M. Nixon.

(4) See Abrahamsen, David, M.D. *Nixon vs. Nixon: An Emotional Tragedy* (Farrar, Straus & Giroux, New York, 1977), p.59. Also see Mazo, Earl. *Richard Nixon: A Political and Personal Portrait* (Harper & Brothers, 1959).

(5) See *Good Housekeeping* magazine, June 1960: *My Son Richard Nixon. A Mother's Story*, by Hannah M. Nixon.

(6) See Morris, Roger. *Richard Milhous Nixon: The Rise of an American Politician* (Henry Holt, New York, 1990), p.97.

(7) See Schulte, Renée K. *The Young Nixon: An Oral Inquiry* (Fullerton, Cal., California State University, 1978), p.78.

(8) See Aitken, Jonathan. *Nixon: A Life* (Regnery Publ., Washington D.C., 1993), p.24.

(9) See Guinn, Jeff. *Manson: The Life and Times of Charles Manson* (Simon & Schuster, New York, 2013), p.96.

(10)   See Guinn, Jeff. Op. cit., p.59-61.

(11)   Please note the passage of Nixon's secondary progressed Moon through the 10th house between June of 1922 (10 years old) and June of 1924 (11 years old). It was on his Pluto skipped step in March-April 1923, that is, after he had turned ten two months earlier (i.e. 9th January 1923). A full analysis of transits & secondary progressions for key events in the life of Richard Nixon is offered in **the EA School Online's Module 3**: https://www.easchoolonline.com

(12)   See Schulte, Renée. Op. cit., p.55, interview with Nixon's aunt Jane Beeson.

(13)   See Aitken, Jonathan. Op. cit., p.27.

(14)   See Summers, Anthony. Op. cit., p.15. Also see Morris, Roger. Op. cit., p.110; Aitken, Jonathan. Op. cit., p.31.

(15)   See Nixon Eisenhower, Julie. *Pat Nixon: The Untold Story* (Simon & Schuster, New York, 1986), p.85; Aitken, Jonathan. Op. cit., p.30;

Nixon, Richard. *The Memoirs of Richard Nixon* (Simon & Schuster, New York, 1990), p.14.

(16)   See Hallett, Douglas. New York Times article *A low-level memoir of the Nixon White House, New York Times:* October 20, 1974.

(17)   See Solberg, Carl. *Hubert Humphrey: A Biography* (W.W. Norton, New York, 1984), p.313.

(18)   The dark tower of power (Pluto H10 skipped step) Nixon would lock himself up in and become the sole inhabitant of.

(19)   See Morris, Roger. Op. cit., p.281.

(20)   Spalding, Henry D. *The Nixon Nobody Knows* (Jonathan David Publ., New York, 1972), p.137.

(21)   See Summers, Anthony. Op. cit., p.33.

(22)   See White, Theodore H. *Breach of Faith: The Fall of Richard Nixon* (Atheneum, 1975); Costello, William. *The Facts About Richard Nixon: An Unauthorized Biography* (Viking Press, 1960), p.23.

(23)   See Brodie, Fawn. *Richard Nixon: The Shaping of His Character* (W.W. Norton, New York, 1981), p.81.

(24)   See Abrahamsen, David. Op. cit., p.111.

(25)   See Brodie, Fawn. Op. cit., p.127.

(26)   See *Good Housekeeping* magazine, June 1960: *My Son Richard Nixon. A Mother's Story*, by Hannah M. Nixon.

(27)   See Hoyt, Edwin P. *The Nixons: An American Family* (Random House, New York, 1972), p.214; Kornitzer, Bela. *The Real Nixon: An Intimate Biography* (Rand McNally, New York, 1960), p.120.

(28)   The Brookings Institution episode is well-documented and features in Summers, Anthony. Op. cit., pp.385-88.

(29)   Transcript taken from Youtube: *Richard Nixon Orders Brookings institute Break-In July 1971.*

(30)   See Nixon, Richard. *The Memoirs of Richard Nixon* (Simon & Schuster, New York, 1990), p.512.

(31)   See Woolger, Roger. Op. cit., chapter 5: *The Multidimensional Psyche.*

(32)   See Grof, Stanislav. *Beyond the Brain: Birth, Death and Transcendence in Psychotherapy* (State University of New York Press, Albany, 1985).

(33)   See Woolger, Roger. Op. cit., p.148.

(34)   The quote Woolger uses on page 147 of *Other Lives, other Selves*, can be found in Doniger O'Flaherty, Wendy. *Karma and Rebirth in Classical Indian Traditions* (University of California Press, Berkeley, Cal., 1980).

(35)   See Woolger, Roger. Op. cit., p.148.

(36)   It is important to remember that in the *Trauma Helix*, memory traces of physical trauma lie embedded in those belonging to the emotional impact of the trauma, which are formed by Neptune's emotion-

laden sense of meaninglessness on the one hand and by the way Pluto emotionally and psychologically identifies with the Neptune and Uranus strand on the other, pulling both into its own story. Needless to say, its identification with Neptune's emotionally highly charged meaninglessness is much stronger than with Uranus' mental content. This content, however, must not be thought of as lying separate from the emotional impact. The words, thoughts and images corresponding with the traumatic event(s) are inextricably linked to their emotional charge, which is why the image of a helix is used to graphically illustrate the phenomenon.

Horizontal representation of the Chiron – *Trauma Helix* Model

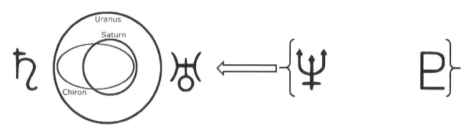

Chiron's own emotional *and* physical wounding
resonates with memory traces of
both past-life physical *and* emotional trauma
when he gets to Uranus

memory traces of physical trauma (S)
lie embedded in the lines of force belonging to
the emotional impact of the trauma (Neptune-Pluto)

(37)   In EA, not Aries but Cancer is associated with the birth of personality. The Chiron pain cannot be made conscious until personality is fully formed. To be known for what it is, it first needs a conscious self-image (Cancer). When the initial contours of personality have been shaped, around the age of six, the pain may be felt but it will need many more years of life experience for it to come into consciousness well and proper.

(38)   We are reminded of the eternal return of Prometheus' liver and Hydra's chopped-off heads in the Chiron myth discussed in chapter 1.

(39)   James Bassett to his wife Wilma, in: Bassett, James. *The Bassett Papers*, Oct. 24, 1960. See https://library.bowdoin.edu

(40)   Baughman, Urbanus Edmund. *Secret Service Chief* (Harper, New York, 1962), p.249.

(41)   Nixon, Richard. *Six Crises* (Doubleday, New York, 1962), p.326.

(42)   The medical term for the affliction being *phlebitis*. See Nixon Eisenhower, Julie. *Pat Nixon: The Untold Story* (Simon & Schuster, New York, 1986), p.223.

(43)   Please do not infer from this that anyone with weak knees suffers from a lack of moral fibre. No such thing is implied here.

(44)   Via this link you can hear Lyndon B. Johnson discuss with Senator Richard Russell how he believed Nixon, through his intermediary Anna Chennault, was effectively sabotaging the Vietnam was peace talks.

https://www.bbc.com/news/av/world-21802132/president-johnson-discusses-nixon-s-vietnam-tactics

(45)   All three of which are described in much detail in Summers, Anthony. Op. cit., chapter 5 (J. Voorhis), chapters 7 & 8 (A. Hiss) and chapter 9 (H. Douglas).

Chapter 7 – Nina Simone

(1) Taken from an interview with Stephen Cleary, July 5, 1989.

(2) See Light, Alan. Op. cit., p.52.

(3) It is important to understand that the Virgoan impulse to self-better is not for its own sake but to prepare the self for equality in relationship. Ideally, when Virgo reaches the threshold of the 7th house/Libra, she is on an equal footing with herself, neither more (Leo) nor less (Virgo) than what she actually is, neither inflating (Leo) nor deflating (Virgo) the self. To reach this state, inner discernment (Virgo) is needed, which is why Mercury is turned inward in Virgo. Only when there is this kind of inward equality (Virgo) can there be outward equality in relationship (Libra). Equality in relationship is of the utmost importance to Virgo because what she has her sights set on is a fair and just society in Capricorn as the culmination of the Earth archetypes. This is why she is seen holding a sheaf of wheat in one of her hands: not bread itself, which in Libra and Scorpio will have to be shared (Scorpio) equally (Libra), but *the promise of bread*. For wheat to become bread people need to work together in a meaningful social context (Libra).

(4) See Light, Alan. Op. cit., p.69. (Andrew Stroud, in an interview with Joe Hagan, 2009). As we move to a more archetypal interpretation of this 6th house Cancer placement, we ask ourselves what the Cancerian attachment would do to the Virgo issues. What it does is, that the attachment to outside sources of emotional security (Pluto in Cancer) will exacerbate the feeling that there is something fundamentally missing in me, something fundamentally not good enough about myself (Pluto H6). Through the emotional leaning on others inherent in Cancer, Virgo concludes there must be something chronically unworthy about herself. This deeper analysis of this Pluto placement is going to be rather important when we get to the PPP in the 12th house Capricorn, so do make a note of it here, so that we have it at the ready when we get there. Pluto by house & sign is the first step in setting up the Evolutionary Axis. I hope you see how much time I take here. I do not proceed to the next step until I feel I have accurately mapped and worded the soul issue(s). If I get this first step wrong, I know all my subsequent steps will be wobbly, and eventually the whole edifice of the Evolutionary Axis will tumble and fall.

(5) When I project onto you what I expect you to do or be, I am not listening (Venus, H7) to you but to myself. Venus in EA is associated with the act of listening to other since this is what the Libra scales do: the slightest movement in one scale causes movement in the other and is registered there. When I register what is happening on the other side, I am listening to it.

(6) This, of course is the big Virgoan dilemma: discernment is needed to determine what criticism is my own as I seek to purify myself and what criticism comes from the outside and gets into my system because I am so susceptible to it due to my self-critical stance. When this discernment is not developed in Virgo, the typical guilt and shame skein is formed, where it becomes very difficult indeed for Virgo to untangle what comes from within and what from without and what needs to be acted upon and what can be left alone.

(7) In therapeutic EA retrogradation indicates the soul wanting the vehicle to deeply reflect on whatever issue comes out of the combination of the house and sign the planet is in. For Richard Nixon that was *the consolidation of truthfulness* (his Saturn is in the 9th house Taurus). The need for reflection inherent in a retrograde planet is linked to the repeat assignment it denotes: when certain circumstances keep repeating in your life, you tend to pause for reflection by asking yourself why this or that thing keeps happening. For Nina Simone the Virgo signature of her Mars placement heightens the need for reflection (on 8th house power, powerlessness and self-empowerment) since both are inward directed movements.

(8) A crisis (inconjunct), therefore, between the lives lived by prior-life selves and the subconscious memories (Ascendant) of non-integration, i.e. segregation (Uranus H3), keeping prior-life selves away from their identity, freedom and right to exist (Uranus in Aries) - see chart sample below.

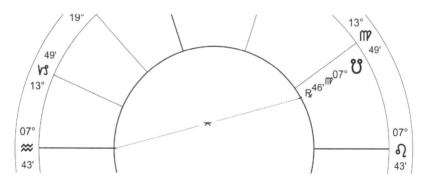

(9) Forgiveness is the last thing Virgo needs to hear for it implies an acknowledgement of guilt. Virgo is already plagued by guilt and does not

need an extra dose of it. What she needs to hear, or feel rather, is the Cosmic Piscean Embrace in which she experiences (feels) that there was nothing to forgive to begin with, that her chronic self-debasement was simply the result of the Mercury frenzy turning inward, creating a hopelessly tangled skein of self-recrimination, effectively hollowing out Virgo from the center and creating what in EA is often called 'a deep existential void.' As Virgo feels this void, she turns to Pisces, whom through religious conditioning she has come to see as 'Perfect' and then tries to fill the gaping hole inside of herself with that presumed perfection. There can be forgiveness in the sextile from Pisces to Capricorn when the latter has done something wrong and then owns up to it, that is, shows integrity (Capricorn). *Then* Pisces can say to Capricorn *"I forgive you."* But never in the opposition to Virgo.

(10)   This is why earlier I pointed out to you the deeper, archetypal meaning of Simone's 6th house Cancer Pluto placement.

(11)   Taken from an interview with Stephen Cleary, June 12, 1989.

(12)   In music, counterpoint is the relationship between voices which are harmonically interdependent (polyphony) yet independent in rhythm and contour. It has been most commonly identified in the European classical tradition, strongly developing in the Baroque era and culminating in the music of Johann Sebastian Bach (1685-1750). This is not the place to go into the intricacy of Simone's musical textures, but as a trained musician I can assure you they show incredible sophistication. Also see Alan, op. cit., p.31.

(13)   Taken from *Nina Simone: La Légende*, TV documentary produced by La Sept., System TV, and BBC, 1992.

(14)   We saw an example of Uranus in contact with the 1st house / Aries / Mars in the chart of Charles Lindbergh in chapter 5, pointing to the untimely death of Abraham Lincoln. Another case in point is the chart of Josef Mengele, which we will have a look at in chapter 11. Yet another example of Uranus in contact with the 1st house / Aries / Mars is found in the chart of Jim Jones (chapter 10), pointing to the premature death of a flock of followers having come under the spell of his words (Uranus H3 Aries). Anne Frank's Uranus, finally, too is in contact with the 1st house / Aries / Mars. It features in the 10th house Aries, pointing to having died young at the hands of dysfunctional authority. Uranus in contact with the Aries archetype indicating dying young or prematurely is not a hard and fast rule. In some of these cases (Lincoln, Frank, Jones), however, it is borne out by biographical fact, warranting the conclusion.

(15)   See chapter 15 in this book. Also see De Baker, Michael, Op. cit., chapter 9. (Anne Frank-Barbro-Karlén comparative chart study).

(16)   The subject is dealt with in Light, Allen. Op. cit., from chapter 5 onwards.

Chapter 8 – The Missing Moon

(1) Why I interpret Nina Simone's and Jim Jones's identical Uranus H3 in Aries placement differently is explained in chapter 16 – *Chiron Miscellaneous*.

(2) Please see Chapter 16 – *Chiron Miscellaneous* for a full elaboration of this train of thought. The fallacy of cookie-cutter descriptions is shown using the example of David Duke's Chiron in the 3rd house Sagittarius.

(3) The fact that the Moon is a skipped step in Lincoln's chart is the soul letting us know in no uncertain terms that it considers this a major unresolved issue coming from one or more prior lives, corroborating at once Yogananda's claim of Lincoln having been a Himalayan yogi who died with the unfulfilled wish of bringing about racial parity. As we discussed in chapter 4, the H12 Capricorn Moon issue resolves through Lincoln's *deep commitment* (NN of the Moon in Scorpio) *to the cause of liberty* (NN of the Moon H9).

The Moon skipped step resolving via the NN of the Moon *does not mean that the NN of the Moon is the 'solution' to the unresolved Moon issue.* All it means is that *the way to* that solution is the counterweight provided by the NN of the Moon. In the case of Lincoln: *the way to* assuming responsibility (Capricorn), *through law* (Capricorn) *for the whole issue of slavery* (H12) – i.e. the Moon's new response - is a deep commitment (NN of the Moon in Scorpio) to the cause of liberty (NN of the Moon H9). The only thing that is evolutionary relevant is the Moon's new response. **It is the Moon itself, i.e. Lincoln the person, who will have to come up with the new 12th house Capricorn response**. Where the resolution node to a Moon skipped step is the SN of the Moon – as is the case in the chart of Greta Garbo [chart discussed in my book *Intercepted Signs: Encoded Messages from the Soul*, chapter 10] the person (Moon) is sent back to the past (SN of the Moon) and challenged to deal with it differently. In other words: *the way to* the Moon's new response is via a return to the past. That past is still confronted by the NN of the Moon's counterforce so that the Moon may formulate this new response. What those circumstances were in the case of Garbo and how she dealt with them differently is explained in said book and chapter. The Moon's new 12th house Taurus response is not.

(4) Honesty compels me to state that incorporating the planetary nodes in chart analysis is not my invention. Others have come before me who have worked assiduously trying to promote it: Dane Rudhyar, Theodor Landscheidt, Jeffrey Green, Zipporah Dobyns, and currently Mark Jones.

(5) Reading the south node descriptions in the upcoming chapters on Richard Nixon, Jim Jones, and Josef Mengele may lead you to think otherwise. Please remember that prior-life selves in these three cases would have been immersed in some pretty dark dynamics to get to their current-life chart placements and corresponding behavior. I therefore suggest you

look at the south nodes, both lunar and planetary, in the charts of Lincoln, Lindbergh, Barbro Karlén and Anne Frank to offset this impression. A description of Lincoln's Mars orbit would look like this: (See chapter 15 - Barbro Karlén-Anne Frank for more examples of this)

Lincoln - SN of Mars H10 Sagittarius	resistance	Lincoln - NN of Mars H2 Aries
conscious actions and desires aimed at having the principle of liberty (Sagittarius) laid down in law (H10), encountering opposition from political forces (H10)	< >	to consolidate (H2) my and others' identity, freedom and right to exist (Aries)
the past streaming into the present and determining the old response: H8 Libra	**Mars's choices**	**new response as the result of the resistance between the planet's SN and NN and its familiarity with the former: H8 Libra**
feeling powerless (H8) in the fight for equality (Libra)	< >	conscious actions and desires aimed at personal and social empowerment (H8) in the context of equality in relationship (Libra)

Chapter 9 – Trauma, Pain and Healing in Orbit

(1) Please take into account that the timeline images used to illustrate these opening sentences of this chapter are incorrect for not representing the actual orbital movement of both the Moon and Neptune.

(2) For some, as is the case for Anne Frank, for example, the SN of Chiron reaches 1 degree Taurus, with its NN in the latter 8 degrees of Libra. Barbro Karlén has her SN of Chiron at 0 degrees Taurus, with the NN of Chiron at 24 degrees Libra. Chiron's highly elliptical orbit has it remain in Pisces and Aries for a long time, after which it gathers speed somewhat through Taurus and races through the signs of Gemini to Sagittarius, slowing down only in Capricorn and then even more so in Aquarius. The result is that it stays in Libra for a mere 21 months yet a good 8 years and 3 months in Aries. Also see footnote (2), chapter 1.

(3) The dynamics of the resolution node (and its ruler) to Nixon's Pluto skipped step are not discussed. The chart of Jim Jones (chapters 10 & 14) is used to illustrate how a Pluto skipped step might resolve through one of the lunar nodes.

(4) Paradoxical planet or nodal placements, that is, placements where the astrologer is faced with archetypal polarities, are easily solved when the

correct filtering - 1. What is the planet about? 2. House conditions planet 3. Sign contextualizes planet in the house – is followed. Nixon's SN of the Moon in Aries did not pose any kind of problem using these interpretative steps, nor does the NN of Chiron H2 Scorpio.

(5) Some evolutionary astrologers will look at the rulers of the planetary nodes for further information on their dynamics. While there may be validity in this approach, that analysis is not undertaken here so as not to unduly complicate matters.

(6) This past dynamic of twisting (Sag) the facts (Gem) sheds additional and crucial light on why the soul chose to have consciousness in its vehicle Nixon structured in such a way as to allow for *the consolidation* (Saturn in Taurus) *of truthfulness* (Saturn H9).

(7) See Woolger, Roger. Op. cit., chapter 5: *The Multidimensional Psyche*.

(8) See Newton, Michael. *Destiny of Souls* (Llewellyn Publ., Woodbury, Minnesota, 2000), pp.126-130.

(9) See De Baker, Michael. *Intercepted Signs: Encoded Messages from the Soul* (Kindle, Publ., 2019), chapter 3, p.26, where the image of a Möbius strip is used to illustrate the *Divine Dance of Consciousness* Source, Soul and Ego are involved in.

Chapter 10 – Jim Jones

(A website which offers extensive Peoples Temples resource material is: *The Jonestown Institute*, https://jonestown.sdsu.edu)

(1) See Guinn, Jeff. *The Road to Jonestown: Jim Jones and Peoples Temple* (Simon & Schuster, New York, 2017), chapter 3 – *Jimmy*.

(2) See Layton, Deborah. *Seductive Poison: A Jonestown Survivor's Story of Life and Death in the Peoples Temple*, p.204. Also see: Scheeres, Julia. *A Thousand Lives: The Untold Story of Jonestown* (Free Press, New York, 2011), p.199.

(3) The title of a book on Jonestown written by one of its survivors, Leslie Wagner-Wilson, aptly condenses Jones' SN of the Moon to two words: *Slavery* [Libra, brackets by me, MDB] *of Faith* [H9, brackets by me, MDB], (iUniverse, Revised Edition, 2009). It is a riveting tale of one woman and her son; a personal account of her life in and escape from (November 17, 1978, leaving her family and relatives behind to face death) Jonestown, painting a detailed portrait of the total control Jones wielded over his followers. Unlike other books on Jonestown, Wagner-Wilson lists the nine hundred plus victims of the Jonestown massacre in the back of her book.

(4) RYMUR (F.B.I. files RYan MURder) 89-4286-O-1-B-1

(5) I associate Libra with socialism since it seeks a fair and equal distribution of wealth between both scales as a result of each listening carefully to what the other needs. This is the new action (cardinal sign) which needs

to be taken if there is to be the fair and just form (Libra square Capricorn) we call *society* (Capricorn) in which inner individual integrity (Capricorn) manifests as outer collective integrity. In Libra this form is in the making, uneasily searched for through tentatively gauging and probing one's own and others' needs.

To give you an idea of the actual socialism Jim Jones practiced: elaborate schemes were devised by him to get his millions into foreign bank accounts. Members of his inner circle were sent on long trips to a variety of countries (among which Switzerland and Panama), often making unusual stopovers to throw the FBI off their scent. See Layton, Deborah. Op. cit., p. 85. No People Temples member ever saw a dime of that money. They lived in abject poverty in Jonestown, working their fingers to the bone and receiving corporal punishment if they so much as entertained 'treasonous thoughts.' (i.e. having a cigarette, spending some time alone, etc.)

Layton, Deborah, Op. cit., (p.176) details what punishment in Jonestown would consist of: rebellious or unruly followers, adults and children alike, would get locked up for days in *the Box*, an underground, six by four feet pitch-dark cubicle which felt like an oven because of the sweltering jungle heat. Alternatively, and especially designed for children, use was made of *the Well*: in the middle of the night sinners would get hung upside down by a rope attached to their ankles and lowered and dunked into the dark water, where they would feel the groping hands of adults hiding inside the well. This punishment was commonly referred to as *'Big Foot.'* For a detailed description of *The Box* and *The Well*, see Scheeres, Julia. Op. cit., p.141.

(6) See Guinn, Jeff. Op. cit., pp.56-57.

(7) Jones is quoted as having spoken words along the lines of: *"I began tearing the bastard* [i.e. God, brackets by me, MDB] *to pieces and chucked him in the bin."* See Guinn, Jeff. Op. cit., p.53.

(8) Like Leslie Wagner-Wilson's *Slavery* [Libra, brackets by me, MDB] *of Faith* [H9, brackets by me, MDB], the term 'evangelical socialism' perfectly captures Jones' 9th house Libra SN of the Moon. With regards to the former, Libra in EA is associated with slavery for in slavery one person does the other person's bidding (i.e. what is expected – Libra – of them) and is totally dependent on them, creating a situation of extreme inequality in relationship. Harry Jaffa's *"A New Birth* [Lincoln's NN of the Moon in Scorpio, brackets by me, MDB] *of Freedom* [Lincoln's NN of the Moon in H9, brackets by me, MB] is another good example of a book title perfectly capturing a nodal dynamic. (See Bibliography: Jaffa, Harry V. *A New Birth of Freedom: Abraham Lincoln and the Coming of the Civil War* (Rowman & Littlefield, Publ., Lanham, Maryland, 2000)

(9) See Layton, Deborah. Op. cit., p.36.

(10)   See Guinn, Jeff. Op. cit., p.215.

(11)   See Guinn, Jeff. Op. cit., p.100.

(12)   See Guinn, Jeff. Op. cit., p.102.

(13)   See Guinn, Jeff. Op. cit., p.280. Also see Youtube: *Jonestown Part 2: How Jim Jones rose to power with his Peoples Temple*, (06:49 mins. in): Laura Johnston Kohl, former Peoples Temple member: *"Jim started early on having people sign blank pieces of paper."* (*Jonestown Part 1-5* on Youtube may serve as a substitute for those readers who want to obtain background information on Jim Jones and his Peoples Temple yet do not wish to read the books listed in the Bibliography).

Additionally, members of Jones' inner circle during weekly meetings of the Planning Commission were made to confess the worst things they had ever done. Admissions of guilt, often made up to please and impress Jones and ranging from shoplifting to having made plans to assassinate the President, were subsequently taped or written down in signed affidavits [SN ruler H3] for later use by Jones should the need arise to blackmail someone. See Layton, Deborah. Op. cit., pp.68-69.

On the theme of false affidavits, also see Scheeres, Julia. Op. cit., p.64. Scheeres mentions the case of Jim Bogue, who had his false confession used against him as he tried to quit the church. His wife Edith told Jones about her husband's wish to leave and she was given instructions by Jones on how to deal with the matter. The next day, Jim Bogue was handed an eviction order and a separation notice by the Mendocino County Sheriff's Department. A day later, he found out his wife had emptied their joint bank account and removed his name from their joint business venture. The final blow in the series of three came the following day, when one of Jones' cronies paid Bogue a visit and reminded him of the affidavit he had signed stating he had laid hands on his daughters.

Equally applicable to the SN ruler H3 Aries are the *"reverse tactics"* letters Jones would send to politicians. He made these letters look as if they had been drafted by white supremacists angry at Jones' efforts on behalf of the less affluent and black population. It was his way (SN ruler H3: letters) of drawing government officials' attention to his person and cause (SN ruler Aries). See, Layton, Deborah. Op. cit., p.62.

Yet another fine example of SN ruler H3 Aries tactics, were the poison-impregnated letters Jones would send defectors, warning them they had better keep schtum because, as the letter clearly showed, they knew where to find them. See Scheeres, Julia. Op. cit., p.43. Also see Layton, Deborah. Op. cit., p.92.

And finally, the so-called "write-ups" [SN ruler H3] expected of Jonestown settlers also fall under the SN ruler H3 Aries: followers were expected to write up their sins and 'capitalist thoughts' (i.e. wishing to start a family, going to the cinema, visiting a relative, etcetera) and submit these to

Jones so that they may be punished [i.e. Jones imposing his will on them: SN ruler Aries], through disciplinary action in the much-feared 'Learning Crew,' which meant doing double shifts in the scorching jungle heat and refraining from speaking to anyone, or, if Jones considered the trespass a major offense, through spending time in *the Box*, [Layton, Deborah. Op. cit., p. 176] or through being injected with coma-inducing Thorazine after which they would wither away in the Extended Care Unit (as happened to Shanda James for no longer wishing to give in to Jones' sexual advances). See Layton, Op. cit., p.300. Also see Reiterman, Tim. *Raven*, p.452. Also see Scheeres, Julia. Op. cit., p.177.

(14)   See Guinn, Jeff. Op. cit., p.394. Also see Layton, Deborah. Op. cit., p. 6, p.151.

(15)   Again, as stated in footnote (5) chapter 4, it is important to grasp the essence of the Gemini archetype as having to do with synthesis followed by integration.

(16)   See Layton, Deborah. Op. cit., Foreword written by Charles Krause, p. xxii.

(17)   Jones' final words towards the end of a 45-minute tape of the 'suicide' in progress, as later recovered by the F.B.I., commonly referred to as *'the death tape.'*

(18)   See Guinn, Jeff. Op. cit., pp.320-321.

(19)   See Guinn, Jeff. Op. cit., p.189. Also see Mills, Jeannie. *Six Years With God: Life Inside Jones' Peoples Temple*, written by Temple inner circle defectors Elmer and Deanna Mertle after they legally changed their names. Possibly the most informative book about Jones and his Temple after *The Road to Jonestown* (Guinn, Jeff), *Seductive Poison* (Layton, Deborah) and *A Thousand Lives* (Scheeres, Julia). See Bibliography.

(20)   In a way we could say that what happened in Jonestown on November 18, 1978 was the ultimate reenactment of this trauma: all had to die prematurely (Uranus in Aries) so that Jones could have the final word (Uranus H3). See Guinn, Jeff. Op. cit., p.452. Why I interpret Jim Jones´s and Nina Simone's identical 3rd house Aries Uranus placement differently is explained in Chapter 16 – *Chiron Miscellaneous.*

(21)   See Layton, Deborah. Op. cit. (Epilogue) p.299.

(22)   Congressman Leo Ryan eventually did get near it but perished in the effort as he was brutally gunned down and killed by Jones' henchmen on the Port Kaituma airstrip. See chapter 16, footnote (4).

(23)   How Jones during his 'healings,' with the help of chicken offal, would lead audiences to believe he could remove cancers is described in detail in Guinn, Jeff. Op. cit., pp.77-78.

(24)   See Guinn, Jeff. Op. cit., pp.68-69.

(25)   Jones, on occasions, stated that he believed he had been Vladimir Lenin in a previous life. (Layton, Deborah, Op. cit., p.45). Jones' mother

Lynetta, even in ripe old age, told the story of how as a young woman she knew she had given birth to a great man, a leader. His mother, Jones claimed, had been Mark Twain in a previous life. For more on Jones' reincarnational delusions, see Guinn, Jeff. Op. cit., p.109.

(26)   For more on Jones' 'Rainbow Family,' see Guinn, Jeff. Op. cit., p.94.

(27)   This is not a play on words. As we saw in chapter 6 – The 'Multidimensional Psyche,' the in**form**ation held in the energy field matrix that is the subtle body – made up of lines of force which coincide with the 3 elements of the Trauma Helix – **form** an etheric cast upon which physical dispositions in the vehicle's body (Saturn), in addition to its structure of consciousness (Saturn), are shaped, **form**ed. Chiron is the astrological equivalent of that energy field matrix. (see chapter 6, p.92)

(28)   The fact that the Moon is conjunct her own north node, pledging allegiance to its 3rd house Aries intentions, does not mean it does not still feel the pull of its own 9th house Libra south node. (see p.166-167 for the particulars of how it is shaped by its own H9 Libra past). In the orbital approach I am building a case for in this book it will *always* feel that pull. Here, with Jones, the Moon might well be conjunct its own north node to help it get over the road hump of the formidable Pluto-Jupiter H7 Cancer skipped step on one end of the see-saw and the Saturn H1 Capricorn skipped step on the other.

Chapter 11 – Josef Mengele in Full Evolutionary Orbit

(1) See Völklein, Ulrich. *Josef Mengele: Der Artz von Auschwitz* (Steidl Verlag, Göttingen, 1999), p.47. The notion that physicians murdering Jews were contributing to preserving the racial purity of the *"Volk,"* i.e. the German nation, is, among other things, explored in Lifton, Robert J. *The Nazi Doctors: Medical Killing and the Psychology of Genocide* (Basic Books, New York, 1986).

(2) For an in-depth exploration of how a small occult lodge was behind the Nazis' distorted worldview, see Luhrssen, David. *Hammer of the Gods: The Thule Society and the Birth of Nazism* (Potomac Books, Washington, D.C., 2012).

(3) See Bruns, Florian. *Turning Away from the Individual: Medicine and Morality Under the Nazis*. In *Nazi Ideology and Ethics*, edited by Wolfgang Bialas and Lothar Fritze, pp.211-36, Newcastle upon Tyne, Cambridge Scholars, 2014), p.216.

(4) See Marwell, David G. *Mengele: Unmasking the "Angel of Death"* (W.W. Norton & Company, New York, 2020). Also see: Proctor, Robert. *Racial Hygiene: Medicine Under the Nazis* (Cambridge, Massachusetts, Harvard University Press, 1988).

(5) See Chapter 7, footnote (7) for an explanation of why a planet's retrogradation denotes a repeat assignment.

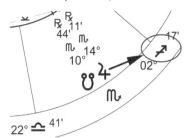

Jupiter's rulership of the 6th house conjures up uncomfortable images of this perverted (Scorpio) ideology (Jupiter) directly affecting (i.e. ruling) a process of filtering out perceived impurities (H6).

(6) This is not the first time we have come across a Pluto placement whose combination of house and sign may lead to a very literal interpretation: in Anne Frank's Pluto H12 Cancer we literally see *a family* (Cancer*) in hiding* (H12) – coming back in Barbo Karlén's subconscious memories of what happened to the family as expressed in her Uranus H12 Cancer conjunct the SN of the Moon H12 Cancer. In Nina Simone's Pluto H6 Cancer we literally see the *interjected inferiority and unworthiness* (H6) *in the context of race and gender* (Cancer). Although we have sought to interpret these placements at a deeper, archetypal level also, the more literal one seems equally valid, warranting the conclusion that both can exist alongside each other. This coexistence of the two levels – the inner, archetypal and the outer, circumstantial one - makes all the more sense when we also look at Pluto as the soul's emotional and psychological identification with the Uranus and Neptune strand of the *Trauma Helix*, which in Mengele's case points to *having sacrificed* (H12), *in vain, one's youth* (Gemini) *for a deluded* (H12) *antagonistic* (Gemini) *idea* (Gemini), something which ultimately was no more than a thought construct (Gemini).

(7) The focus of Mengele's medical activities at Auschwitz is detailed in Marwell, David G. Op. cit., chapter 4.

(8) See Marwell, David G. Op. cit., p.83.

(9) This is that deeper, archetypal interpretation I refer to in footnote (6). David G. Marwell, Op. cit., (p.8), mentions an interesting and perhaps key moment in the life of the young Mengele when he has what appears to be a casual encounter with a fellow university student by the name of Diesbach, who convinces him to choose medicine over dentistry, which is what Mengele had initially shown an interest in. Looking back at this moment when he changed course, Mengele suggested his friend had rekindled something that had lain dormant inside of him and ascribed almost mythic meaning to the encounter, as if it had set him on the path of his destiny. The anecdote is noteworthy for it shows how the past-life dynamics described in my analysis of the Pluto placement, the SN of the Moon and its ruler can be triggered by encounters like these precisely because the soul comes into the current-life with memories of them. The

mythic significance ascribed to it by Mengele is a reflection of his Pluto in the 12th house sensing that science (Gemini) once again might be used to further the cause of the delusional, mythical, elevated and purified collective (H12).

(10)	How Mengele used the Nazi escape route through South Tyrol and Italy is detailed in Steinacher, Gerald. *Nazis on the Run: How Hitler's Henchmen Fled Justice* (Oxford University Press, 2011), which sheds much light on the role of the Red Cross and the Vatican in allowing Nazi war criminals to slip through the hands of justice. Also see Marwell, David G. Op. cit., Part III: *Flight*.

(11)	As we shall see shortly, and in line with the work done on the Moon dynamics in chapters 8 & 9, we will define the new response of Mengele's Moon - <u>not</u> *the NN of the Moon* - as the facilitator of soul evolution. His 11th house Taurus NN of the Moon is *the catalyst* for change. His 4th house Libra Moon itself *the agent of change*.

(12)	See Marwell, David G. Op. cit., p.82. The trial against Auschwitz physician Horst Fischer, who joined the SS in 1933 at the age of 20 and the Nazi party at the age of 24, took place in what was then called the German Democratic Republic (i.e. east Germany) only after he had been allowed to practice medicine there undisturbed for a period of twenty years after WWII had ended. The GDR Supreme Court found him guilty of crimes committed at the Auschwitz-Birkenau concentration camp and executed him by guillotine in the city of Leipzig on 8 July 1966. The trial is recounted in Dirks, Christian. *Die Verbrechen der Anderen: Auschwitz und der Auschwitz-Prozess der DDR. Das Verfahren gegen die ZZ-Artz Dr. Horst Fischer* (Schöning Ferdinand GMBH, Publ.).

(13)	The same way our fated economy is based on debt, that is, the financial equivalent of guilt.

(14)	Free translation after the Hippocratic Oath, in Greek, from the 1923 Loeb edition.

(15)	See Marwell, David G. Op. cit., Epilogue: *Father and Son*, p.342. Also see: "The Meeting," September 30, 1985, Posner Papers, Box 34, Folder 13, Gotlieb Archival Research Center, Boston University.

(16)	Quoted in Zofka, Efraim. *Der KZ-Artz Mengele. Zur Typologie eines NS-Verbrechers*, in Vierteljahrshefte für Zeitgeschichte 34, no.2 (1986), p.266.

(17)	See Marwell, David G. Op. cit., p.126.

(18)	See Marwell, David G. Op. cit., p.9, Also see Bruns, Florian. Op. cit., p.216.

(19)	This is not the place to go into interceptions, but you can see how both of Venus' responses – the old and the new one – rule Taurus intercepted in the 11th house: *the (non) survival* (Taurus) *of large groups of people* (H11).

(20)　　　See Dirks, Christian. *Die Verbrechen der Anderen: Auschwitz und der Auschwitz-Prozess der DDR. Das Verfahren gegen der ZZ-Artz Dr. Horst Fischer* (Schöning Ferdinand GMBH, Publ.), pp.158-159.

(21)　　　Forming a T-square with Neptune in the 1st house Cancer and the Moon in the 4th house Libra, with the latter as its apex (the compartmentalization of the emotional body and the need to decompartmentalize it).

Chapter 12 – Richard Nixon in Full Evolutionary Orbit

(1) Youtube: *Richard Nixon Accepts the 1968 Republican Presidential Nomination*. Video. The words on truth are spoken 06:30 mins. into the video.

(2) See Summers, Anthony. Op. cit., p.22. Also see Aitken, Jonathan. *Nixon: A Life* (Regnery Publ., Washington D.C., 1993), p.61.

(3) Please note the SN of Mars's proximity to the SN of Uranus H3 Sagittarius: conscious actions directed at the distortion (Sag) of the facts (H3) and dishonest (Sag) use of information (H3) – of which there were many recurrences in the life of Richard Nixon – found to lie near the origin of his 5th house Aquarius trauma, i.e. his sudden dissociation (Aquarius) from leadership (H5) through a removal from office (Uranus ruling H6).

(4) Having defined the *Trauma Helix* the way we have, the NN of Saturn H11 Cancer might also be thought of as the need for consciousness to be structured in such a way as to allow for the emotional body (Cancer) to in-*divi*-duate, (H11) understood as becoming in-*divis*-ible, i.e. no longer fractalized.

(5) We are beginning to understand the sextile between Saturn and Neptune: there is an ease in the energy flow between the fracturing of the emotional body (Neptune H11 Cancer) and the curbing of truthfulness (Saturn H9 Taurus), the same way there is one between Nixon feeling at home with who he truly is – or, alternatively: the indivisibility of the emotional body (Neptune H11 Cancer) - and the consolidation of truthfulness (Saturn H9 Taurus). Once the key players have been identified – through determining planetary function – we understand the dialogue (i.e. the aspect) going on between them. We understand, to choose yet another aspect from Nixon's chart, why there would be a crisis (inconjunct) between the consolidation of truthfulness (Saturn H9 Taurus) and the emotional dishonesty of Mars as the NN ruler in its capacity as skipped step. What you are witnessing in these chapters is how looking at a planet in its full orbit can be helpful in determining planetary function and, subsequently, aspects.

Chapter 13 – Nina Simone in Full Evolutionary Orbit

(1) Interview clip in *Nina Simone Live at Ronnie Scott's London*.

(2) Nina Simone interview in Taylor, Arthur R. *Notes and Tones: Musician-to-Musician Interviews* (Da Capo Press, New York, 1982).

(3) See Light, Alan. Op. cit., p.169.

(4) Or, to phrase this differently, meaninglessness trauma (Neptune) incurred as a result of past-life selves' identity (H1) having been determined in the context of a large collective of people made equally *un*important (Aquarius).

(5) Nina Simone interview in Taylor, Arthur R. Op. cit.

Chapter 14 – Jim Jones in Full Evolutionary Orbit

(1) Using one again that most useful title of Leslie Wagner-Wilson's book *"Slavery of Faith"*. See chapter 10, footnotes (3) and (8). Also see *Bibliography*.

(2) Fostering independent (Aries) thinking (H3) by allowing people to connect (H3) with their own free will (Aries) can be said to be the great promise of the 3rd house Aries NN of the Moon, buoyed up in a recent past life by Uranus (Uranus H3 Aries conjunct NN of the Moon H3 Aries).

(3) Observing how close the SN of Pluto is to Jones' Saturn in Capricorn skipped step, looming large in the 1st house – with the NN of Pluto sandwiched between his Pluto and Jupiter skipped step at the rear end in H7 - you may want to draw your own conclusions with regards to the larger soul mission I referred to in the final paragraphs of Chapter, where we came to speak of the nodes of Pluto.

(4) The SN of Venus is bang on the Moon H3 Aries (in its conjunction to her own NN), representing an energy the current-life Moon and its NN seek to invert.

(5) Here, again, we see how vitally important it is to understand Gemini in its capacity of connect**ing**, as opposed to Libra already being connec**ted**. For more on this, see Chapter 4, footnote (7).

(6) See Guinn, Jeff. Op. cit., p.224. For a more detailed account of the bus rape scene - in the victim's own words - see Layton, Deborah. Op. cit., pp.71-74, chapter 5: *Father Loves Us*.

(7) See Charles Krause (reporter for the *Washington Post* who, having sustained light injuries as a bullet grazed his hip, survived the Port Kaituma airstrip assault by playing dead) in the Foreword to Layton, Deborah. Op. cit., p. xiv.

(8) Closely aligned with the Sun H5 22° Taurus 24'.

(9) See Guinn, Jeff. Op. cit., p.218.

(10)   See Guinn, Jeff. Op. cit., p.204.

Chapter 15 – From Barbro Karlén back to Anne Frank via the planetary south nodes: *'trauma continuity and healing continuity'*

(1) Libra in EA is associated with projections from one person onto another (i.e. one of the scales onto the other). Aquarius and the 11th house in EA are associated with projections from the group onto the individual, from the individual onto the group, or from one group onto another.

(2) The square being 'out of sign' in EA does not disqualify it as a square. Quite the contrary: if Barbro's SN of Chiron had been neatly in Aries, falling in the 10th house or in the final minutes of the 29th degree in the 11th house, we would have got none of the information leading us to uncover the all-important trauma continuity. Also see chapter 2, footnote (5) and chapter 4, footnote (9).

(3) Recounted in Karlén, Barbro. *And the Wolves Howled* (Clairview Books, London 2000).

(4) Because of the biographical information available to us, I would be willing to stretch my orbs considerably and count Abraham Lincoln's (out of sign) Chiron 11° Aquarius-SN Chiron 25° Aries (16 degrees) and Charles Lindbergh's Chiron 10° Capricorn-SN Chiron 25° Aries (15 degrees) as squares as well.

(5) Here, again, it is important to see why Libra has to do with things affecting you: the slightest movement in one of the scales affects the other and vice versa (i.e. if one goes up, the other goes down). Each of the two scales - welded together and therefore condemned to listen to each other - registers and reflects what happens at the other end.

(6) This is what actually happened in Barbro's fight against what seemed like a never-ending fusillade of false accusations against her person and good name, chronicled in her book *And the Wolves Howled*. She stood up to her accusers and so stopped the barrage of false allegations leveled at her. Barbo ends her book with the following words: *"The howling of the wolves has finally stopped."* Karlén, Barbro, Op. cit., p.236.

(7) See Meyer, Thomas. *What would people say if she claimed that she had been Anne Frank?*, Afterword in Karlén, Barbro. Op. cit., p.247.

(8) Two short works of fiction in which 11-year-old Barbro Karlén in exquisite poetry and prose depicts the catastrophic effects of man´s disrespect for Mother Earth. She also shows the way forward towards a more respectful coexistence between guest (man) and host (earth).

(9) See Meyer, Thomas. *What would people say if she claimed that she had been Anne Frank?*, Afterword in Karlén, Barbro, Op. cit., pp.247-248.

(10)   See Karlén, Barbro. *And the Wolves Howled,* p.230.

(11)   We are looking at Libra one-to-one projection here since the entire German nation (H4), with a few negligible exceptions (in terms of number, not importance) stood as one against the Jewish people (H4 race). We

would be looking at Aquarius projection if a large group of people projected something onto an individual, an individual projected something onto a group, or one group onto another one. The German nation is not a group of people. A group of people is 150,000 far-right extremists, eugenicists, anti-abolitionists, etc.

(12)   You can see the inconjunct (crisis) between the ruler of the SN of the Moon (Moon H8 Aquarius) and the SN of the Moon (H12 Cancer). It is almost exact (ruler of the SN of the Moon 15° Aquarius 35' – SN of the Moon 15° Cancer 30'), indicating a state of acute crisis between the two.

(13)   Just like in Barbro's chart, there is a close contact between Neptune and the Moon in Anne's. In the former it is between the SN of Neptune and the Moon, in the latter between the Moon and Neptune itself.

(14)   As pointed out in footnote (5), why Libra has to do with one thing affecting another can be gleaned from the physical object the archetype derives its name and glyph from: the slightest movement in one of the scales *affects* the other.

(15)   See Meyer, Thomas. *What would people say if she claimed that she had been Anne Frank?*, Afterword in Karlén, Barbro. Op. cit., p.249.

(16)   See Karlén, Barbro. *And the Wolves Howled,* p.19.

(17)   When, interestingly, her transiting Uranus and Saturn were in the 11th house Gemini squaring her transiting SN of the Moon H8 Pisces-NN of the Moon H2 Virgo, with the ruler of the former in H3 Virgo and her secondary progressed Moon inconjunct the latter from H7 Aquarius.

(18)   Frank, Anne. *The Diary of Anne Frank: The Revised Critical Edition* (Doubleday, New York, 2003).

(19)   This continuity in the nature of will from lifetime to the next we already examined in the Lincoln-Lindbergh chart comparison in chapters 4 and 5.

(20)   We are not talking about Mars as a skipped step here, but Mars defined in terms of its planetary function. In Chapter 9 of my book *Intercepted Signs: Encoded Messages from the Soul*, Anne's Mars skipped step was defined as *"a will* (Mars) *directed at establishing my creative* (Leo) *identity* (H1) *was thwarted* (Mars skipped step)." Since we are dealing with the same archetypes (i.e. Aries and Leo) the descriptions, inevitably, overlap.

(21)   See Marwell, David G. *Mengele: Unmasking the "Angel of Death"* p.125 (in Posner Papers, Box 18, Folder 3, Gotlieb Archival Research Center, Boston University, "Gespräch mit Frau Irene Maria Hackenjos, geschiedene 1. Ehefrau von Josef Mengele," Freiburg, September 20, 1985).

(22)   See Posner, Gerald L. *Hitler's Children: Sons and Daughters of Leaders of the Third Reich Talk About Their Fathers and Themselves*

(Random House, New York, 1991). Also see Marwell, David G. Op. cit., p.126.

(23)   See Karlén, Barbro. *And the Wolves Howled,* pp.12-13, where Barbro´s *"Letter to the Man wo was Afraid to Die"* is reproduced in full.

(24)   See Meyer, Thomas. *What would people say if she claimed that she had been Anne Frank?*, Afterword in Karlén, Barbro. Op. cit., p.249.

(25)   Wordsworth, William. *Ode: Intimations of Immortality* (a.k.a. "Ode", "Immortality Ode" or "Great Ode"), published in *Poems, in Two Volumes* (1807), reprinted under its full title *Ode: Intimations of Immortality from Recollections of Early Childhood* in the 1815 collection *Poems.*

Chapter 16 – Chiron Miscellaneous

(1) Birth data for David Duke: 1 July 1950, 11:37 hrs., Tulsa, Oklahoma, RR:AA. For an explanation of dissociation in the sign of Gemini, please turn to Chapter 5, footnote (8).

(2) These so-called 'White Nights' and their goings-on are described in detail in Scheeres, Julia. *A Thousand Lives: The Untold Story of Jonestown* (Free Press, New York, 2011), pp.93, 99, 165, 170, 178, 215, 231.

(3) See Scheeres, Julia. Op. cit., p.170.

(4) The damning articles would appear in the *New West* magazine, the custody battle was with once very loyal but now-defected Grace Stoen, and the questions being asked in Congress in November of 1978 would lead to congressman Leo Ryan visiting Jonestown that same month, a visit he would not survive for he was gunned down by Jones' guards on the Port Kaituma airstrip where aircraft was waiting that would have taken him, congresswoman Jackie Speier, a selection of journalists and Temple members wishing to leave back to Georgetown airport and from there to the United Sates.

Interestingly, the *New West* article Jones had so feared was published 1 August 1977, which is when Jones' transiting SN of the Moon was bang on his Uranus in the 3rd house Aries, with the transiting SN ruler Mars in the 5th house Gemini: the full scope of Jones' megalomania (H5) was exposed in writing (Gemini). You can read the article here: https://jonestown.sdsu.edu/wp content/uploads/2013/10/newWestart.pdf

(5) See Scheeres, Julia. Op. cit., pp.93-94.

(6) Using, once again, Leslie Wagner-Wilson's book title *"Slavery of Faith"* (iUniverse, Revised Edition, 2009).

(7) See Guinn, Jeff. Op. cit., p.53.

(8) See Scheeres, Julia. Op. cit., pp.155-156.

(9) See Scheeres, Julia. Op. cit., p.94.

(10)   See Scheeres, Julia. Op. cit., p.151.

(11)   See Scheeres, Julia. Op. cit., p.149.

(12)   At this point it is important, I feel, to once again emphasize the undeniable fact that not only did Jones not believe in God but that he also did not give two pins about socialism. The SN ruler in the 3rd house Aries – in this context - unequivocally points to him having used the word, the Book (H3, SN ruler linked back to the SN of the Moon), to impose his will (SN ruler Aries) on people.

(13)   Without wanting to unduly complicate matters, it is perhaps noteworthy that Jones' secondary progressed Venus touched the NN of Uranus at 12 degrees Gemini 36 minutes in August of 1973, which is when membership of the Peoples Temple peaked. It was listed as 2,570. This was also the year when the church's Planning Commission, made up of Jones' inner circle, decided on establishing its agricultural mission in Guyana. Instead of allowing the congregation to have an equal say (Gemini) in matters, rule became ever more autocratic as membership swelled. On the day of the Jonestown tragedy, secondary progressed Venus was half-sextile the Pluto skipped step in the 7th house Cancer on one side of it (almost exact) and half-sextile Chiron in the 4th house Taurus on the other.

(14)   RYMUR (F.B.I. files for RYan MURder) 89-4286-2233-EE-2-I-5B.

About the Author

Michael De Baker is a licensed regression therapist and evolutionary astrologer from Holland, who currently lives in Spain where he holds a private practice.

Trained by evolutionary astrologer Mark Jones (www.plutoschool.com) and regression therapist Andy Tomlinson (www.regressionacademy.com), he combines the two disciplines in his psychotherapeutic work with clients.

He runs the **EA School Online** (https://www.easchoolonline.com) where he trains students who wish to become certified therapeutic evolutionary astrologers.

His first book, *Intercepted Signs: Encoded Messages from the Soul* is available on Amazon.

For information about private consultations and psychotherapeutic counseling (either in English, Spanish or Dutch), please visit https://www.michaeldebaker.com or e-mail michaeldebaker896@gmail.com

Facebook Closed Group: Therapeutic Evolutionary Astrology

Bibliography

Abrahamsen, David, M.D. *Nixon vs. Nixon: An Emotional Tragedy* (Farrar, Straus & Giroux, New York, 1977)

Aitken, Jonathan. *Nixon: A Life* (Regnery Publ., Washington D.C., 1993)

Bak, Richard. *Lindbergh: Triumph and Tragedy* (Taylor Trade Publ., 2000)

Baughman, Urbanus Edmund. *Secret Service Chief* (Harper, New York, 1962)

Berg, Scott. *Lindbergh* (G.P. Putnam's Sons Publ., New York, 1998)

Brodie, Fawn. *Richard Nixon: The Shaping of His Character* (W.W. Norton, New York, 1981)

Bruns, Florian. *Turning Away from the Individual: Medicine and Morality Under the Nazis* (in *Nazi Ideology and Ethics*, edited by Wolfgang Bialas and Lothar Fritze, Newcastle upon Tyne, Cambridge Scholars, 2014)

Costello, William. *The facts About Richard Nixon: An Unauthorized Biography* (Viking Press, 1960)

De Baker, Michael. *Intercepted Signs: Encoded Messages from the Soul* (Kindle Publ. 2019)

Dobyns, Zipporah P. *The Node Book* (American Federation of Astrologers Inc., 2010)

Donald, David Herbert. *"We are Lincoln Men": Abraham Lincoln and His Friends* (Simon & Schuster, New York, 2003)

Doniger O'Flaherty, Wendy. *Karma and Rebirth in Classical Indian Traditions* (University of California Press, Berkely, Cal., 1980)

Feinsod, Ethan. *Awake in a Nightmare: Jonestown, the Only Eyewitness Account* (W.W. Norton & Company, 1981)

Frank, Anne. *The Diary of Anne Frank: The Revised Critical Edition* (Doubleday, New York, 2003)

Garbus, Liz. *What Happened, Miss Simone?* (Netflix documentary, 2015)

Goodwin, Doris Kearns. *Team of Rivals* (Simon & Schuster, Reprint edition 2005)

Grof, Stanislav. *Beyond the Brain: Birth, Death and Transcendence in Psychotherapy* (State University of New York Press, Albany, 1985)

Guinn, Jeff. *The Road to Jonestown: Jim Jones and Peoples Temple* (Simon & Schuster, New York, 2017)

--- *Manson: The Life and Times of Charles Manson* (Simon & Schuster, New York, 2013)

Hoyt, Edwin P. *The Nixons: An American Family* (Random House, New York, 1972)

Jaffa, Harry V. *A New Birth of Freedom: Abraham Lincoln and the Coming of the Civil War* (Rowman & Littlefield, Publ., Lanham, Maryland, 2000)

Karlén, Barbro. *And the Wolves Howled* (Clairview Books, London 2000)

--- *When the Storm Comes* and *A Moment in the Blossom Kingdom* (Clairview Books, London 2001)

Kohl, Laura Johnston. *Jonestown Survivor: An Insider's Look* (Bloomington, iUniverse, 2010

Korff, Baruch. *The President and I: Richard Nixon's Rabbi Reveals his Role in the Saga that Traumatized the Nation* (Ktav, Publ. Inc. 1995)

--- *The Personal Nixon: Staying on the Summit* (Fairness Publ., 1974)

Kornitzer, Bela. *The Real Nixon: An Intimate Biography* (Rand McNally, New York, 1960)

Kriyananda, Swami. *The Path: Autobiography of a Western Yogi* (Ananda Publications, Nevada City, Cal., 1977)

Kubica, Helena. *The Crimes of Josef Mengele*. In: Gutman, Yisrael and Berenbaum, Michael. *Anatomy of the Auschwitz Death Camp*, Part III, Chapter 13. (Indiana University Press, Bloomington, 1994)

Lagnado, Lucette, and Cohn Dekel, Sheila. *Children of the Flames: Dr. Josef Mengele and the Untold Story of the Twins at Auschwitz* (William Morrow, New York, 1991)

Luhrssen, David. *Hammer of the Gods: The Thule Society and the Birth of Nazism* (Potomac Books, Washington, D.C., 2012)

Landscheidt, Theodor. *Cosmic Cybernetics: The Foundations of a Modern Astrology* (Ebertin Verlag, Aalen, Germany, 1973)

Layton, Deborah. *Seductive Poison: A Jonestown Survivor's Story of Life and Death in the Peoples Temple* (A.&W. Publ. 1999)

Lifton, Robert J. *The Nazi Doctors: Medical Killing and the Psychology of Genocide* (Basic Books, New York, 1986)

--- *What made this Man?* Art. New York Times, July 21, 1985 (freely available on the Internet)

Light, Alan. *What Happened Miss Simone? A Biography* (Crown Archetype, 2016)

Lindbergh, Reeve. *Under a Wing: A Memoir* (Simon & Schuster, New York, 1998)

Madison, James H. *A Lynching in the Heartland: Race and Memory in America* (Palgrave MacMillan, new York, 2001)

Marwell, David G. *Mengele: Unmasking the "Angel of Death"* (W.W. Norton & Company, New York, 2020)

Mazo, Earl. *Richard Nixon: A Political and Personal Portrait* (Harper & Brothers, 1959)

Mills, Jeannie. *Six Years With God: Life Inside Jim Jones' Peoples Temple* (A. & W. Publ., 1979)

Milton, Joyce. *Loss of Eden: A Biography of Charles and Anne Morrow Lindbergh* (Harper Collins, New York, 1993)

Morris, Roger. *Richard Milhous Nixon: The Rise of an American Politician* (Henry Holt, New York, 1990)

Newton, Michael. *Destiny of Souls* (Llewellyn Publ., Woodbury, Minnesota, 2000)

Nixon, Richard. *In the Arena: A Memoir of Victory, Defeat and Renewal* (Easton Press, New York, 1990)

--- *The Memoirs of Richard Nixon* (Simon & Schuster, New York, 1990)

--- *Six Crises* (Doubleday, New York, 1962)

Nixon Eisenhower, Julie. *Pat Nixon: The Untold Story* (Simon & Schuster, New York, 1986)

Nyiszli, Miklós. *I Was Doctor Mengele's Assistant: The Memoirs of an Auschwitz Physician* (Oswiecim, 2001)

Posner, Gerald L. *Hitler's Children: Sons and Daughters of Leaders of the Third Reich Talk About Themselves and Their Fathers* (Random House, New York, 1991)

Posner, Gerald, and Ware, John. *Mengele: The Complete Story* (McGraw-Hill, New York, 1986)

Proctor, Robert. *Racial Hygiene: Medicine Under the Nazis* (Cambridge, Massachusetts, Harvard University Press, 1988)

Reiterman, Tim. Raven: *The Untold Story of the Rev. Jim Jones and His People* (Tarcher Perigree, 2008. Orig. publ. by Dutton Adult, 1982)

Rudhyar, Dane. *The Planetary and Lunar Nodes* (CSA Press, 1971)

Sarna, Jonathan D. and Shapell, Benjamin. *Lincoln and the Jews: A History* (Thomas Dunne Books, New York, 2015)

Schafft, Gretchen E. *From Racism to Genocide: Anthropology in the Third Reich* (University of Illinois Press, Urbana, 2004)

Scheeres, Julia. *A Thousand Lives: The Untold Story of Jonestown* (Free Press, New York, 2011)

Schnabel, Ernst. *The Footsteps of Anne Frank: Essential Companion to The Diary of a Young Girl* (Southbank Publ. London, 2015)

Schulte, Renée. *The Young Nixon: An Oral Enquiry* (Fullerton, Cal., California State University, 1978)

Silva, Richard. *The Reincarnation of Abraham Lincoln* (Crystal Clarity Publ. Nevada City, Cal. 2009)

Solberg, Carl. *Hubert Humphrey: A Biography* (W.W. Norton, New York, 1984)

Spalding, Henry D. *The Nixon Nobody Knows* (Jonathan David Publ., New York, 1972)

Steinacher, Gerald. *Nazis on the Run: How Hitler's Henchmen Fled Justice* (Oxford University Press, 2011)

Summers, Anthony. *The Arrogance of Power: The Secret World of Richard Nixon* (Viking Publ., Penguin Group, 2000)

Taylor, Arthur R. *Notes and Tones: Musician-to-Musician Interviews* (Da Capo Press, New York, 1982)

Völklein, Ulrich. *Josef Mengele: Der Artz von Auschwitz* (Steidl Verlag, Göttingen, 1999)

Wagner-Wilson, Leslie. *Slavery of Faith* (iUniverse, Revised Edition, 2009)

White, Theodore H. *Breach of Faith: The Fall of Richard Nixon* (Atheneum, 1975)

Woolger, Roger. *Other Lives, Other Selves: a Jungian Psychotherapist Discovers Past Lives* (Bantam Books, 1988)

Zimmer, Heinrich. *Philosophies of India* (Bollingen Series, Princeton University Press, 1951)

Made in United States
Troutdale, OR
01/11/2024

16905358R00204